Final Report of the Fortieth Antarctic Treaty Consultative Meeting

ANTARCTIC TREATY
CONSULTATIVE MEETING

Final Report
of the Fortieth
Antarctic Treaty
Consultative Meeting

Beijing, China
22 May - 1 June 2017

Volume II

Secretariat of the Antarctic Treaty
Buenos Aires
2017

Published by:

Secretariat of the Antarctic Treaty
Secrétariat du Traité sur l' Antarctique
Секретариат Договора об Антарктике
Secretaría del Tratado Antártico

Maipú 757, Piso 4
C1006ACI Ciudad Autónoma
Buenos Aires - Argentina
Tel: +54 11 4320 4260
Fax: +54 11 4320 4253

This book is also available from: *www.ats.aq* (digital version)
and online-purchased copies.

ISSN 2346-9897
ISBN (vol. II): 978-987-4024-55-8
ISBN (complete work): 978-987-4024-42-8

Contents

VOLUME I

3. Resolutions

VOLUME II

PART IV. ADDITIONAL DOCUMENTS FROM XL ATCM

Acronyms and Abbreviations

ACAP	Agreement on the Conservation of Albatrosses and Petrels
ACBR	Antarctic Conservation Biogeographic Region
ASMA	Antarctic Specially Managed Area
ASOC	Antarctic and Southern Ocean Coalition
ASPA	Antarctic Specially Protected Area
ATS	Antarctic Treaty System or Antarctic Treaty Secretariat
ATCM	Antarctic Treaty Consultative Meeting
ATME	Antarctic Treaty Meeting of Experts
BP	Background Paper
CCAMLR	Convention on the Conservation of Antarctic Marine Living Resources and/or Commission for the Conservation of Antarctic Marine Living Resources
CCAS	Convention for the Conservation of Antarctic Seals
CCRWP	Climate Change Response Work Programme
CEE	Comprehensive Environmental Evaluation
CEP	Committee for Environmental Protection
COMNAP	Council of Managers of National Antarctic Programs
EIA	Environmental Impact Assessment
EIES	Electronic Information Exchange System
HSM	Historic Site and Monument
IAATO	International Association of Antarctica Tour Operators
IBA	Important Bird Area
ICAO	International Civil Aviation Organization
ICG	Intersessional Contact Group
IEE	Initial Environmental Evaluation
IGP&I Clubs	International Group of Protection and Indemnity Clubs
IHO	International Hydrographic Organization
IMO	International Maritime Organization
IOC	Intergovernmental Oceanographic Commission
IOPC Funds	International Oil Pollution Compensation Funds
IP	Information Paper
IPCC	Intergovernmental Panel on Climate Change
IUCN	International Union for Conservation of Nature

MARPOL	International Convention for the Prevention of Pollution from Ships
MPA	Marine Protected Area
RCC	Rescue Coordination Centre
SAR	Search and Rescue
SCAR	Scientific Committee on Antarctic Research
SC-CAMLR	Scientific Committee of CCAMLR
SGCCR	Subsidiary Group on Climate Change Response
SGMP	Subsidiary Group on Management Plans
SOLAS	International Convention for the Safety of Life at Sea
SOOS	Southern Ocean Observing System
SP	Secretariat Paper
UAV/RPAS	Unmanned Aerial Vehicle / Remotely Piloted Aircraft System
UNEP	United Nations Environment Programme
UNFCCC	United Nations Framework Convention on Climate Change
WMO	World Meteorological Organization
WP	Working Paper
WTO	World Tourism Organization

PART II

Measures, Decisions and Resolutions (Cont.)

4. Management Plans

Management Plan for Antarctic Specially Protected Area No. 109

MOE ISLAND, SOUTH ORKNEY ISLANDS

Introduction

The primary reason for the designation of Moe Island, South Orkney Islands (Latitude 60°44'S, Longitude 045°41'W), as Antarctic Specially Protected Area (ASPA) No. 109 is to protect environmental values, and primarily the terrestrial flora and fauna within the Area.

The Area was originally designated in Recommendation IV-13 (1966, SPA No. 13) after a proposal by the United Kingdom on the grounds that the Area provided a representative sample of the maritime Antarctic ecosystem, that intensive experimental research on the neighbouring Signy Island might alter its ecosystem and that Moe Island should be specially protected as a control area for future comparison.

These grounds are still relevant. Whilst there is no evidence that research activities at Signy Island have significantly altered the ecosystems there, a major change has occurred in the low altitude terrestrial system as a result of the rapidly expanding Antarctic fur seal (*Arctocephalus gazella*) population. Plant communities on nearby Signy Island have been physically disrupted by trampling by fur seals and nitrogen enrichment from the seals' excreta has resulted in replacement of bryophytes and lichens by the macro-alga *Prasiola crispa*. Low-lying lakes have been significantly affected by enriched run-off from the surrounding land. So far Moe Island has only been invaded by fur seals to a limited extent and its topography makes it less likely that seals will penetrate to the more sensitive areas inland. Moe Island has been visited on few occasions and has never been the site of occupation for periods of more than a few hours.

Resolution 3 (2008) recommended that the "Environmental Domains Analysis for the Antarctic Continent", be used as a dynamic model for the identification of Antarctic Specially Protected Areas within the systematic environmental-geographical framework referred to in Article 3(2) of Annex V of the Protocol (see also Morgan et al., 2007). Using this model, ASPA 109 is contained within Environment Domain G (Antarctic Peninsula off-shore islands geologic). The scarcity of Environment Domain G, relative to the other environmental domain areas, means that substantial efforts have been made to conserve the values found within this environment type elsewhere: other protected areas containing Domain G include ASPAs 111, 112, 125, 126, 128, 145, 149, 150, and 152 and ASMAs 1 and 4.

Resolution 6 (2012) recommended that the Antarctic Conservation Biogeographic Regions (ACBRs) be used for the 'identification of areas that could be designated as Antarctic Specially Protected Areas within the systematic environmental-geographic framework referred to in Article 3(2) of Annex V to the Environmental Protocol. ASPA 109 sits within Antarctic Conservation Biogeographic Region (ACBR) 2 South Orkney Islands.

Through Resolution 5 (2015) Parties recognised the usefulness of the list of Antarctic Important Bird Areas (IBAs) in planning and conducting activities in Antarctica. Within the boundary of ASPA 109 is located IBA ANT020 Moe Island, which was identified due to its extensive colonies of chinstrap penguins, cape petrels and Antarctic prions.

The two other ASPAs present within the South Orkney Islands (ASPA 110 Lynch Island and ASPA 111 Southern Powell Island and adjacent islands) were designated primarily to protect terrestrial vegetation and bird communities. Moe Island complements the local network of

ASPAs by protecting a representative sample of the maritime Antarctic ecosystem including cryptogam-dominated terrestrial and coastal communities.

1. Description of values to be protected

Following a visit to the ASPA in February 2016, the values specified in the earlier designation were reaffirmed. These values are set out as follows:

- The Area contains exceptional environmental values associated with the biological composition and diversity of a near-pristine example of the maritime Antarctic terrestrial and littoral marine ecosystems.
- Moe Island contains the greatest continuous expanses of *Chorisodontium-Polytrichum* moss turf found in the Antarctic.

2. Aims and objectives

Management of Moe Island aims to:

- avoid major changes to the structure and composition of the terrestrial vegetation, in particular the moss turf banks;
- prevent unnecessary human disturbance to the Area;
- prevent or minimise the introduction to the Area of non-native plants, animals and microorganisms;
- allow scientific research in the Area provided it is for compelling reasons which cannot be served elsewhere and which will not jeopardise the natural ecological system in that Area
- allow visits for management purposes in support of the aims of the management plan;
- minimise the possibility of introduction of pathogens which may cause disease in bird populations within the Area;

3. Management activities

The following management activities are to be undertaken to protect the values of the Area:

- Visits shall be made as necessary to assess whether the ASPA continues to serve the purposes for which it was designated and to ensure management and maintenance measures are adequate.
- The Management Plan shall be reviewed at least every five years and updated as required.
- Markers, signs or other structures erected within the Area for scientific or management purposes shall be secured and maintained in good condition and removed when no longer required.
- In accordance with the requirements of Annex III of the Protocol on Environmental Protection to the Antarctic Treaty, abandoned equipment or materials shall be removed to the maximum extent possible provided doing so does not adversely impact on the environment and the values of the Area.

- A copy of this Management Plan shall be made available at Signy Research Station (UK; 60°42′30″ S, 045°36′30″ W) and Orcadas Station (Argentina; 60°44′15″ S, 044°44′20″ W).

- Where appropriate, National Antarctic Programmes are encouraged to liaise closely to ensure management activities are implemented. In particular, National Antarctic Programmes are encouraged to consult with one another to prevent excessive sampling of biological material within the Area. Also, National Antarctic Programmes are encouraged to consider joint implementation of guidelines intended to minimize the introduction and dispersal of non-native species within the Area.

- All scientific and management activities undertaken within the Area should be subject to an Environmental Impact Assessment, in accordance with the requirements of Annex I of the Protocol on Environmental Protection to the Antarctic Treaty.

4. Period of designation

Designated for an indefinite period.

5. Maps

Figure 1. Map of the location of Moe Island in relation to the South Orkney Islands and the other protected areas in the region. Inset: the location of the South Orkney Islands in Antarctica. Map specifications: Projection: WGS84 Antarctic Polar Stereographic. Standard parallel: 71 °S. Central meridian 45 °W.

Figure 2. Map of Moe Island in greater detail. Map specifications: Projection: WGS84 Antarctic Polar Stereographic. Standard parallel: 71 °S. Central meridian 45 °W.

6. Description of the Area

6(i) *Geographical co-ordinates, boundary markers and natural features*

BOUNDARIES AND CO-ORDINATES

The boundary co-ordinates of the Area, starting with the most north-westerly position and moving clockwise, are shown in Table 1.

Number	Latitude	Longitude
1	60°43′40″ S	045°42′15″ W
2	60°43′40″ S	045°40′30″ W
3	60°43′55″ S	045°40′10″ W
4	60°44′40″ S	045°40′10″ W
5	60°44′40″ S	045°42′15″ W

The Area includes all of Moe Island and unnamed adjacent islands and islets. The Area encompasses all of the ice-free ground, permanent ice and semi-permanent ice found within the boundaries, but excludes the marine environment extending greater than 10 m offshore from the low tide water line (Figure 2). Boundary markers have not been installed..

GENERAL DESCRIPTION OF THE AREA

Moe Island, South Orkney Islands, is a small irregularly-shaped island lying 300 m off the south-western extremity of Signy Island, from which it is separated by Fyr Channel. It is about 1.3 km from the northeast to southwest and 1 km from northwest to southeast (1.22 km²). It should be noted that the position of Moe Island on Admiralty Chart No. 1775 (60°44'S, 45°45'W), does not agree closely with the more accurate coordinates in Figure 2 (60°44'S, 45°41'W).

The island rises precipitously on the north-eastern and south-eastern sides to Snipe Peak (226 m altitude). There is a subsidiary summit above South Point (102 m altitude) and lower hills on each of three promontories on the western side above Corral Point (92 m), Conroy Point (39 m) and Spaull Point (56 m). Small areas of permanent ice remain on the east- and south-facing slopes with late snow lying on the steeply dipping western slopes. There are no permanent streams or pools.

GEOLOGY

The rocks are metamorphic quartz mica schists, with occasional biotite and quartz-rich beds. There is a thin bed of undifferentiated amphibolite on the northeastern coast. Much of the island is overlain with glacial drift and scree. Soils are predominantly immature deposits of fine to coarse clays and sands intermixed with gravels, stones and boulders. They are frequently sorted by freeze-thaw action in high or exposed locations into small-scale circles, polygons, stripes and lobes. There are deep accumulations of peat (up to 2 m thick on western slopes), considerable expanses of the surface of which are bare and eroded.

TERRESTRIAL BIOLOGICAL COMMUNITIES

The dominant plant communities are *Andreaea-Usnea* fellfield and banks of *Chorisodontium-Polytrichum* moss turf (the largest known example of this community type in the Antarctic). Use of satellite remote sensing techniques (Normalised Difference Vegetation Index) showed the area of green vegetation within the ASPA to be 0.58 km² (48% of the ASPA area; Figures 3 and 4). These moss banks constitute a major biological value and a reason for the designation of the Area. The cryptogamic flora is diverse. The majority of these moss banks have received little damage from fur seals, and show few visible sign of degradation. However, the exception to this observation is the northern-most banks located around Spaull Point. Here, although still extensive, the moss turf was estimated to have suffered about 50% damage from Antarctic fur seal (*Arctocephallus gazella*) activity during a survey in January 2006 and still evident during observations in February 2016. One sub-adult male Antarctic fur seal was present on this area of moss turf during the survey in January 2006. Almost certainly fur seals gain access to this plant community via the gentle slope leading inland from the small shingle beach located at the north-eastern corner of Landing Cove.

The mites *Gamasellus racovitzai* and *Stereotydeus villosus* and the springtail *Cryptopygus antarcticus* are common under stones.

VERTEBRATE FAUNA

There were five colonies of chinstrap penguins (*Pygoscelis antarctica*) totalling about 11,000 pairs in 1978-79. A visit in February 1994 noted fewer than 100 pairs on the northern side of Landing Cove and more than a thousand on the southern side. A visit in February 2011 noted c. 75 pairs on the northern side of Landing Cove and c. 750 pairs on the southern side. Approximately 100 breeding pairs were observed on Spaull Point during a visit in January 2006. Numerous other birds breed on the island, notably about 2,000 pairs of cape petrels (*Daption capensis*) in 14 colonies (1966) and large numbers of Antarctic prions (*Pachyptila desolata*). Snow Petrels (*Pagodroma nivea*) were recorded breeding on Moe Island in 1957/58 when the colony comprised 34 breeding pairs (Croxall *et al*. 1995), and were confirmed breeding during a survey in 2005/06 (R. Fijn pers. comm. 2015, quoted in Harris et al., 2015).

Weddell seals (*Leptonychotes weddellii*), crabeater seals (*Lobodon carcinophaga*) and leopard seals (*Hydrurga leptonyx*) are found in the bays on the west side of the island. Increasing numbers of fur seals (*Arctocephalus gazella*), mostly juvenile males, come ashore on the north side of Landing Cove and have caused some damage to vegetation in that area (25 seals were counted in this area in February 2016). However, it is possible that the nature of the terrain will restrict these animals to this small headland where damage may intensify.

6(ii) Access to the Area

- Where possible, access shall be by small boat. There are no restrictions on landing from the sea. Landings are usually most safely made at the northeast corner of Landing Cove (Lat. 60°43'55" S, Long. 045°41'06" W; Figure 2). If Landing Cove is inaccessible due to the ice conditions, an alternative landing site is at the western-most point of Spaull Point (Lat. 60°43'54" S, Long. 045°41'15" W), directly opposite an offshore rock of 26 m altitude.
- Under exceptional circumstances, necessary for purposes consistent with the objectives of the Management Plan, helicopters may be permitted to land within the Area.
- Helicopters may land only on the col between hill 89 m and the western slope of Snipe Peak (Lat. 60°44'09" S, Long. 045°41'23" W, Figure 2). Landing on vegetation in the col should be avoided to the maximum extent practicable. To avoid overflying bird colonies, approach should preferably be from the south, though an approach from the north is permissible.
- Within the Area the operation of aircraft should be carried out, as a minimum requirement, in compliance with the 'Guidelines for the Operation of Aircraft near Concentrations of Birds' contained in Resolution 2 (2004). When conditions require aircraft to fly at lower elevations than recommended in the guidelines, aircraft should maintain the maximum elevation possible and minimise the time taken to transit the Area.
- Use of helicopter smoke grenades is prohibited within the Area unless absolutely necessary for safety. If used, all smoke grenades should be retrieved.

6(iii) Location of structures within and adjacent to the Area

A marker board is located at the back of the small shingle beach in the northeast corner of Landing Cove, beyond the splash zone on top of a flat rock, to which it is bolted (Lat. 60°43'55" S, Long. 045°41'05" W). During periods of heavy snowfall, the marker board may be buried and difficult to locate.

There is a cairn and the remains of a survey mast, erected in 1965-66, on Spaull Point (Lat. 60°43'49" S, Long. 045°41'05" W). This mast is of interest for lichenometric studies and should not be removed. There are no other structures on Moe Island.

6(iv) Location of other Protected Areas in the vicinity

ASPA No. 110, Lynch Island, lies about 10 km north-north-east of Moe Island. ASPA No. 111, Southern Powell Island and adjacent islands, is about 41 km to the east (Figure 1).

6(v) Special zones within the Area

None

7. Permit conditions

7(i) General permit conditions

Entry into the Area is prohibited except in accordance with a Permit issued by an appropriate national authority as designated under Article 7 of Annex V of the Protocol on Environmental Protection to the Antarctic Treaty.

Conditions for issuing a Permit to enter the Area are that:
- it is issued for a compelling scientific purpose which cannot be served elsewhere; or
- it is issued for essential management purposes such as inspection, maintenance or review;
- the actions permitted will not jeopardise the natural ecological system in the Area;
- any management activities are in support of the objectives of this Management Plan;
- the actions permitted are in accordance with this Management Plan;
- the Permit, or an authorised copy, must be carried within the Area;
- permits shall be issued for a stated period;
- a report or reports are supplied to the authority or authorities named in the Permit;
- the appropriate authority should be notified of any activities/measures undertaken that were not included in the authorised Permit.

7(ii) Access to and movement within or over the Area
- Land vehicles are prohibited within the Area

- Movement within the Area shall be on foot.

- Pilots, helicopter or boat crew, or other people on helicopters or boats, are prohibited from moving on foot beyond the immediate vicinity of their landing site unless specifically authorised by Permit.

- Pedestrian traffic should be kept to the minimum consistent with the objectives of any permitted activities and every reasonable effort should be made to minimise trampling effects, i.e. all movement should be undertaken carefully so as to minimise disturbance to the soil and vegetated surfaces, walking on rocky terrain if practical.

- Overflight of bird colonies within the Area by Remotely Piloted Aircraft Systems (RPAS) shall not be permitted unless for scientific or operational purposes, and in accordance with a permit issued by an appropriate national authority.

7(iii) Activities which may be conducted in the Area

- Compelling scientific research which cannot be undertaken elsewhere and which will not jeopardize the ecosystem of the Area
- Essential management activities, including monitoring

7(iv) Installation, modification or removal of structures

No new structures are to be erected within the Area, or scientific equipment installed, except for compelling scientific or management reasons and for a pre-established period, as specified in a permit. Installation (including site selection), maintenance, modification or removal of structures and equipment shall be undertaken in a manner that minimises disturbance to the values of the Area. All structures or scientific equipment installed in the Area shall be clearly identified by country, name of the principal investigator and year of installation. All such items should be free of organisms, propagules (e.g. seeds, eggs) and non-sterile soil, and be made of materials that can withstand the environmental conditions and pose minimal risk of contamination of the Area. Removal of specific structures or equipment for which the Permit has expired shall be a condition of the Permit. Permanent structures or installations are prohibited.

7(v) Location of field camps

Camp in the Area is not normally permitted. If camping is essential for reasons of safety, tents should be erected having regard to causing the least damage to vegetation or disturbance to fauna.

7(vi) Restrictions on materials and organisms that may be brought into the Area

No living animals, plant material or microorganisms shall be deliberately introduced into the Area. To ensure that the floristic and ecological values of the Area are maintained, special precautions shall be taken against accidentally introducing microbes, invertebrates or plants from other Antarctic sites, including stations, or from regions outside Antarctica. All sampling equipment or markers brought into the Area shall be cleaned or sterilized. To the maximum extent practicable, footwear and other equipment used or brought into the Area (including bags or backpacks) shall be thoroughly cleaned before entering the Area. Further guidance can be found in the CEP Non-native Species Manual (Edition 2011) and COMNAP/SCAR Checklists for supply chain managers of National Antarctic Programmes for the reduction in risk of transfer of non-native species. In view of the presence of breeding bird colonies within the Area, no poultry products, including wastes from such products and products containing uncooked dried eggs, shall be released into the Area or into the adjacent sea.

No herbicides or pesticides shall be brought into the Area. Any other chemicals, including radio-nuclides or stable isotopes, which may be introduced for scientific or management purposes specified in the Permit, shall be removed from the Area at or before the conclusion of the activity for which the Permit was granted. Release of radio-nuclides or stable isotopes directly into the environment in a way that renders them unrecoverable should be avoided. Fuel or other chemicals shall not be stored in the Area unless specifically authorised by Permit condition. They shall be stored and handled in a way that minimises the risk of their accidental introduction into the environment. Materials introduced into the Area shall be for a stated period only and shall be removed by the end of that stated period. If release occurs which is likely to compromise the values of the Area, removal is encouraged only where the impact of removal is not likely to be greater than that of leaving the material in situ. The appropriate authority should be notified of anything released and not removed that was not included in the authorised Permit.

7(vii) Taking of, or harmful interference with, native flora and fauna

Taking of or harmful interference with native flora or fauna is prohibited, except by Permit issued in accordance with Annex II to the Protocol on Environmental Protection to the Antarctic Treaty. Where taking of or harmful interference with animals is involved, the *SCAR Code of Conduct for the Use of Animals for Scientific Purposes in Antarctica* should be used as a minimum standard.

7(viii) The collection or removal of materials not brought into the Area by the Permit holder

Collection or removal of anything not brought into the Area by the permit holder shall only be in accordance with a Permit and should be limited to the minimum necessary to meet scientific or management needs.

Other material of human origin likely to compromise the values of the Area which was not brought into the Area by the permit holder or otherwise authorised, may be removed from the Area unless the environmental impact of the removal is likely to be greater than leaving the material in situ; if this is the case the appropriate Authority must be notified and approval obtained.

7(ix) Disposal of waste

As a minimum standard, all waste shall be disposed of in accordance with Annex III to the Protocol on Environmental Protection to the Antarctic Treaty. In addition, all wastes shall be removed from the Area. Liquid human wastes may be disposed of into the sea. Solid human waste should not be disposed of to the sea, but shall be removed from the Area. No solid or liquid human waste shall be disposed of inland.

7(x) Measures that may be necessary to ensure that the aims and objectives of the Management Plan continue to be met

- Permits may be granted to enter the Area to carry out scientific research, monitoring and site inspection activities, which may involve the collection of a small number of samples for analysis, to erect or maintain signboards, or to carry out protective measures.

- Any long-term monitoring sites shall be appropriately marked and the markers or signs maintained.

- Scientific activities shall be performed in accordance with *SCAR's environmental code of conduct for terrestrial scientific field research in Antarctica.*

7(xi) Requirements for reports

The principal permit holder for each visit to the Area shall submit a report to the appropriate national authority as soon as practicable, and no later than six months after the visit has been completed. Such reports should include, as appropriate, the information identified in the visit report form contained in the Guide to the Preparation of Management Plans for Antarctic Specially Protected Areas. If appropriate, the national authority should also forward a copy of the visit report to the Party that proposed the Management Plan, to assist in managing the Area and reviewing the Management Plan. Wherever possible, Parties should deposit the original or copies of the original visit reports, in a publicly accessible archive to maintain a record of usage, for the purpose of any review of the Management Plan and in organising the scientific use of the Area.

8. Supporting documentation

Croxall, J. P., Rootes, D. M. & Price, R. A. 1981. Increases in penguin populations at Signy Island, South Orkney Islands. *British Antarctic Survey Bulletin* 54, 47-56.

Croxall, J. P., Steele, W. K, McInnes, S. J., and Prince, P.A. 1995. Breeding distribution of the Snow Petrel *Pagodroma nivea. Marine Ornithology* 23, 69-99.

Harris, C.M., Lorenz, K., Fishpool, L.D.C., Lascelles, B., Cooper, J., Coria, N.R., Croxall, J.P., Emmerson, L.M., Fijn, R.C., Fraser, W.L., Jouventin, P., LaRue, M.A., Le Maho, Y., Lynch, H.J., Naveen, R., Patterson-Fraser, D.L., Peter, H.-U., Poncet, S., Phillips, R.A., Southwell, C.J., van Franeker, J.A., Weimerskirch, H., Wienecke, B., and Woehler, E.J. 2015. *Important Bird Areas in Antarctica 2015*. BirdLife International and Environmental Research & Assessment Ltd., Cambridge.

Longton, R.E. 1967. Vegetation in the maritime Antarctic. In Smith, J.E., *Editor*, A discussion of the terrestrial Antarctic ecosystem. *Philosophical Transactions of the Royal Society of London*, B, 252, 213-235.

Morgan, F., Barker, G., Briggs, C., Price, R. and Keys, H. 2007. Environmental Domains of Antarctica Version 2.0 Final Report, Manaaki Whenua Landcare Research New Zealand Ltd. 89 pp.

Ochyra, R., Bednarek-Ochyra, H. and Smith, R.I.L. *The Moss Flora of Antarctica*. 2008. Cambridge University Press, Cambridge. 704 pp.

Øvstedal, D.O. and Smith, R.I.L. 2001. *Lichens of Antarctica and South Georgia. A Guide to their Identification and Ecology*. Cambridge University Press, Cambridge, 411 pp.

Peat, H., Clarke, A., and Convey, P. 2007. Diversity and biogeography of the Antarctic flora. *Journal of Biogeography,* 34, 132-146.

Poncet, S., and Poncet, J. 1985. A survey of penguin breeding populations at the South Orkney Islands. *British Antarctic Survey Bulletin* 68, 71-81.

Smith, R. I. L. 1972. British Antarctic Survey science report 68. British Antarctic Survey, Cambridge, 124 pp.

Smith, R. I. L. 1984. Terrestrial plant biology of the sub-Antarctic and Antarctic. In: Antarctic Ecology, Vol. 1. Editor: R. M. Laws. London, Academic Press.
Figure 1. Map showing the location of Moe Island in relation to the South Orkney Islands and the other protected areas in the region. Inset: the location of the South Orkney Islands in Antarctica.

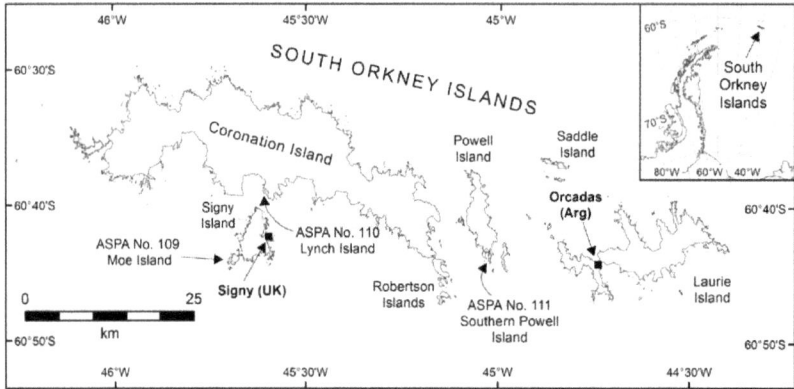

Figure 2. Map of Moe Island in greater detail.

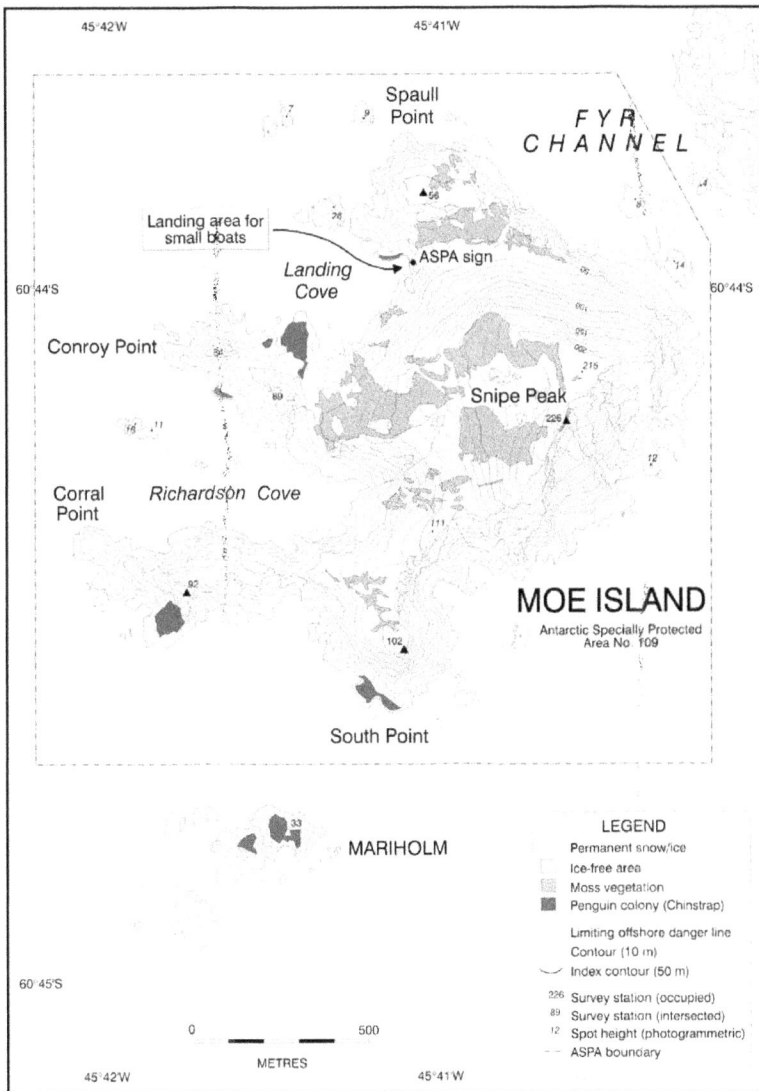

Figure 3. False colour satellite image of ASPA No. 109 Moe Island, South Orkney Islands, which highlights vegetation in red.

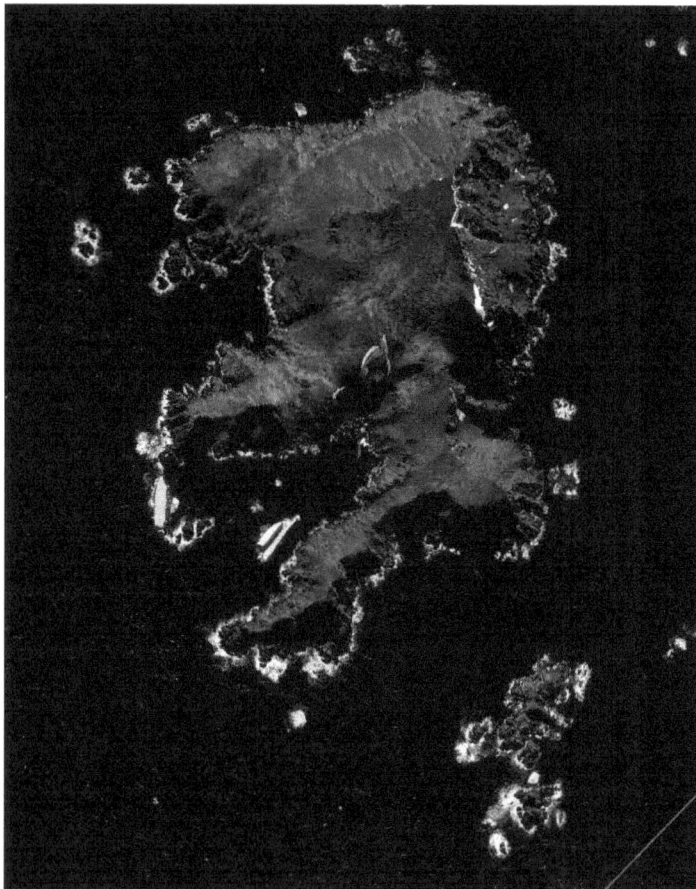

Figure 4. Normalised Difference Vegetation Index (NDVI), derived from satellite imagery, for ASPA No. 109 Moe Island, South Orkney Islands, showing vegetation cover using a colour scale of white → orange → red, with red indicating the highest NDVI values.

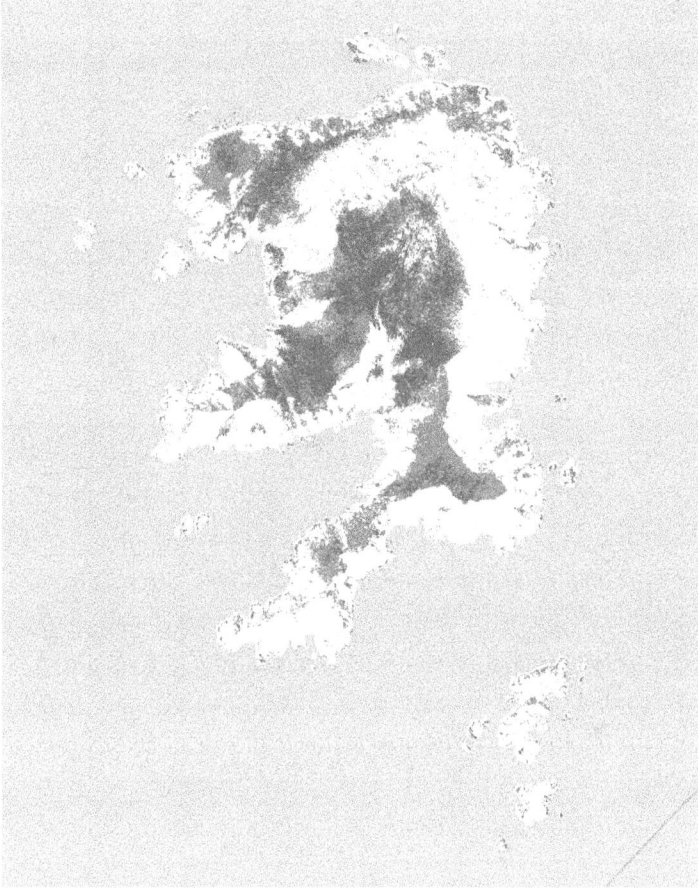

Management Plan for Antarctic Specially Protected Area No. 110

LYNCH ISLAND, SOUTH ORKNEY ISLANDS

Introduction

The primary reason for the designation of Lynch Island, South Orkney Islands (Latitude 60°39'10'' S, Longitude 045°36'25'' W; 0.14 km²), as Antarctic Specially Protected Area (ASPA) 110 is to protect environmental values, and primarily the terrestrial flora within the Area.

Lynch Island, Marshal Bay, South Orkney Islands, was originally designated as a Specially Protected Area through Recommendation IV-14 (1966, SPA No. 14) after a proposal by the United Kingdom. It was designated on the grounds that the island "supports one of the most extensive and dense areas of grass (*Deschampsia antarctica*) known in the Treaty area and that it provides an outstanding example of a rare natural ecological system". These values were amplified and extended by Recommendation XVI-6 (1991) when a management plan for the site was adopted.

Lynch Island is 2.4 km from Signy Island, the location of Signy Research Station (UK), and about 200 m from Coronation Island, the largest of the South Orkney Islands. The Area has been afforded special protection for most of the modern era of scientific activity in the region, with entry permits having been issued only for compelling scientific reasons. Thus, the island has not been subjected to frequent visits, scientific research or sampling. Since 1983, the numbers of Antarctic fur seals in the South Orkney Islands as increased significantly, with consequent destruction of accessible areas of vegetation where the seals come ashore. Some vegetated areas on Lynch Island have been damaged, for example, accessible *Polytrichum* and *Chorisodontium* moss banks and *Deschampsia* on the north-eastern and eastern sides of the island have been extensively damaged in some locations. A visit in February 2011 reported fur seals were present over the eastern side of the island [roughly drawing a line between the boat landing site (Lat. 60°39'05" S, Long. 045°36'12" W; Figure 2) and the island's summit (Lat. 60°39'05" S, Long. 045°36'12" W)]. Seals were present to the highest point of the island with about 30 seals on the summit. Despite this, both the Antarctic hair grass; *Deschampsia Antarctica* and *Colobanthus quitensis* appeared to be thriving. The area covered by *Deschampsia*, as reported in February 2011, is more extensive than in the previous report (February 1999). The grass has now increased its abundance and distribution range in an area to the east of the island, extending west to the highest point on the island with good cover to the summit and all over the area around the summit cairn (Figure 3). During a visit in February 1999 it was observed that the most luxuriant areas of grass on the northern and north-western slopes had not yet been affected and this observation was confirmed during a visit in February 2011. Notwithstanding some localised destruction, to date the primary values of the island, as noted above, have not been significantly compromised by either human or seal access to the island.

Resolution 3 (2008) recommended that the "Environmental Domains Analysis for the Antarctic Continent", be used as a dynamic model for the identification of Antarctic Specially Protected Areas within the systematic environmental-geographical framework referred to in Article 3(2) of Annex V of the Protocol (see also Morgan et al., 2007). ASPA 110 is not categorised within Morgan et al.; however, ASPA 110 is likely to be contained within Environment Domain G (Antarctic Peninsula off-shore islands geologic). The scarcity of Environment Domain G, relative to the other environmental domain areas, means that substantial efforts have been made to conserve the values found within this environment type elsewhere: other protected areas containing Domain G include ASPAs 109, 111, 112, 125, 126, 128, 145, 149, 150, and 152 and ASMAs 1 and 4.

Resolution 6 (2012) recommended that the Antarctic Conservation Biogeographic Regions (ACBRs) be used for the 'identification of areas that could be designated as Antarctic Specially Protected Areas within the systematic environmental-geographic framework referred to in Article 3(2) of Annex V to the Environmental Protocol. ASPA 110 sits within Antarctic Conservation Biogeographic Region (ACBR) 2 South Orkney Islands.

The two other ASPAs present within the South Orkney Islands (ASPA No. 109 Moe Island, and ASPA No. 111 Southern Powell Island and adjacent islands) were designated primarily to protect terrestrial vegetation and bird communities. ASPA No. 110 Lynch Island complements the local network of ASPAs by protecting a representative sample of the maritime Antarctic ecosystem including phanerogam-dominated terrestrial communities.

1. Description of values to be protected

Following a visit to the ASPA in February 2016, the values specified in the earlier designation were reviewed. Values within the Area are set out as follows:

- The Area contains luxuriant swards of Antarctic hair grass *Deschampsia antarctica* and the only other Antarctic flowering plant, Antarctic pearlwort (*Colobanthus quitensis*), is also abundant. It is also one of few sites where the grass *Deschampsia* is known to grow directly on *Polytrichum-Chorisodontium* moss banks.
- The cryptogamic vegetation is typical of the region; however, several species of moss found on the island (*Polytrichastrum alpinum* (=*Polytrichum alpinum*) and *Muelleriella crassifolia*) are unusually fertile for their southerly location. It is also possibly the only known location in Antarctica where *Polytrichastrum alpinum* develops sporophytes in profusion annually. Furthermore, *Polytrichum strictum* (=*Polytrichum alpestre*) occasionally produces male inflorescences in local abundance, which is a rare occurrence in this species in Antarctica and the rare moss *Plagiothecium ovalifolium* occurs in moist shaded rock crevices near the shore.
- The shallow loam-like soil associated with the grass swards was contains a rich invertebrate fauna. The population density of the arthropod community associated with *Deschampsia* on Lynch Island appears unusually high, with some measurements suggesting it is one of the highest in the world. The site also shows unusual diversity for an Antarctic site. A rare enchytraeid worm was also found in moist moss in rock crevices on the northern side of the island. One arthropod species (*Globoppia loxolineata*) is near the northernmost limit of its known distribution, and specimens collected from Lynch Island exhibited unusual morphological characteristics compared to specimens collected elsewhere in the South Orkney-Antarctic Peninsula region.

- *Chromobacterium* bacteria, yeasts and fungi are found in higher densities than on Signy Island, thought to be a result of the lower acidity of the soils associated with *Deschampsia* and the more favourable microclimate at Lynch Island.

- The shallow gravelly loam-like soil beneath the dense swards of *Deschampsia* may represent one of the most advanced soil types in the Antarctic.

2. Aims and objectives

Management at Lynch Island aims to:

- avoid major changes to the structure and composition of the terrestrial vegetation;
- prevent unnecessary human disturbance to the Area;
- prevent or minimise the introduction to the Area of non-native plants, animals and microorganisms;
- allow scientific research in the Area provided it is for compelling reasons which cannot be served elsewhere and which will not jeopardise the natural ecological system in that Area;
- ensure that the flora and fauna are not adversely affected by excessive sampling within the Area;
- allow visits for management purposes in support of the aims of the management plan;
- minimise the possibility of introduction of pathogens which may cause disease in vertebrate populations within the Area;

3. Management activities

The following management activities shall be undertaken to protected the values of the Area

- Visits shall be made as necessary to assess whether the ASPA continues to serve the purposes for which it was designated and to ensure management and maintenance measures are adequate.
- The Management Plan shall be reviewed at least every five years and updated as required.
- Markers, signs or other structures erected within the Area for scientific or management purposes shall be secured and maintained in good condition and removed when no longer required.
- In accordance with the requirements of Annex III of the Protocol on Environmental Protection to the Antarctic Treaty, abandoned equipment or materials shall be removed to the maximum extent possible provided doing so does not adversely impact on the environment and the values of the Area.
- A copy of this Management Plan shall be made available at Signy Research Station (UK; 60°42′30″ S, 045°36′30″ W) and Orcadas Station (Argentina; 60°44′15″ S, 044°44′20″ W).
- Where appropriate, National Antarctic Programmes are encouraged to liaise closely to ensure management activities are implemented. In particular, National Antarctic Programmes are encouraged to consult with one another to prevent excessive sampling of biological material within the Area. Also, National Antarctic Programmes are encouraged to consider joint implementation of guidelines intended to minimize the introduction and dispersal of non-native species within the Area.
- All scientific and management activities undertaken within the Area should be subject to an Environmental Impact Assessment, in accordance with the requirements of Annex I of the Protocol on Environmental Protection to the Antarctic Treaty.

4. Period of designation

Designated for an indefinite period.

5. Maps and images

Figure 1. Map of the location of Lynch Island in relation to the South Orkney Islands and the other protected areas in the region. Inset: the location of the South Orkney Islands in Antarctica. Map specifications: Projection: WGS84 Antarctic Polar Stereographic. Standard parallel: 71 °S. Central meridian 45 °W.

Figure 2. ASPA No. 110, Lynch Island, South Orkney Islands, topographic map. Projection: Lambert Conformal Conic. Standard parallels: 1st 60°40'00'' W; 2nd 63°20'00'' S. Central Meridian: 045°26'20'' W. Latitude of Origin: 63°20'00'' S. Spheriod: WGS84. Datum: Mean Sea Level. Horizontal accuracy of control points: ±1 m.

Figure 3. Normalised Difference Vegetation Index (NDVI), derived from satellite imagery, for ASPA No. 110 Lynch Island, South Orkney Islands, showing green vegetation cover using a colour scale of yellow → orange → red, with red indicating the highest NDVI values.

6. Description of the Area

6(i) Geographical co-ordinates, boundary markers and natural features

BOUNDARIES AND CO-ORDINATES
The Area encompasses all of Lynch Island but excludes all unnamed adjacent islands and islets. The Area encompasses all of the ice-free ground, permanent ice and semi-permanent ice found within Lynch Island, but excludes the marine environment extending greater than 10 m offshore from the low tide water line (Map 2). Boundary markers have not been installed because the coast itself is a clearly defined and visually obvious boundary.

GENERAL DESCRIPTION
Lynch Island (Latitude 60°39'10" S, Longitude 045°36'25" W; area) is a small island situated at the eastern end of Marshall Bay in the South Orkney Islands, about 200 m south of Coronation Island and 2.4 km north of Signy Island (Map 1). The 500 m x 300 m island has low cliffs of up to 20 m in height on the south, east and west sides, dissected by boulder-filled gullies. The northern side has a low cliff below a rock terrace at about 5-8 m altitude, above which moderate slopes rise to a broad plateau at about 40-50 m, with a maximum altitude of 57 m. A beach at the eastern end of the northern coast affords easy access to relatively gentle slopes leading to the central plateau area. The coastal cliffs generally make access to the upper island by other routes difficult, although access is feasible via one or two of the gullies on the eastern and northern sides. Small temporary melt-streams occur on the slopes in summer, but there are no permanent streams or pools, and only a few small late-lying snow patches occur on the southern side of the island. No meteorological data are available for Lynch Island, but conditions are broadly expected to be similar to those experienced at Signy Research Station. However, anecdotal observations suggest that significant microclimatic differences exist on Lynch Island, as the more profuse growth of plant communities would seem to attest. The island is exposed to the south-west and to katabatic and föhn winds descending from Coronation Island to the north. However, in other respects the island is relatively sheltered from regional northerly, easterly and southerly winds by Coronation Island, Cape Hansen and Signy Island respectively. The föhn effect can briefly raise local air temperatures by as much as 10°C at Signy Island. Lynch Island has often been observed to receive sunshine when the surrounding region is shrouded in low cloud. The angle of solar incidence is also relatively high on the northern side of the island because of its general slope and aspect. The above factors may be important reasons for the abundance of the two flowering plants found on the island.

GEOLOGY

The bedrock of Lynch Island consists of quartzo-feldspathic and micaceous schists of the Scotia metamorphic complex, but is poorly exposed and equivalent rocks are much better displayed in the Cape Hansen area, to the east on Coronation Island.

PEDOLOGY

Three main soil types have been identified on Lynch Island:

(i) An acidic (pH 3.8 – 4.5) moss peat, formed by the tall turf-forming mosses *Chorisodontium aciphyllum* and *Polytrichum strictum* (=*Polytrichum alpestre*), occurs mainly at the north-eastern end of the island. This peat reaches a depth of about 50 cm and is similar to peat on Signy Island where it reaches a depth of 2 m. Where the peat depth exceeds about 30 cm there is permafrost. In a few places where the substratum is moist, shallow peat of 10-15 cm depth (pH 4.8 - 5.5) has accumulated beneath the carpet-forming mosses *Warnstorfia laculosa* (=*Calliergidium austro-stramineum*) and *Sanionia uncinata* (=*Drepanocladus uncinatus*).

(ii) A shallow, gravelly loam-like soil resembling tundra brown soil occurs beneath dense swards of the grass *Deschampsia antarctica*. It is seldom more than about 30 cm in depth (pH 5.0 – 5.8) and probably represents one of the most advanced soil types in the Antarctic.

(iii) A glacial till with material ranging from fine clay (pH 5.2 – 6.0) and sand to gravel and larger stones. This covers the summit plateau and occurs in rock depressions throughout the island, as well as on parts of the rock terrace. On the plateau cryoturbation has in several places sorted the material into patterned features with small stone circles and polygons on level ground and stone stripes on sloping ground. At the north-eastern end of the island, the deposition of limpet shells (*Nacella concinna*) by gulls (*Larus dominicanus*) has resulted in a more calcareous mineral soil in rock depressions with a pH of 6.5 - 6.8.

TERRESTRIAL FLORA

Cryptogamic and phanerogamic vegetation typical of the maritime Antarctic is found over much of the island (Figure 3). Use of satellite remote sensing techniques (Normalised Difference Vegetation Index) showed the area of green vegetation within the ASPA to be 35,000 m² (25% of the ASPA area). The most significant aspect of the vegetation is the abundance and reproductive success of the two native Antarctic flowering plants, the Antarctic hair grass (*Deschampsia antarctica*) and Antarctic pearlwort (*Colobanthus quitensis*), found especially on the northern slopes (Map 3). Both species flower in profusion and seed viability appears to be much greater than on Signy Island. Lynch Island possesses the largest stands of *Deschampsia* and the greatest abundance of *Colobanthus* known in the South Orkney Islands and one of the most extensive anywhere in the Antarctica Treaty area. On the rock terrace and moist slope rising above the northern coast, the grass forms extensive swards of up to 15 × 50 m. These swards range from continuous stands of relatively luxuriant plants on the moister sites and ledges to small, yellowish, more isolated plants on the drier, stonier and more exposed terrain. *Colobanthus* is generally associated with the grass, but here the plants do not coalesce to form closed patches. This is one of very few sites where *Deschampsia* is known to grow directly on *Polytrichum-Chorisodontium* moss banks. Elsewhere on the island, the grass and, to a lesser extent, the pearlwort are frequent associates in other communities, especially stands of denser fellfield vegetation where there is quite high cover afforded by various mosses and lichens (particularly towards the western end of the northern terrace).

Shallow but occasionally extensive (about 50 m²) banks of *Chorisodontium aciphyllum and Polytrichum strictum* are frequent at the north-eastern end of the island and, to a lesser extent, on the southern side. These are typical of the moss banks which occur on Signy Island and elsewhere in the northern maritime Antarctic, with several fruticose and crustose lichens growing epiphytically on the moss surface. In small moist depressions, there are carpets of *Warnstorfia laculosa* and *Sanionia uncinata*, with some *Warnstorfia sarmentosa* (=*Calliergon sarmentosum*) and *Cephaloziella varians* (= *C. exiliflora*). On wet soil and rock ledges, *Brachythecium austro-salebrosum* is common. On the drier, more windswept, stonier soils and rock surfaces – notably in the plateau area – a typical open fellfield community of many bryophyte and lichen taxa form a complex mosaic. The dominant species in this locality are the lichens *Usnea antarctica* and *U. aurantiaco-atra* (=*U. fasciata*) and the moss *Andreaea depressinervis*; *Sphaerophorus globosus* and other species of *Alectoria, Andreaea, Cladonia,* and *Stereocaulon* are also common, while *Himantormia lugubris* and *Umbilicaria antarctica* are infrequent. Crustose lichens are abundant on all rock surfaces. The mosses and macrolichens in this area are loosely attached on thin soils and are easily damaged. Large thalli of *Usnea spp.* and *Umbilicaria antarctica* are found on moist sheltered boulders and rock faces, especially on the southern side of the island.

Communities of crustose lichen occur in the cliffs above the high water mark, especially where the rock is influenced by breeding or roosting birds. The distribution of several species forms distinctive zones in relation to inundation by sea spray and exposure to wind. The best developed communities of brightly coloured ornithocoprophilous taxa occur at the western end of the island where *Caloplaca spp., Haematomma erythromma, Mastodia tesselata, Physcia caesia, Xanthoria candelaria, X. elegans,* and species of *Buellia* and *Verrucaria* are frequent. The uncommon halophilous moss *Muelleriella crassifolia* also occurs within the spray zone around the island.

The only rare moss recorded on Lynch Island is *Plagiothecium ovalifolium*, found in moist, shaded rock crevices near the shore. However, the island is possibly the only site known in the Maritime Antarctic where the moss *Polytrichastrum alpinum* develops sporophytes in profusion each year; this occurs among *Deschampsia, Colobanthus* and cryptogams on the northern side of the island; elsewhere in the Antarctic sporophytes are in some years very rare. Also, *Polytrichum strictum* produces male inflorescences in local abundance, a rare phenomenon in this species in the Antarctic. While the thalloid liverwort *Marchantia berteroana* is locally common on Signy Island, Lynch Island is one of very few other localities where it is known in the South Orkney Islands. Several cryptogamic species of very restricted distribution in the Antarctic, but which are locally common on Signy Island and the mainland of Coronation Island only a few hundred metres away, have not been observed at Lynch Island.

TERRESTRIAL INVERTEBRATES

The microinvertebrate fauna associated with the rich *Deschampsia* swards described thus far comprises 13 taxa: three springtails (*Cryptopygus antarcticus, Friesea woyciechowskii* and *Isotoma* (*Folsomotoma*) *octooculata* (=*Parisotoma octooculata*), one mesostigmatid mite (*Gamasellus racovitzai*), two cryptostigmatid mites (*Alaskozetes antarcticus* and *Globoppia loxolineata*), and seven prostigmatid mites (*Apotriophtydeus sp., Ereynetes macquariensis, Nanorchestes berryi, Stereotydeus villosus,* and three species of *Eupodes*). The number of taxa identified is likely to increase with greater sampling. The community is dominated by the Collembolla, especially *Cryptopygus antarcticus* (84% of all arthropods extracted), with relatively large numbers of *I. octooculata*; the principal mite was an undetermined species of *Eupodes. Globoppia loxolineata* is near the northernmost limit of its known distribution. In general, the population density of the arthropod community of grass stands on Lynch Island appears unusually high, with some measurements suggesting it is one of the highest in the world. It also shows considerable diversity for an Antarctic site, although this observation was based on a small number of sample replicates and further sampling would be required to establish densities with greater reliability: this is difficult to achieve on Lynch Island given the very limited extent of communities available for sampling.

Lynch Island was the first site in the Antarctic where a terrestrial enchytraeid was found (in soil beneath a moss *Hennediella antarctica* on a rock ledge above the northern shore); only in a few other sites in the South Orkney Islands have these worms been found – although few samples have been gathered and the species has yet to be identified. Of the tardigrade fauna, most of the 16 individuals isolated from a sample of *Brachythecium* were *Hypsibius alpinus* and *H. pinguis* with some *H. dujardini*, while of 27 isolated from a *Prasiola crispa* sample, almost all were the latter species with a few that were other species of *Hypsibius*.

MICROORGANISMS

The mineral and organic soils of Lynch Island have a slightly higher pH than corresponding soils on nearby Signy Island. This higher base and nutrient status, together with the more favourable microclimate, is reflected in larger numbers of bacteria (including *Chromobacterium*), yeasts and fungi than occur in comparable soils on Signy Island. Bacterial numbers in the *Polytrichum* peat on Lynch Island are about eight times, and in the *Warnstorfia* peat about six times, greater than in corresponding Signy Island peats; yeasts and fungi are similarly much more abundant. Soil associated with the two flowering plants yielded several nematophagous fungi: in *Deschampsia* soil *Acrostalagmus goniodes*, *Cephalosporium balanoides* and *Dactylaria gracilis*; in *Colobanthus* soil, *Cephalosporium balanoides*, *Dactylaria gracilis*, *Dactylella stenobrocha* and *Harposporium anguillulae* were found. The basidiomycete fungi *Galerina antarctica* and *G. longinqua* occur on moist moss.

VERTEBRATES

The island has no penguin colonies or substantial breeding colonies of other birds. Groups of chinstrap (*Pygoscelis antarctica*), Adélie (*P. adeliae*) and gentoo (*P. papua*) penguins and, sometimes, blue-eyed cormorants (*Phalacrocorax atriceps*) often congregate at the north-eastern and the western ends of the island. Several pairs of brown skuas (*Catharacta lonnbergii*) and at least two pairs of kelp gulls (*Larus dominicanus*) were observed in the early 1980s to nest at the north-eastern corner. A small colony of Antarctic terns (*Sterna vittata*) may also occur in this vicinity, although in February 1994 breeding was not observed. Cape petrels (*Daption capense*) and snow petrels (*Pagodroma nivea*) breed on the higher cliffs at the eastern end and along the north-western coast of the island. A few pairs of snow petrels and Wilson's storm petrels (*Oceanites oceanicus*) nest on ledges and beneath boulders on the south side of the island.

Weddell seals (*Leptonychotes weddellii*), crabeater seals (*Lobodon carcinophgus*),occasional leopard seals (*Hydrurga leptonyx*), and small groups of southern elephant seals (*Mirounga leonina*) are regularly seen on the coast and on ice floes in the vicinity; none have been known to breed on Lynch Island. Since the early 1980s increasing numbers of Antarctic fur seals (*Arctocephalus gazella*), virtually all being immature non-breeding males, have been observed on Lynch Island, some gaining access up the more gentle north-eastern slopes to vegetated areas, where they have caused local, but severe, damage to *Polytrichum-Chorisodontium* moss banks and other communities.

Seal access to the island is principally from a beach on the northeast coast. Once seals have gained access, there are no further substantial geographical impediments to their more extensive travel over the island. Groups of seals have been observed near the summit. Destruction of swards of *Deschampsia* was first reported in 1988. At the time of the most recent inspection of the island (February 2016), it was observed that the most luxuriant areas of *Deschampsia* and *Colobanthus* on the northern and north-western slopes had not yet been affected. Accessible areas of vegetation in the eastern and north-eastern sides of the island, particularly *Polytrichum* and *Chorisodontium* moss banks, have been severely damaged by Antarctic fur seals. In some eastern and north-eastern areas that have been heavily impacted by fur seals, *Deschampsia and Colobanthus* have either been damaged or have died, but at less impacted locations at higher altitudes, these plants continue to grow and may be increasing their abundance and extending their distribution range on the island (see Map 3).

6(ii) Access to the Area

- Where possible, access shall be by small boat. Landings from the sea should be at the beach on the eastern end of the northern coast of the island (Lat. 60°39'05" S, Long. 045°36'12" W; Map 2), unless specifically authorised by Permit to land elsewhere, or when landing at this location is impractical because of adverse conditions.
- Under exceptional circumstances, necessary for purposes consistent with the objectives of the Management Plan, helicopters may be permitted to land within the Area.
- Landing of helicopters within the Area shall be at the designated location on the rock platform (8 m) on the north-western end of the island (Lat. 60°39'04.5" S, Long. 045°36'12" W; Map 2).

- Within the Area the operation of aircraft should be carried out, as a minimum requirement, in compliance with the 'Guidelines for the Operation of Aircraft near Concentrations of Birds' contained in Resolution 2 (2004). When conditions require aircraft to fly at lower elevations than recommended in the guidelines, aircraft should maintain the maximum elevation possible and minimise the time taken to transit.
- Use of helicopter smoke grenades is prohibited within the Area unless absolutely necessary for safety. If used, all smoke grenades should be retrieved.

6(iii) Location of structures within and adjacent to the Area

There are no structures present in the Area apart from several cairns marking sites used for topographical survey. The island's summit cairn is located at Lat. 60°39'05" S, Long. 045°36'12" W. A sign notifying the protected status of Lynch Island was erected on a prominent rock outcrop above the recommended landing beach in February 1994, but this was destroyed by strong winds.

Signy Research Station (UK) is 6.4 km south at Factory Cove, Borge Bay, on Signy Island.

6(iv) Location of other protected areas in the vicinity

The nearest protected areas to Lynch Island are Moe Island (ASPA No. 109), which is about 10 km SSW, and Southern Powell Island and adjacent islands (ASPA No. 111), which is about 35 km to the east (Map 1).

6(v) Special zones within the Area

None.

7. Permit conditions

7(i) General permit conditions

Entry into the Area is prohibited except in accordance with a Permit issued by an appropriate national authority as designated under Article 7 of Annex V of the Protocol on Environmental Protection to the Antarctic Treaty.

Conditions for issuing a Permit to enter the Area are that:
- it is issued for a compelling scientific purpose which cannot be served elsewhere; or

- it is issued for essential management purposes such as inspection, maintenance or review;
- the actions permitted will not jeopardise the natural ecological system in the Area;
- any management activities are in support of the objectives of this Management Plan;
- the actions permitted are in accordance with this Management Plan;
- the Permit, or an authorised copy, must be carried within the Area;
- permits shall be issued for a stated period;
- a report or reports are supplied to the authority or authorities named in the Permit;
- the appropriate authority should be notified of any activities/measures undertaken that were not included in the authorised Permit.

7(ii) Access to, and movement within or over, the Area

- Land vehicles are prohibited within the Area

- Movement within the Area shall be on foot.

- Pilots, helicopter or boat crew, or other people on helicopters or boats, are prohibited from moving on foot beyond the immediate vicinity of their landing site unless specifically authorised by Permit.

- Pedestrian traffic should be kept to the minimum consistent with the objectives of any permitted activities and every reasonable effort should be made to minimise trampling effects, i.e. all movement should be undertaken carefully so as to minimise disturbance to the soil and vegetated surfaces, walking on rocky terrain if practical.

- Overflight of bird colonies within the Area by Remotely Piloted Aircraft Systems (RPAS) shall not be permitted unless for scientific or operational purposes, and in accordance with a permit issued by an appropriate national authority.

7(iii) Activities which may be conducted in the Area

- Compelling scientific research which cannot be undertaken elsewhere and which will not jeopardize the ecosystem of the Area
- Essential management activities, including monitoring

7(iv) Installation, modification or removal of structures

No new structures are to be erected within the Area, or scientific equipment installed, except for compelling scientific or management reasons and for a pre-established period, as specified in a permit. Installation (including site selection), maintenance, modification or removal of structures and equipment shall be undertaken in a manner that minimises disturbance to the values of the Area. All structures or scientific equipment installed in the Area shall be clearly identified by country, name of the principal investigator and year of installation. All such items should be free of organisms, propagules (e.g. seeds, eggs) and non-sterile soil (see Section *7(vi)*), and be made of materials that can withstand the environmental conditions and pose minimal risk of contamination of the Area. Removal of specific structures or equipment for which the Permit has expired shall be a condition of the Permit. Permanent structures or installations are prohibited.

7(v) Location of field camps

Camping should be avoided within the Area. However, when absolutely necessary for purposes specified in the Permit, camping is allowed at the designated site at the north-western end of the island (Lat. 60°39'04" S, Long. 045°36'37" W; Map 2).

7(vi) Restrictions on materials and organisms which may be brought into the Area

No living animals, plant material or microorganisms shall be deliberately introduced into the Area. To ensure that the floristic and ecological values of the Area are maintained, special precautions shall be taken against accidentally introducing microbes, invertebrates or plants from other Antarctic sites, including stations, or from regions outside Antarctica. All sampling equipment or markers brought into the Area shall be cleaned or sterilized. To the maximum extent practicable, footwear and other equipment used or brought into the Area (including bags or backpacks) shall be thoroughly cleaned before entering the Area. Further guidance can be found in the *CEP non-native species manual* (CEP, 2016) and the *Environmental code of conduct for terrestrial scientific field research in Antarctica* (SCAR, 2009).

No herbicides or pesticides shall be brought into the Area. Any other chemicals, including radio-nuclides or stable isotopes, which may be introduced for scientific or management purposes specified in the Permit, shall be removed from the Area at or before the conclusion of the activity for which the Permit was granted. Release of radio-nuclides or stable isotopes directly into the environment in a way that renders them unrecoverable should be avoided. Fuel or other chemicals shall not be stored in the Area unless specifically authorised by Permit condition. They shall be stored and handled in a way that minimises the risk of their accidental introduction into the environment. Materials introduced into the Area shall be for a stated period only and shall be removed by the end of that stated period. If release occurs which is likely to compromise the values of the Area, removal is encouraged only where the impact of removal is not likely to be greater than that of leaving the material in situ. The appropriate authority should be notified of anything released and not removed that was not included in the authorised Permit.

7(vii) Taking, or harmful interference with, native flora or fauna

Taking or harmful interference with native flora or fauna is prohibited, except by Permit issued in accordance with Annex II to the Protocol on Environmental Protection to the Antarctic Treaty. Where taking or harmful interference with animals is involved, the *SCAR Code of Conduct for the Use of Animals for Scientific Purposes in Antarctica* should be used as a minimum standard.

7(viii) The collection or removal of materials not brought into the Area by the Permit holder

Collection or removal of anything not brought into the Area by the permit holder shall only be in accordance with a Permit and should be limited to the minimum necessary to meet scientific or management needs.

Permits shall not be granted if there is a reasonable concern that the sampling proposed would take, remove or damage such quantities of soil, native flora or fauna that their distribution or abundance within the Area would be significantly affected.

Other material of human origin likely to compromise the values of the Area which was not brought into the Area by the permit holder or otherwise authorised, may be removed from the Area unless the environmental impact of the removal is likely to be greater than leaving the material in situ; if this is the case the appropriate Authority must be notified and approval obtained.

7(ix) Disposal of waste

As a minimum standard, all waste shall be disposed of in accordance with Annex III to the Protocol on Environmental Protection to the Antarctic Treaty. In addition, all wastes shall be removed from the Area. Liquid human wastes may be disposed of into the sea. Solid human waste should not be disposed of to the sea, but shall be removed from the Area. No solid or liquid human waste shall be disposed of inland.

7(ix) Measures that may be necessary to continue to meet the aims of the Management Plan

- Permits may be granted to enter the Area to carry out scientific research, monitoring and site inspection activities, which may involve the collection of a small number of samples for analysis, to erect or maintain signboards, or to carry out protective measures.

- Any long-term monitoring sites shall be appropriately marked and the markers or signs maintained.

- Scientific activities shall be performed in accordance with *SCAR's environmental code of conduct for terrestrial scientific field research in Antarctica.*

7(xi) Requirements for reports

The principal permit holder for each visit to the Area shall submit a report to the appropriate national authority as soon as practicable, and no later than six months after the visit has been completed. Such reports should include, as appropriate, the information identified in the visit report form contained in the Guide to the Preparation of Management Plans for Antarctic Specially Protected Areas. If appropriate, the national authority should also forward a copy of the visit report to the Party that proposed the Management Plan, to assist in managing the Area and reviewing the Management Plan. Wherever possible, Parties should deposit the original or copies of the original visit reports, in a publicly accessible archive to maintain a record of usage, for the purpose of any review of the Management Plan and in organising the scientific use of the Area.

8. Supporting documentation

Convey, P. 1994. Modelling reproductive effort in sub- and maritime Antarctic mosses. *Oecologica* **100**: 45-53.

Block, W. and Christensen, B. 1985. Terrestrial Enchytraeidae from South Georgia and the Maritime Antarctic. *British Antarctic Survey Bulletin* **69**: 65-70.

Bonner, W.N. and Smith, R.I.L. (Eds) 1985. *Conservation areas in the Antarctic.* SCAR, Cambridge: 73-84.

Bonner, W.N. 1994. Active management of protected areas. In Smith, R.I.L., Walton, D.W.H. and Dingwall, P.R. (Eds) *Developing the Antarctic Protected Area system. Conservation of the Southern Polar Region I.* IUCN, Gland and Cambridge: 73-84.

Booth, R.G., Edwards, M. and Usher, M.B. 1985. Mites of the genus Eupodes (Acari, Prostigmata) from maritime Antarctica: a biometrical and taxonomic study. *Journal of the Zoological Society of London (A)* **207**: 381-406. (samples of Eupodes analysed)

Buryn, R. and Usher, M.B. 1986. A morphometric study of the mite, *Oppia loxolineata*, in the Maritime Antarctic. *British Antarctic Survey Bulletin* **73**: 47-50.

Chalmers, M.O. 1994. Lynch Island fur seal exclosure report 01/01/94. Unpublished British Antarctic Survey report BAS Ref AD6/2H/1993/NT2.

Greene, D.M and Holtom, A. 1971. Studies in *Colobanthus quitensis* (Kunth) Bartl. and *Deschampsia antarctica* Desv.: III. Distribution, habitats and performance in the Antarctic botanical zone. *British Antarctic Survey Bulletin* **26**: 1-29.

Hodgson, D.A. and Johnston, N.M. 1997. Inferring seal populations from lake sediments. *Nature* **387**(1 May).

Hodgson, D.A., Johnston, N.M., Caulkett, A.P., and Jones, V.J. 1998. Palaeolimnology of Antarctic fur seal *Arctocephalus gazella* populations and implications for Antarctic management. *Biological Conservation* **83**(2): 145-54.

Hooker, T.N. 1974. Botanical excursion to Lynch Island, 13/03/74. Unpublished British Antarctic Survey report BAS Ref AD6/2H/1973-74/N12.

Hughes, K. A., Ireland, L., Convey, P., Fleming, A. H. 2016. Assessing the effectiveness of specially protected areas for conservation of Antarctica's botanical diversity. *Conservation Biology*, **30**: 113-120.

Jennings, P.G. 1976. Tardigrada from the Antarctic Peninsula and Scotia Ridge region. *British Antarctic Survey Bulletin* **44**: 77-95.

SCAR (Scientific Committee on Antarctic Research). 2009. Environmental code of conduct for terrestrial scientific field research in Antarctica. ATCM XXXII IP4.

Shears, J.R. and Richard, K.J. 1994. Marking and inspection survey of Specially Protected Areas in the South Orkney Islands, Antarctica 07/01/94 – 17/02/94. Unpublished British Antarctic Survey report BAS Ref AD6/2H/1993/NT5.

Smith, R.I. Lewis 1972. Vegetation of the South Orkney Islands. *BAS Scientific Report* **68**, British Antarctic Survey, Cambridge.

Smith, R.I. Lewis 1990. Signy Island as a paradigm of environmental change in Antarctic terrestrial ecosystems. In K.R. Kerry and G. Hempel. *Antarctic Ecosystems: ecological change and conservation*. Springer-Verlag, Berlin: 32-50.

Smith, R.I. Lewis 1994. Introduction to the Antarctic Protected Area System. In Smith, R.I.L., Walton, D.W.H. and Dingwall, P.R. (Eds) *Developing the Antarctic Protected Area system. Conservation of the Southern Polar Region I*. IUCN, Gland and Cambridge: 14-26.

Smith, R.I. Lewis 1997. Impact of an increasing fur seal population on Antarctic plant communities: resilience and recovery. In Battaglia, B. Valencia, J. and Walton, D.W.H. *Antarctic communities: species, structure and survival*. Cambridge University Press, Cambridge: 432-36.

Star, J. and Block, W. 1998. Distribution and biogeography of oribatid mites (Acari: Oribatida) in Antarctica, the sub-Antarctic and nearby land areas. *Journal of Natural History* **32**: 861-94.

Usher, M.B. and Edwards, M. 1984. The terrestrial arthropods of the grass sward of Lynch Island, a specially protected area in Antarctica. *Oecologica* **63**: 143-44.

Usher, M.B. and Edwards, M. 1986. A biometrical study of the family Tydeidae (Acari, Prostigmata) in the Maritime Antarctic, with descriptions of three new taxa. *Journal of the Zoological Society of London (A)* **209**: 355-83.

Wynn-Williams, D.D. 1982. The microflora of Lynch Island, a sheltered maritime Antarctic site. *Comité National Française Recherche en Antarctiques* **51**: 538.

Figure 1. Map showing the location of Lynch Island in relation to the South Orkney Islands and the other protected areas in the region. <u>Inset</u>: the location of the South Orkney Islands in Antarctica.

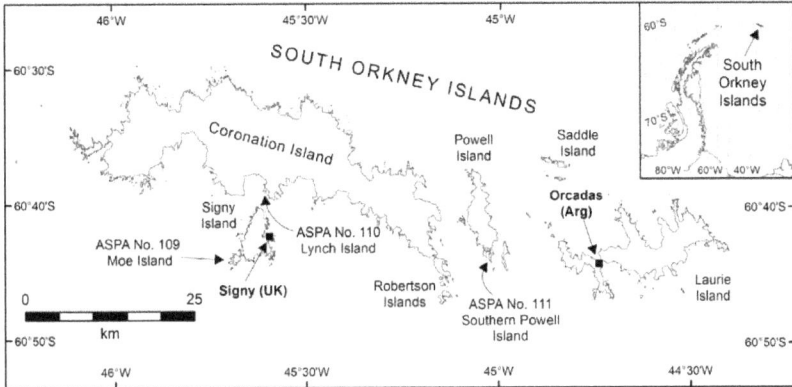

Figure 2. ASPA No. 110, Lynch Island, South Orkney Islands, topographic map.

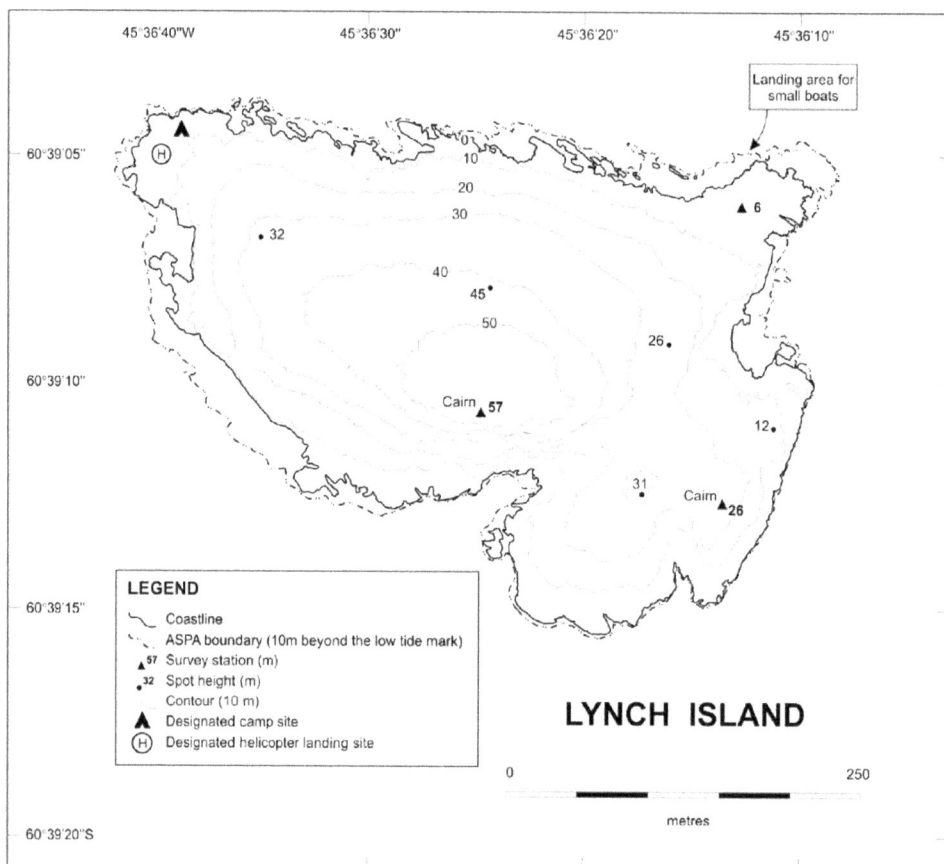

Figure 3. Normalised Difference Vegetation Index (NDVI), derived from satellite imagery, for ASPA No. 110 Lynch Island, South Orkney Islands, showing green vegetation cover using a colour scale of yellow → orange → red, with red indicating the highest NDVI values

Management Plan for Antarctic Specially Protected Area No. 111

SOUTHERN POWELL ISLAND AND ADJACENT ISLANDS, SOUTH ORKNEY ISLANDS

Introduction

The primary reason for the designation of Southern Powell Island and Adjacent Islands, South Orkney Islands (Lat. 62°57'S, Long. 60°38'W) as an Antarctic Specially Protected Area (ASPA) is to protect environmental values, predominantly the breeding bird and seal populations, and to a lesser extent, the terrestrial vegetation within the Area.

The Area was originally designated in Recommendation IV-15 (1966, SPA No. 15) after a proposal by the United Kingdom on the grounds that southern Powell Island and the adjacent islands support substantial vegetation and a considerable bird and mammal fauna. The Area was representative of the natural ecology of the South Orkney Islands, and was rendered more important by the presence of a small colony of Antarctic fur seals (*Arctocephalus gazella*).

The Area is also recognised as having scientific value. It is now well established that climate change is affecting the Southern Ocean, and that the region around the Antarctic Peninsula, Scotia Sea and South Orkney Islands is showing some of the most evident impacts of climate change. Air temperatures and ocean temperatures have increased, some ice shelves have collapsed and seasonal sea ice is now much reduced. This has important consequences for biological communities with some of the most obvious consequences of environment change have been reported for pygoscelid penguins. In particular, Adélie penguins, a species of the pack ice, are now though to be declining at most localities along the Peninsula and at the South Orkney Islands. Chinstrap penguins, a species of the more open ocean, are now also thought to be in decline. Consequently, understanding penguin foraging behaviour in an attempt to relate it to their preferred foraging habitat is particularly important. Understanding how pygoscelid penguins utilise the ocean around them is critical if we are to adequately protect their breeding colonies, including in highly biodiverse protected areas such as southern Powell Island.

Resolution 3 (2008) recommended that the "Environmental Domains Analysis for the Antarctic Continent", be used as a dynamic model for the identification of Antarctic Specially Protected Areas within the systematic environmental-geographical framework referred to in Article 3(2) of Annex V of the Protocol (see also Morgan et al., 2007). Using this model, ASPA 111 is contained within Environment Domain G (Antarctic Peninsula off-shore islands geologic). The scarcity of Environment Domain G, relative to the other environmental domain areas, means that substantial efforts have been made to conserve the values found within this environment type elsewhere: other protected areas containing Domain G include ASPAs 109, 112, 125, 126, 128, 140, 145, 149, 150, and 152 and ASMAs 1 and 4. Environment Domain A is also present (Antarctic Peninsula northern geologic). Other protected areas containing Environment Domain A include ASPAs 128, 151 and ASMA 1.

Resolution 6 (2012) recommended that the Antarctic Conservation Biogeographic Regions (ACBRs) be used for the 'identification of areas that could be designated as Antarctic Specially Protected Areas within the systematic environmental-geographic framework referred to in Article 3(2) of Annex V to the Environmental Protocol. ASPA 111 sits within Antarctic Conservation Biogeographic Region (ACBR) 2 South Orkney Islands.

Through Resolution 5 (2015) Parties recognised the usefulness of the list of Antarctic Important Bird Areas (IBAs) in planning and conducting activities in Antarctica. Important Bird Area ANT015 Southern Powell Island and adjacent islands has the same boundary as ASPA 111, and was identified due to its extensive colonies of chinstrap penguins, Adélie penguins, gentoo penguins, blue-eyed cormorants and southern giant petrels.

The two other ASPAs present within the South Orkney Islands (ASPA 109 Moe Island and ASPA 110 Lynch Island) were designated primarily to protect terrestrial vegetation. Therefore, ASPA 111 Southern Powell Island and adjacent islands complements the local network of ASPAs by protecting primarily breeding bird and seal populations, but also terrestrial vegetation.

1. Description of values to be protected

Following a visit to the ASPA in February 2016, the values specified in the original designation were reaffirmed and expanded. These values are set out as follows:

- The breeding avifauna within the Area is diverse, including up to four species of penguin [chinstrap (*Pygoscelis antarctica), gentoo (*P. papua*), Adélie (*P. adeliae*) and macaroni penguins (*Eudyptes chrysolophus*)], Wilson's storm petrels (*Oceanites oceanicus*), cape petrels (*Daption capense*), Dominican gulls (*Larus dominicanus*), southern giant petrels (*Macronectes giganteus*), black-bellied storm petrels (*Fregetta tropica*), blue-eyed cormorants (*Phalacrocorax atriceps*), brown skuas (*Catharacta loennbergi*), sheathbills (*Chionis alba*), snow petrels *(Pagodroma nivea*) and possibly Antarctic prions (*Pachyptila desolata*)

- The longest known breeding site of fur seals in the Antarctic, since their near extermination in the nineteenth century, is found within the Area.

- A diverse flora, typical of the region, including moss banks with underlying peat, moss carpet in wet areas, snow algae and the nitrophilous macroalga *Prasiola crispa* associated with the penguin colonies, is found within the Area.

- The Area has scientific value as a location for the collection of telemetry data in order to explore penguin foraging behaviour. This information will contribute to the development of habitat models that will describe the relationship between penguin foraging behaviour and seasonal sea ice extent.

2. Aims and objectives

Management of southern Powell Island and adjacent islands aims to:

- avoid degradation of, or substantial risk to, the values of the Area by preventing unnecessary human disturbance to the Area;

- allow scientific research in the Area provided it is for compelling reasons which cannot be served elsewhere and which will not jeopardise the natural ecological system in that Area;

- prevent or minimise the introduction to the Area of non-native plants, animals and microorganisms;

- minimise the possibility of introduction of pathogens which may cause disease in bird populations within the Area;

- preserve the natural ecosystem of the Area as a reference area for future comparative studies and for monitoring floristic and ecological change, colonisation processes and community development;

- allow visits for management purposes in support of the aims of the management plan;

- allow for the gathering of data on the population status of the resident penguins and seals on a regular basis and in a sustainable manner

3. Management activities

- Visits shall be made as necessary to assess whether the ASPA continues to serve the purposes for which it was designated and to ensure management and maintenance measures are adequate.

- The Management Plan shall be reviewed at least every five years and updated as required.

- Markers, signs or other structures erected within the Area for scientific or management purposes shall be secured and maintained in good condition and removed when no longer required.

- In accordance with the requirements of Annex III of the Protocol on Environmental Protection to the Antarctic Treaty, abandoned equipment or materials shall be removed to the maximum extent possible provided doing so does not adversely impact on the environment and the values of the Area.

- A copy of this Management Plan shall be made available at Signy Research Station (UK; 60°42′30″ S, 045°36′30″ W) and Orcadas Station (Argentina; 60°44′15″ S, 044°44′20″ W).

- Where appropriate, National Antarctic Programmes are encouraged to liaise closely to ensure management activities are implemented. In particular, National Antarctic Programmes are encouraged to consult with one another to prevent excessive sampling of biological material within the Area. Also, National Antarctic Programmes are encouraged to consider joint implementation of guidelines intended to minimize the introduction and dispersal of non-native species within the Area.

- All scientific and management activities undertaken within the Area should be subject to an Environmental Impact Assessment, in accordance with the requirements of Annex I of the Protocol on Environmental Protection to the Antarctic Treaty.

4. Period of designation

ASPA 111 is designated for an indefinite period.

5. Maps

Map 1. The location of southern Powell Island and adjacent island in relation to the South Orkney Islands and the other protected areas in the region. Inset: the location of the South Orkney Islands in Antarctica. Map specifications: Projection: WGS84 Antarctic Polar Stereographic. Standard parallel: 71 °S. Central meridian 45 °W.

Map 2 shows the Area in greater detail.

6. Description of the Area

6(i) Geographical coordinates and natural features

BOUNDARIES AND CO-ORDINATES
The corner co-ordinates of the Area are shown in Table 1.

Corner	Latitude	Longitude
northwest	60°42′35″ S	45°04′00″ W
northeast	60°42′35″ S	44°58′00″ W
southwest	60°45′30″ S	45°04′00″ W

southeast	60°45'30'' S	44°58'00'' W

The Area includes all of Powell Island south of the southern summit of John Peaks (415 m altitude), together with the whole of Fredriksen Island, Michelsen Island (a tidal peninsula at the southern tip of Powell Island), Christoffersen Island, Grey Island and unnamed adjacent islands. The Area encompasses all of the ice-free ground, permanent ice and semi-permanent ice found within the boundaries, but excludes the marine environment extending greater than 10 m offshore from the low tide water line. All but the Crutchley Ice Piedmont of southern Powell Island are ice-free in summer, though there are patches of semi-permanent or late-lying snow in places.

GEOLOGY

The rocks of southern Powell Island, Michelsen Island and Christoffersen Island are conglomerates of Cretaceous-Jurassic age. The two promontories to the west of John Peaks are Carboniferous greywacke-shales. There are boulders containing plant fossils in the glacial deposits around Falkland Harbour. Much of central and southern Fredriksen Island is composed of sandstone and dark phyllitic shales. The north-east and probably most of the north of this island is highly sheared conglomerate with laminated mudstone. The Area has a thick mantle of glacial till, strongly influenced by seabird guano.

BIOLOGICAL COMMUNITIES

Michelsen Island has little land vegetation, although on the rocks there are extensive communities of lichens dominated by nitrophilous crustose species. These are also widespread on Fredriksen Island and elsewhere on bird-influenced cliffs and rocks near the shore. The most diverse vegetation on Powell Island occurs on the two promontories and associated scree west of Falkland Harbour. Here, and on Christoffersen Island and the northern part of Fredriksen Island, moss banks with underlying peat occur. Wet areas support stands of moss carpet. There are extensive areas of the nitrophilous macroalga *Prasiola crispa* associated with the penguin colonies in the area. Snow algae are prominent on the ice piedmont and snow patches in late summer. Use of satellite remote sensing techniques (Normalised Difference Vegetation Index) showed the area of green vegetation within the ASPA to be 0.8 km^2 (c. 3% of the ASPA area).

No information is available on the arthropod fauna, but this is probably very similar to that at Signy Island. The springtails *Cryptopygus antarcticus* and *Parisotoma octoculata* and the mites *Alaskozetes antarcticus*, *Stereotydeus villosus* and *Gamasellus racovitzai* occur in great numbers beneath stones.

There are few observations on marine invertebrates and biota in the Area, but this is likely to be very similar to the well-researched Signy Island area. The relatively enclosed Falkland-Ellefsen Harbour area and the bay on the east side of the peninsula are highly influenced by glacial run-off from the ice piedmont.

Large numbers of penguins and petrels breed throughout the Area. There are many thousand pairs of chinstrap penguins (*Pygoscelis antarctica*), mostly on Fredriksen Island. Similarly large numbers of Adélie penguins (*P. adeliae*) occur principally on the southern Powell-Michelsen Island area. Here there are also several thousand pairs of gentoo penguins (*P. papua*) and a very few scattered pairs of macaroni penguins (*Eudyptes chrysolophus*) breeding among the gentoos (for more information see Harris et al., 2015).

Other breeding birds include southern giant petrels (*Macronectes giganteus*), cape petrels *(Daption capensis)*, snow petrels *(Pagodroma nivea)*, Wilson's storm petrels (*Oceanites oceanicus*), blue-eyed shags (*Phalacrocorax atriceps*), Dominican gulls (*Larus dominicanus*), brown skuas (*Catharacia lonnbergi*), sheathbills (*Chionis alba*), and possibly Antarctic prions (*Pachyptila desolata*) and blackbellied storm petrels (*Fregetta tropica*).

Michelsen Island is the longest known breeding site in the Antarctic of fur seals since their near extermination in the nineteenth century. The number of pups born annually has increased slowly but fairly steadily from 11 in 1956 to about 60 in 1989. Thirty-four live pups were recorded in January 1994. However, numbers have declined, with only four pups recorded during the 2013-14 and 2015-15 breeding seasons. Nevertheless, many transient non-breeding males and juveniles visit the Area during the summer. Other seals are frequent on the beaches, mainly elephant seals (*Mirounga leonina*) and Weddell seals (*Leptopychotes weddelli*). Leopard seals (*Hydrurga leptonyx*) and crabeater seals (*Lobodon carcinophagus*) are occasionally seen on ice floes.

6(ii) Access to the Area

- Access shall be by small boat.
- There are no special restrictions on boat landings from the sea, or that apply to the sea routes used to move to and from the Area. Due to the large extent of accessible coast around the Area, landing is possible at many locations. Nevertheless, if possible, landing of cargo and scientific equipment should be close to the recommended field camp at 60°43'20''S, 045°01'32''W.
- Under exceptional circumstances necessary for purposes consistent with the objectives of the Management Plan helicopters may be permitted to land at the designated landing site located beside the recommended field camp at 60°43'20''S, 045°01'32''W. Helicopters shall not land elsewhere within the Area.
- To prevent disturbance of breeding avifauna, helicopters landings are prohibited within the Area between the period 1 November to 15 February.
- Within the Area the operation of aircraft should be carried out, as a minimum requirement, in compliance with the 'Guidelines for the Operation of Aircraft near Concentrations of Birds' contained in Resolution 2 (2004). When conditions require aircraft to fly at lower elevations than recommended in the guidelines, aircraft should maintain the maximum elevation possible and minimise the time taken to transit.
- Overflying helicopters should avoid sites where there are concentrations of birds (e.g. southern Powell-Michelsen Island area or Fredriksen Island).
- Use of helicopter smoke grenades is prohibited within the Area unless absolutely necessary for safety. If used all smoke grenades should be retrieved.

6(iii) Location of structures within and adjacent to the Area

Marker boards denoting the Area's protected status are positioned in the following locations:

- Christoffersen Island: on a small promontory on the north-eastern shore of the island at the entrance to Falkland Harbour. The board is located at the back of the beach just below a small Adélie penguin rookery (60°43'36''S, 045°02'08''W).
- Fredriksen Island: at the northern end of the pebble boulder beach on the western side of the island, below a small chinstrap penguin rookery. The board is at the back of the beach on top of a small rock outcrop (60°44'06''S, 044°59'25''W).

Other structures in the area include a marker posts on top of a small rock outcrop at the back of the shingle beach on the east side of the southern promontory of Powell Island (60°43'20''S, 045°01'40''W) and various mooring chains, posts and rings associated with the use of Ellefsen and Falkland Harbours by floating whale factories in the 1910s that are located on the shore.

6(iv) Location of other protected areas within close proximity of the Area

ASPA No. 109, Moe Island, and ASPA No. 110, Lynch Island, are located approximately 35 km west of the Area (see Map 1).

6(v) Restricted zones within the Area

None.

7. Permit Conditions

7(i) General permit conditions

Entry into the Area is prohibited except in accordance with a Permit issued by an appropriate national authority as designated under Article 7 of Annex V of the Protocol on Environmental Protection to the Antarctic Treaty.

Conditions for issuing a Permit to enter the Area are that:

- it is issued for a compelling scientific purpose which cannot be served elsewhere;
- it is issued for essential management purposes such as inspection, maintenance or review;
- the actions permitted will not jeopardise the natural ecological system in the Area;
- any management activities are in support of the objectives of this Management Plan;
- the actions permitted are in accordance with this Management Plan;
- the Permit must be carried within the Area;
- permits shall be issued for a stated period;
- a report or reports are supplied to the authority or authorities named in the Permit;
- the appropriate authority should be notified of any activities/measures undertaken that were not included in the authorised Permit.

7(ii) Access to and movement within or over the Area

- Land vehicles are prohibited in the Area.

- No pedestrian routes are designated within the Area, but persons on foot should avoid walking on vegetated areas or disturbing wildlife wherever possible.

- To reduce disturbance of bird species, anchoring within Falkland Harbour and Ellefsen Harbour is strongly discouraged, except in an emergency.

- Pilots, air and boat crew, or other people on aircraft or boats, are prohibited from moving on foot beyond the immediate vicinity of their landing site unless specifically authorised by Permit.

- Overflight of bird colonies within the Area by Remotely Piloted Aircraft Systems (RPAS) shall not be permitted unless for scientific or operational purposes, and in accordance with a permit issued by an appropriate national authority.

7(iii) Activities which may be conducted in the Area

Activities include:

- compelling scientific research which cannot be undertaken elsewhere
- essential management activities, including monitoring.

7(iv) Installation, modification or removal of structures

No new structures are to be erected within the Area, or scientific equipment installed, except for compelling scientific or management reasons and for a pre-established period, as specified in a permit. Installation (including site selection), maintenance, modification or removal of structures and equipment shall be undertaken in a manner that minimises disturbance to the values of the Area. All structures or scientific equipment installed in the Area shall be clearly identified by country, name of the principal investigator and year of installation. All such items should be free of organisms, propagules (e.g. seeds, eggs) and non-sterile soil (see Section *7(vi)*), and be made of materials that can withstand the environmental conditions and pose minimal risk of contamination of the Area. Removal of specific structures or equipment for which the Permit has expired shall be a condition of the Permit. Permanent structures or installations are prohibited.

7(v) Location of field camps

In order to minimise the area of ground within the ASPA impacted by camping activities, tents should be erected at the designated field campsite, located at 60°43'20''S, 045°01'32''W. When necessary for purposes specified in the Permit, temporary camping beyond the designated field campsite is allowed within the Area. Camps should be located on non-vegetated sites, such as on the drier parts of the raised beaches, or on thick (>0.5 m) snow-cover when practicable, and should avoid concentrations of breeding birds or mammals.

7(vi) Restrictions on materials and organisms which may be brought into the Area

No living animals, plant material or microorganisms shall be deliberately introduced into the Area. To ensure that the floristic and ecological values of the Area are maintained, special precautions shall be taken against accidentally introducing microbes, invertebrates or plants from other Antarctic sites, including stations, or from regions outside Antarctica. All sampling equipment or markers brought into the Area shall be cleaned or sterilized. To the maximum extent practicable, footwear and other equipment used or brought into the Area (including bags or backpacks) shall be thoroughly cleaned before entering the Area. Further guidance can be found in the CEP Non-native Species Manual (Edition 2011) and COMNAP/SCAR Checklists for supply chain managers of National Antarctic Programmes for the reduction in risk of transfer of non-native species. In view of the presence of breeding bird colonies within the Area, no poultry products, including wastes from such products and products containing uncooked dried eggs, shall be released into the Area or into the adjacent sea.

No herbicides or pesticides shall be brought into the Area. Any other chemicals, including radio-nuclides or stable isotopes, which may be introduced for scientific or management purposes specified in the Permit, shall be removed from the Area at or before the conclusion of the activity for which the Permit was granted. Release of radio-nuclides or stable isotopes directly into the environment in a way that renders them unrecoverable should be avoided. Fuel or other chemicals shall not be stored in the Area unless specifically authorised by Permit condition. They shall be stored and handled in a way that minimises the risk of their accidental introduction into the environment. Materials introduced into the Area shall be for a stated period only and shall be removed by the end of that stated period. If release occurs which is likely to compromise the values of the Area, removal is encouraged only where the impact of removal is not likely to be greater than that of leaving the material in situ. The appropriate authority should be notified of anything released and not removed that was not included in the authorised Permit.

7(vii) Taking or harmful interference with native flora and fauna

Taking of or harmful interference with native flora or fauna is prohibited, except by Permit issued in accordance with Annex II to the Protocol on Environmental Protection to the Antarctic Treaty. Where taking of or harmful interference with animals is involved, the *SCAR Code of Conduct for the Use of Animals for Scientific Purposes in Antarctica* should be used as a minimum standard.

7(viii) Collection and removal of materials not brought into the Area by the Permit holder

Collection or removal of anything not brought into the Area by the permit holder shall only be in accordance with a Permit and should be limited to the minimum necessary to meet scientific or management needs.

Other material of human origin likely to compromise the values of the Area which was not brought into the Area by the permit holder or otherwise authorised, may be removed from the Area unless the environmental impact of the removal is likely to be greater than leaving the material in situ; if this is the case the appropriate Authority must be notified and approval obtained.

7(ix) Disposal of waste

As a minimum standard, all waste shall be disposed of in accordance with Annex III to the Protocol on Environmental Protection to the Antarctic Treaty. In addition, all wastes shall be removed from the Area. Liquid human wastes may be disposed of into the sea. Solid human waste should not be disposed of to the sea, but shall be removed from the Area. No solid or liquid human waste shall be disposed of inland.

7(ix) Measures that may be necessary to ensure that the aims and objectives of the Management Plan continue to be met

- Permits may be granted to enter the Area to carry out scientific research, monitoring and site inspection activities, which may involve the collection of a small number of samples for analysis, to erect or maintain signboards, or to carry out protective measures.

- Any long-term monitoring sites shall be appropriately marked and the markers or signs maintained.

- Scientific activities shall be performed in accordance with *SCAR's environmental code of conduct for terrestrial scientific field research in Antarctica.*

7(xi) Requirements for reports

The principal permit holder for each visit to the Area shall submit a report to the appropriate national authority as soon as practicable, and no later than six months after the visit has been completed. Such reports should include, as appropriate, the information identified in the visit report form contained in the Guide to the Preparation of Management Plans for Antarctic Specially Protected Areas. If appropriate, the national authority should also forward a copy of the visit report to the Party that proposed the Management Plan, to assist in managing the Area and reviewing the Management Plan. Wherever possible, Parties should deposit the original or copies of the original visit reports, in a publicly accessible archive to maintain a record of usage, for the purpose of any review of the Management Plan and in organising the scientific use of the Area.

8. Supporting documentation

Cantrill, D. J. 2000. A new macroflora from the South Orkney Islands, Antarctica: evidence of an Early to Middle Jurassic age for the Powell Island Conglomerate. Antarctic Science 12: 185-195.

Harris, C.M., Lorenz, K., Fishpool, L.D.C., Lascelles, B., Cooper, J., Coria, N.R., Croxall, J.P., Emmerson, L.M., Fijn, R.C., Fraser, W.L., Jouventin, P., LaRue, M.A., Le Maho, Y., Lynch, H.J., Naveen, R., Patterson-Fraser, D.L., Peter, H.-U., Poncet, S., Phillips, R.A., Southwell, C.J., van Franeker, J.A., Weimerskirch, H., Wienecke, B., and Woehler, E.J. 2015. *Important Bird Areas in Antarctica 2015*. BirdLife International and Environmental Research & Assessment Ltd., Cambridge.

Holmes, K. D. 1965. *Interim geological report on Matthews and Powell islands.* British Antarctic Survey AD6/2H/1965/G2. 2pp

Longton, R.E. 1967. Vegetation in the maritime Antarctic. In Smith, J.E., *Editor*, A discussion of the terrestrial Antarctic ecosystem. *Philosophical Transactions of the Royal Society of London*, B, **252**, 213-235.

Morgan, F., Barker, G., Briggs, C., Price, R. and Keys, H. 2007. *Environmental Domains of Antarctica Version 2.0 Final Report*. Manaaki Whenua Landcare Research New Zealand Ltd, 89 pp.

Ochyra, R., Bednarek-Ochyra, H. and Smith, R.I.L. *The Moss Flora of Antarctica*. 2008. Cambridge University Press, Cambridge. 704 pp.

Øvstedal, D.O. and Smith, R.I.L. 2001. *Lichens of Antarctica and South Georgia. A Guide to their Identification and Ecology*. Cambridge University Press, Cambridge, 411 pp.

Peat, H., Clarke, A., and Convey, P. 2007. Diversity and biogeography of the Antarctic flora. *Journal of Biogeography*, 34, 132-146.

Poncet, S., and Poncet, J. 1985. A survey of penguin breeding populations at the South Orkney Islands. *British Antarctic Survey Bulletin*, No. 68, 71-81.

Smith, R. I. L. 1972. *British Antarctic Survey science report 68*. British Antarctic Survey, Cambridge, 124 pp.

Smith, R. I. L. 1984. Terrestrial plant biology of the sub-Antarctic and Antarctic. In: *Antarctic Ecology*, Vol. 1. Editor: R. M. Laws. London, Academic Press.

Thomson, J. W. 1973. The geology of Powell, Christoffersen and Michelsen islands, South Orkney Islands. *British Antarctic Survey Bulletin*, Nos. 33 & 34, 137-167.

Thomson, M. R. A. 1981. Late Mesozoic stratigraphy and invertebrate palaeontology of the South Orkney Islands. *British Antarctic Survey Bulletin*, No. 54, 65-83.

Map 1. The location of Southern Powell Island and adjacent island in relation to the South Orkney Islands and the other protected areas in the region. <u>Inset</u>: the location of the South Orkney Islands in Antarctica.

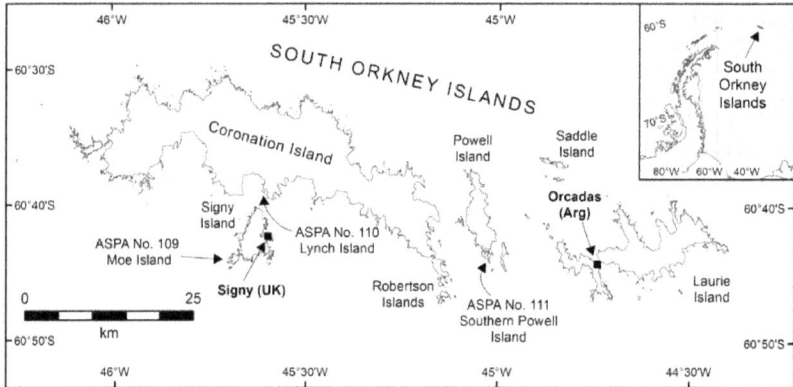

Map 2. Southern Powell Island and adjacent islands Antarctic Specially Protected Area No. 111.

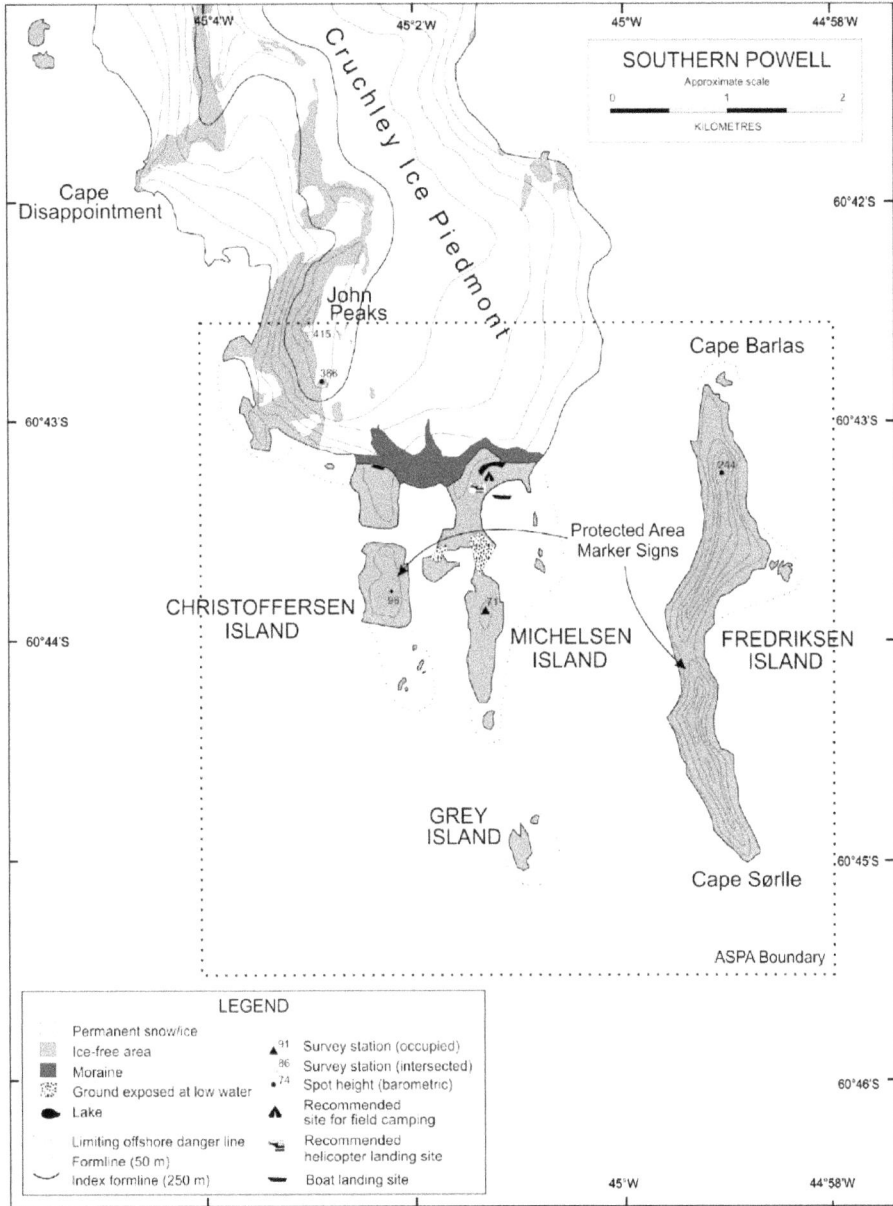

Management Plan for Antarctic Specially Protected Area No. 115

LAGOTELLERIE ISLAND, MARGUERITE BAY, GRAHAM LAND

Introduction

The primary reason for the designation of Lagotellerie Island, Marguerite Bay, Graham Land (Latitude 67°53'20" S, Longitude 67°25'30" W; area 1.58 km^2) as an Antarctic Specially Protected Area (ASPA) is to protect environmental values, and primarily the terrestrial flora and fauna but also the avifauna within the Area.

Lagotellerie Island is approximately 2 km by 1.3 km, oriented generally in an east-west direction. The Area is 11 km south of Porquois Pas Island and 3.25 km west of the south end of Horseshoe Island. Lagotellerie Island was first mapped by Jean-Baptiste Charcot during the Deuxième Expédition Antarctiques Française in 1908-10. There are no records of further visits until the 1940s, when the island was visited occasionally by American, Argentine and British field parties from nearby scientific stations. The island has not been the subject of any major scientific investigations and is thus largely undisturbed by human activities.

Lagotellerie Island was originally designated as a Specially Protected Area through Recommendation XIII-II (1985, SPA No. 19) after a proposal by the United Kingdom. It was designated on the grounds that the island contains a rich and diverse flora and fauna typical of the southern Antarctic Peninsula region. These values were reiterated in Recommendation XVI-6 (1991) when a management plan for the site was adopted, and are largely reaffirmed again in the present management plan.

Resolution 3 (2008) recommended that the Environmental Domains Analysis for the Antarctic Continent, be used as a dynamic model for the identification of Antarctic Specially Protected Areas within the systematic environmental-geographical framework referred to in Article 3(2) of Annex V of the Protocol (see also Morgan et al., 2007). Using this model, ASPA 115 is contained within Environment Domain B (Antarctic Peninsula mid-northern latitudes geologic). Other protected areas containing Domain B include ASPAs 108, 134, 140 and 153 and ASMAs 4. Resolution 6 (2012) recommended that the Antarctic Conservation Biogeographic Regions (ACBRs) be used for the identification of areas that could be designated as Antarctic Specially Protected Areas within the systematic environmental-geographic framework referred to in Article 3(2) of Annex V to the Environmental Protocol. ASPA 115 Lagotellerie Island sits within ACBR 3 Northwest Antarctic Peninsula (Terauds et al., 2012). Through Resolution 5 (2015) Parties recognised the usefulness of the list of Antarctic Important Bird Areas (IBAs) in planning and conducting activities in Antarctica. Important Bird Area ANT098 Lagotellerie Island has the same boundary as ASPA 115, and was identified due to the presence of a large colony of blue-eyed cormorants.

The three other ASPAs are present within the Marguerite Bay area (ASPA 107 Emperor Island, Dion Islands, ASPA 117 Avian Island and ASPA 129 Rothera Point). ASPA 107 Emperor Island and ASPA 117 Avian Island were designated to protect predominantly the avifauna of the area, while ASPA 129 Rothera Point was designated to monitor the impact of the nearby station on an Antarctic fellfield ecosystem. Therefore, Lagotellerie Island complements the local network of ASPAs by primarily protecting terrestrial biological communities.

1. Description of values to be protected

Following a visit to the ASPA in February 2017, the values specified in the earlier designation were reaffirmed. These values are set out as follows:

- Lagotellerie Island contains a relatively diverse flora typical of the southern Antarctic Peninsula region. Of particular interest is the abundance of the only two Antarctic flowering plants *Deschampsia antarctica* and *Colobanthus quitensis* which form stands up to 10 m^2. These are amongst the largest stands known south of the South Shetland Islands, being only 90 km north of their southern limit. Both species flower profusely and the seeds have a greater viability than those produced in the South Orkney or South Shetland Islands.

- Numerous mosses and lichens form well-developed communities on the island. A few of the mosses are fertile, which is a rare phenomenon in most Antarctic localities.

- The island is notable for the occurrence of *Deschampsia antarctica* at the highest recorded altitude south of 56° S, with scattered small plants observed at heights of up to 275 m. The island therefore has a particular future scientific value for study of the influence of altitudinal gradient on biological viability for plant species represented at this site.

- The invertebrate fauna is rich and the island is one of the southernmost sites for the apterous midge *Belgica antarctica*

- The shallow loamy soil developed beneath the vegetation and its associated invertebrate fauna and microbiota are probably unique at this latitude

- There is a colony of Adélie penguins (*Pygoscelis adeliae*) and one of the farthest south colonies of a few dozen blue-eyed cormorants (*Phalacrocorax atriceps*) at the south-east corner of the island. Numerous pairs of brown and south polar skuas (*Catharacta lonnbergii* and *C. maccormicki*) breed on the island.

- The values associated with the penguin and skua colonies are now considered to be their ecological interrelationship with the other biological features of exceptional value noted above.

- Fossiliferous strata present at the eastern end of the island are of particular geological value, as such formations are not commonly exposed in the Antarctic Peninsula Volcanic Group.

- The island has not been subject to frequent visits, scientific research or sampling and therefore may be regarded as one of the most pristine highly vegetated areas in the region.

2. Aims and objectives

Management at Lagotellerie Island aims to:

- avoid degradation of, or substantial risk to, the values of the Area by preventing unnecessary human disturbance to the Area;

- allow scientific research in the Area provided it is for compelling reasons which cannot be served elsewhere which will not jeopardise the natural ecological system in that Area;

- allow visits for management purposes in support of the aims of the management plan;

- prevent or minimise the introduction to the Area of non-native plants, animals and microorganisms;

- minimise the possibility of introduction of pathogens which may cause disease in bird populations within the Area;

- preserve the natural ecosystem of the Area as a reference area for future studies.

3. Management activities

The following management activities are to be undertaken to protect the values of the Area:

- Visits shall be made as necessary to assess whether the ASPA continues to serve the purposes for which it was designated and to ensure management and maintenance measures are adequate.

- The Management Plan shall be reviewed at least every five years and updated as required.

- Markers, signs or other structures erected within the Area for scientific or management purposes shall be secured and maintained in good condition and removed when no longer required.

- In accordance with the requirements of Annex III of the Protocol on Environmental Protection to the Antarctic Treaty, abandoned equipment or materials shall be removed to the maximum extent possible provided doing so does not adversely impact on the environment and the values of the Area.

- A copy of this Management Plan shall be made available at Rothera Research Station (UK; Latitude 67°34' S, Longitude 68°07' W) and General San Martín Station (Argentina; Latitude 68°08' S, Longitude 67°06' W).

- All scientific and management activities undertaken within the Area should be subject to an Environmental Impact Assessment, in accordance with the requirements of Annex I of the Protocol on Environmental Protection to the Antarctic Treaty.

4. Period of designation

The ASPA is designated for an indefinite period.

5. Maps

Figure 1. Lagotellerie Island Antarctic Specially Protected Area No. 115, Marguerite Bay, location map, showing the location of General San Martín Station (Arg.), the station Teniente Luis Carvajal (Chile), Adelaide Island, Rothera Research Station (UK) and nearby ASPA 129 at Rothera Point, also on Adelaide Island, and the location of the other protected areas in the region [Emperor Island, Dion Islands (ASPA 107) and Avian Island (ASPA 117)]. 'Base Y' (UK) (Historic Monument No. 63) on Horseshoe Island is shown. Inset: the location of Lagotellerie Island along the Antarctic Peninsula.

Figure 2. Lagotellerie Island (ASPA 115) topographic map. Map specifications: Projection: Lambert Conformal Conic. Standard parallels: 1st 63° 20' 00" S; 2nd 76° 40' 00"S. Central Meridian: 65° 00' 00" W. Latitude of Origin: 70° 00' 00" S. Spheroid: WGS84. Datum: Mean Sea Level. Vertical contour interval 20 m. Horizontal and vertical accuracy expected to be better than ±5 m.

Figure 3. Lagotellerie Island (ASPA 115) geological sketch map.

Figure 4. Normalised Difference Vegetation Index (NDVI), derived from satellite imagery, for ASPA No. 115 Lagotellerie Island, Marguerite Bay, Graham Land, showing green vegetation cover using a colour scale of yellow → orange → red, with red indicating the highest NDVI values

6. Description of the Area

6(i) Geographical coordinates and natural features

BOUNDARIES AND CO-ORDINATES
The corner co-ordinates of the Area are shown in Table 1.

Corner	Latitude	Longitude
northwest	67°52'30'' S	67°27'00'' W

northeast	67°52'30'' S	67°22'00'' W
southwest	67°54'00'' S	67°27'00'' W
southeast	67°54'00'' S	67°22'00'' W

The Area includes all of Lagotellerie Island and unnamed adjacent islands and islets. The Area encompasses all of the ice-free ground, permanent ice and semi-permanent ice found within the boundaries, but excludes the marine environment extending greater than 10 m offshore from the low tide water line (Figure 2). Boundary markers have not been installed because the coast itself is a clearly defined and visually obvious boundary.

Lagotellerie Island is steep-sided and rocky, with about 13% permanent ice cover, most of which is on the southern slopes. The island rises to twin peaks of 268 m and 288 m separated by a broad saddle at around 200 m, with precipitous cliffs up to this height on the south, west and east sides. The upper northern slopes also have steep cliffs, intersected by gullies, screes and traversed by broad rock terraces. The lower northern slopes are more gentle, particularly on the eastern half of the island, with a broad rocky terrace at an elevation of about 15 m which is formed of frost-shattered raised beach debris.

GEOLOGY

The bulk of Lagotellerie Island is formed of quartz diorite of unknown age, cut by pink, coarse-grained granodiorite and numerous basic and felsic dykes (Figure 3). At the eastern end of the island the plutonic rocks are in fault contact with folded, mildly hornfelsed volcanic rocks of Jurassic–Cretaceous age. These consist of agglomerates, andesitic lavas and tuffs of the Antarctic Peninsula Volcanic Group, with plant remains – probably Jurassic – present in shaly beds interbedded with tuff. Such fossiliferous strata are not commonly exposed in the Antarctic Peninsula Volcanic Group, and are therefore of particular geological importance.

Locally extensive areas of coarse sand and gravel derived from weathered quartz-diorite occur on slopes, ledges, gullies and depressions; the most extensive accumulations are on the saddle between the two summits where the soil is sorted into well-developed stone polygons, circles and stripes. On the broad rock terraces closed stands of moss and grass have developed a relatively rich loamy earth up to 25 cm in depth. Glacial erratics are common on the island.

TERRESTRIAL BIOLOGICAL COMMUNITIES

The island has a relatively diverse flora and luxuriant development of plant communities, representative of the southern maritime Antarctic region. Use of satellite remote sensing techniques (Normalised Difference Vegetation Index) showed the area of green vegetation within the ASPA to be 0.06 km² (c. 3.7% of the ASPA area) (see Figure 4). The rich terrestrial biology of Lagotellerie Island was first noted by Herwil Bryant, biologist at East Base (US, on Stonington Island; now Historic Monument No. 55), during a visit in 1940-41 when he observed growths of moss, the Antarctic hair grass *Deschampsia antarctica*, and "a small flowering plant" (almost certainly the Antarctic pearlwort *Colobanthus quitensis*), in a small gully – believed to be that found at the north-eastern end of the island – which he considered of such unusual richness for the region that he unofficially referred to it as "Shangri-la Valley". He did not describe the less luxuriant but more extensive communities of *Deschampsia antarctica* and *Colobanthus quitensis* found on the higher north-facing slopes of the island. These slopes and terraces also provide favourable microclimatic conditions for growth, with a relatively long snow-free growing season, and support an abundance of *Deschampsia antarctica* and *Colobanthus quitensis*, the grass forming closed swards of up to 10 m² on some of the terraces. These are among the largest stands of these plants known south of the South Shetland Islands. Both species flower abundantly and the seeds have a greater viability than those produced in the South Orkney or South Shetland Islands, yet they are close to the southern limit of their range. Lagotellerie Island, however, is notable for the growth of *Deschampsia antarctica* at the highest altitude recorded south of

56° S, with scattered small plants observed at heights of up to 275 m. *Colobanthus quitensis* has been observed growing up to 120 m on the island.

Lagotellerie Island also has a rich cryptogamic flora, with small stands of well-developed communities containing several mosses and lichens which are rare at this latitude (notably the mosses *Platydictya jungermannioides* and *Polytrichastrum alpinum*, and lichens *Caloplaca isidioclada*, *Fuscoparmelia gerlachei* and *Usnea trachycarpa*). The number of bryophyte species thus far identified include 20 mosses and two liverworts (*Barbilophozia hatcheri* and *Cephaloziella varians*), and there are at least 60 lichen species. A comprehensive floristic survey of the island has not yet been undertaken, and numerous species, especially of crustose lichens, remain to be accurately determined.

Vegetation is best developed on a series of rock terraces at around 30-50 m a.s.l. on the northern side of the island. Here, both *Deschampsia* and *Colobanthus* are abundant, and closed grass swards form stands of several square metres. Associated with these, especially on the moister terraces, are usually the mosses *Brachythecium austro-salebrosum*, *Bryum* spp., *Pohlia nutans*, *Polytrichastrum alpinum* and *Sanionia uncinata*, and liverworts *Barbilophozia hatcheri* and *Cephaloziella varians*. Many of these grass swards are used as nest sites by skuas.

In drier habitats, especially on scree and rock faces, there are locally dense stands dominated by the macrolichens *Usnea sphacelata* and *U. subantarctica*, with *Pseudephebe minuscula*, *Umbilicaria decussata*, and a large number of crustose taxa. Several lichens are associated with the grass and moss communities (e.g. *Cladonia* spp., *Leproloma* spp., *Leptogium puberulum*, *Ochrolechia frigida*, *Psoroma* spp.). Near the penguin and cormorant colonies several colourful nitrophilous lichens are abundant (e.g. *Buellia* spp., *Caloplaca* spp., *Fuscoparmelia gerlachei*, *Xanthoria* spp.).

Numerous lichens (notably *Caloplaca isidioclada*, *Pseudephebe minuscula*, *Usnea sphacelata*, *Umbilicaria decussata* and many crustose taxa) and a few mosses (notably *Grimmia refelxidens*) occur close to the summit of the island, as do scattered individual plants of *Deschampsia*. Few bryophytes produce sporophytes at far southern latitudes, but several mosses are fertile on Lagotellerie Island (e.g. *Andreaea regularis*, *Bartramia patens*, *Bryum amblyodon*, *B. pseudotriquetrum*, *Grimmia reflexidens*, *Hennediella heimii*, *Pohlia nutans*, *Schistidium antarctici*, *Syntrichia princeps*).

Specific studies of the invertebrate fauna have not been conducted on Lagotellerie Island. However, at least six species of arthropod have been recorded: *Alaskozetes antarcticus*, *Gamasellus racovitzai*, *Globoppia loxolineata* (Acari), *Cryptopygus antarcticus*, *Friesea grisea* (Collembola), and *Belgica antarctica* (Diptera, Chironomidae). Several species of nematophagous fungi have been isolated from the soils associated with mosses and *Deschampsia* on Lagotellerie Island (*Cephalosporium balanoides*, *Dactylaria gracilis*, *Dactylella ellipsospora*), species widely distributed in similar habitats throughout the Antarctic and also commonly found in temperate soils.

Bryant reported several small pools present on the island in the early 1940s, which presumably are the same as, or close to, those observed more recently on the extensive flat low-lying ground on the northern side of the island. He recorded the pools contained many phyllopod crustaceans identified as *Branchinecta granulosa*. Rocks in one of the pools were coated in a bright green filamentous alga, on which the mites *Alaskozetes antarcticus* were observed. *A. antarcticus* was also common under pebbles on the pool floor. Other microorganisms of the trochelminth type were observed living in the algae, with a pink rotifer identified as *Philodina gregaria* being especially numerous. Small tufts of a grey-green alga were observed on large pebbles close to the pool bottom. The algae have not been described in more detail, although the presence of *Prasiola crispa* has been noted. More recent observations in the early 1980s suggested there were no permanent freshwater bodies on the island, but temporary runnels in summer were found, with some brackish pools in rock depressions near the northern coast. Inspection visit January 1989 and more recently noted the presence of several small melt pools of around 5-10 m², some with fringing wet moss carpets, and suggested these were probably the habitat of *Belgica antarctica*.

VERTEBRATE FAUNA

A small Adélie penguin (*Pygoscelis adeliae*) colony occupies the eastern promontory of the island (Figure 2). Numbers have varied from a low of perhaps 350-400 pairs based on an estimate made in December 1936 to a high of 2402 pairs recorded in an accurate nest count in November 1955. A count of the colony made on 19 February 2011 noted approximately 1850 adult and juvenile birds (accurate to within 10%). The colony was regularly used as a source of eggs for personnel stationed at the nearby British Base Y on Horseshoe Island between 1955-60. It was reported that some 800 eggs were taken during 1955. The number of breeding pairs dropped to around 1000 in 1959 and 1960. Adélie penguin colonies are known to exhibit high interannual change in numbers as a result of a variety of natural factors, and in March 1981 it was observed that all of the approximately 1000 chicks in the colony had died. A chick count made in February 1983 suggested the colony consisted of approximately 1700 pairs, which is considered accurate to within 15-25%.

A small colony of blue-eyed cormorants (*Phalacrocorax atriceps*) has been observed on the eastern promontory of the island, which is one of the most southerly breeding sites reported for the species. Some 200 immature birds were observed close to the island, within view of the colony, on 16 January 1956. The colony was reported to consist of 10 nests on 17 February 1983. The colony was not seen in the January 1989 inspection on Lagotellerie Island; however, in February 2011, c. 250 adults and chicks were observed and with many nest containing two large chicks.

Brown and south polar skuas (*Catharacta loenbergi* and *C. maccormicki*) are also present, with 12 nests reported in 1956, when it was noted that many of the chicks were definitely south polar skua (*C. maccormicki*). It was estimated in 1958 that five pairs nested around the penguin colony and that both species occurred. A group of 59 non-breeding birds of both species was recorded on 12 January 1989 mid-way along the northern side of the island. Two Wilson's storm petrel (*Oceanites oceanicus*) nests were recorded on 14 January 1956. A kelp gull (*Larus dominicanus*) nest, with eggs, was recorded in the 'Shangri-La Valley' by Bryant in December 1940 (for more information on bird life in the Area see Harris et al., 2015).

The inspection visit in January 1989 reported 12 Weddell seals (*Leptonychotes weddellii*) hauled out on a small shingle beach at the base of a rocky spit on the north coast, but no other seals were seen. In contrast, the inspection visit of February 2011 noted c. 200 fur seals on northern side of the island and within the Adélie penguins colony (particular to the south of the colony above the pebble beaches). Twenty Weddell seals were also observed.

HUMAN IMPACT

The most significant environmental impact at Lagotellerie Island appears to have been from the practice of egg harvesting to feed personnel at bases operating nearby in the period 1955-60. The inspection visit of February 2017 reported there was no evidence of any recent physical or biological change on the island and it was concluded that the Area was continuing to serve the purpose for which it was designated.

6(ii) Access to the Area

- Access to the Area shall be by boat. Access from the sea should be to the northern coast of the island (Figure 2), unless specifically authorised by Permit to land elsewhere or when landing along this coast is impractical because of adverse conditions. The coastline is generally rocky and recommended landing sites are located on the north coast at Lat. 67°52'57'' Long. 067°24'03'' and Lat. 67°53'04'' Long. 067°23'30'' (see Figure 2).

- Access to the Area is not permitted 100 m either side of the gulley on the northeast coast at Lat. 67°53'10'' Long. 067°23'13'' (i.e. the coast below the valley unofficially referred to as "Shangri-la Valley" by Bryant; see Figure 2). The valley inland of this coastline contains the richest vegetation growth on the island, and to reduce trampling impacts, non-essential activity within this area is discouraged (Figure 2). These restrictions apply equally to persons wishing to access the Area via sea ice in the winter.

- Under exceptional circumstances necessary for purposes consistent with the objectives of the Management Plan helicopters may be permitted to land at the designated landing site located beside the recommended field camp on the broad rock/permanent snow platform about half-way along the northwest coast at about 15 m altitude, and 200 m inland from the sea (Lat. 67°53'04'' Long. 067°23'43''). Helicopters shall not land elsewhere within the Area unless specifically authorized by Permit.
- Within the Area the operation of aircraft should be carried out, as a minimum requirement, in compliance with the 'Guidelines for the Operation of Aircraft near Concentrations of Birds' contained in Resolution 2 (2004). When conditions require aircraft to fly at lower elevations than recommended in the guidelines, aircraft should maintain the maximum elevation possible and minimise the time taken to transit.
- Overflight of the eastern end of the island over the penguin/cormorant colony is prohibited below 610 m (2000 feet) (Figure 2).
- Use of helicopter smoke grenades is prohibited within the Area unless absolutely necessary for safety. If used all smoke grenades should be retrieved.

6(iii) Location of structures within and adjacent to the Area

A cairn and the remains of a mast erected for survey purposes in the 1960s are present on the summit of the island. During the inspection visit in February 2011, some of the cabling and the remains of black survey flag associated with the mast were removed. The five 8-10 m long bamboo posts, from which the original mast was constructed, were collected together and secured along with six metal stakes near the eastern summit of the island (288 m). In February 2017 all of the bamboo posts and metal stakes were removed.

A cairn (c. 1 m high) is present on the north coast of the island (Lat. 67°53'16'' Long. 067°22'51'') and a 30 cm high pile of stones containing a short wooden post with a 2.5 cm diameter metal disc at one end inscribed with the number '10' is present on cliffs west of the penguin colony (Lat. 67°53'17'' Long. 067°22'46''). No other structures are known to exist on the island.

Two year-round scientific research stations operate in the vicinity: General San Martín (Argentina; Lat. 68°08' S, Long. 67°06' W) which is 29.5 km south-southeast, and Rothera Research Station (UK; Lat. 67°34' S, Long. 68°07' W) which is 46 km to the northwest. A summer-only station, Teniente Luis Carvajal (Lat. 67°46' S, Long. 68°55' W), has been operated by Chile at the southern end of Adelaide Island since 1985.

6(iv) Location of other protected areas in the vicinity

The nearest protected areas to Lagotellerie Island are Emperor Island, Dion Islands (ASPA 107) about 55 km west, Avian Island (ASPA 117) 65 km west and Rothera Point (ASPA 129) 46 km to the northwest (Figure 1). Several Historic Sites and Monuments are located in the vicinity: 'Base Y' (UK) on Horseshoe Island (HSM No. 63); 'Base E' (UK) (HSM No. 64) and buildings and artefacts at and near East Base (US) (HSM No. 55), both on Stonington Island; and installations of San Martín Station (Argentina) at Barry Island (HSM No. 26).

6(v) Special zone within the Area
None.

7. Permit conditions

7(i) General permit conditions

Entry into the Area is prohibited except in accordance with a Permit issued by an appropriate national authority as designated under Article 7 of Annex V of the Protocol on Environmental Protection to the Antarctic Treaty.

Conditions for issuing a Permit to enter the Area are that:

- it is issued for a compelling scientific purpose which cannot be served elsewhere;
- it is issued for essential management purposes such as inspection, maintenance or review;
- the actions permitted will not jeopardise the natural ecological system in the Area;
- any management activities are in support of the objectives of this Management Plan;
- the actions permitted are in accordance with this Management Plan;
- the Permit must be carried within the Area;
- permits shall be issued for a stated period;
- a report or reports are supplied to the authority or authorities named in the Permit;
- the appropriate authority should be notified of any activities/measures undertaken that were not included in the authorised Permit.

7(ii) Access to and movement within over the Area

- Vehicles are prohibited within the Area

- Movement within the Area shall be on foot.

- Pilots, helicopter or boat crew, or other people on helicopters or boats, are prohibited from moving on foot beyond the immediate vicinity of their landing site unless specifically authorised by Permit.

- Pedestrian traffic should be kept to the minimum consistent with the objectives of any permitted activities and every reasonable effort should be made to minimise trampling effects, i.e. all movement should be undertaken carefully so as to minimise disturbance to the soil and vegetated surfaces, walking on rocky terrain if practical.

- Overflight of bird colonies within the Area by Remotely Piloted Aircraft Systems (RPAS) shall not be permitted unless for scientific or operational purposes, and in accordance with a permit issued by an appropriate national authority.

7(iii) Activities which may be conducted in the Area

- Scientific research that will not jeopardise the ecosystem or scientific values of the Area and which cannot be served elsewhere;
- Essential management activities, including monitoring.

7(iv) Installation, modification or removal of structures

No new structures are to be erected within the Area, or scientific equipment installed, except for compelling scientific or management reasons and for a pre-established period, as specified in a permit. Installation (including site selection), maintenance, modification or removal of structures and equipment shall be undertaken in a manner that minimises disturbance to the values of the Area. All structures or scientific equipment installed in the Area shall be clearly identified by country, name of the principal investigator and year of installation. All such items should be free of organisms, propagules (e.g. seeds, eggs) and non-sterile soil, and be made of materials that can withstand the environmental conditions and pose minimal risk of contamination of the Area (see Section *7(vi)*). Removal of specific structures or equipment for which the Permit has expired shall be a condition of the Permit. Permanent structures or installations are prohibited.

7(v) Location of field camps

When necessary for purposes specified in the Permit, temporary camping is allowed at the designated site on the broad rock/permanent snow platform about half-way along the northwest coast at about 15 m altitude, and 200 m inland from the sea (Lat. 67°53'04'' Long. 067°23'43''; Figure 2).

7(vi) Restrictions on materials and organisms which can be brought into the Area

No living animals, plant material or microorganisms shall be deliberately introduced into the Area. To ensure that the floristic and ecological values of the Area are maintained, special precautions shall be taken against accidentally introducing microbes, invertebrates or plants from other Antarctic sites, including stations, or from regions outside Antarctica. All sampling equipment or markers brought into the Area shall be cleaned or sterilized. To the maximum extent practicable, footwear and other equipment used or brought into the Area (including bags or backpacks) shall be thoroughly cleaned before entering the Area. Further guidance can be found in the *CEP non-native species manual* (CEP, 2016) and the *Environmental code of conduct for terrestrial scientific field research in Antarctica* (SCAR, 2009). In view of the presence of breeding bird colonies within the Area, no poultry products, including wastes from such products and products containing uncooked dried eggs, shall be released into the Area or into the adjacent sea.

No herbicides or pesticides shall be brought into the Area. Any other chemicals, including radio-nuclides or stable isotopes, which may be introduced for scientific or management purposes specified in the Permit, shall be removed from the Area at or before the conclusion of the activity for which the Permit was granted. Release of radio-nuclides or stable isotopes directly into the environment in a way that renders them unrecoverable should be avoided. Fuel or other chemicals shall not be stored in the Area unless specifically authorised by Permit condition. They shall be stored and handled in a way that minimises the risk of their accidental introduction into the environment. Materials introduced into the Area shall be for a stated period only and shall be removed by the end of that stated period. If release occurs which is likely to compromise the values of the Area, removal is encouraged only where the impact of removal is not likely to be greater than that of leaving the material in situ. The appropriate authority should be notified of anything released and not removed that was not included in the authorised Permit.

7(vii) Taking or harmful interference with native flora or fauna

Taking or harmful interference with native flora or fauna is prohibited, except by Permit issued in accordance with Annex II to the Protocol on Environmental Protection to the Antarctic Treaty. Where taking or harmful interference with animals is involved, the *SCAR Code of Conduct for the Use of Animals for Scientific Purposes in Antarctica* should be used as a minimum standard.

To prevent human disturbance of the breeding cormorant colony and in particular the premature fledging of juvenile cormorants, visitors shall not approach within 10 m of the cormorant colony on the eastern tip of the island between 15 October and 28 February, unless authorised by Permit for specific scientific or management purposes.

7(viii) Collection and removal of materials not brought into the Area by the Permit holder

Collection or removal of anything not brought into the Area by the Permit holder shall only be in accordance with a Permit and should be limited to the minimum necessary to meet scientific or management needs. Permits shall not be granted in instances where it is proposed to take, remove or damage such quantities of soil, native flora or fauna that their distribution or abundance on Lagotellerie Island would be significantly affected. Anything of human origin likely to compromise the values of the Area, which was not brought into the Area by the Permit Holder or otherwise authorised, may be removed unless the impact of removal is likely to be greater than leaving the material *in situ*: if this is the case the appropriate authority should be notified.

7(ix) Disposal of waste

As a minimum standard, all waste shall be disposed of in accordance with Annex III to the Protocol on Environmental Protection to the Antarctic Treaty. In addition, all wastes shall be removed from the Area. Liquid human wastes may be disposed of into the sea. Solid human waste should not be disposed of to the sea, but shall be removed from the Area. No solid or liquid human waste shall be disposed of inland.

7(x) Measures that may be necessary to ensure that the aims and objectives of the Management Plan continue to be met

- Permits may be granted to enter the Area to carry out scientific research, monitoring and site inspection activities, which may involve the collection of a small number of samples for analysis, to erect or maintain signboards, or to carry out protective measures.

- Any long-term monitoring sites shall be appropriately marked and the markers or signs maintained.

- Scientific activities shall be performed in accordance with *SCAR's environmental code of conduct for terrestrial scientific field research in Antarctica.*

7(xi) Requirements for reports

The principal permit holder for each visit to the Area shall submit a report to the appropriate national authority as soon as practicable, and no later than six months after the visit has been completed. Such reports should include, as appropriate, the information identified in the visit report form contained in the Guide to the Preparation of Management Plans for Antarctic Specially Protected Areas. If appropriate, the national authority should also forward a copy of the visit report to the Party that proposed the Management Plan, to assist in managing the Area and reviewing the Management Plan. Wherever possible, Parties should deposit the original or copies of the original visit reports, in a publicly accessible archive to maintain a record of usage, for the purpose of any review of the Management Plan and in organising the scientific use of the Area.

8. Supporting documentation

Bryant, H.M. 1945. Biology at East Base, Palmer Peninsula, Antarctica. Reports on scientific results of the United States Antarctic Service Expedition 1939-1941. In *Proceedings of the American Philosophical Society* **89**(1): 256-69.

Block, W. and Star, J. 1996. Oribatid mites (Acari: Oribatida) of the maritime Antarctic and Antarctic Peninsula. *Journal of Natural History* **30**: 1059-67.

Convey, P. and Smith, R.I. Lewis 1997. The terrestrial arthropod fauna and its habitats in northern Marguerite Bay and Alexander Island, maritime Antarctic. *Antarctic Science* **9**(1):12-26.

Croxall, J.P. and Kirkwood, E.D. 1979. The distribution of penguins on the Antarctic Peninsula and the islands of the Scotia Sea. British Antarctic Survey, Cambridge.

Farquharson, G.W and Smellie, J.L. 1993. Sedimentary section, Lagotellerie Island. Unpublished document, British Antarctic Survey Archives Ref 1993/161.

Gray, N.F. and Smith, R.I. Lewis. 1984. The distribution of nematophagous fungi in the maritime Antarctic. *Mycopathologia* **85**: 81-92.

Harris, C.M., Lorenz, K., Fishpool, L.D.C., Lascelles, B., Cooper, J., Coria, N.R., Croxall, J.P., Emmerson, L.M., Fijn, R.C., Fraser, W.L., Jouventin, P., LaRue, M.A., Le Maho, Y., Lynch, H.J.,

Naveen, R., Patterson-Fraser, D.L., Peter, H.-U., Poncet, S., Phillips, R.A., Southwell, C.J., van Franeker, J.A., Weimerskirch, H., Wienecke, B., and Woehler, E.J. 2015. *Important Bird Areas in Antarctica 2015*. BirdLife International and Environmental Research & Assessment Ltd., Cambridge.

Lamb, I.M. 1964. Antarctic lichens: the genera *Usnea, Ramalina, Himantormia, Alectoria, Cornicularia*. *BAS Scientific Report* **38**, British Antarctic Survey, Cambridge.

Matthews D.W. 1983. The geology of Horseshoe and Lagotellerie Islands, Marguerite Bay, Graham Land. *British Antarctic Survey Bulletin* **52**: 125-154.

McGowan, E.R. 1958. Base Y Ornithological report 1958-59. Unpublished BAS internal report AD6/2Y/1958/Q.

Morgan, F., Barker, G., Briggs, C., Price, R. and Keys, H. 2007. Environmental Domains of Antarctica Version 2.0 Final Report, Manaaki Whenua Landcare Research New Zealand Ltd, 89 pp.

Poncet, S. and Poncet, J. 1987. Censuses of penguin populations of the Antarctic Peninsula, 1983-87. *British Antarctic Survey Bulletin* **77**: 109-129.

SCAR (Scientific Committee on Antarctic Research). (2009). Environmental code of conduct for terrestrial scientific field research in Antarctica. ATCM XXXII IP4.

Smith, H.G. 1978. The distribution and ecology of terrestrial protozoa of sub-Antarctic and maritime Antarctic islands. *BAS Scientific Report* **95**, British Antarctic Survey, Cambridge.

Smith, R.I. Lewis, 1982. Farthest south and highest occurrences of vascular plants in the Antarctic. *Polar Record* **21**: 170-73.

Smith, R.I. Lewis, 1996. Terrestrial and freshwater biotic components of the western Antarctic Peninsula. In Ross, R.M., Hofmann, E.E. and Quetin, L.B. *Foundations for ecological research west of the Antarctic Peninsula*. Antarctic Research Series **70**: American Geophysical Union, Washington D.C.: 15-59.

Star, J., and Block, W. 1998. Distribution and biogeography of oribatid mites (Acari: Oribatida) in Antarctica, the sub-Antarctic and nearby land areas. *Journal of Natural History* **32**: 861-94.

Terauds, A., Chown, S. L., Morgan, F., Peat, H. J., Watt, D., Keys, H., Convey, P., and Bergstrom, D. M. 2012. Conservation biogeography of the Antarctic. Diversity and Distributions 18: 726–41.

United Kingdom. 1997. *List of protected areas in Antarctica*. Foreign and Commonwealth Office, London.

Usher, M.B. 1986. Further conserved areas in the maritime Antarctic. *Environmental Conservation* 13: 265-66.

Vaughan, A. 1994. A geological field report on N and E Horseshoe Island and SE Lagotellerie Island, Marguerite Bay, and some adjoining areas of S. Graham Land. 1993/94 Field Season. Unpublished report, BAS Archives Ref R/1993/GL5.

Woehler, E.J. (ed) 1993. The distribution and abundance of Antarctic and sub-Antarctic penguins. SCAR, Cambridge

Figure 1. Lagotellerie Island Antarctic Specially Protected Area No. 115, Marguerite Bay, location map, showing the location of General San Martín Station (Arg.), the station Teniente Luis Carvajal (Chile), Adelaide Island, Rothera Research Station (UK) and nearby ASPA 129 at Rothera Point, also on Adelaide Island, and the location of the other protected areas in the region [Emperor Island, Dion Islands (ASPA 107) and Avian Island (ASPA 117)]. 'Base Y' (UK) (Historic Monument No. 63) on Horseshoe Island is shown. Inset: the location of Lagotellerie Island along the Antarctic Peninsula.

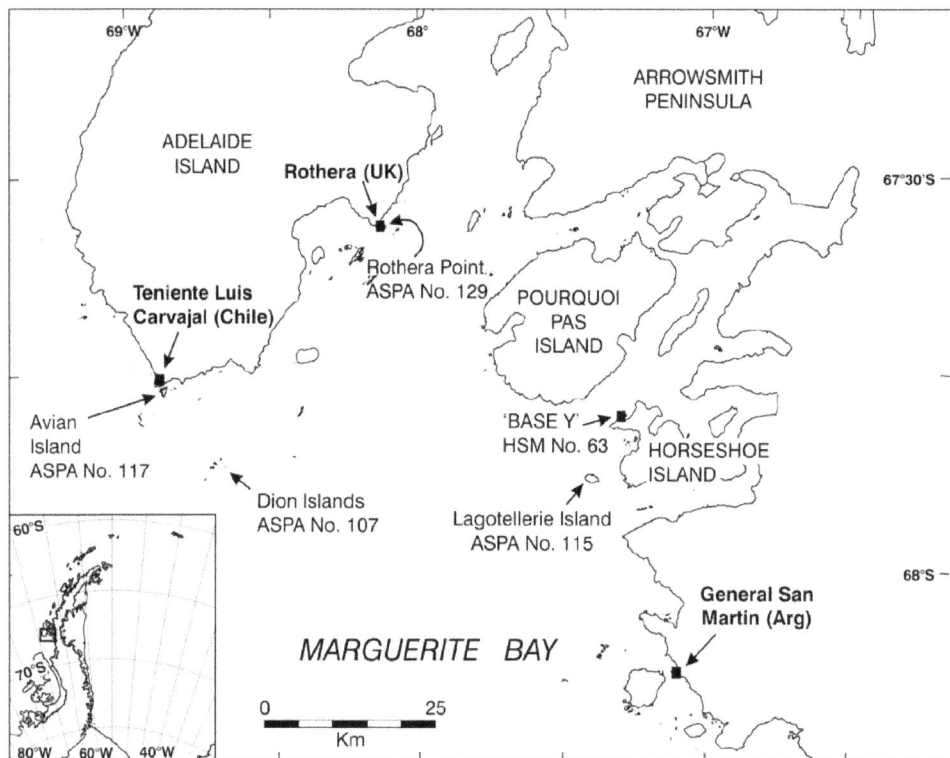

Figure 2. Lagotellerie Island (ASPA 115) topographic map.

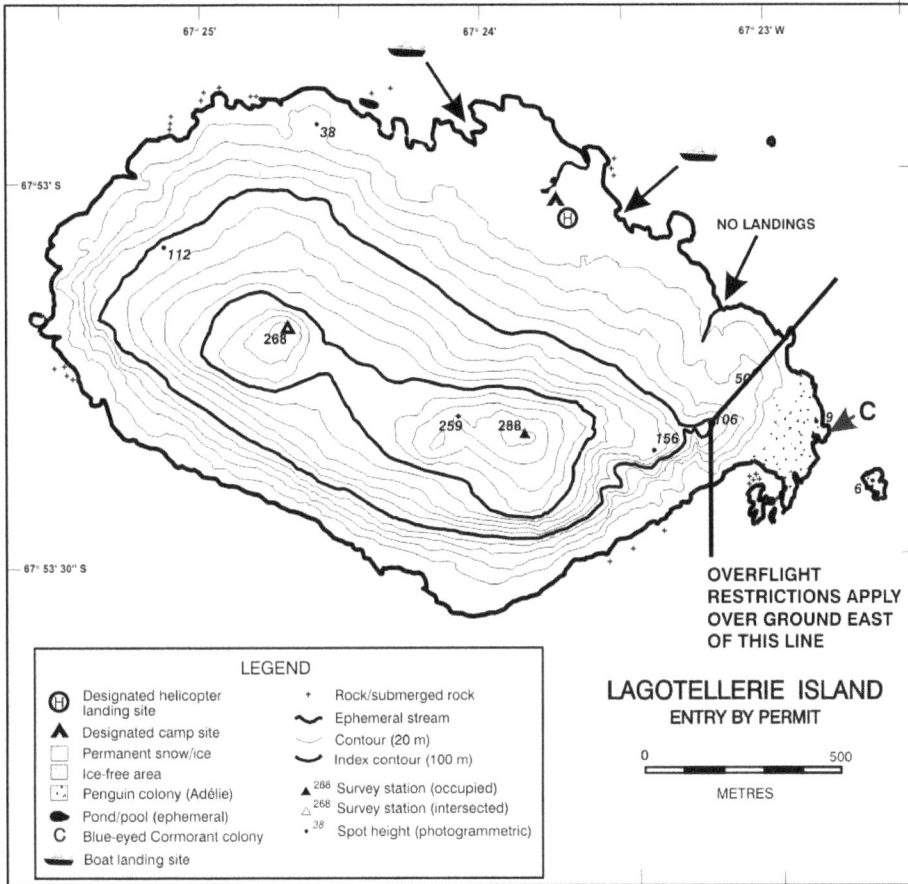

LEGEND

Ⓗ	Designated helicopter landing site	+	Rock/submerged rock
▲	Designated camp site	∼	Ephemeral stream
☐	Permanent snow/ice	‿	Contour (20 m)
☐	Ice-free area	‿	Index contour (100 m)
⠂	Penguin colony (Adélie)	▲ 288	Survey station (occupied)
●	Pond/pool (ephemeral)	△ 268	Survey station (intersected)
C	Blue-eyed Cormorant colony	• 38	Spot height (photogrammetric)
⬗	Boat landing site		

NO LANDINGS

OVERFLIGHT
RESTRICTIONS APPLY
OVER GROUND EAST
OF THIS LINE

LAGOTELLERIE ISLAND
ENTRY BY PERMIT

0   500

METRES

Figure 3. Lagotellerie Island (ASPA 115) geological sketch map.

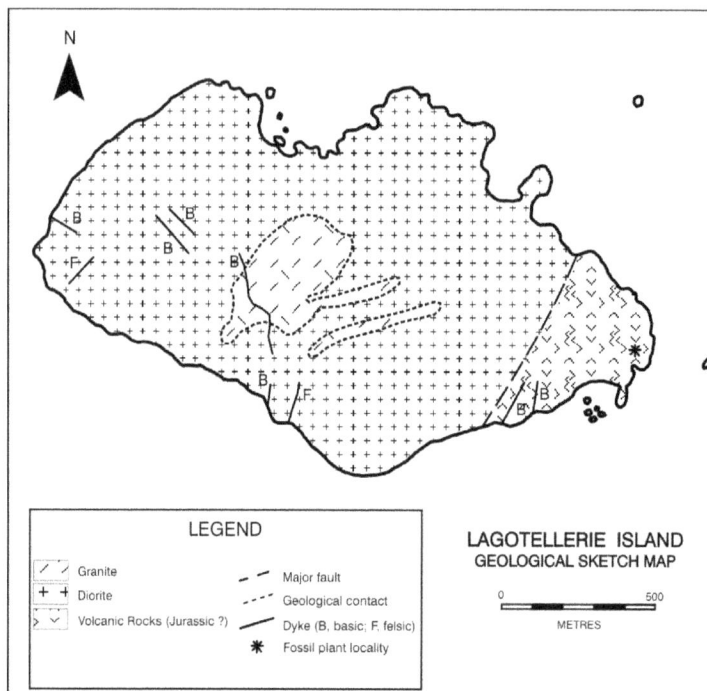

Figure 4. Normalised Difference Vegetation Index (NDVI), derived from satellite imagery, for ASPA No. 115 Lagotellerie Island, Marguerite Bay, Graham Land, showing green vegetation cover using a colour scale of yellow → orange → red, with red indicating the highest NDVI values

Management Plan for Antarctic Specially Protected Area (ASPA) No. 129

ROTHERA POINT, ADELAIDE ISLAND

Introduction

The primary reason for the designation of Rothera Point, Adelaide Island (Lat. 68°07'S, Long. 67°34'W), South Shetland Islands, as an Antarctic Specially Protected Area (ASPA) is to protect scientific values, primarily that the Area would serve as a control area, against which the effects of human impact associated with the adjacent Rothera Research Station (UK) could be monitored in an Antarctic fellfield ecosystem. Rothera Point was originally designated in Recommendation XIII-8 (1985, SSSI No. 9) after a proposal by the United. The Area itself has little intrinsic nature conservation value.

The Area is unique in Antarctica as it is the only protected area currently designated solely for its value in the monitoring of human impact. The objective is to use the Area as a control area which has been relatively unaffected by direct human impact, in assessing the impact of activities undertaken at Rothera Research Station on the Antarctic environment. Monitoring studies undertaken by the British Antarctic Survey (BAS) began at Rothera Point in 1976, before the establishment of the station later that year. On-going environmental monitoring activities within the Area and Rothera Point include:(i) assessment of heavy metal concentrations in lichens; (ii) measurement of hydrocarbon and heavy metal concentrations in gravel and soils and (iii) survey of the breeding bird populations.

Resolution 3 (2008) recommended that the "Environmental Domains Analysis for the Antarctic Continent", be used as a dynamic model for the identification of Antarctic Specially Protected Areas within the systematic environmental-geographical framework referred to in Article 3(2) of Annex V of the Protocol (see also Morgan et al., 2007). Using this model, Rothera Point is predominantly Environment Domain E (Antarctic Peninsula and Alexander Island main ice fields) which is also found in ASPAs 113, 114, 117, 126, 128, 129, 133, 134, 139, 147, 149, 152 and ASMAs 1 and 4. However, given that Rothera Point is predominantly ice-free this domain may not be full representative of the environment encompassed within the Area. Although not specifically described as such, Rothera Point may also contain Environment Domain B (Antarctic Peninsula mid-northern latitudes geologic). Other protected areas containing Environment Domain B include ASPAs 108, 115, 134, 140 and 153 and ASMA 4. Resolution 6 (2012) recommended that the Antarctic Conservation Biogeographic Regions (ACBRs) be used for the 'identification of areas that could be designated as Antarctic Specially Protected Areas within the systematic environmental-geographic framework referred to in Article 3(2) of Annex V to the Environmental Protocol. ASPA No. 129 sits within Antarctic Conservation Biogeographic Region (ACBR) 3 Northwest Antarctic Peninsula.

1. Description of values to be protected

- The Area itself has little intrinsic nature conservation value. However, it has scientific value as a control area, against which the effects of human impact associated with the adjacent Rothera Research Station (UK) could be monitored in an Antarctic fellfield ecosystem.
- The Area also has value as a biological research site, particularly for scientists working in the Bonner Laboratory (Rothera Research Station).

2. Aims and objectives

Management of the Area aims to:

- avoid degradation of, or substantial risk to, the values of the Area by preventing unnecessary human disturbance to the Area;

- avoid major changes to the structure and composition of the terrestrial ecosystems, in particular to the fellfield ecosystem and breeding birds, by (i) preventing physical development within the site, and (ii) limiting human access to the Area to maintain its value as a control area for environmental monitoring studies;

- allow scientific research and monitoring studies in the Area provided it is for compelling reasons which cannot be served elsewhere and which will not jeopardise the natural ecological system in that Area;

- minimize to the maximum extent practicable, the introduction of non-native species, which could compromise the scientific values of the Area;

- preserve the natural ecosystem of the Area as a reference area for future comparative studies

- allow regular visits for management purposes in support of the objectives of the management plan.

3. Management activities

The following management activities are to be undertaken to protect the values of the Area:

- Signboards illustrating the location and boundary of the Area and stating entry restrictions shall be erected at the major access points and serviced on a regular basis;

- A map showing the location and boundaries of the Area and stating entry requirements shall be displayed in a prominent position at Rothera Research Station;

- Visits shall be made as necessary to assess whether the Area continues to serve the purposes for which it was designated and to ensure management and maintenance measures are adequate.

- Abandoned equipment or materials shall be removed to the maximum extent possible provided doing so does not adversely impact on the environment and the values of the Area.

4. Period of designation

Designated for an indefinite period.

5. Maps

Map 1. ASPA No. 129 Rothera Point, location map.
Map specifications: Projection: WGS84 Antarctic Polar Stereographic. Standard parallel: 71°S. Central meridian 67°45'W.

Map 2. ASPA No. 129 Rothera Point, topographic map.
Map specifications: Projection: WGS84 Antarctic Polar Stereographic. Standard parallel: 71°S. Central meridian 67°45'W.

6. Description of the Area
6 (i) Geographical coordinates, boundary markers and natural features

BOUNDARIES AND CO-ORDINATES
Rothera Point (67°34'S, 68°08'W) is situated in Ryder Bay, at the south-east corner of Wright Peninsula on the east side of Adelaide Island, south-west Antarctic Peninsula (Map 1). The Area is the north-eastern one-third of Rothera Point (Map 2), and is representative of the area as a whole. It is extends about 280 m from west to east and 230 m from north to south, and rises to a maximum altitude of 36 m. At the coast, the Area boundary is the 5 m contour. No upper shore, littoral or sublittoral areas of Rothera Point are therefore included within the ASPA. The southern boundary of the Area, running across Rothera Point, is partially marked by rock filled gabions, in which are placed ASPA boundary signs. The remaining boundary is unmarked. There are two signboards just outside the perimeter of the Area located at the starting points of the pedestrian access route around Rothera Point (see Map 2). The boundary is broadly represented by the following co-ordinates, listed in a clockwise direction, starting with the most northerly point:

Area	Number	Latitude	Longitude
ASPA 129 Rothera Point	1	67°33'59'' S	068°06'47'' W
	2	67°34'06'' S	068°06'48'' W
	3	67°34'06'' S	068°07'00'' W
	4	67°34'02'' S	068°07'08'' W

Rothera Research Station (UK) lies about 250 m west of the western boundary of the Area (see inset on Map 2).

GENERAL DESCRIPTION
Small areas of permanent ice occur to the north and south of the summit of the ASPA. There are no permanent streams or pools. The rocks are predominantly heterogeneous intrusions of diorite, granodiorite and adamellite of the mid-Cretaceous-Lower Tertiary Andean Intrusive Suite. Veins of copper ore are prominent bright green stains on the rock. Soil is restricted to small pockets of glacial till and sand on the rock bluffs. Local deeper deposits produce scattered small circles and polygons of frost sorted material. There are no extensive areas of patterned ground. Accumulations of recent and decaying limpet (*Nacella concinna*) shells forming patches of calcareous soil around prominent rock outcrops used as bird perches by Dominican gulls (*Larus dominicanus*). There are no accumulations of organic matter.There are no special or rare geological or geomorphological features in the Area.

The limited terrestrial biological interest within the Area is confined to the rock bluffs where there is a locally abundant growth of lichens. The vegetation is representative of the southern "maritime" Antarctic fellfield ecosystem and is dominated by the fruticose lichens *Usnea antarctica, Usnea sphacelala*, and *Pseudephebe minuscula*, and the foliose lichen *Umbilicaria decussata*. Numerous crustose lichens are found, but bryophytes (mainly *Andreaea* spp.) are sparse. The invertebrate fauna is impoverished and consists only of a few species of mites and springtails, of which *Halozetes belgicae* and *Cryptopygus antarcticus* are the most common. There are no special or rare terrestrial flora or fauna in the Area. During monitoring studies undertaken in January 2015, no non-native springtails were found within the ASPA or elsewhere on Rothera Point.

Brown and south polar skuas (*Catharacta lonnbergii* and *C. maccormicki*) are the most abundant breeding birds found in the Area, with up to five pairs of skuas recorded nesting. A pair of Dominican gulls (*Larus dominicanus*) nest in the Area and one Wilson's storm petrels (*Oceanites oceanicus*) nest has been found.

6(ii) Access to the Area
- Access to the Area shall be by foot.
- Helicopter landings are prohibited within the Area.
- The operation of aircraft should be carried out, to the maximum extent possible, in compliance with the 'Guidelines for the Operation of Aircraft near Concentrations of Birds' contained in Resolution 2 (2004). However, the Area is only c. 250 m from the Rothera Research Station runway and for reasons of safety it is recognized that full compliance may not always be possible.
- The Area boundary extends to the 5 m contour at the coast. There is unrestricted pedestrian access below this contour height around the boundary of the Area. The recommended pedestrian access route follows the Mean High Water Mark (MHWM) and is shown on Map 2. During periods when the ground is snow-covered and sea ice has formed, pedestrians should ensure that they are at a safe distance from the shoreline and are not in danger of straying onto unreliable sea ice or into tide cracks.

6 (iii) Location of structures within and adjacent to the Area
A rock cairn marks the summit of the Area (36 m; Lat. 68°34'01.5'' S, Long. 068°06'58'' W) and 35 m to the east south east of it there is another cairn marking a survey station (35.4 m; Lat. 68°34'02'' S, Long. 068°06'55'' W).

Rothera Research Station (UK) lies about 250 m west of the western boundary of the Area (see inset on Map 2). A number of masts and aerials exist on the raised beach that is adjacent to the southern boundary of the Area.

6 (iv) Location of other protected areas in the vicinity
ASPA No. 107, Emperor Island, Dion Islands, Marguerite Bay, lies about 15 km south of Adelaide Island. ASPA No. 115, Lagotellerie Island, Marguerite Bay, lies about 11 km south of Pourquoi Pas Island. ASPA No. 117, Avian Island, Marguerite Bay, lies about 0.25 km south of the south-west tip of Adelaide Island. The locations of these ASPAs are shown on Map 1.

6 (v) Special zones within the Area
None.

7. Permit Conditions

7(i) General permit conditions
Entry into the Area is prohibited except in accordance with a Permit issued by an appropriate national authority. Conditions for issuing a Permit to enter the Area are that:
- it is issued only for compelling scientific reasons which cannot be served elsewhere or it is issued for essential management purposes such as inspection, maintenance or review;
- the actions permitted will not jeopardise the environmental or scientific values of the Area;
- any management activities are in support of the objectives of the Management Plan;
- the actions permitted are in accordance with this Management Plan;
- the Permit, or an authorised copy, must be carried within the Area;
- permits shall be issued for a stated period;
- the appropriate authority should be notified of any activities/measures undertaken that were not included in the authorised Permit.

7(i) Access to, and movement within or over, the Area
- Access to, and movement within, the Area shall be on foot.
- Land vehicles are prohibited in the Area.

- Landing of helicopters within the Area is prohibited.
- All movement shall be undertaken carefully so as to minimize disturbance to soil and vegetation.
- Overflight of bird colonies within the Area by Remotely Piloted Aircraft Systems (RPAS) shall not be permitted unless for scientific or operational purposes, and in accordance with a permit issued by an appropriate national authority.

7(iii) Activities which may be conducted in the Area
Activities which are or may be conducted within the Area are:
- scientific research or monitoring which will not jeopardise the ecosystems of the Area;
- essential management activities.

7(iv) Installation, modification or removal of structures
No new structures are to be erected within the Area, or scientific equipment installed, except for compelling scientific or management reasons and for a pre-established period, as specified in a permit. Installation (including site selection), maintenance, modification or removal of structures and equipment shall be undertaken in a manner that minimises disturbance to the values of the Area. All structures or scientific equipment installed in the Area shall be clearly identified by country, name of the principal investigator and year of installation. All such items should be free of organisms, propagules (e.g. seeds, eggs) and non-sterile soil, and be made of materials that can withstand the environmental conditions and pose minimal risk of contamination of the Area. Removal of specific structures or equipment for which the Permit has expired shall be a condition of the Permit. Permanent structures or installations are prohibited.

7(v) Location of field camps
Camping in the Area is prohibited. Accommodation may be available at Rothera Research Station.

7(vi) Restrictions on materials and organisms that may be brought into the Area
No living animals, plant material or microorganisms shall be deliberately introduced into the Area. To ensure that the values of the Area are maintained, special precautions shall be taken against accidentally introducing microbes, invertebrates or plants from other Antarctic sites, including stations, or from regions outside Antarctica. All sampling equipment or markers brought into the Area shall be cleaned or sterilized. To the maximum extent practicable, footwear and other equipment used or brought into the Area (including bags or backpacks) shall be thoroughly cleaned before entering the Area. No poultry or egg products shall be taken into the Area. Further guidance can be found in the CEP Non-native Species Manual and COMNAP/SCAR Checklists for supply chain managers of National Antarctic Programmes for the reduction in risk of transfer of non-native species. No herbicides or pesticides shall be brought into the Area. Any other chemicals, including radio-nuclides or stable isotopes, which may be introduced for scientific or management purposes specified in the permit, shall be removed from the Area at or before the conclusion of the activity for which the permit was granted. Release of radio-nuclides or stable isotopes directly into the environment in a way that renders them unrecoverable shall not be permitted. Fuel, food and other materials are not to be deposited within the Area, unless authorized by Permit for specific scientific or management purposes. Permanent depots are not permitted. All materials introduced shall be for a stated period only, shall be removed at or before the conclusion of the stated period, and shall be stored and handled so that risk of their introduction into the environment is minimised. If release occurs which is likely to compromise the values of the Area, removal is encouraged only where the impact of removal is not likely to be greater than that of leaving the material in situ. The appropriate authority shall be notified of any materials released and not removed that were not included in the authorised Permit.

7(vii) Taking of, or harmful interference with, native flora and fauna
Taking of or harmful interference with native flora and fauna is prohibited, except in accordance with a Permit issued in accordance with Annex II to the Protocol on Environmental Protection to the Antarctic Treaty. Where taking of, or harmful interference with, animals is involved this should in

accordance with the SCAR Code of Conduct for the use of Animals for Scientific Purposes in Antarctica, as a minimum standard.

7 (viii) The collection or removal of materials not brought into the Area by the Permit holder
Material of a biological or geological nature may be collected and/or removed from the Area only in accordance with a Permit and should be limited to the minimum necessary to meet scientific or management needs. Permits shall not be granted if there is reasonable concern that the sampling proposed would take, remove or damage such quantities of soil, sediment, flora or fauna that their distribution or abundance within the Area would be significantly affected. Material of human origin not brought into the site by the Permit holder, or otherwise authorised, which is likely to compromise the values of the Area shall be removed unless the impact of removal is likely to be greater than leaving the material in situ. In the latter case the appropriate authority shall be notified.

7 (ix) Disposal of wastes
All wastes shall be removed from the Area in accordance with Annex III (Waste disposal and waste management) of the Protocol on Environmental Protection to the Antarctic Treaty (1998). All solid and/or liquid human waste shall be removed from the Area.

7 (x) Measures that may be necessary to continue to meet the aims of the Management Plan
- Permits may be granted to enter the Area to carry out scientific research, monitoring and site inspection activities, which may involve the collection of a small number of samples for analysis, to erect or maintain signboards, or to carry out protective measures.
- Any long-term monitoring sites shall be appropriately marked and the markers or signs maintained.
- Scientific activities shall be performed in accordance with SCAR's environmental code of conduct for terrestrial scientific field research in Antarctica.

7 (xi) Requirements for reports
The principal permit holder for each visit to the Area shall submit a report to the appropriate national authority as soon as practicable and no later than six months after the visit has been completed. Such visit reports should include, as applicable, the information identified in the recommended visit report form (contained as an Appendix in the Guide to the Preparation of Management Plans for Antarctic Specially Protected Areas (available from the website of the Secretariat of the Antarctic Treaty; www.ats.aq)). If appropriate, the national authority should also forward a copy of the visit report to the Party that proposed the Management Plan, to assist in managing the Area and reviewing the Management Plan. Wherever possible, Parties should deposit the original or copies of the original visit reports, in a publicly accessible archive to maintain a record of usage, for the purpose of any review of the management plan.

8. Supporting documentation

Block, W., and Star, J. 1996. Oribatid mites (Acari: Oribatida) of the maritime Antarctic and Antarctic Peninsula. Journal of Natural History 30: 1059-67.

Bonner, W. N. 1989. Proposed construction of a crushed rock airstrip at Rothera Point, Adelaide Island - final Comprehensive Environmental Evaluation. NERC, Swindon. 56 pp.

Convey, P., and Smith, R.I.L. 1997. The terrestrial arthropod fauna and its habitats in northern Marguerite Bay and Alexander Island, maritime Antarctic. Antarctic Science 9:12-26.

Downie, R., Ingham, D., Hughes, K. A., and Fretwell, P. 2005. Initial Environmental Evaluation: proposed redevelopment of Rothera Research Station, Rothera Point, Adelaide Island, Antarctica. British Antarctic Survey, Cambridge, 29 pp.

Hughes, K. A., Greenslade, P., Convey, P. The fate of the non-native Collembolon, *Hypogastrura viatica*, at the southern extent of its introduced range in Antarctica. In submission.

Milius, N. 2000. The birds of Rothera, Adelaide Island, Antarctic Peninsula. Marine Ornithology 28: 63-67.

Morgan, F., Barker, G., Briggs, C., Price, R., and Keys, H. 2007. Environmental Domains of Antarctica Version 2.0 Final Report. Manaaki Whenua Landcare Research New Zealand Ltd, 89 pp.

Øvstedal, D.O. and Smith, R.I.L. 2001. Lichens of Antarctica and South Georgia. A Guide to their Identification and Ecology. Cambridge University Press, Cambridge, 411 pp.

Ochyra, R., Bednarek-Ochyra, H. and Smith, R. I. L. 2008. The Moss Flora of Antarctica. Cambridge University Press, Cambridge. pp 704.

Peat, H., Clarke, A., and Convey, P. 2007. Diversity and biogeography of the Antarctic flora. Journal of Biogeography, 34: 132-146.

Riley. T. R., Flowerdew, M. J. and Whitehouse, M. J. 2012. Chrono- and lithostratigraphy of a Mesozoic–Tertiary fore- to intra-arc basin: Adelaide Island, Antarctic Peninsula. Geological Magazine 149: 768-782.

Shears, J. R. 1995. Initial Environmental Evaluation – expansion of Rothera Research Station, Rothera Point, Adelaide Island, Antarctica. British Antarctic Survey, Cambridge, 80 pp.

Shears, J. R., and Downie, R. 1999. Initial Environmental Evaluation for the proposed construction of an accommodation building and operations tower at Rothera Research Station, Rothera Point, Adelaide Island, Antarctica. British Antarctic Survey, Cambridge, 22 pp.

Map 1. ASPA No. 129 Rothera Point, location map.

Map specifications: Projection: WGS84 Antarctic Polar Stereographic. Standard parallel: 71°S. Central meridian 67°45'W.

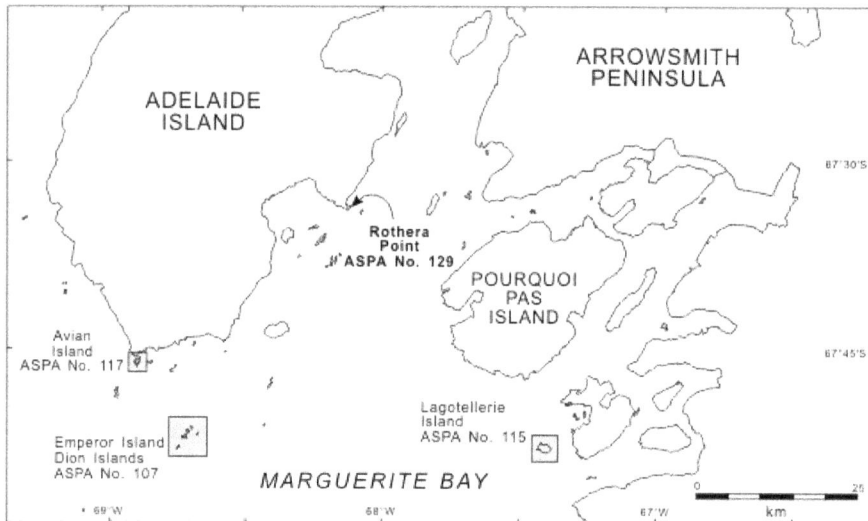

Map 2. ASPA No. 129 Rothera Point, topographic map.

Map specifications: Projection: WGS84 Antarctic Polar Stereographic. Standard parallel: 71°S. Central meridian 67°45'W.

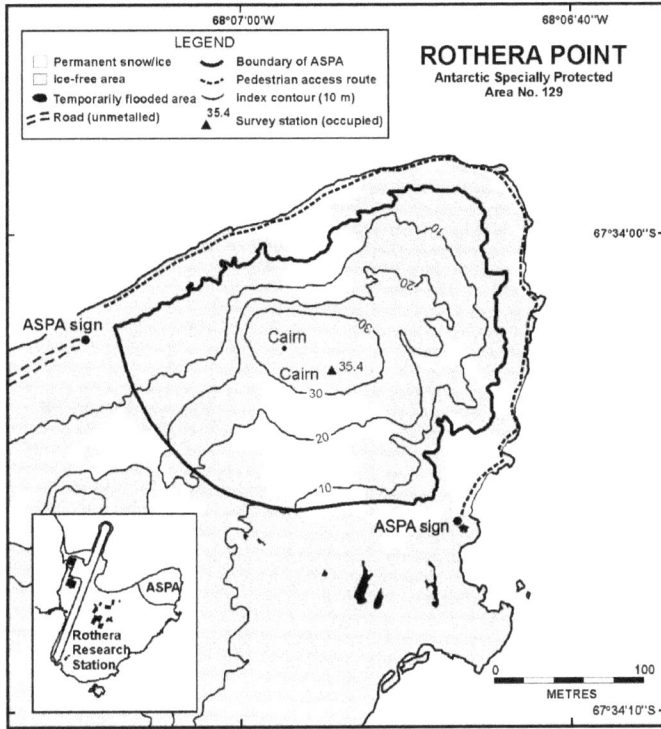

Management Plan for Antarctic Specially Protected Area No 140

PARTS OF DECEPTION ISLAND, SOUTH SHETLAND ISLANDS

Introduction

The primary reason for the designation of Parts of Deception Island, (Lat. 62°57'S, Long. 60°38'W), South Shetland Islands, as an Antarctic Specially Protected Area (ASPA) is to protect environmental values, predominantly the terrestrial flora within the Area. The flora of the island is unique in Antarctic terms, particularly where associated with these geothermal areas, but also because of the recently formed surfaces that provide known-age habitats for the study of colonisation and other dynamic ecological processes by terrestrial organisms (Smith 1988).

Deception Island is an active volcano. Recent eruptions occurring in 1967, 1969 and 1970 (Baker *et al*. 1975) altered many of the topographical features of the island and created new, and locally transient, surfaces for the colonisation of plants and other terrestrial biota (Collins 1969; Cameron & Benoit 1970; Smith 1984a,b,c). There are a number of sites of geothermal activity, some with fumaroles (Smellie *et al*. 2002).

Five small Sites around the coast of Port Foster were adopted under Recommendation XIII–8 (ATCM XIII, Brussels, 1985) as Site of Special Scientific Interest No 21 on the grounds that '*Deception Island is exceptional because of its volcanic activity, having had major eruptions in 1967, 1969 and 1970. Parts of the island were completely destroyed, new areas were created, and others were covered by varying depths of ash. Few areas of the interior were unaffected. The island offers unique opportunities to study colonization processes in an Antarctic environment*'. Following an extensive scientific survey, protection of the island's botanical values was enhanced through Measure 3 (2005) when the number of Sites of botanical interest included within the ASPA was increased to 11.

ASPA 140 makes a substantial contribution to the Antarctic protected areas system as it (a) contains a particularly wide diversity of species, (b) is distinct from other areas due to the geothermally-heated ground in some parts of the island which create habitats of great ecological importance unique to the Antarctic Peninsula region and (c) is vulnerable to human interference, in particular, due to highly restricted spatial distribution of many plant species, particularly those associated with heated ground. While ASPA 140 is protected primarily for its outstanding environmental values (specifically its biological diversity) it is also protected for its scientific values (ie, for terrestrial biology, zoology, geomorphology and geology). In particular, scientific research includes long-term colonisation studies and ground temperature measurements.

The 11 Sites within the Area (c. 2.7 km^2) encompass terrestrial and lagoon habitats around geo-thermally heated ground, areas of rich flora and known-age surfaces created following eruptions of 1967, 1969 and 1970, which are potentially useful for recolonisation studies. The Area is considered to be of sufficient size to provide adequate protection of the values identified, which may be highly susceptible to direct physical disturbance, due to activities of national and non-governmental visitors, and the identified boundaries provide an adequate buffer around sensitive features.

Deception Island is predominantly Environment Domain G (Antarctic Peninsula off-shore islands geologic) under the "Environmental Domains Analysis for the Antarctic Continent" (Resolution 3 (2008)). Environment Domain G is scarce relative to the other environmental domain and substantial efforts are required to conserve the values found within this environment type.

ASPA 140 sits within Antarctic Conservation Biogeographic Region (ACBR) 3 Northwest Antarctic Peninsula (Resolution 6 (2012)).

No IBAs are within the boundaries of the ASPA sites (Resolution 5 (2015)).

1. Description of values to be protected

Following a detailed botanical survey of the island in 2002 (reviewed in 2010 and 2014/15), 11 Sites of unique botanical interest were identified. Consequently, the values specified in the original designation were reaffirmed and considerably augmented.

These values are set out as follows:

- The island has the greatest number of rare (i.e., known to grow at a few localities in the Antarctic and often in small quantity) and extremely rare (i.e., known to grow at only one or two localities in the Antarctic) plant species of any site in the Antarctic. Twenty eight of the 54 mosses recorded on the island, four of the eight liverworts and 14 of the *c*. 75 lichens are considered to be rare or extremely rare. Annex 1 lists the plant species classed as rare or extremely rare in the Antarctic Treaty area, which occur on Deception Island. These represent 25%, 17% and *c*. 4% of the total number of mosses, liverworts and lichens, respectively, known from the Antarctic (Aptroot & van der Knaap 1993; Bednarek-Ochyra *et al.* 2000; Ochyra *et al.* 2008; Øvstedal & Lewis Smith 2001). Thirteen species of moss (including two endemics), two species of liverwort and three species of lichen growing on Deception Island have not been recorded elsewhere in the Antarctic. No other site in the Antarctic is comparable. This suggests that there is a significant deposition of immigrant propagules (by wind and seabirds), particularly of southern South American provenance, over the Antarctic, which become established only where favourable germinating conditions prevail (eg, the heat and moisture provided around fumaroles) (Smith 1984b; c). Such sites are unique in the Antarctic Treaty area.

- The more stable geothermal areas, some of which have fumaroles issuing steam and sulphurous gas, have developed bryophyte communities of varying complexity and density, each with a distinct and unique flora. Most of these areas were created during the 1967-70 series of eruptions, but at least one (Mt. Pond) predates that period. Species growing close to active vents are continuously subjected to temperatures between 30 to 50°C, thereby posing important questions regarding their physiological tolerance.

- Areas of volcanic ash, mudflows, scoria and lapilli deposited between 1967 and 1970 provide unique known-age surfaces. These are currently being colonised by vegetation and other terrestrial biota, allowing the dynamics of immigration and colonisation to be monitored. These areas are unstable and subject to wind and water erosion, so exposing some areas to continual surface change and a cycle of recolonisation.

- Kroner Lake, the only intertidal lagoon with hot springs in Antarctica, supports a unique community of brackish-water algae.

- Several Sites within the Area, unaffected by ash deposits during the 1967-70 eruptions, support long-established mature communities with diverse vegetation and are typical of the older stable ecosystems on the island.

- The largest known stand of Antarctic pearlwort (*Colobanthus quitensis*), one of only two flowering plants in the Antarctic, is located within the Area. After being virtually eradicated by burial in ash during the 1967 eruption, it has recovered and is now spreading at an unprecedented rate. This correlates with the current trend in regional climate change, particularly increasing temperature.

- The Area contains some Sites where on-going scientific research is performed including long-term colonization experiments (Collins Point) and long-term ground temperature variation measurements (Caliente Hill).

- The Area also contains some Sites with surfaces that date from the eruption in 1967, which allowing accurate monitoring of colonisation by plants and other biota and are of important scientific value.

2. Aims and objectives

Management of the Area aims to:

- avoid degradation of, or substantial risk to, the values of the Area by preventing unnecessary human disturbance to the Area;
- allow scientific research in the Area provided it is for compelling reasons which cannot be served elsewhere and which will not jeopardise the natural ecological system in that Area;
- prevent or minimise the introduction to the Area of alien plants, animals and microorganisms;
- ensure that the flora is not adversely affected by excessive sampling within the Area;
- preserve the natural ecosystem of the Area as a reference area for future comparative studies and for monitoring floristic and ecological change, colonisation processes and community development;

3. Management activities

The following management activities shall be undertaken to protect the values of the Area:

- Visits shall be made as necessary to assess whether the individual Sites continue to serve the purposes for which they were designated and to ensure management and maintenance measures are adequate.
- Markers, signs or other structures (e.g., fences, cairns) erected within the Area for scientific or management purposes shall be secured and maintained in good condition and removed when no longer required.
- In accordance with the requirements of Annex III of the Protocol on Environmental Protection to the Antarctic Treaty, abandoned equipment or materials shall be removed to the maximum extent possible provided doing so does not adversely impact on the environment and the values of the Area.
- A map showing the location of each Site on Deception Island (stating any special restrictions that apply) shall be displayed prominently and a copy of this Management Plan shall be made available at Gabriel de Castilla Station (Spain) and Decepción Station (Argentina). Copies of the Management Plan shall be freely available and carried aboard all vessels planning visits to the island.
- Where appropriate, National Antarctic Programmes are encouraged to liaise closely to ensure management activities are implemented (including through the Deception Island Antarctic Specially Managed Area Management Group). In particular, National Antarctic Programmes are encouraged to consult with one another to prevent excessive sampling of biological material within the Area, particularly given the often slow rate of re-growth and limited quantity and distribution of some flora. Also, National Antarctic Programmes are encouraged to consider joint implementation of guidelines intended to minimize the introduction and dispersal of non-native species within the Area.
- At Site K Ronald Hill to Kroner Lake, any wind-blown debris from HSM No 71 shall be removed. At Site G Pendulum Cove, any wind-blown debris from HSM No 76 shall be removed (see Section 7(viii)).
- At Site A Collins Point, the existing staked plots should be maintained to allow continued monitoring of vegetation change since 1969.

3

4. Period of designation

Designated for an indefinite period.

5. Maps

Figure 1: Antarctic Specially Protected Area No 140, Deception Island, showing the location of Sites A – L (Scale 1:100 000).

Figures 1a–d: Topographic Maps of Antarctic Specially Protected Area No 140 showing Sites A – L (Scale 1: 25 000). The 'hill shade' effect has been added to highlight the topography of the areas.

6. Description of the Area

6 (i) Geographical co-ordinates, boundary markers and natural features

GENERAL DESCRIPTION

Research by Smith (1984a) and Peat *et al.* (2007) described the recognised biogeographical regions present within the Antarctic Peninsula. Antarctica can be divided into three major biological provinces: northern maritime, southern maritime and continental. Deception Island lies within the northern maritime zone (Smith 1984a).

NATURAL FEATURES, BOUNDARIES, AND SCIENTIFIC VALUES

ASPA 140 comprises 11 Sites, shown in Figures 1 and 1a-1d. Annotated photographs of each Site are shown in Annex 2. This fragmented distribution is characteristic of the vegetation cover of Deception Island. Because of the patchy nature of stable and moist substrata not subjected to erosion, the vegetation has a disjunct distribution and is consequently restricted to widely scattered, and often very small, habitats. Use of satellite remote sensing techniques (Normalised Difference Vegetation Index) showed the area of green vegetation within the ASPA sites to be 0.10 km^2 (4% of the ASPA area).

The Sites are lettered A to L (but excluding I), in a clockwise direction from the south-west of the caldera and referred to by the most prominent named geographical feature associated with each Site. Photographs of each Site are shown in Annex 2. Boundary co-ordinates are listed in Annex 3, but as many of the boundaries follow natural features, the boundary description outlines below should also be consulted.

Site A - Collins Point

Area encompassed. The north-facing slopes between Collins Point and the unnamed point 1.15 km to the east (0.6 km west of Entrance Point), directly opposite Fildes Point, and extending from the back of the beach to a ridge extending up to *c.* 1 km inland from the shoreline.

Boundaries. The eastern boundary of Site A runs south from the shore at the unnamed point 0.6 km west of Entrance Point, following the outline of a ridge to an elevation of 184 m. The western boundary extends from Collins Point, following a ridge south to an elevation of 145 m. The southern boundary is delimited by the arcuate ridge crest (following a line of summits east to west at 172, 223 and 214 m) joining points 184 and 145 m. The beach area, including the Collins Point light beacon (maintained by the Chilean Navy), to the 10 m contour is excluded from the Site.

Scientific value. No geothermally-heated ground is known within the Site boundary. The Site contains some of the best examples of the island's longest established vegetation, largely unaffected by the recent eruptions, with high species diversity and several Antarctic rarities, some in considerable abundance. A few small plants of *Colobanthus quitensis* have recently become established, while the large liverwort (*Marchantii berteroana*) is a fairly recent and spreading colonist. Research on seals is undertaken on the beach to the north of the Site, and the Site also contains a colony of kelp gulls in the low cliffs above the beach. Six 50 × 50 cm plots marked with wooden corner stakes (Lat. 62°60'00''S, Long. 060°34'48''W) were established by the British Antarctic Survey in 1969 to monitor changes in the vegetation in subsequent years (Collins 1969).

Human impact. The non-native springtail *Hypogastrura viatica* is found within the Site A.

Site B - Crater Lake

Area encompassed. Crater Lake and its shoreline, the flat ground to its north and the scoria-covered lava tongue to the south.

Boundaries. The northern boundary extends along the foot of the slope to the north of the broad valley *c.* 300 m north of Crater Lake (at *c.* 30 m altitude). The western boundary follows the ridgeline immediately west of the lake, and to the east of the small unnamed lake at Lat. 62°59'00''S, Long. 060°40'30''W. The southwestern and southern boundaries follow the top of the slope (at altitude *c.* 80 m) that extend to the southwest and south of the lake. The eastern boundary passes to the east of the lava tongue south of Crater Lake, around the eastern rim of the lake and *c.* 300 m across the flat plain to the north of the Crater Lake.

Scientific value. No geothermally-heated ground is known within the Site boundary. The principal area of botanical interest lies on a scoria-covered lava tongue south of the lake. The Site was unaffected by the recent eruptions. The vegetation on the scoria tongue has a diverse cryptogamic flora, including several Antarctic rarities, and exceptional development of turf-forming moss, dominated by one relatively common species (*Polytrichastrum alpinum*). Of particular interest is that it reproduces sexually in great abundance here. Sporophytes of this species are not known in such profusion in this, or any other moss, anywhere else in the Antarctic. The extensive, virtually monospecific, moss carpet (*Sanionia uncinata*), on the flat ground to the north of Crater Lake, is one of the largest continuously vegetated stands on the island.

Site C – Caliente Hill, southern end of Fumarole Bay

Area encompassed. A narrow line of fumaroles extending c. 40 × 3 m along the gently sloping summit ridge at *c.* 95 to 107 m elevation on Caliente Hill above the north-west side of Albufera Lagoon northwest of Decepción Station (Argentina) at the southern end of Fumarole Bay.

Boundaries. The area includes all the ground above the 90 m contour on the hill, with the exception of the ground south east of a point 10 m north west of the cairn (Lat. 62°58'27''S, Long. 060°42'31''W) at the southeast end of the ridge. Access to the cairn at the southeast end of the ridge is not restricted.

Scientific value. Geothermally-heated ground is included within the Site. Several rare species of moss, some unique to the island, colonise the heated soil crust close to the vents, of which only two or three are visible. The vegetation is extremely sparse and not obvious, in total encompassing less than *c.* 1 m² in area, and is therefore particularly vulnerable to trampling and over-sampling. Structures within the Site include experimental apparatus monitoring long-term ground temperature variations (operated by the Spanish Antarctic programme) and several short metal stakes arranged along the ridgeline near the highest point of the ridge.

Human impact. The non-native springtail *Proisotoma minuta* is found within the Site C. In recent years, the sparse vegetation, containing rare and very rare bryophite asemblages, has been subject to cumulative human trampling, which has reduced the vegetation cover in the area. Minimizing new entries and sample collections within the site is highly advisory given the delicate nature and endangered status of the local plant communities.

5

Site D - Fumarole Bay

Area encompassed. The unstable moist scree slopes below the precipitous lava cliffs on the east side of the southern end of Stonethrow Ridge to the break of slope beyond the beach west of mid-Fumarole Bay. No structures are located within the Site, although much timber debris is found at the back of the beach several metres above the high tide mark. The timber may have been deposited at this location by a tsunami generated by earlier vulcanological activity.

Boundaries. The southern end of the cliffs terminate in a prominent ridge sloping southeastward down to the beach. The southern boundary of the Site extends from the base of this ridge (at altitude *c.* 10 m) along the ridge line to the base of the cliffs at an altitude of *c.* 50 m. The western boundary follows the limit of the scree at the base of the cliffs roughly northwards for 800m at altitude of approximately 50 m. The eastern boundary extends northwards along the break-of-slope at the back of the beach for 800 m including all the large boulders. The northern boundary (*c.* 100 m in length) joins the break of slope at the back of the beach to the scree at the base of the lava flow cliffs. The flat beach area from the shore, including two prominent inter-tidal fumaroles to the south of Fumarole Bay, to the break-of-slope is excluded from the Site.

Scientific value. No geothermally-heated ground is known within the Site, although fumarole activity is present in the inter-tidal zone east of the Site. The Site has a complex geology and contains the most diverse flora on the island, including several Antarctic rarities. It was unaffected by the recent eruptions.

Site E – west of Stonethrow Ridge

Area encompassed. The Site encompasses an area of fumarole activity and includes a red scoria cone at *c.* 270 m altitude, on the northern side of the east-west trending ridge, *c.* 600 m south-southwest of the highest point on Stonethrow Ridge (330 m), west of central Fumarole Bay. It comprises two fumaroles about 20 m apart, the more easterly fumarole being more highly vegetated with lichens, mosses and liverworts covering an area of *c.* 15 × 5 m.

Boundaries. The boundary extends to 10 m beyond all evidence of geothermal activity and the non-heated ground linking the two fumaroles.

Scientific value. Areas of geothermally-heated ground are present within the Site. The Site possesses several very rare mosses, liverworts and lichens, two of the dominant species being a liverwort (*Clasmatocolea grandiflora*) and lichen (*Stereocaulon condensatum*), neither of which is known elsewhere in Antarctica. Photographs taken in the mid-1980s indicate that the development and diversity of this vegetation has advanced considerably. A skua nest (noted in 1993 and 2002 and occupied in 2010) is present within the vegetation. These birds may be responsible for introducing some of the plants from Tierra del Fuego, notably the dominant liverwort.

Site F - Telefon Bay

Area encompassed. The Site incorporates several features created during the 1967 eruption in Telefon Bay: Pisagua Hill on the south side of the Site, the small shallow Ajmonecat Lake on the ash plain north of Stancomb Cove and the low flat ash plain extending from the shoreline of Telefon Bay to the steep slopes and lava outcrops *c.* 0.5 km inland. Pisagua Hill was created as a new island in 1967, but is now joined to the main island by the aforementioned ash plain. At the northern end of the plain is Extremadura Cove, which was a lake until the narrow isthmus (*c.* 2 m wide and 50 m long) separating it from Port Foster was breached sometime around 2006. Extremadura Cove is excluded from the Site.

Boundaries. The north shoreline of the lagoon (Stancomb Cove) at the southwest of Telefon Bay marks the southern boundary of the Site, while the southwest shore of the Extremadura

Cove to the north of Telefon Bay marks the northeastern boundary of the Site. The southeast boundary extends along the shore south of Pisagua Hill, northwards to the shoreline of the Extremadura Cove at the northern end of Telefon Bay. The northwest boundary is roughly delineated by the 10 m contour of Telefon Ridge that links Stancomb Cove to Extremadura Cove. Ajmonecat Lake (Lat. 62°55'23''S, Long. 060°40'45''W), including its shoreline, is included in the Site. The shoreline of Telefon Bay is excluded from the Site to allow access past the Site. Those boating within Extremadura Cove without a permit to enter the ASPA should be careful not to land passengers on the southwest shore of the Cove, as this marks the boundary of Site F (see Figure 1c).

Scientific value. No geothermally-heated ground is known within the Site. The main point of botanical interest is that all surfaces within the Site date from 1967, thereby allowing accurate monitoring of colonisation by plants and other biota. The Site has a generally barren appearance, but close inspection reveals an abundance of inconspicuous mosses and lichens. In the absence of geothermal activity here, colonisation processes may be related to aspects of the current trend in climate change. Although species diversity is low, the developing communities are typical of non-heated habitats throughout the island.

Human impact. The non-native springtail *Hypogastrura viatica* is found within the Site F.

Site G - Pendulum Cove

Area encompassed. The Site comprises the uneven gentle slope of coarse grey, crimson, and red scoria and occasional disintegrating blocks of yellowish tuff, east-northeast of Crimson Hill and *c.* 0.4 – 0.8 km east of Pendulum Cove. It extends *c.* 500m from west to east and is up to *c.* 400m wide from north to south. It was created largely by the 1969 eruption which destroyed the nearby abandoned Chilean Base (Historic Site and Monument No 76). The Site includes the slope and undulating "plateau" behind Pendulum Cove.

Boundaries. The western boundary follows the 40m contour line and the eastern boundary follows the 140 m contour line east-southeast of Pendulum Cove. The northern and southern boundaries follow the edge of the volcanic debris-covered permanent ice that borders the Site.

Scientific value. Geothermal activity was recorded during a survey in 1987, with substantial heat being emitted from crevices amongst scoria. There was no such evidence in 2002. Although vegetation is very sparse, this known-age site is being colonised by numerous moss and lichen species. Two of the mosses (*Racomitrium lanuginosum* and *R. heterostichoides*) are unique both on the island and in the Antarctic, and both are very rare here. Several other mosses are Antarctic rarities.

Human impact. The non-native springtail *Deuteraphorura cebennaria* has been found in Pendulum Cove, but just outside Site G.

Site H - Mt. Pond

Area encompassed. The Site is situated *c.* 1.4 to 2 km north-north-west of Mount Pond summit. The extensive area of geothermally-heated ground includes an area (c. 150 × 500 m) on the north eastern side of the gently sloping upper part of a broad ridge at *c.* 385 to 500m elevation (Smith 1988). At the northern end of the Site there are numerous inconspicuous fumarole vents in low mounds of very fine, compacted baked soil. The higher, southern, part of the Site is close to a large rime dome at 512 m, in the lee of which (at c. 500 to 505 m) are numerous active fumaroles, also surrounded by fine, compacted baked soil, on a steep, moist, sheltered slope. The extensive areas of heated ground surrounding the fumaroles comprise a fine soil with a soft crust that is extremely vulnerable to trampling. There are several stands of dense, thick (up to 10 cm) bryophyte vegetation associated with these areas. The adjacent yellowish tuff outcrops support a different community of mosses and lichens.

7

Boundaries. The northern boundary is marked by Lat. 62°55'51''S, the southern boundary by Lat. 62°56'12''S and the eastern boundary is marked by Long. 060°33'30''W. The western boundary follows the ridgeline of the broad ridge that slopes north northwest from the summit of Mt. Pond between Long. 060°33'48''W and Long. 060°34'51''W.

Scientific value. This is an outstanding site of botanical interest, unique in the Antarctic. It possesses several moss species which are either unique to the Antarctic or are extremely rare in Antarctica. The development of the moss turf (*Dicranella hookeri* and *Philonotis polymorpha*) in the main upper part of the Site is exceptional, and two or more species have colonised profusely since last inspected in 1994. The large liverwort (*Marchantii berteroana*) is rapidly colonising the warm moist soil crust at the periphery of the moss stands. At least one species of toadstool fungus also occurs amongst the moss, the highest known record for these organisms in Antarctica. A totally different community of mosses and lichens occurs on the rock outcrops, and also includes several extremely rare species (notably *Schistidium andinum* and *S. praemorsum*).

Site J - Perchuc Cone

Area encompassed. This ash cone lies *c.* 750 m northeast of Ronald Hill and comprises a very narrow line of fumaroles and adjacent heated ground on the west-facing slope at *c.* 160-170 m elevation (Lat. 62°58'00.9" S; Long. 060°33'39.7" W). The geothermal area covers *c.* 25 × 10 m, and the fine ash and lapilli surface of the entire slope is very vulnerable to pedestrian damage.

Boundaries. The northern boundary is marked by Lat. 62°57'50''S, the southern boundary by Lat. 62°58'05''S, the eastern boundary is marked by Long. 060°33'25''W and the western boundary by Long. 060°33'50''W. Site J Perchuć Cone has been designated as a Prohibited Zone to protect the vulnerable vegetation and soil structures at this location. Access to Site J Perchuć Cone is strictly prohibited.

Scientific value. The Site contains several mosses that are extremely rare in Antarctica. Photographic evidence suggests that the extent of moss colonisation has decreased since the mid-1980s.

Site K – Ronald Hill to Kroner Lake

Area encompassed. This Site includes the circular flat plain of the crater immediately to the south of Ronald Hill, and extends along the prominent broad shallow outwash gulley with a low bank on either side, leading southwards from here to Kroner Lake. The substratum throughout the area is consolidated mud, fine ash and lapilli deposited by the lahar during the 1969 eruption. Part of the Site, notably the gulley, remains geothermally active. The Site also includes the intertidal geothermal lagoon (Kroner Lake) as it is part of the same volcanological feature. This small, shallow, circular, brackish crater lake was broached by the sea during the 1980's, and is now the only geothermally heated lagoon in the Antarctic.

Boundaries. The boundary surrounds the crater basin, gulley, Kroner Lake and an area between *c.* 100 – 150 m wide around the lake. A corridor below Ronald Hill, from the break-of-slope to the lowermost massive boulders about 10 to 20 m beyond, remains outside the boundary to allow access past the Area.

Scientific value. The surfaces of this Site are of a known age and are being colonised by numerous moss, liverwort and lichen species, several of which are extremely rare in the Antarctic (eg, the mosses *Notoligotrichum trichodon* and *Polytrichastrum longisetum*, and a rare lichen, *Peltigera didactyla*, is colonising >1 ha of the crater floor). The geothermal northern intertidal shore of Kroner Lake possesses a unique community of algae.

Human impact. The non-native springtails *Hypogastrura viatica* , *Mesaphorura macrochaeta* and *Proisotoma minuta* and mites *Speleorchestes* sp., *Terpnacarus gibbosus* and

Coccotydaeolus cf. *krantzii* are found at several site around Whalers Bay and may be present within Site K. The non-native springtails *Protaphorura fimata* and *Folsomia candida* were reported from Whalers Bay in the 1960s but have not be found in subsequent surveys.

Site L - South East Point

Area encompassed. An east-west trending rocky ridge *c.* 0.7 km north of South East Point, extending from the top of the sea cliff (*c.* 20 m altitude) westwards for *c.* 250 m, to a point about 80m altitude. The north edge of the ridge is a low vertical lava outcrop, giving way to a steep unstable slope leading to the floor of a gully parallel to the ridge. The south side of the Site is the gently sloping ridge crest covered with ash and lapilli.

Boundaries. The Site extends 50 m north and south of the lava outcrop.

Scientific value. This Site has the most extensive population of Antarctic pearlwort (*Colobanthus quitensis*) known in the Antarctic. It was the largest population before the 1967 eruption (Longton 1967), covering *c.* 300 m^2, but was almost completely destroyed by ash burial. It gradually recovered, but since about 1985-1990 there has been a massive increase in seedling establishment and the population has expanded downwind (westwards, uphill). It is now very abundant in an area of *c.* 2 ha. It is also remarkable for the absence of the other native vascular plant, Antarctic hairgrass (*Deschampsia antarctica*), almost always associated with this plant. Photographs of the Site immediately after the eruption revealed almost total loss of lichens, but these too have recolonised rapidly and extensively, the large bushy *Usnea antarctica* being particularly abundant and attaining a considerable size after the relatively short period since recolonisation. The cryptogamic flora of the Site is generally sparse and typical of most of the island. The Site is particularly important for monitoring the reproduction and spread of the pearlwort in a known-age site.

6(ii) Access to the Area

- Access to the Sites shall be by foot or small boat.
- Helicopter landings are prohibited within the Area. The Management Plan for Deception Island ASMA 4 shows recommended helicopter landing sites on Deception Island, which are also shown in Figure 1. Helicopter landings sites which may be useful for accessing Sites are located at: Decepción Station (Argentina; Lat. 62°58'30''S, Long. 060°42'00''W), northern Fumarole Bay (Lat. 62°57'18''S, Long. 060°42'48''W), the south of Cross Hill (Lat. 62°56'39''S, Long. 060°41'36''W), eastern Telefon Bay (Lat. 62°55'18''S, Long. 060°38'18''W), Pendulum Cove (Lat. 62°56'12''S, Long. 060°35'45''W) and Whalers Bay (Lat. 62°58'48''S, Long. 060°33'12''W).
- All travel to the Sites shall be undertaken carefully so as to minimize disturbance to soil and vegetation en route.
- The operation of aircraft should be carried out, as a minimum requirement, in compliance with the 'Guidelines for the Operation of Aircraft near Concentrations of Birds' contained in Resolution 2 (2004). Particular care should be taken when overflying Site A Collins Point, which contains a colony of kelp gulls in the low cliffs above the beach.

6(iii) Location of structures within and adjacent to the Area

Two research stations are found close to the ASPA sites: Decepción Station (Argentina; Lat. 62°58'30''S, Long. 060°41'54''W) and Gabriel de Castilla Station (Spain; Lat. 62°58'36''S, Long. 060°40'30''W). Two Historic Sites or Monuments are found close to the ASPA sites: Whalers Bay (HSM 71; Lat. 62°58'42''S, Long. 060°33'36''W) and the ruins of the Base Pedro Aguirre Cerda Station (HSM 76; Lat. 62°56'12''S, Long. 060°35'36''W). Collins Point navigation beacon is situated at Lat. 62°59'42''S, Long. 060°35'12''W. At Site A, Collins Point, there are six 50 × 50cm plots marked with wooden corner stakes, although not all of the

9

four stakes per plot remain (Lat. 63°00'00''S, Long. 060°34'48''W). These were established by the British Antarctic Survey in 1969 to monitor changes in the vegetation in subsequent years (Collins 1969); data were obtained in 1969 and 2002. These markers should be maintained.

Structures within the Site C, Caliente Hill, include some experimental apparatus monitoring long-term ground temperature variations (operated by the Spanish National Antarctic Programme) and several short metal stakes arranged along the ridgeline near the summit.

Other structures near to the Area are listed in the ASMA Management Plan for Deception Island.

6(iv) Location of other protected areas in the vicinity

ASPA 145 comprises two sites of benthic importance within Port Foster. Deception Island and Port Foster are managed within ASMA 4 Deception Island.

6(v) Special zones within the Area

Site J Perchuć Cone has been designated as a Prohibited Zone to protect the vulnerable vegetation and soil structures at this location. Access to Site J Perchuć Cone is strictly prohibited.

7. Permit conditions

7(i) General permit conditions

Entry into the Area is prohibited except in accordance with a Permit issued by an appropriate national authority. Conditions for issuing a Permit to enter the Area are that:

- it is issued only for compelling scientific reasons which cannot be served elsewhere; or
- it is issued for essential management purposes such as inspection, maintenance or review;
- the actions permitted will not jeopardise the floristic, ecological or scientific values of the Area;
- any management activities are in support of the objectives of the Management Plan;
- the actions permitted are in accordance with this Management Plan;
- the Permit, or an authorised copy, must be carried within the Area;
- permits shall be issued for a stated period;
- the appropriate authority should be notified of any activities/measures undertaken that were not included in the authorised Permit.

7(ii) Access to, and movement within or over, the Area

- Land vehicles are prohibited in the Area.
- Helicopter landings are prohibited within the Area. The Management Plan for Deception Island ASMA 4 shows recommended helicopter landing sites on Deception Island (see also Figure 1).
- Rowing boats are permitted for sampling purposes in the lakes in Site B - Crater Lake and Site F - Telefon Bay, and the lagoon in Site K - Ronald Hill to Kroner Lake. Prior to use at each Site, boats shall be cleaned to reduce the risk of introductions of non-native species from outside the Treaty area and other Antarctic locations, including other Sites within ASPA 140. Engine powered boats must not be used.

- Movement within the Area Sites shall be on foot.
- Movements into the Area shall consider the *SCAR Code of Conduct for Activity within Terrestrial Geothermal Environments in Antarctica.*
- All movement shall be undertaken carefully so as to minimize disturbance to soil and vegetation:
  - The vegetation at Site C - Caliente Hill is sparse and not obvious and is therefore particularly vulnerable to trampling. <u>Extreme care</u> should be taken to avoid trampling of vegetation when visiting this site.
  - The soil in the vicinity of Site J Perchuć Cone is extremely friable and exceptionally vulnerable to damage by trampling. Compared to other fumeroles on Deception Island, Perchuć Cone has experienced relatively little human visitation and associated trampling impact and may provide a representative site for future scientific studies. Consequently, Site J has been designated as a Prohibited Zone and entry is strictly prohibited.

7(iii) Activities which may be conducted in the Area

Activities include:

- compelling scientific research which cannot be undertaken elsewhere and which will not jeopardize the flora and ecology of the Area;
- essential management activities, including monitoring.
- surveys, to be undertaken as necessary, to determine the state of the botanical values for which each Site has been designated, in support of the aims of this Management Plan.

7(iv) Installation, modification or removal of structures

Structures shall not be erected within the Area except as specified in a Permit. All scientific equipment, botanical quadrats or other markers installed in the Area must be approved by Permit and clearly identified by country, name of the principal investigator and year of installation. All such items should be made of materials that pose minimal risk of contamination of the Area (see Section *7(vi)*).

7(v) Location of field camps

Camping is not permitted within the Area. The ASMA Management Plan for Deception Island shows recommended sites for field camps on the island, but outside ASPA 140. Campsites which may be useful for accessing Sites are located at: northern Fumarole Bay (Lat. 62°57'18''S, Long. 060°42'42''W), the south of Cross Hill (Lat. 62°56'36''S, Long. 060°41'30''W), eastern Telefon Bay (Lat. 62°55'18''S, Long. 060°38'12''W), Pendulum Cove (Lat. 62°56'12''S, Long. 060°35'42''W) and Whalers Bay (Lat. 62°58'54''S, Long. 060°33'0''W) (see Figure 1). When planning camping locations and activities, recommendation within the SCAR *Code of Conduct for Activity within Terrestrial Geothermal Environments in Antarctica*, should be taken into consideration, as appropriate.

7(vi) Restrictions on materials and organisms which may be brought into the Area

The deliberate introduction of animals, plant material, microorganisms and non-sterile soil into the Area shall not be permitted. To ensure that the floristic and ecological values of the Area are maintained, special precautions shall be taken to prevent the accidental introduction of animals, plant material, micro-organisms and non-sterile soil from other biologically distinct regions (within or beyond the Antarctic Treaty area). Care should be taken to prevent distribution of species between ASPA sites. Visitors should take into consideration the recommendations contained within the biosecurity guidelines that are found in Appendix 11 of the Antarctic Specially Managed Area No. 4 Deception Island management plan as well as the SCAR *Environmental code of conduct for terrestrial scientific field research in Antarctica* and in the

11

SCAR *Code of Conduct for Activity within Terrestrial Geothermal Environments in Antarctica* as appropriate (both available at: http://www.scar.org/codes-of-conduct). Visitors should also consult and follow, as appropriate, recommendations contained in the *CEP non-native species manual* (available at: http://www.ats.aq/e/ep_faflo_nns.htm). In particular, all sampling equipment or markers brought into the Area shall be cleaned or sterilized. To the maximum extent practicable, footwear and other equipment used or brought into the Area (including bags or backpacks) shall be thoroughly cleaned before entering the Area. No poultry or egg products shall be taken into the Area.

No herbicides or pesticides shall be brought into the Area. Any other chemicals, including radio-nuclides or stable isotopes, which may be introduced for scientific or management purposes specified in the permit, shall be removed from the Area at or before the conclusion of the activity for which the permit was granted. Release of radio-nuclides or stable isotopes directly into the environment in a way that renders them unrecoverable shall not be permitted.

Fuel, food and other materials are not to be deposited within the Area, unless authorized by Permit for specific scientific or management purposes. Permanent depots are not permitted. All materials introduced shall be for a stated period only, shall be removed at or before the conclusion of the stated period, and shall be stored and handled so that risk of their introduction into the environment is minimised. If release occurs which is likely to compromise the values of the Area, removal is encouraged only where the impact of removal is not likely to be greater than that of leaving the material *in situ*. The appropriate authority shall be notified of any materials released and not removed that were not included in the authorised Permit.

7(vii) Taking of, or harmful interference with, native flora and fauna

Taking or harmful interference with native flora or fauna is prohibited, except by Permit issued in accordance with Annex II to the Protocol on Environmental Protection to the Antarctic Treaty. Where taking of or harmful interference with animals is involved, the SCAR *Code of Conduct for the Use of Animals for Scientific Purposes in Antarctica* should be used as a minimum standard.

7(viii) The collection or removal of materials not brought into the Area by the Permit holder

Material of a biological, geological (including soil and lake sediment), or hydrological nature may be collected or removed from the Area only in accordance with a Permit and should be limited to the minimum necessary to meet scientific or management needs. Permits shall not be granted if there is reasonable concern that the sampling proposed would take, remove or damage such quantities of soil, sediment, flora or fauna that their distribution or abundance within the Area would be significantly affected. Material of human origin likely to compromise the values of the Area, which was not brought into the Area by the Permit Holder or otherwise authorised, may be removed unless the impact of removal is likely to be greater than leaving the material *in situ*; if this is the case the appropriate authority should be notified. If wind-blown debris is found in the Area it should be removed. Plastic debris should be disposed of in accordance with Annex III (Waste disposal and waste management) of the Protocol on Environmental Protection to the Antarctic Treaty (1998). Other wind-blown material should be returned to the Historic Site or Monument from which it originated and secured to prevent further dispersal by wind. A report describing the nature of the material removed from the ASPA and the location within the Historic Site and Monument where it has been secured and stored, should be submitted to the Deception Island Antarctic Specially Managed Area (ASMA) Management Group, via the Chair, to establish the most appropriate way to deal with the debris (ie, conservation to preserve any historic value or appropriate disposal) (see Deception Island ASMA website: *http://www.deceptionisland.aq/contact.php*).

7(ix) Disposal of waste

All wastes shall be removed from the Area in accordance with Annex III (Waste disposal and waste management) of the Protocol on Environmental Protection to the Antarctic Treaty (1998).

In order to avoid anthropogenic microbial and nutrient enrichment of soils, no solid or liquid human waste should be deposited within the Area. Human wastes may be disposed of within Port Foster, but avoiding ASPA 145.

7(x) Measures that may be necessary to continue to meet the aims of the Management Plan

- Permits may be granted to enter the Area to carry out biological, vulcanological or seismic monitoring and site inspection activities.
- Any long-term monitoring sites shall be appropriately marked and the markers or signs maintained.
- Permits may be granted to allow for monitoring of the Area, or to allow for some active management as set out in Section 3.

7(xi) Requirements for reports

The principal permit holder for each visit to the Area shall submit a report to the appropriate national authority as soon as practicable, and no later than six months after the visit has been completed. Such visit reports should include, as applicable, the information identified in the recommended visit report form (contained as an Appendix in the Guide to the Preparation of Management Plans for Antarctic Specially Protected Areas (available from the website of the Secretariat of the Antarctic Treaty; *www.ats.aq*)). If appropriate, the national authority should also forward a copy of the visit report to the Party that proposed the Management Plan, to assist in managing the Area and reviewing the Management Plan. Wherever possible, Parties should deposit the original or copies of the original visit reports, in a publicly accessible archive to maintain a record of usage, for the purpose of any review of the Management Plan and in organising the scientific use of the Area.

13

8. Supporting documentation

Aptroot, A. and van der Knaap, W.O. 1993. The lichen flora of Deception Island, South Shetland Islands. *Nova Hedwigia*, **56**, 183-192.

Baker, P.E., McReath, I., Harvey, M.R., Roobol, M., & Davies, T.G. 1975. The geology of the South Shetland Islands: V. Volcanic evolution of Deception Island. *British Antarctic Survey Scientific Reports,* No. 78, 81 pp.

Bednarek-Ochyra, H., Váňa, J., Ochyra, R. and Lewis Smith, R.I. 2000. *The Liverwort Flora of Antarctica*. Polish Academy of Sciences, Krakow, 236 pp.

Cameron, R.E. and Benoit, R.E. 1970. Microbial and ecological investigations of recent cinder cones, Deception Island, Antarctica – a preliminary report. *Ecology*, **51**, 802-809.

Collins, N.J. 1969. The effects of volcanic activity on the vegetation of Deception Island. *British Antarctic Survey Bulletin*, **21**, 79-94.

Greenslade, P., Potapov, M., Russell, D., and Convey, P. (2012) Global collembola on Deception Island. *Journal of Insect Science*, **12**, 111. http://www.insectscience.org/12.111

Hack, W.H. 1949. Nota sobre un colémbolo de la Antartida Argentina *Achorutes viaticus* Tullberg. *Notas del Museo de la Plata,* **14**, 211–212.

Longton, R.E. 1967. Vegetation in the maritime Antarctic. In Smith, J.E., *Editor*, A discussion of the terrestrial Antarctic ecosystem. *Philosophical Transactions of the Royal Society of London*, B, **252**, 213-235.

Morgan F, Barker G, Briggs C, Price R and Keys H. 2007. Environmental Domains of Antarctica Version 2.0 Final Report, Manaaki Whenua Landcare Research New Zealand Ltd, 89 pages.

Ochyra, R., Bednarek-Ochyra, H. and Smith, R.I.L. *The Moss Flora of Antarctica*. 2008. Cambridge University Press, Cambridge. pp 704.

Øvstedal, D.O. and Smith, R.I.L. 2001. *Lichens of Antarctica and South Georgia. A Guide to their Identification and Ecology*. Cambridge University Press, Cambridge, 411 pp.

Peat, H., Clarke, A., and Convey, P. 2007. Diversity and biogeography of the Antarctic flora. *Journal of Biogeography,* **34**, 132-146.

Smellie, J.L., López-Martínez, J., Headland, R.K., Hernández-Cifuentes, Maestro, A., Miller, I.L., Rey, J., Serrano, E., Somoza, L. and Thomson, J.W. 2002. *Geology and geomorphology of Deception Island*, 78 pp. BAS GEOMAP Series, Sheets 6-A and 6-B, 1:25,000, British Antarctic Survey, Cambridge.

Smith, R. I. L. 1984a. Terrestrial plant biology of the sub-Antarctic and Antarctic. In: Antarctic Ecolgy, Vol. 1. Editor: R. M. Laws. London, Academic Press.

Smith, R.I.L. 1984b. Colonization and recovery by cryptogams following recent volcanic activity on Deception Island, South Shetland Islands. *British Antarctic Survey Bulletin*, **62**, 25-51.

Smith, R.I.L. 1984c. Colonization by bryophytes following recent volcanic activity on an Antarctic island. *Journal of the Hattori Botanical Laboratory*, **56**, 53-63.

Smith, R.I.L. 1988. Botanical survey of Deception Island. *British Antarctic Survey Bulletin*, **80**, 129-136.

Figure 1. Map of Deception Island showing the 11 sites that make up ASPA 140 Parts of Deception Island, South Shetland Islands.

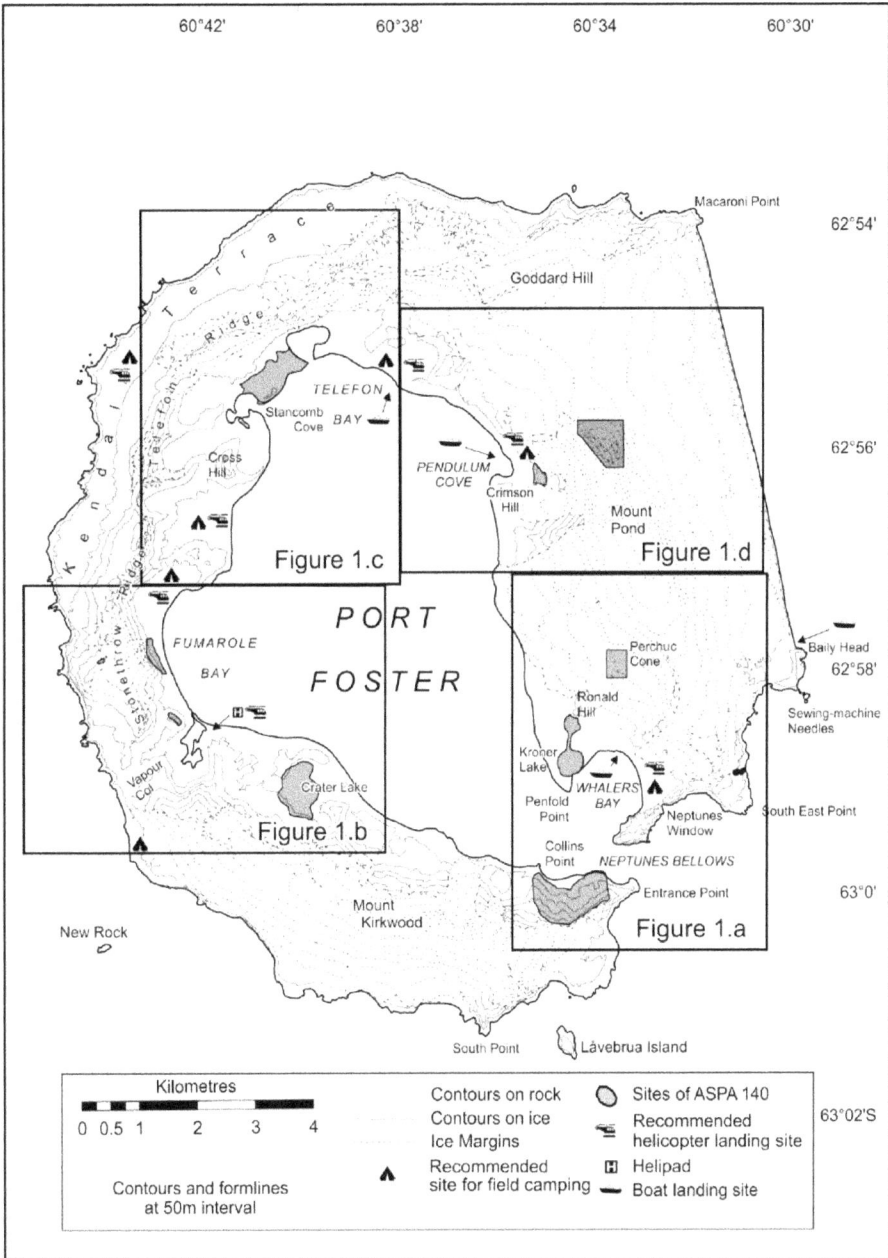

15

Figure 1a. Map showing the location of ASPA No. 140 Sites A, J, K and L.

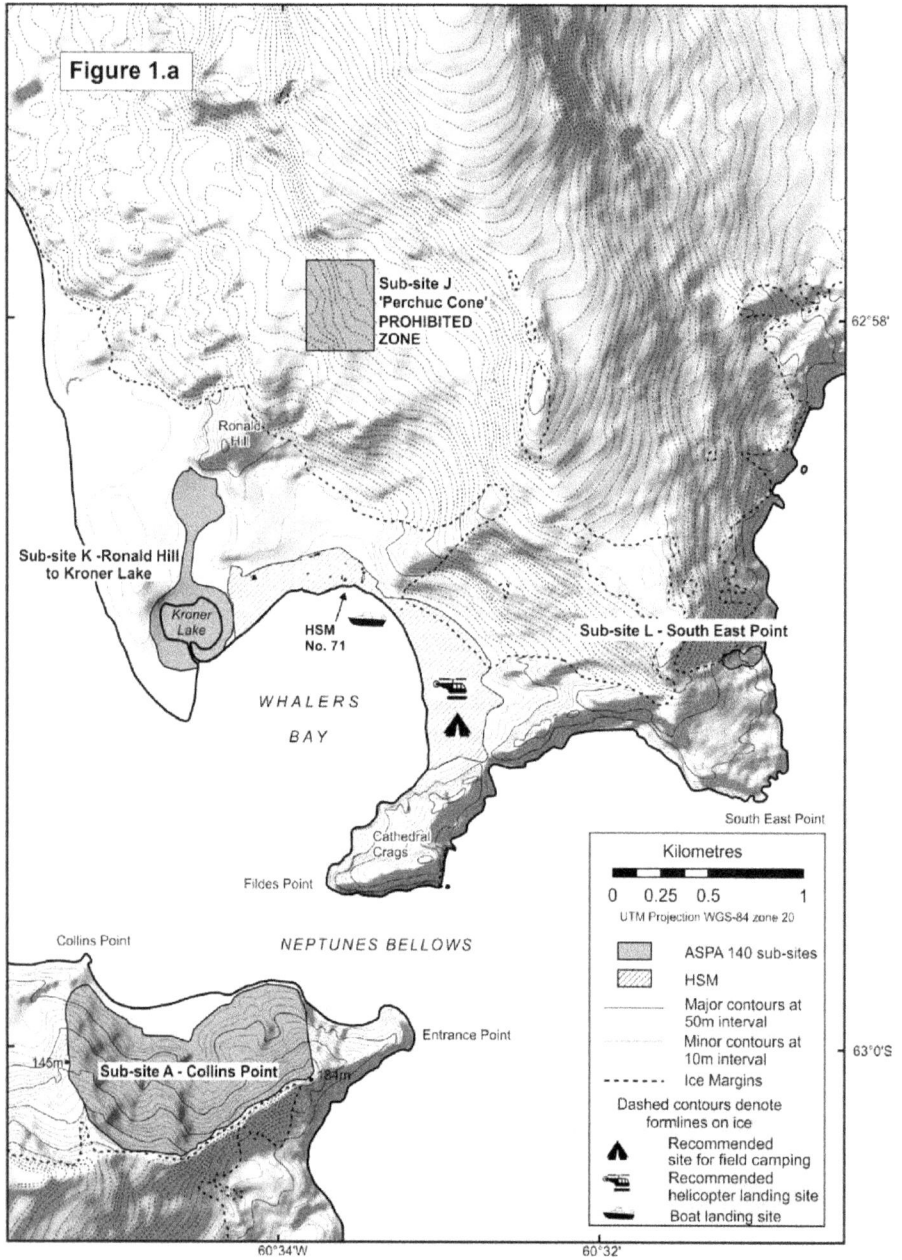

Figure 1b. Map showing the location of ASPA No. 140 Sites B, C, D and E.

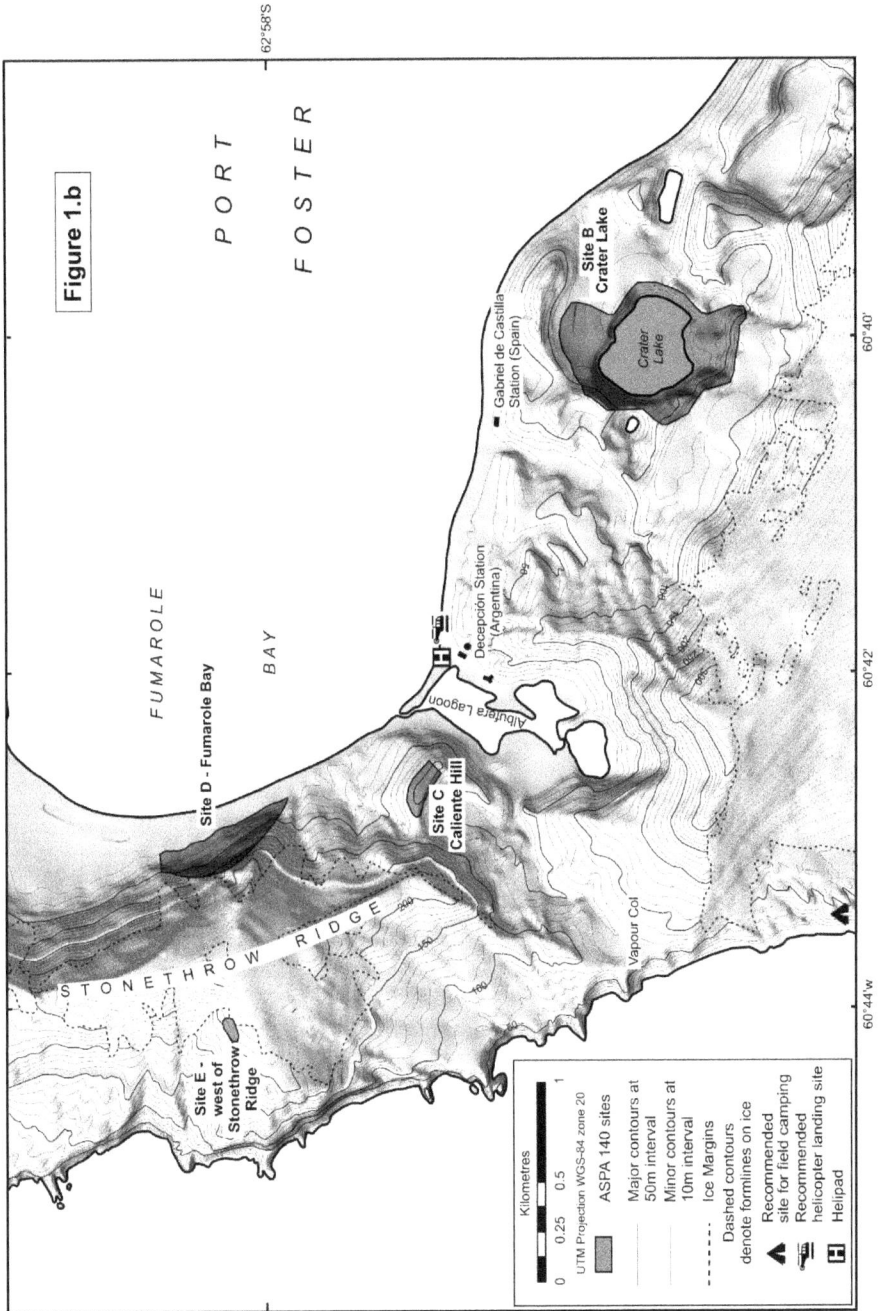

17

Figure 1c. Map showing the location of ASPA No. 140 Site F.

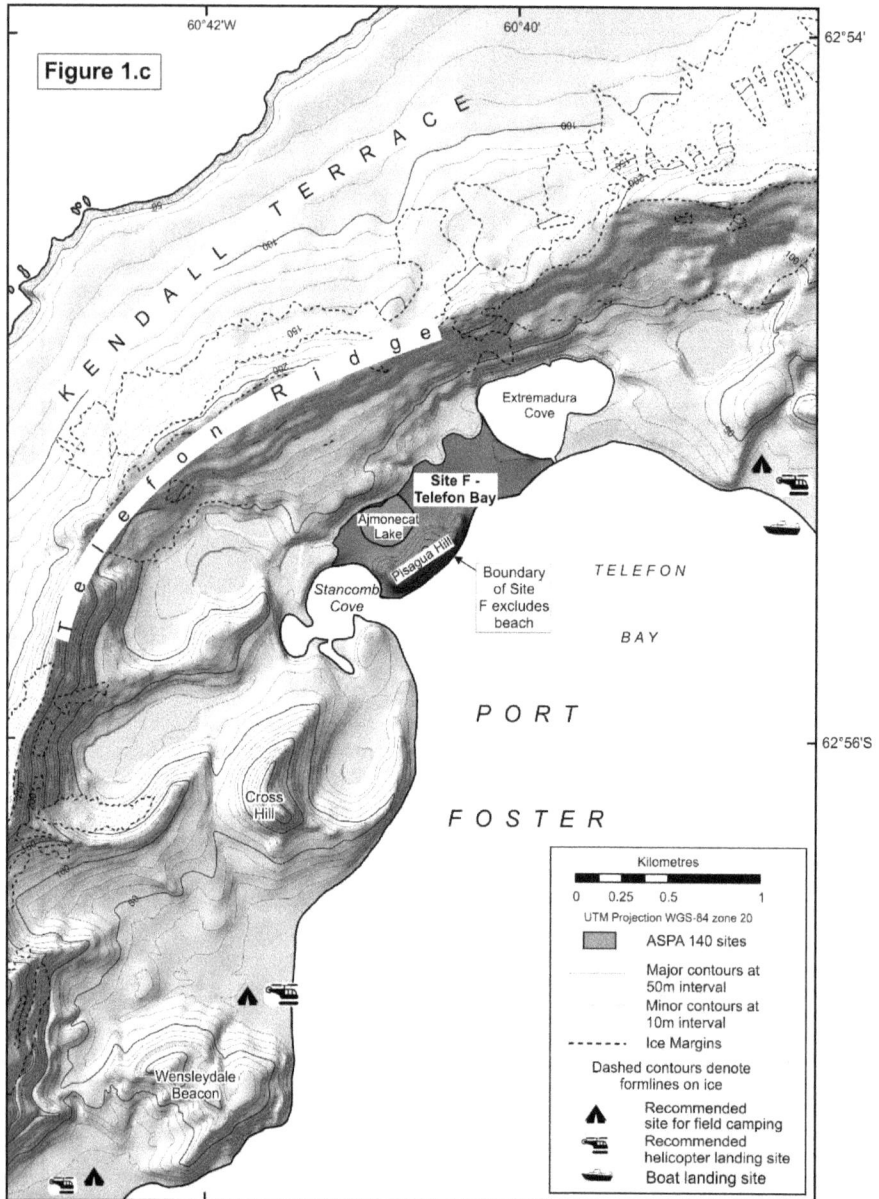

Figure 1d. Map showing the location of ASPA No. 140 Sites G and H.

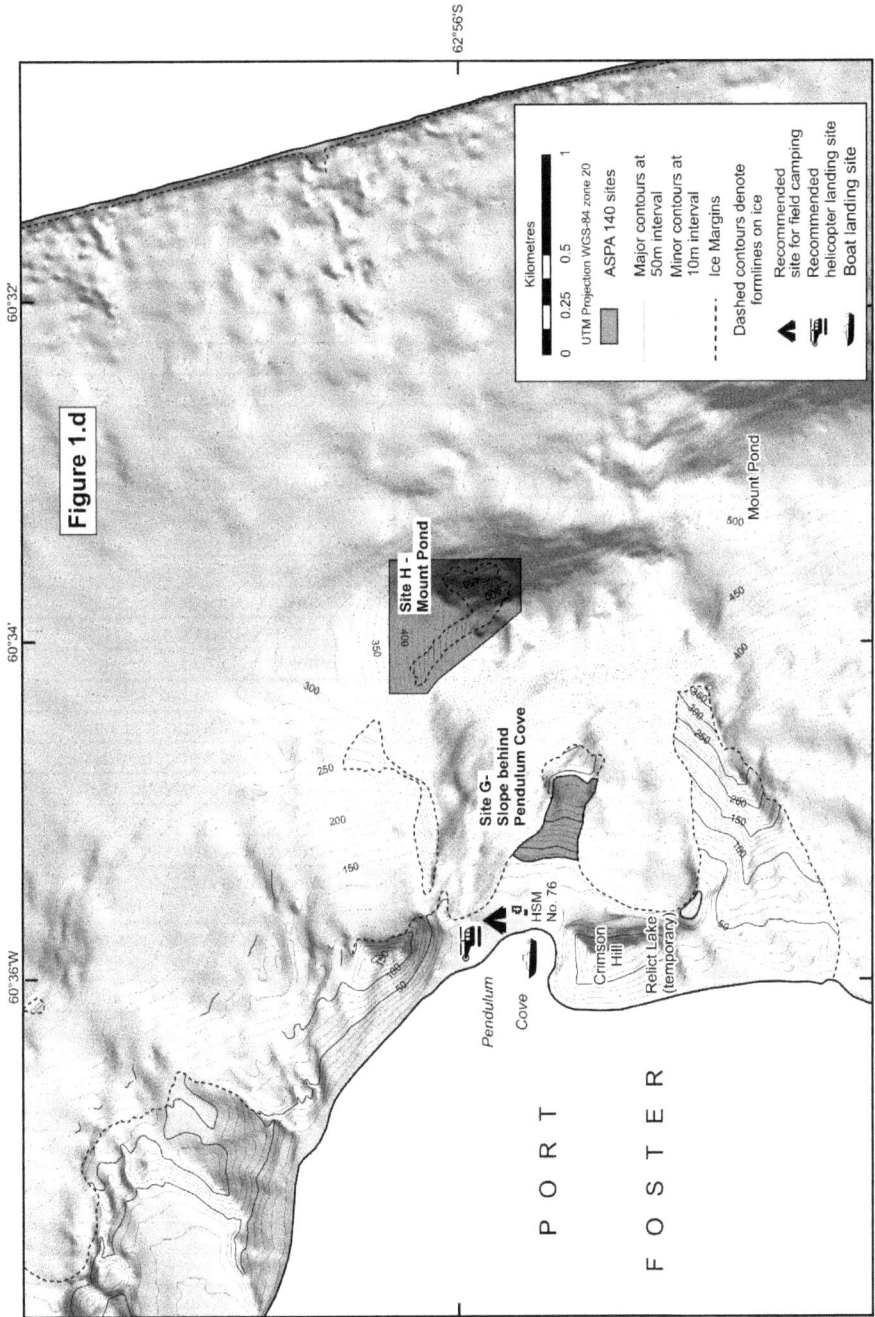

Annex 1. List of plant species, classed as rare or very rare in the Antarctic Treaty Area, occurring on Deception Island.

A. Bryophytes (L = Liverwort)

Species	Sites where species occurs	Notes
Brachythecium austroglareosum	D	Few other known Antarctic sites
B. fuegianum	G	Only known Antarctic site
Bryum amblyodon	C, D, G, K	Few other known Antarctic sites
B. dichotomum	C, E, H, J	Only known Antarctic site
B. orbiculatifolium	H, K	One other known Antarctic site
B. pallescens	D	Few other known Antarctic sites
Cryptochila grandiflora (L)	E	Only known Antarctic site
Dicranella hookeri	C, E, H	Only known Antarctic site
Didymodon brachyphillus	A, D, G, H	Locally more abundant than any other known Antarctic site
Ditrichum conicum	E	Only known Antarctic site
D. ditrichoideum	C, G, J	Only known Antarctic site
D. heteromallum	C, H	Only known Antarctic site
D. hyalinum	G	Few other known Antarctic sites
D. hyalinocuspidatum	G	Few other known Antarctic sites
Grimmia plagiopodia	A, D, G	A continental Antarctic species
Hymenoloma antarcticum	B, C, D, E, G, K	Few other known Antarctic sites
H. crispulum	G	Few other known Antarctic sites
Notoligotrichum trichodon	K	One other known Antarctic site
Philonotis polymorpha	E, H	Only known Antarctic site
Platyneurum jungermannioides	D	Few other known Antarctic sites
Polytrichastrum longisetum (L)	K	One other known Antarctic site
Pohlia wahlenbergii	C, E, H	One other known Antarctic site
Racomitrium heterostichoides	G	Only known Antarctic site
R. lanuginosum	G	Only known Antarctic site
R. subsecundum	C	Only known Antarctic site
S. amblyophyllum	C, D, G, H	Few other known Antarctic sites
S. andinum	H	Few other known Antarctic sites
S. deceptionensis sp. nov.	C	Deception endemic
S. leptoneurum sp. nov.	D	Deception endemic
Schistidium praemorsum	H	One other known Antarctic site
Syntrichia andersonii	D, L	Only known Antarctic site

B. Lichens

Species	Sites where species occurs	Notes
Acarospora austroshetlandica	A	One other known Antarctic site
Caloplaca johnstonii	B, D, F, L	Few other known Antarctic sites
Catapyrenium lachneoides	?	Few other known Antarctic sites
Cladonia galindezii	A, B, D	More abundant than any other known site
Degelia sp.	K	Only known Antarctic site
Ochrolechia parella	A, B, D	More abundant than any other known site
Peltigera didactyla	B, K	Very rare in B; very small colonising form abundant in K
Pertusaria excludens	D	Few other known Antarctic sites
P. oculae-ranae	G	Only known Antarctic site
Placopsis parellina	A, B, D, G, H	More abundant than any other known site
Protoparmelia loricata	B	Few other known Antarctic sites
Psoroma saccharatum	D	Only known Antarctic site
Stereocaulon condensatum	E	Only known Antarctic site
S. vesuvianum	B, G	Few other known Antarctic sites

21

Annex 2. Photographs of the Sites comprising ASPA 140. Photographs were taken between 19-26 Jan 2010 (K. Hughes: A, B, C, E, F, G, J, K, L; P. Convey: D, H).

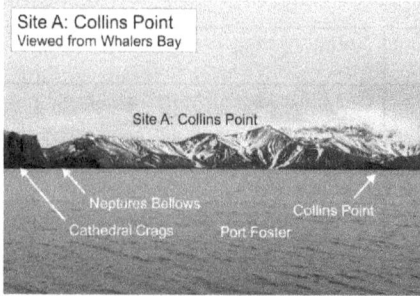

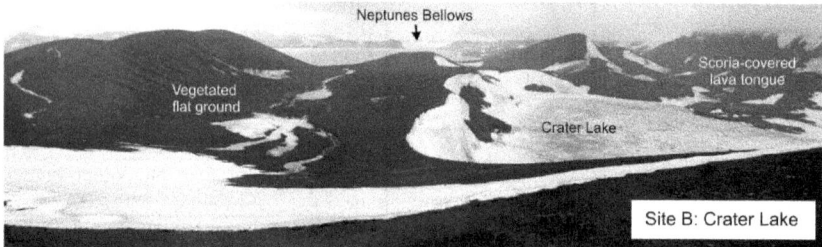

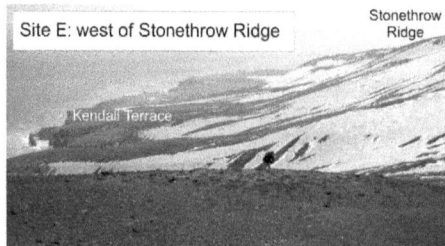

Site A: Collins Point
Viewed from Whalers Bay

Site B: Crater Lake
Scoria-covered lava tongue south of the lake

Site B: Crater Lake

Site C: Caliente Hill

Site C: Caliente Hill

Site D: Fumerole Bay

Site E: west of Stonethrow Ridge

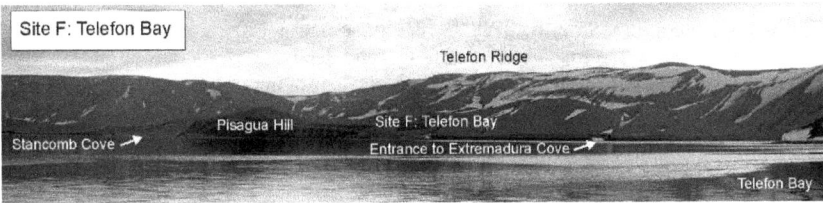

Site F: Telefon Bay

Telefon Ridge

Pisagua Hill

Site F: Telefon Bay

Stancomb Cove

Entrance to Extremadura Cove

Telefon Bay

Site G: Pendulum Cove

Mount Pond

Site G: Pendulum Cove

Crimson Hill

HSM No. 76

Pendulum Cove

Site H: Mount Pond

Mount Pond summit

Site H: Mount Pond

RIDGE

Port Foster

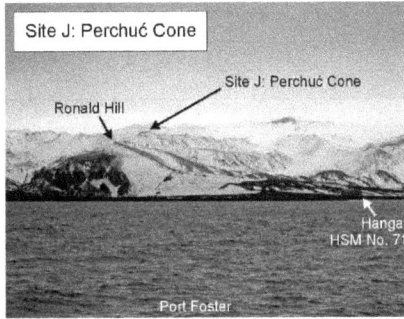

Site J: Perchuć Cone

Site J: Perchuć Cone

Ronald Hill

Hangar HSM No. 71

Port Foster

Site K: Ronald Hill to Kroner Lake

Ronald Hill

Penfold Point

Kroner Lake

Whalers Bay

Hangar HSM No. 71

Port Foster

Site L: South East Point

Cathedral Crags

Site L: South East Point

South East Point

Bransfield Strait

23

Annex 3. Boundary coordinates for the Sites that comprise ASPA 140 Parts of Deception Island. Many of the boundaries follow natural features and detailed descriptions of the boundaries are found in Section 6. The boundary coordinates are numbered, with number 1 the most northerly co-ordinate and further coordinates numbered sequentially in a clockwise direction around each Site.

Site	Number	Latitude	Longitude
A: Collins Point	1	62°59'50'' S	060°33'55'' W
	2	63°00'06'' S	060°33'51'' W
	3	63°00'16'' S	060°34'27'' W
	4	63°00'15'' S	060°34'53'' W
	5	63°00'06'' S	060°35'15'' W
	6	62°59'47'' S	060°35'19'' W
	7	62°59'59'' S	060°34'48'' W
	8	62°59'49'' S	060°34'07'' W
B: Crater Lake	1	62°58'48'' S	060°40'02'' W
	2	62°58'50'' S	060°39'45'' W
	3	62°58'56'' S	060°39'52'' W
	4	62°59'01'' S	060°39'37'' W
	5	62°59'11'' S	060°39'47'' W
	6	62°59'18'' S	060°39'45'' W
	7	62°59'16'' S	060°40'15'' W
	8	62°59'04'' S	060°40'31'' W
	9	62°58'56'' S	060°40'25'' W
C: Caliente Hill	1	62°58'33'' S	060°42'12'' W
	2	62°58'27'' S	060°42'28'' W
	3	62°58'29'' S	060°42'33'' W
	4	62°58'25'' S	060°42'51'' W
D: Fumarole Bay	1	62°57'42'' S	060°43'05'' W
	2	62°58'04'' S	060°42'42'' W
	3	62°57'53'' S	060°43'08'' W
	4	62°57'43'' S	060°43'13'' W
E: west of Stonethrow Ridge	1	62°57'51'' S	060°44'00'' W
	2	62°57'54'' S	060°44'00'' W
	3	62°57'54'' S	060°44'10'' W
	4	62°57'51'' S	060°44'10'' W
F: Telefon Bay	1	62°55'02'' S	060°40'17'' W
	2	62°55'11'' S	060°39'45'' W
	3	62°55'35'' S	060°40'43'' W
	4	62°55'30'' S	060°41'13'' W
	5	62°55'21'' S	060°41'07'' W
G: Pendulum Cove	1	62°56'10'' S	060°35'15'' W
	2	62°56'20'' S	060°34'41'' W
	3	62°56'28'' S	060°34'44'' W

	4	62°56'21'' S	060°35'16'' W
H: Mt. Pond	1	62°55'51'' S	060°33'30'' W
	2	62°56'12'' S	060°33'30'' W
	3	62°56'12'' S	060°33'48'' W
	4	62°55'57'' S	060°34'42'' W
	5	62°55'51'' S	060°34'42'' W
J: Perchuć Cone	1	62°57'50'' S	060°33'50'' W
	2	62°57'50'' S	060°33'25'' W
	3	62°58'05'' S	060°33'25'' W
	4	62°58'05'' S	060°33'50'' W
K: Ronald Hill to Kroner Lake	1	62°58'25'' S	060°34'22'' W
	2	62°58'32'' S	060°34'20'' W
	3	62°58'34'' S	060°34'27'' W
	4	62°58'41'' S	060°34'30'' W
	5	62°58'44'' S	060°34'18'' W
	6	62°58'50'' S	060°34'18'' W
	7	62°58'58'' S	060°34'38'' W
	8	62°58'49'' S	060°34'53'' W
	9	62°58'41'' S	060°34'40'' W
	10	62°58'24'' S	060°34'44'' W
L: South-east Point	1	62°58'53'' S	060°31'01'' W
	2	62°58'56'' S	060°30'59'' W
	3	62°58'57'' S	060°31'13'' W
	4	62°58'55'' S	060°31'14'' W

25

Annex 4. Recommended access to the Sites that comprise ASPA 140.

Site	Name	Recommended access route
A	Collins Point	By boat: land at the coast to the north of the site (Port Foster)
B	Crater Lake	Overland: traverse the west side of the ridge that rises to the south of Gabriel de Castilla Station for 500m, then travel east for 200 m until the western boundary of the Areas is reached.
C	Caliente Hill	Overland: access the site from Fumarole Bay to the north of the site, or along the prominent ridge that lies to the south west of the summit of Caliente Hill.
D	Fumarole Bay	By boat: access anywhere along the coast of Fumarole Bay.
E	west of Stonethrow Ridge	Overland: from Fumarole Bay, head southwest pass Albufera Lagoon then head north, traversing the west slope of Stonethrow Ridge. The Site lies on the north side of the east-west trending ridge that lies *c.* 600m south-southwest of the highest point on Stonethrow Ridge.
F	Telefon Bay	By boat: access the Site from either Telefon Bay or Stancomb Cove.
G	Pendulum Cove	By boat: access the site from Pendulum Cove, Port Foster, then overland past HSM No 76.
H	Mt. Pont	Overland: access with caution from Pendulum Cove via the prominent ice-free ridge to the west of the Site.
J	Perchuć Cone	Prohibited Zone: DO NOT ENTER
K	Ronald Hill to Kroner Lake	By boat: land in Whalers Bay, south of the Site - do not take boats into Kroner Lake to access the site (see Section *7(ii)* for details) Over land: access from Whalers Bay to the east of the Site.
L	South-east Point	On foot: Access overland, with caution, from either Whalers Bay (to the west of the Site) or Bailey Head (to the north of the Site)

Management Plan for
Antarctic Specially Protected Area No. 165

EDMONSON POINT, WOOD BAY, VICTORIA LAND, ROSS SEA

1. Description of values to be protected

Edmonson Point (74°20' S, 165°08' E, 5.49 km^2), Wood Bay, Victoria Land, Ross Sea, is proposed as an Antarctic Specially Protected Area (ASPA) by Italy on the grounds that it has outstanding ecological and scientific values which require protection from possible interference that might arise from unregulated access. The Area includes ice-free ground and a small area of adjacent sea at the foot of the eastern slopes of Mount Melbourne (2732 m), which is of limited extent and is the subject of ongoing and long-term scientific research.

The terrestrial and freshwater ecosystem at Edmonson Point is one of the most outstanding in northern Victoria Land. An exceptional diversity of freshwater habitats is present, with numerous streams, lakes, ponds and seepage areas, exhibiting nutrient conditions ranging from eutrophic to oligotrophic. Such a range of freshwater habitats is rare in Victoria Land. Consequently, these habitats support a high diversity of algal and cyanobacterial species, with over 120 species so far recorded, and the stream network is the most extensive and substantial in northern Victoria Land. The volcanic lithology and locally nutrient-enriched (by birds) substrata, together with a localised abundance of water, provides a habitat for relatively extensive bryophyte development. Plant communities are highly sensitive to changes in the hydrological regime, and environmental gradients produce sharply defined community boundaries. Thus, the range of vegetation is diverse, and includes epilithic lichen communities, some of which are dependent on high nitrogen input from birds, communities associated with late-lying snow patches, and moss-dominated communities that favour continually moist or wet habitats. The site represents one of the best examples of the latter community-type in Victoria Land. Invertebrates are unusually abundant and extensively distributed for this part of Antarctica.

The nature and diversity of the terrestrial and freshwater habitats offer outstanding scientific opportunities, especially for studies of biological variation and processes along moisture and nutrient gradients. The site is considered one of the best in Antarctica for studies of algal ecology. These features were among those that led to the selection of Edmonson Point as a key site in the Scientific Committee on Antarctic Research's Biological Investigations of Terrestrial Antarctic Systems (BIOTAS) programme in 1995-96. A coordinated multinational research programme, known as BIOTEX-1, established study sites and made extensive collections of soil, rock, water, snow, guano, bacteria, vegetation (cyanobacterial mats, fungi, algae, lichens, bryophytes) and of terrestrial invertebrates.

The scientific value of Edmonson Point is also considered exceptional for studies on the impact of climate change on terrestrial ecosystems. Its location at approximately the mid-point in a north- south latitudinal gradient extending along Victoria Land is complementary to other sites protected for their important terrestrial ecological values, such as Cape Hallett (ASPA No. 106) and Botany Bay, Cape Geology (ASPA No. 154), which are about 300 km to the north and south respectively. This geographical position is recognised as important in a continent-wide ecological research network (e.g. the Scientific Committee on Antarctic Research 'RiSCC' programme). In addition, the lakes are among the best in northern Victoria Land for studies of biogeochemical processes with short- and long-term variations. Together with the unique properties of the permafrost active layer, which is unusually thick in this location, these features are considered particularly useful as sensitive indicators of ecological change in response to levels of UV radiation and in shifting climate.

A colony of approximately 2000 pairs of Adélie penguins (*Pygoscelis adeliae*) has been a focus of ongoing research since 1994-95 together with a colony of approximately 120 pairs of south polar skuas (*Catharacta maccormicki*). The Edmonson Point Adélie penguin colony is included in the ecosystem monitoring network of the Commission for the Conservation of Antarctic Marine Living Resources (CCAMLR). The site is considered a good example of this species assemblage, which is representative of those found elsewhere. It is unusual, however, for the diverse range of breeding habitat available for south polar skuas, and also because of the unusually high skua to penguin ratio (1:20). The geographical position, the size of the colonies, the terrain and habitat features of the site, the natural protection given by the summer fast ice extension and the distance from Mario Zucchelli Station at Terra Nova Bay (which isolates the colony from research station disturbance but allows for logistic support) make Edmonson Point particularly suitable for the research being undertaken on these birds. The research contributes to the CCAMLR Ecosystem Monitoring Programme (CEMP), focusing on population monitoring, reproductive success, feeding and foraging strategies, migration, and behaviour. This research is important to broader studies of how natural and human-induced variations in the Antarctic ecosystem may affect the breeding success of Adélie penguins, and to understand the potential impact of harvesting of Antarctic krill (*Euphausia superba*).

The near-shore marine environment is a good and representative example of the sea-ice habitat used by breeding Weddell seals to give birth and wean pups early in the summer season. Only one other ASPA in the Ross Sea region has been designated to protect Weddell seals (ASPA No. 137 Northwest White Island, McMurdo Sound), although this site is designated because the small breeding group of seals in that locality is highly unusual; in contrast, inclusion here is as a representative example similar to breeding sites throughout the region.

In addition to the outstanding biological values, a diversity of geomorphic features is present, including a series of ice-cored moraines incorporating marine deposits, raised beaches, patterned ground, a cuspate foreland, and fossil penguin colonies. The cuspate foreland at Edmonson Point is a rare feature in Victoria Land, and is one of the best examples of its kind. It is unusual in that it is not occupied by a breeding colony of penguins, as is the case at Cape Hallett and Cape Adare. The glacial moraines that incorporate marine deposits, including seal bones and shells of the bivalves *Laternula elliptica* and *Adamussium colbecki*, are particularly valuable for dating regional glacier fluctuations. Sedimentary sequences in the north-west of Edmonson Point contain fossils from former penguin colonies. These are useful for dating the persistence of bird breeding at the site, which contributes to reconstructions of Holocene glacial phases and palaeoclimate.

The wide representation and the quality of phenomena at Edmonson Point have attracted interest from a variety of disciplines and research has been carried out at the site for more than 20 years. Over this period, substantial scientific databases have been established, which adds to the value of Edmonson Point for current, on-going and future research. It is important that pressures from human activities in the Area are managed so that the investments made in these long-term data sets are not inadvertently compromised. These factors also make the site of exceptional scientific value for multi-disciplinary studies.

Given the duration and range of past activities, Edmonson Point cannot be considered pristine. Some environmental impacts have been observed, such as occasional damage to soils and moss communities by trampling, dispersal of materials from scientific equipment by wind, and alteration of habitat by construction of facilities. In contrast, the ice-free area at Colline Ippolito (Ippolito Hills) (1.67 km^2) approximately 1.5 km to the north-west, has received relatively little visitation and human disturbance at this site is believed to be minimal. As such, Colline Ippolito is considered particularly valuable as a potential reference area for comparative studies to the main Edmonson Point, and it is important that this potential scientific value is maintained. While the precise effects of scientific research and human presence at both sites are uncertain, because detailed studies on human impact have not yet been undertaken, contaminants in the local marine ecosystem remain very low and human impacts on the ecosystem as a whole, particularly at Colline Ippolito, are considered to be generally minor.

The biological and scientific values at Edmonson Point and Colline Ippolito are vulnerable to human disturbance. The vegetation, water-saturated soils and freshwater environments are susceptible to damage from trampling, sampling and pollution. Scientific studies could be compromised by disturbance to phenomena or to installed equipment. It is important that human activities are managed so that the risks of impacts on the outstanding values of the Area are minimised.

The total Area of 5.49 km^2 comprises the ice-free area of Edmonson Point (1.79 km^2), the smaller but similar ice-free area at Colline Ippolito (1.12 km^2) approximately 1.5 km to its north which is designated a Restricted Zone, and the adjacent marine environment (2.58 km^2) extending 200 m offshore from Edmonson Point and Colline Ippolito and including Baia Siena (Siena Bay) (Map 1).

2. Aims and objectives

Management at Edmonson Point aims to:

- avoid degradation of, or substantial risk to, the values of the Area by preventing unnecessary human disturbance;
- allow scientific research while ensuring protection from mutual interference and/or over-sampling;
- allow scientific research provided it is for reasons which cannot reasonably be served elsewhere;
- protect sites of long-term scientific studies from disturbance;
- preserve a part of the natural ecosystem as a potential reference area for the purpose of future comparative studies;
- minimise the possibility of introduction of alien plants, animals and microbes to the Area;
- allow visits for management purposes in support of the aims of the Management Plan.

3. Management activities

The following management activities shall be undertaken to protect the values of the Area:

- Copies of this management plan, including maps of the Area, shall be made available at Mario Zucchelli Station at Terra Nova Bay (Italy), Gondwana Station (Germany), and at any other permanent stations established within 100 km of the Area;
- Structures, markers, signs, fences or other equipment erected within the Area for scientific or management purposes shall be secured and maintained in good condition and removed when no longer necessary;
- Durable wind direction indicators should be erected close to the designated helicopter landing sites whenever it is anticipated there will be a number of landings in a given season;
- Markers, which should be clearly visible from the air and pose no significant risk to the environment, should be placed to mark the designated helicopter landing sites;
- Markers, such as a series of durable sticks, should be placed to mark the preferred inland walking routes between the Adélie penguin colony and the designated helicopter landing sites;
- Visits shall be made as necessary (no less than once every five years) to assess whether the Area continues to serve the purposes for which it was designated and to ensure management and maintenance measures are adequate;
- National Antarctic Programmes operating in the region shall consult together with a view to ensuring these steps are carried out.

3(i)   Management issues

Key management issues relate to the protection of potentially sensitive features, such as: moist soils that can be easily disturbed; the extensive but fragile vegetation cover; a variety of lakes and streams; two species of breeding birds and one breeding species of seal.

Priority issues are also the management of activities that may be harmful or interfere with fauna and flora including aircraft access, movements within the area, camping, facilities, installation/removal of equipment, use of materials, waste disposal and coordination of the multidisciplinary scientific activities.

Logistics constraints imposed restrictions to the study seasons that often started after penguins arrival at the colony. The necessity to decrease impacts for nesting penguins and skuas, made impossible to put in activity the CEMP research camp (Map 2 and 4). Moreover snow coverage and distance from the colony made difficult the use of the alternative camping site (site A Map 2). For this reason during the 2011 summer campaign, a new camp position, suitable for research activity with reduced impacts on birds, was identified. Its position, 74°19'44.58"S 165° 8'4.99"E, is near the helicopter landing site B (Map 2 and 4). The camp included 1 big apple, 1 toilet tent and 1 generator and some fuel drums for 40 days of autonomy and was removed at the end of the study season. It is recommended to use this location for future CEMP research activities.

4. Period of designation

Designated for an indefinite period.

5. Maps and photographs

Map 1: Edmonson Point ASPA No. 165, Wood Bay, Victoria Land, Ross Sea. Map specifications: Projection: UTM Zone 58S; Spheroid: WGS84; Ice-free areas and coastline derived from rectified Quickbird satellite image with a ground pixel resolution of 70 cm, acquired 04/01/04 by Programma Nazionale di Ricerche in Antartide (PNRA), Italy. Horizontal accuracy approx ±10 m; elevation information unavailable. Inset 1: the location of Wood Bay in Antarctica. Inset 2. The location of Map 1 in relation to Wood Bay and Terra Nova Bay. The location of Mario Zucchelli Station (Italy), Gondwana Station (Germany), and the nearest protected areas are shown.

Map 2: Edmonson Point, ASPA No. 165, Physical / human features and access guidelines. Map derived from digital orthophotograph with ground pixel resolution of 25 cm, from ground GPS surveys and observations, and from Quickbird satellite image (04/01/04).

Map specifications: Projection: Lambert Conformal Conic; Standard parallels: 1st 72° 40' 00" S; 2nd 75° 20' 00"S; Central Meridian: 165° 07' 00" E; Latitude of Origin: 74° 20' 00" S; Spheroid: WGS84; Vertical datum: Mean Sea Level. Vertical contour interval 10 m. Horizontal accuracy: ±1 m; vertical accuracy expected to be better than ±1 m.

Map 3: Restricted Zone, Colline Ippolito: Edmonson Point ASPA No. 165. Map derived from Quickbird satellite image (04/01/04). Map specifications as for Map 2, except for horizontal accuracy which is approx ±10 m, and elevation information is not available. Sea level is approximated from coastline evident in satellite image.

Map 4: Edmonson Point ASPA No. 165, topography, wildlife and vegetation. Map specifications as for Map 2, except for contour interval which is 2 m.

Map data and preparation: PNRA, Dipartimento di Scienze Ambientali (Università di Siena), Environmental Research & Assessment (Cambridge), Gateway Antarctica (Christchurch).

6. Description of the Area

6(i) Geographical coordinates, boundary markers and natural features

GENERAL DESCRIPTION

Edmonson Point (74°20' S, 165°08' E) is a coastal ice-free area of 1.79 km^2 situated at Wood Bay, 50 km north of Terra Nova Bay, and 13 km east of the summit and at the foot of Mount Melbourne (2732 m), Victoria Land. The Area comprises a total of 5.49 km^2, including the entire ice-free ground of Edmonson Point (1.79 km^2), the separate ice-free area of Colline Ippolito (Ippolito Hills) (1.12 km^2) approximately 1.5 km north-west of Edmonson Point, and the nearshore marine environment and intervening sea of Baia Siena (Siena Bay) between these ice-free areas (2.58 km^2), which lie east and at the foot of the permanent ice sheet extending from Mount Melbourne (Map 1). Part of the glacier from Mount Melbourne separates the two ice-free areas on land. A broad pebbly beach extends the length of the coastline of Edmonson Point, above which cliffs rise up to 128 m towards the south of the Area. The topography of the Area is rugged, with several hills of volcanic origin of up to 134 m in height, and ice-free slopes rising to around 300 m adjacent to the ice sheet, although accurate elevation information in these areas is not currently available. Undulating ice-cored moraines, boulder fields and rock outcrops are separated by small ash plains and shallow valleys. The Area is dissected by numerous valleys and melt streams, with several small lakes, and seepage areas being common features throughout the Area. In the central region of Edmonson Point are several wide shallow basins, at about 25 m elevation, covered by fine scoria and coarse sand, mixed with extensive carpets of vegetation and areas of patterned ground. The northern coast of Edmonson Point is a cuspate foreland comprising several raised beaches.

The environmental character of Colline Ippolito is similar to that of Edmonson Point. This area has a narrow boulder beach backed by a ridge running parallel to the coast. Small meltwater streams run through shallow gullies and across flats into two lakes behind the coastal ridge in the north. Ridges and cones rise to about 200 m before merging with the snow fields and glaciers of Mount Melbourne in the south.

BOUNDARIES

The margin of the permanent ice sheet extending from Mount Melbourne is defined as the boundary in the west, north and south of the Area (Maps 1-3). The eastern boundary is marine, which in the southern half of the Area follows the coastline 200 m offshore from the southern to northern extremities of the ice-free area of Edmonson Point. From the northern extremity of Edmonson Point, the eastern boundary extends NW across Baia Siena for a distance of 2 km to a position 200 m due east from the coast of the northern extremity of Colline Ippolito. Baia Siena is thus enclosed within the Area. Boundary markers have not been installed because the ice sheet margin and the coast are obvious boundary references.

CLIMATE

No extended meteorological records are available for Edmonson Point, although annual data for McMurdo Station, Scott Base and Cape Hallett suggest the average mean temperature in the Edmonson Point vicinity would be around -16° C, and the mean annual snow accumulation about 20-50 cm, equivalent to 10-20 cm of water (Bargagli *et al.*, 1997). Short-term data are available for December 1995 – January 1996, collected during the BIOTEX 1 expedition. During this period temperatures ranged from -7° C to 10° C, with 0° C exceeded every day. Relative humidity was low (15-40% day, 50-80% night), precipitation occasional as light snow and wind speeds mostly low. From late January weather conditions deteriorated, with frequent subzero daytime temperatures, snow-fall and high winds. Data available for summer seasons in 1998-99 and 1999-00 from a weather station installed near the penguin colony suggest prevailing summer winds at Edmonson Point come from the east, southeast and south. Daily average wind speeds were generally in the range of 3-6 knots, with daily maximums usually being of 6-10 knots, occasionally reaching up to

25-35 knots. Daily average air temperatures ranged from around -15°C in October, -6°C in November, -2.5°C in December to -1°C in January, decreasing to -3.5°C again in February (Olmastroni, pers. comm., 2000). The highest daily maximum in the two summer periods was recorded as 2.6°C on 25 December 1998. The average air temperature recorded over both summers was approximately -4°C, while the average wind speed was 4.5 knots. Average daily relative humidity generally ranged between 40-60%.

GEOLOGY AND SOILS

The geology at Edmonson Point is derived from Cenozoic eruptive activity of Mount Melbourne (Melbourne Volcanic Province), part of the McMurdo Volcanic Group (Kyle, 1990), combined with glacial deposits from the marine-based ice sheet that covered much of the Victoria Land coastline during the last glacial maximum (7500 to 25000 years B.P) (Baroni and Orombelli, 1994). The volcanic complex at Edmonson Point is composed of a large subaerial tuff ring, scoria cones, lava flows, and subaquatic megapillow lava sequences (Wörner and Viereck, 1990). The rocks are mainly of basaltic and/or trachytic composition, and include various additional volcanic products, such as accumulations of tuffs, pumices and debris deposits (Simeoni *et al.*, 1989; Bargagli *et al.*, 1997). The ground surface is composed mainly of dry, coarse-textured volcanic materials with a low proportion of silt and clay (Bargagli *et al.*, 1997). These exposed surfaces, as well as beneath the surfaces of stones and boulders, are often coated with white encrustations or efflorescences of soluble salts. Most of the ground is dark-coloured, with brownish or yellowish patches of scoria and tuffite. Unstable scree is common on hill slopes, which are dry and mostly unvegetated. Valley and basin floors are covered by fine scoria and coarse sand (Bargagli *et al.*, 1999).

GEOMORPHOLOGY

A series of marine deposits are visible on the cuspate foreland at the northern extremity of Edmonson Point. The gently sloping raised beaches of the foreland are composed of differing ratios of sands, pebbles and boulders distributed over lava flows (Simeoni *et al.*, 1989). Numerous small crater-like pits, many containing melt-water or ice, can be observed just above the high tide mark in this locality; these are thought to have been formed by extreme tides and the melting of coastal ice accumulations. South of the cuspate foreland, volcanic bedrock exposures are common over much of the ground extending up to about 800 m inland from the coast, most evident in the prominent hills of about 120 m in height in the central northern part of Edmonson Point. A series of late-Pleistocene moraines and related tills lie on the western side of these exposures, with bands of Holocene ice-cored moraine, talus and debris slopes adjacent to the glacier ice which extends from Mount Melbourne (Baroni and Orombelli, 1994).

STREAMS AND LAKES

There are six lakes on Edmonson Point, ranging in length up to 350 m, and in area from approximately 1600 m^2 up to 15,000 m^2 (Map 2). Two further lakes occur behind the coastal ridge at Colline Ippolito, the largest of which is approximately 12,500 m^2 (Map 3). In addition, on Edmonson Point there are approximately 22 smaller ponds of diameters of less than 30 m (Broady, 1987). The larger ponds are permanently ice-covered, with peripheral moats forming during the summer. Detailed physico-chemical characteristics and limnology of the lakes of Edmonson Point are reported in Guilizzoni *et al.* (1991). There are numerous streams throughout the Area, some of which are supplied with meltwater from the adjacent ice sheet, while others are fed by lakes and general ice / snow melt. Several stream beds have flood terraces of fine soil covered by pumice-like pebbles of 5-10 mm diameter. Many of the streams and pools are transient, drying up shortly after the late snow patches in their catchments disappear.

PLANT BIOLOGY

Compared to several other sites in central Victoria Land, Edmonson Point does not have a particularly diverse flora, and there are only a few extensive closed stands of vegetation. Six moss species, one liverwort, and at least 30 lichen species have been recorded within the Area (Broady,

1987; Lewis Smith, 1996, 1999; Lewis Smith pers. comm., 2004; Castello, 2004). Cavacini (pers. comm., 2003) noted that recent analyses have identified at least 120 alga and cyanobacteria species present at Edmonson Point. These are present in a range of forms including algal mats on soil and as epiphytes on mosses, and in a range of habitats such as in lakes, streams and snow, and on moist ornithogenic and raw mineral soils. At the onset of summer, snow melt reveals small stands of algae and moss on valley floors, although much of these lie buried by up to 5 cm of wind-blown and melt-washed fine mineral particles. This community is capable of rapid growth during December, when moisture is available and soil temperatures are relatively high, bringing shoot apices up to a centimetre above the surface as the surface accumulation of sand is washed or blown away. Increased water flow or strong winds can quickly bury these stands, although sufficient light for growth can penetrate 1-2 cm below the surface (Bargagli *et al.*, 1999).The principal moss communities occur on more stable substrata which are not subjected to burial by sand, for example in sheltered depressions or along the margins of ponds and meltwater streams, and seepage areas below late snow beds where moisture is available for several weeks. Some of these are among the most extensive stands found in continental Antarctica, being of up to 3000 m^2, most notably the stand of *Bryum subrotundifolium* (= *B. argenteum*) several hundred metres west of the main Adélie colony (Map 4). Other, less extensive, notable stands occur near the lake adjacent to the Adélie colony (Map 4), and smaller localized stands of *Ceratodon purpureus* (with relatively thick deposits of dead organic material) being found in a valley in the north of Edmonson Point and in the upper area of the principal stream in the northern ice-free area. Greenfield *et. al.* (1985) suggested that, apart from Cape Hallett, no area in the Ross Sea has a comparable abundance of plants, although in 1996 a similarly extensive area colonised almost exclusively by *Bryum subrotundifolium* (= *B. argenteum*) was discovered on Beaufort Island (ASPA No. 105), approximately 280 km to the south of Edmonson Point.

The moss-dominated communities comprise up to seven bryophyte species, several algae and cyanobacteria and, at the drier end of the moisture gradient, several lichens encrusting moribund moss (Lewis Smith, 1999; Bargagli *et al.*, 1999). There are mixed communities or zones of *Bryum subrotundifolium* (= *B. argenteum*), *B. pseudotriquetrum* and *Ceratodon purpureus*. In some wetter sites the liverwort *Cephaloziella varians* occurs amongst *C. purpureus*. Dry, very open, often lichen-encrusted moss communities usually contain *Hennediella heimii*, and often occur in hollows which hold small late snow patches. *Sarconeurum glaciale* occurs in a stable scree above the large lake in the south of the Area (Lewis Smith, 1996). The upper portions of moss colonies are often coated with white encrustations of soluble salts (Bargagli *et al.*, 1999).

The lichen communities are relatively diverse, with 24 species identified and at least six crustose species so far unidentified, although few are abundant (Castello, 2004; Lewis Smith, pers. comm. 2004). Epilithic lichens are generally sparse and not widespread, being mainly crustose and microfoliose species restricted to rocks used as skua perches and occasionally on stable boulders in scree, moist gullies and temporary seepage areas. Macrolichens are scarce, with *Umbilicaria aprina* and *Usnea sphacelata* found in a few places. The former species is more abundant on the gently sloping intermittently inundated outwash channels of Colline Ippolito, together with *Physcia* spp. and associated with small cushions of *Bryum subrotundifolium* (= *B. argenteum*) (Given, 1985, 1989), *B. pseudotriquetrum* and *Ceratodon purpureus* (Lewis Smith, pers comm. 2004). *Buellia frigida* is the most widespread crustose lichen on the hard lavas, but a distinct community of nitrophilous species occurs on rocks used as skua perches (*Caloplaca, Candelariella, Rhizoplaca, Xanthoria*). In gravelly depressions below late snow beds, moss turves are often colonised by encrusting cyanobacteria and ornithocoprophilic lichens (*Candelaria, Candelariella, Lecanora, Xanthoria*) and, where there is no bird influence, by the white *Leproloma cacuminum* (Lewis Smith, 1996).

Early work on the algal flora at Edmonson Point identified 17 species as Cyanophyta, 10 as Chrysophyta and 15 as Chlorophyta (Broady, 1987). More recent analyses (Cavacini, pers. comm., 2003) have identified 120 alga and cyanobacteria species, which is considerably more than the numbers of species of Cyanophyta (28), Chlorophyta (27), Bacillariophyta (25) and Xanthophyta (5) recorded previously (Cavacini, 1997, 2001; Fumanti *et al.,* 1993, 1994a, 1994b; Alfinito *et al.,* 1998). Broady (1987) observed few areas of algal vegetation on ground surfaces; the most extensive were oscillatoriacean mats in moist depressions in areas of beach sand, which may have been temporary melt ponds prior to when the survey was undertaken. Similar mats were found adjacent to an area of moss with a *Gloeocapsa* sp. as an abundant associate. *Prasiococcus calcarius* was observed in the vicinity of the Adélie penguin colony, both as a small area of rich green crusts on soil and growing on an area of moribund moss cushions. Other epiphytic algae include Oscillatoriaceae, *Nostoc* sp., unicellular chlorophytes including *Pseudococcomyxa simplex*, and the desmid *Actinotaenium cucurbita*. Substantial stream algae were observed with waters containing oscillatoriacean mats over the stream beds, wefts of green filaments attached to the surface of stones (mainly *Binuclearia tectorum* and *Prasiola* spp.), small ribbons of *Prasiola calophylla* on the under-surfaces of stones, and dark brown epilithic crusts of cyanophytes (dominated by *Chamaesiphon subglobosus* and *Nostoc* sp.) coating boulders. Ponds present in beach sand contained *Chlamydomonas* sp. and cf. *Ulothrix* sp., while ponds fertilized by penguin and skua guano contained *Chlamydomonas* sp. and black benthic oscillatoriacean mats. Other ponds also contained rich benthic growths of Oscillatoriaceae, frequently associated with *Nostoc sphaericum*. Other abundant algae were *Aphanothece castagnei, Binuclearia tectorum, Chamaesiphon subglobosus, Chroococcus minutus, C. turgidus¸ Luticola muticopsis, Pinnularia cymatopleura, Prasiola crispa* (particularly associated with penguin colonies and other nitrogen-enriched habitats), *Stauroneis anceps*, various unicellular chlorophytes, and – in the highest conductivity pond in beach sand – cf. *Ulothrix* sp.

Algae and cyanobacteria are locally abundant in moist soils, and filaments and foliose mats of *Phormidium* spp. (dominant on patches of wet ground and in shallow lake bottoms), aggregates of *Nostoc commune* and a population of diatoms have been identified (Wynn-Williams, 1996; Lewis Smith pers. comm., 2004). The fungal species *Arthrobotrys ferox* has been isolated from moss species *Bryum pseudotriquetrum* (= *B. algens*) and *Ceratodon purpureus*. *A. ferox* produces an adhesive secretion which has been observed to capture springtails of the species *Gressittacantha terranova* (about 1.2 mm in length) (Onofri and Tosi, 1992).

7. Scientific values

7(i)   Invertebrate

There is a high diversity of soil nematodes in the moist soils at Edmonson Point when compared to other areas described in Victoria Land. Nematodes found at Edmonson Point include *Eudorylaimus antarcticus, Monhysteridae* sp., *Panagrolaimus* sp., *Plectus antarcticus, P. frigophilus,* and *Scottnema lyndsayea* (Frati, 1997; Wall pers. comm., 2000). The latter species, previously only known from the McMurdo Dry Valleys, was found at Edmonson Point in 1995-96 (Frati, 1997). Less abundant are the springtails, most commonly *Gressittacantha terranova*, which was found under rocks and on soil and mosses in a number of moist microhabitats (Frati, 1997). Red mites (likely to be either *Stereotydeus* sp. or *Nanorchestes*, although species not identified) are common in aggregations beneath stones in moist habitats, and Collembola, rotifers, tardigrades and a variety of protozoans are also found (Frati *et al.,* 1996; Lewis Smith, 1996; Wall pers. comm., 2000; Convey pers. comm., 2003).

7(ii)   Breeding birds

Adélie penguins (*Pygoscelis adeliae*) breed in two groups near the coast in the central and eastern-most part of Edmonson Point, occupying an area of about 9000 m^2 (Map 4). The number of breeding pairs recorded between 1981-2005 is summarised in Table 1, the average number in this period being 2080. In 1994-95 the majority of birds were recorded to arrive around 30-31 October, while the majority of the season's chicks had fledged by 12 February, with fledging complete by 21

February (Franchi *et al.,* 1997). An abandoned nesting site, occupied approximately 2600-3000 years ago, lies about 1 km to the northwest of the current colony, on bedrock adjacent to the cuspate foreland (Baroni and Orombelli, 1994).

Table 1. Adélie penguins (breeding pairs) at Edmonson Point 1981-2005 (data Woehler, 1993; Olmastroni, 2005, *pers. comm.*).

Year	No. of breeding pairs	Year	No. of breeding pairs
1981	1300	1995	1935
1984	1802	1996	1824
1987	2491	1997	1961
1989	1792	1999	2005
1991	1316	2001	1988
1994	1960	2003	2588
		2005	2385
		2007	2303
		2010	2112
		2016	2704

Between 2005 and 2010 according to CEMP procedures, three population counts were made at Edmonson Point, the colony consisting of 2385, 2303 and 2112 occupied nests in 2005, 2007 and 2010 respectively.

The average number since the beginning of the research program being 2112. Thus total population seem stable with respect to the average value 2080 from 1994 to 2005.

The colony, in the last count carried out in November 2016, consists of 3066 breeding pairs distributed in 11 under colonies (data sent to the CCAMLR in June 2016).

The population of skua (Stercorarius maccormicki) was evaluated in about 100 breeding pairs in the whole area, slightly less do as reported by Pezzo *et al*, (2001), although sufficiently in line with that reported by Piece et al, (2001) regarding the relationship between skuas and penguins of about 1:20.

The ratio between skua and penguin remained high (1:20) as previously reported by Pezzo *et al*, (2001). Edmonson Point's skua population nearby Adélie penguin colony remained stable through years consisting of about 130 breeding pairs in 2010 summer season. Also at Edmonson Point North and South 55 and 61 breeding pairs respectively , were counted in 2010 summer season.

A breeding colony of south polar skuas (*Catharacta maccormicki*) within the Area is one of the most numerous in Victoria Land, with over 120 pairs, of which 36 pairs occupy Colline Ippolito (CCAMLR, 1999; Pezzo *et al.*, 2001; Volpi pers. comm. 2005). . Furthermore the Area includes two "club sites", nearby large freshwater ponds, used throughout the breeding seasons by groups of non-breeders ranging between 50 and 70 individuals (Pezzo 2001; Volpi 2005 pers. comm.). Flocks of snow petrels (*Pagodroma nivea*) have been observed flying over the Area, and Wilson's storm petrels (*Oceanites oceanicus*) have been sighted regularly. Neither of these latter two species is known to breed within the Area.

Penguin Nest Camera (NC49)

The System of Digital images PNC49 (Australian Antarctic Division) was installed at Edmonson Point during the 2014-15 antarctic campaign. This tool allows, through the acquisition of images remotely the monitoring of area with about 30 nests of control, external to the APMS area. The Penguin Nest Room, reactivating autonomously after the winter season, thanks to the solar panel and batteries, has allowed us to observe the first arrival into the reproductive area to the 20/10/2015.

All images were collected and sent to colleagues of the Australian Antarctic Division, to become part of an international database for research on reproductive phenology of the Adelie penguin.

7(iii)   Breeding mammals

At Edmonson Point numerous (>50) Weddell seals (Leptonychotes weddellii) regularly breed in the near shore marine environment (on fast ice) within the Area. Females use this area to give birth and raise pups on the fast ice along the coastline of the whole Area. Later in the summer Weddell seals frequently haul out on beaches within the Area.

8.   Scientific Research

8(i)   CCAMLR Ecosystem Monitoring Programme (CEMP) Studies

1. The presence at Edmonson Point of breeding penguin colonies and the absence of krill fisheries within their foraging range make this a critical site for comparative studies and inclusion with other CEMP sites in the ecosystem monitoring network established to meet the objectives of CCAMLR. The purpose of protected area designation is to allow planned research and monitoring to proceed, while avoiding or reducing, to the greatest extent possible, other activities which could interfere with or affect the results of the research and monitoring programme of alter the natural features of the site.

2. The Adélie penguin is a species of particular interest for CEMP routine monitoring and directed research at this site. For this purpose the Adélie Penguin Monitoring Program, a joint research project between Italian and Australian biologists, has been ongoing at Edmonson Point since 1994- 95. An Automated Penguin Monitoring System (APMS) along with on-site observations by researchers, forms the basis of a study of at least 500-600 nests within the northern sector of the colony as part of the CEMP (CCAMLR, 1999; Olmastroni *et al.*, 2000). Fences have been installed to direct penguins over a bridge which registers their weight, identity and crossing direction as they move between the sea and their breeding colony.

3. Parameters routinely monitored include trends in population size, demography, duration of foraging trips, breeding success, chick fledging weight, chick diet and breeding chronology.

4. The studies on Adélie penguin also involve population monitoring, experiments with satellite transmitters and temperature-depth recorders to investigate foraging location and duration. Combined with stomach flushing to record the diet of monitored penguins, this programme is developing comprehensive observations of Adélie penguin feeding ecology (Olmastroni, 2002). Diet data (Olmastroni *et al.*, 2004) confirmed the results of studies from krill distribution in the Ross Sea (Azzali and Kalinowski, 2000; Azzali *et al.,* 2000) and indicate that this colony is located at a transition point in the availability of *E. superba* between northern and more southerly colonies where this species is absent or rare in the diet of penguins (Emison, 1968; Ainley, 2002). These studies also highlighted the importance of fish to the diet of the Adélie penguin, which represented up to 50% of stomach contents in some years.

Local sea ice and weather data contribute to the understanding of possible factors affecting the breeding biology of this species (Olmastroni *et al.*, 2004). Moreover behavioural studies are also part of the research (Pilastro *et al.,* 2001).

Research on the south polar skua colony focuses on breeding biology (Pezzo *et al.*, 2001), population dynamics, biometry, reproductive biology and migratory patterns. Since 1998/99 more than 300 south polar skuas have been banded by metal and coloured rings, which facilitate field research that requires the recognition of individual birds and will allow for identification of birds migrating from the Area.

8(ii)   Scientific Research after 2005

Ecology of marine birds and CCAMLR Ecosystem Monitoring Programme (CEMP) Studies.

The studies on Adélie penguin population involved demographic parameters that were estimated in relation to individual characteristics (sex and age) and to large scale (Ross Sea winter ice extent anomalies and SOI) and local scale (food availability) environmental variables. While large-scale environmental factors affected adult survival, breeding success varied principally according to local variables. Breeding success was particularly low when local stochastic events (storms) occurred at sensitive times of the breeding cycle (immediately after the hatching) (Olmastroni et al. 2004; Pezzo et al, 2007; Ballerini et al., 2009). Also changes in fast-ice extent in front of the breeding area influenced the adult breeders transit times between colony and foraging grounds, and females conducted longer foraging trips, dived for longer periods and made more dives than males. The diving parameters were affected neither by the sex nor by the year, but differed between the breeding stages (Nesti et al, 2010). Annual adult survival probability at Edmonson Point (0.85, range 0.76– 0.94) was similar to that estimated from other Adélie penguin populations in which individuals were marked with passive transponders. An annual average survival rate of 0.85 seems to be typical of the species and is consistent with an expected average lifespan of about 11 years (6.6 years after adulthood) (Ballerini et al., 2009).

Some aspects of the breeding biology of the south polar skua, during five seasons are under investigation being the subject of a doctoral thesis that is being carried out at University of Siena (A. Franceschi, Aspetti della Biologia riproduttiva dello Stercorario di McCormick, *Stercorarius maccormicki*).

Related projects to the vegetation

At Edmonson Point, over the past five years, several research projects on issues related to the vegetation were started.

1) long-term monitoring: installation of n. 3 permanent plot for the monitoring of long-term vegetation, permafrost and soil thermal regime (period of the plot installation 2002)

2) analysis of the CO2 streams: the analyzes were carried out using CO2 portable analyzers (IRGA) by selecting different types of vegetation cover in the vicinity of the long-term monitoring sites

3) during the 2014/2015 campaign, we have fitted manipulation experiments for the study of potential future impacts of climate change. These experiments were made (and are still in progress) along a latitudinal gradient from Finger Point (77 ° S) at Apostrophe Island (73 ° S). For these experiments Edmonson Point is the master site is the site with the largest number of complex experiments and the replicas. In all sites for each experiment it was carried out a plot of treatment accompanied by a control plot (undisturbed).
The types of manipulation are as follows:
 a) An increase of the temperature using open top chambers (OTC) according to the protocol ITEX (International Tundra EXperiment);
b) canopies for the exclusion of the precipitation;
c) barriers for redistribution of the snowpack by wind (Snow fences).
In addition to these manipulations related to the physical environment they were implemented manipulations of the regime of water / snow / nutrients. In particular, the additions include: A) the snow; B) liquid water; C) N-NO3; D) N-Urea; E) P-PO4; F) Guano.

4) further molecular analyzes are being carried out relatively to the phylogeny and filogrografia of mosses of the genus Bryum pan-Antarctic level also using samples of biological material collected at Edmonson Point.

8(iii)   Other Scientific Activities

Studies of terrestrial ecology at Edmonson Point were initiated in the 1980s, although this type of research and other forms of science increased in the 1990s, in particular by Italian scientists. Edmonson Point was the location of BIOTEX 1, the first SCAR Biological Investigation of Antarctic Terrestrial Ecosystems (BIOTAS) research expedition, during December 1995 and January 1996. Ten researchers from three countries participated in a variety of scientific projects which included: taxonomic, ecological, physiological and biogeographical studies on cyanobacteria, algae, bryophytes, lichens (including chasmolithic and endolithic communities), nematodes, springtails and mites; studies of soil and freshwater biogeochemistry; microbial metabolic activity and colonisation studies; and investigations into the photosynthetic responses to ambient and controlled conditions of mosses, lichens and plant pigments that may act as photoprotectants (Bargagli, 1999). While the BIOTAS programme has now formally concluded, it is expected that further studies of this type will be on-going at Edmonson Point.

9.   Human Activities/Impacts

Edmonson Point was probably first visited on 6 February 1900 when Carsten Borchgrevink landed just north of Mount Melbourne on "a promontory almost free of snow .... about 100 acres in extent" and climbed about 200 m up the slopes (Borchgrevink, 1901: 261). The Wood Bay region was rarely mentioned during the following 70 years, and presumably was visited only infrequently. Activity in the area increased in the 1980s, first with visits by the GANOVEX expeditions (Germany). Botanical research was undertaken in December 1984 (Given, 1985; Greenfield *et. al.*, 1985; Broady, 1987) and in January 1989, at which time the first proposals for special protection of the site were made (Given pers. comm. 2003). Italy established a station in close proximity at Terra Nova Bay in 1986-87 and increased research interest in the site followed.

The modern era of human activity at Edmonson Point has been largely confined to science. The impacts of these activities have not been described, but are believed to be minor and limited to items such as campsites, footprints, markers of various kinds, human wastes, scientific sampling, handling of limited numbers of birds (e.g. installation of devices to track birds, stomach lavage, biometric measurements, etc), and potentially some impacts associated with helicopter access and installation and operation of camp and research facilities at the penguin colony and on the northern cuspate foreland. At least one fuel spill of around 500 ml, and other smaller spills, were reported in 1996 as a result of refuelling operations at the generator and fuel store located at the penguin colony (see disturbed sites marked on Map 4). In addition, seaborne litter is occasionally washed onto beaches within the Area. The Restricted Zone at Colline Ippolito has received less human activity than Edmonson Point and impacts in this area are expected to be negligible.

9(i)   Restricted and managed zones within the Area

Restricted Zone

The ice-free area of Colline Ippolito (1.12 km^2) approximately 1.5 km north-west of Edmonson Point is designated as a Restricted Zone in order to preserve part of the Area as a reference site for future comparative studies, while the remainder of the terrestrial Area (which is similar in biology, features and character) is more generally available for research programmes and sample collection. The northern, western and southern boundaries of the Restricted Zone are defined as the margins of the permanent ice extending from Mount Melbourne, and are coincident with the boundary of the Area (Maps 1 and 3). The eastern boundary of the Restricted Zone is the mean low water level along the coastline of this ice-free area.

Access to the Restricted Zone is allowed only for compelling scientific reasons or management purposes (such as inspection or review) that cannot be served elsewhere within the Area.

9(ii) Structures within and near the Area

CEMP Site: A fibreglass cabin for field observation, containing instrumentation and APMS panel, and two Nunsen huts for 4 people were installed by PNRA in 1994/95 to support CEMP research. These structures are located on a rocky knoll at an elevation of 16 m, 80 m from the coast and 40 m south of the northern sub-colony of penguins (Maps 2 and 4). At the beginning of each field season a generator and a number of fuel drums are temporarily stored about 20 m from the camp and removed at the end of each season. Adjacent to the northern penguin sub-colony, fences of metal net (30-50 cm) have been installed to direct penguins over the APMS weigh bridge.

Other activities: Approximately 50 plastic cloches were installed at 10 locations throughout the Area in 1995-96 as part of BIOTEX-1 (Maps 2 and 4). A number of additional cloches were installed the previous year at four locations (Wynn-Williams, 1996). It is not precisely known how many of these cloches remain within the area. Temporary camp facilities were installed at the location of the designated camp site for the duration of the BIOTEX-1 programme, which have now been removed.

During the thirtieth Italian Antarctic expedition has been removed much of the fence surrounding the colony D (Map 4) and the underlying part. It 'been completely eliminated the barrier in the valley under the Automated Penguin Monitoring System (APMS), by limiting only to the fence surrounding the APMS. We have so improved and freed the area from several meters of the fence and over 40 iron bolts that were in the ground. (Map 4).

On 28 October 2016, during the Antarctic campaign XXXII, the old field has been reclaimed: were removed two fuel drums and the Nansen Hut located near the apple. Then remains the apple, APMS and outbuildings, the weather station and the Penguin Nest Camera at A,B observation points (Map 4)

The nearest permanent stations are Mario Zucchelli Station at Terra Nova Bay (Italy), Gondwana Station (Germany) and Jang Bogo Station (Republic of Korea) which lie approximately 50, 44 and 43 Km south respectively.

9(iii) Location of other protected areas within close proximity of the Area

The nearest protected areas to Edmonson Point are the summit of Mount Melbourne (ASPA No. 118), which lies 13 km to the west, and a marine area at Terra Nova Bay (ASPA No. 161), which lies approximately 52 km to the south (Map 1, Inset 2).

10. Permit conditions

Entry into the Area is prohibited except in accordance with a Permit issued by an appropriate national authority. Conditions for issuing a Permit to enter the Area are that:

- it is issued only for scientific research on the Area, or for compelling scientific reasons that cannot be served elsewhere; or
- it is issued for essential management purposes consistent with plan objectives such as inspection, maintenance or review;
- access to the Restricted Zone is allowed only for compelling scientific reasons or management purposes (such as inspection or review) that cannot be served elsewhere within the Area;
- the actions permitted will not jeopardise the ecological or scientific values of the Area;
- any management activities are in support of the objectives of the Management Plan;
- the actions permitted are in accordance with the Management Plan;

- the Permit, or an authorised copy, shall be carried within the Area;
- a visit report shall be supplied to the authority named in the Permit;
- Permits shall be issued for a stated period.
- The appropriate authority should be notified of any activities/measures undertaken that were not included in the authorised Permit.

10(i) Access to and movement within the Area

Access to the Area shall be by small boat, on foot or by helicopter. Movement over land within the Area shall be on foot or by helicopter. Access to the Area by vehicle is restricted according to the conditions described below.

Small boat access

The Edmonson Point part of the Area may be entered at any point where pinnipeds or seabird colonies are not present on or near the beach. Access for purposes other than CEMP research should avoid disturbing pinnipeds and seabirds (Map 1 and 2). There are no special restrictions on landings from the sea, although when accessing the main ice-free area of Edmonson Point visitors shall land at the northern cuspate foreland and avoid landing at breeding bird colonies (Map 2).

Restricted conditions of vehicle access

Use of vehicles within the Area is prohibited, except at the southern boundary of the Area where they may be used on sea ice to gain access to the shore, from where visitors shall proceed on foot. Thus, vehicle use shall avoid interference with animal feeding routes and the Adélie penguin colony. When using vehicles on sea ice care should be exercised to avoid Weddell seals which may be present: speed should be kept low and seals shall not be approached by vehicle closer than 50 m. Access over land by vehicles is allowed to the boundary of the Area. Vehicle traffic shall be kept to the minimum necessary for the conduct of permitted activities.

Aircraft access and overflight

All restrictions on aircraft access and overflight stipulated in this plan shall apply during the period 15 October – 20 February inclusive. Aircraft may operate and land within the Area according to strict observance of the following conditions:

(i)　All overflight of the Area for purposes other than access shall be conducted according to the height restrictions imposed in the following table:

Minimum overflight heights within the Area according to aircraft type

Aircraft type	Number of Engines	Minimum height above ground	
		Feet	Metres
Helicopter	1	2461	750
Helicopter	2	3281	1000
Fixed-wing	1 or 2	1476	450
Fixed-wing	4	3281	1000

(ii)　Helicopter landing is normally allowed at only three designated sites (Maps 1-4). The landing sites with their coordinates are described as follows:

(A) shall be used for most purposes, located on the northern cuspate foreland of Edmonson Point (Map 2) (74°19'24"S, 165°07'12"E);

(B) is allowed in support of the Adélie Penguin Monitoring Programme when necessary for transport of heavy equipment / supplies (Map 2) (74°19'43"S, 165°07'57"E); and

(C) is allowed for access to the Restricted Zone, located at the northern ice-free area (Colline Ippolito, Map 3) (74°18'50"S, 165°04'29"E).

(iii)   In exceptional circumstances, helicopter access may be specifically authorised elsewhere within the Area for the purpose of supporting science or management according to conditions imposed by the Permit on access location(s) and timing. Landing of helicopters at sites of mammals and seabird sites and significant vegetation shall be avoided at all times (Maps 2-4).

(iv)   The designated aircraft approach route is from the west of the Area, from over the lower eastern ice slopes of Mount Melbourne (Maps 1-3). Aircraft shall approach the main designated landing site (A) on the cuspate foreland from the north-west over or near Baia Siena (Siena Bay). When appropriate, access to landing site (B) should follow the same route and proceed a further 700 m SE. The departure route is identical in reverse.

(v)   When appropriate, access to landing site (C) should be from the lower eastern ice slopes of Mount Melbourne and proceed directly to the landing site from the south over the land or where this is not feasible over Baia Siena (Siena Bay), avoiding skuas nesting to the north of the landing site;

(vi)   Use of smoke grenades to indicate wind direction is prohibited within the Area unless absolutely necessary for safety, and any grenades used should be retrieved.

Foot access and movement within the Area

Movement on land within the Area shall be on foot. Visitors should move carefully so as to minimise disturbance to the breeding birds, soil, geomorphological features and vegetated surfaces, and should walk on rocky terrain or ridges if practical to avoid damage to sensitive plants and the often waterlogged soils. Pedestrian traffic should be kept to the minimum consistent with the objectives of any permitted activities and every reasonable effort should be made to minimise trampling effects. Pedestrians that are not undertaking research or management related to the penguins shall not enter the colonies and should maintain a separation distance from the breeding birds of at least 15 m at all times. Care should be exercised to ensure monitoring equipment, fences and other scientific installations are not disturbed.

Pedestrians moving between the helicopter landing sites (A) or (B) to the Adélie colony shall follow the preferred walking routes marked on Maps 2 and 4 or follow a route along the beach.

10(ii) Activities that are or may be conducted in the Area, including restrictions on time or place

- The research programme associated with the CCAMLR CEMP
- Scientific research that will not jeopardise the ecosystem of the Area;
- Essential management activities, including monitoring.

10(iii) Installation, modification or removal of structures

No structures are to be erected within the Area except as specified in a Permit. All scientific equipment installed in the Area must be approved by Permit and clearly identified by country, name of the principal investigator and year of installation. All such items should be made of materials that pose minimal risk of contamination to the Area. Removal of specific equipment for which the Permit has expired shall be a condition of the Permit. Permanent structures are prohibited.

10(iv) Location of field camps

Semi-permanent camps and temporary camping is permitted within the Area at the primary designated site on the cuspate foreland of Edmonson Point (Map 2). Camping at the CEMP Research camp (Maps 2 & 4) is permitted only for purposes of the Adélie Penguin Monitoring Programme. When necessary within the Restricted Zone for purposes specified in the Permit, temporary camping is permitted at the designated site (C) (74°18'51"S, 165°04'16"E) approximately 100 m west of helicopter landing site (Map 3).

10(v) Restrictions on materials and organisms which can be brought into the Area

No living animals, plant material or microorganisms shall be deliberately introduced into the Area and the precautions listed in 7(ix) below shall be taken against accidental introductions. In view of the presence of breeding bird colonies at Edmonson Point, no poultry products, including products containing uncooked dried eggs, including wastes from such products, shall be released into the Area. No herbicides or pesticides shall be brought into the Area. Any other chemicals, including radio-nuclides or stable isotopes, which may be introduced for scientific or management purposes specified in the Permit, shall be removed from the Area at or before the conclusion of the activity for which the Permit was granted. Fuel is not to be stored in the Area, unless authorised by Permit for specific scientific or management purposes. Fuel spill clean-up equipment should be made available for use at locations where fuel is being regularly handled. Anything introduced shall be for a stated period only, shall be removed at or before the conclusion of that stated period, and shall be stored and handled so that risk of any introduction into the environment is minimised. If release occurs which is likely to compromise the values of the Area, removal is encouraged only where the impact of removal is not likely to be greater than that of leaving the material in situ. The appropriate authority should be notified of anything released or not removed that was not included in the authorised Permit.

10(vi) Taking or harmful interference with native flora or fauna

Taking or harmful interference with native flora or fauna is prohibited, except by Permit issued in accordance with Annex II to the Protocol on Environmental Protection to the Antarctic Treaty. Where taking or harmful interference with animals is involved, the *SCAR Code of Conduct for the Use of Animals for Scientific Purposes in Antarctica* should be used as a minimum standard.

10(vii) Collection or removal of anything not brought into the Area by the Permit holder

Collection or removal of anything not brought into the Area by the Permit holder shall only be in accordance with a Permit and should be limited to the minimum necessary to meet scientific or management needs. Permits shall not be granted if there is a reasonable concern that the sampling proposed would take, remove or damage such quantities of rock, soil, native flora or fauna that their distribution or abundance on Edmonson Point would be significantly affected. Anything of human origin likely to compromise the values of the Area, which was not brought into the Area by the Permit Holder or otherwise authorised, may be removed unless the impact of removal is likely to be greater than leaving the material *in situ*: if this is the case the appropriate authority should be notified.

10(viii) Disposal of waste

All wastes, except human wastes, shall be removed from the Area. Human wastes shall either be removed from the Area, or incinerated using purpose-designed technologies such as a propane-burning toilet, or in the case of liquid human wastes may be disposed of into the sea.

10(ix) Measures that are necessary to ensure that the aims and objectives of the Management Plan can continue to be met

1. Permits may be granted to enter the Area to carry out monitoring and site inspection activities, which may involve the small-scale collection of samples for analysis or review, or for protective measures.

2. Any specific long-term monitoring sites shall be appropriately marked.

3. To help maintain the ecological and scientific values of Edmonson Point special precautions shall be taken against introductions. Of concern are microbial, invertebrate or plant introductions from other Antarctic sites, including stations, or from regions outside Antarctica. All sampling equipment or markers brought into the Area shall be thoroughly cleaned. To the maximum extent practicable, footwear and other equipment used or brought into the Area (including backpacks, carry-bags and tents) shall be thoroughly cleaned before entering the Area.

10(x) Requirements for reports

Parties should ensure that the principal holder for each Permit issued submits to the appropriate authority a report describing the activities undertaken. Such reports should include, as appropriate, the information identified in the visit report form contained in the Guide to the Preparation of Management Plans for Antarctic Specially Protected Areas. Parties should maintain a record of such activities and, in the Annual Exchange of Information, should provide summary descriptions of activities conducted by persons subject to their jurisdiction, which should be in sufficient detail to allow evaluation of the effectiveness of the Management Plan. Parties should, wherever possible, deposit originals or copies of such original reports in a publicly accessible archive to maintain a record of usage, to be used both in any review of the Management Plan and in organising the scientific use of the Area.

Bibliography

Ainley, D.G. 2002. *The Adélie Penguin. Bellwether of climate change*. Columbia University Press, New York.

Alfinito, S., Fumanti, B. and Cavacini, P. 1998. Epiphytic algae on mosses from northern Victoria Land (Antarctica). *Nova Hedwigia* **66** (3-4): 473-80.

Ancora, S., Volpi, V., Olmastroni, S., Leonzio, C. and Focardi, S. 2002. Assumption and elimination of trace elements in Adélie penguins from Antarctica: a preliminary study. *Marine Environmental Research* **54**: 341-44.

Azzali M. and J. Kalinowski. 2000. Spatial and temporal distribution of krill *Euphausia superba* biomass in the Ross Sea. In: Ianora A. (ed). *Ross Sea Ecology*. Springer, Berlin, 433-455.

Azzali M., J. Kalinowski, G. Lanciani and G. Cosimi. 2000. Characteristic Properties and dynamic aspects of krill swarms from the Ross Sea. In: Faranda F. G.L., Ianora A. (Ed). *Ross Sea Ecology*. Springer, Berlin, 413-431.

Bargagli, R., Martella, L. and Sanchez-Hernandez, J.C. 1997. The environment and biota at EdmonsonPoint (BIOTEX 1): preliminary results on environmental biogeochemistry. In di Prisco, G., Focardi, S. and Luporini, P. (eds) *Proceed. Third Meet. Antarctic Biology,* Santa Margherita Ligure, 13-15 December 1996. Camerino University Press: 261-71.

Bargagli, R. 1999. Report on Italian activities. *BIOTAS Newsletter* No. 13. Austral Summer 1998/99. A.H.L. Huiskes (ed) Netherlands Institute of Ecology: 16-17.

Bargagli, R., Sanchez-Hernandez, J.C., Martella, L. and Monaci, F. 1998. Mercury, cadmium and lead accumulation in Antarctic mosses growing along nutrient and moisture gradients. *Polar Biology* 19: 316-322.

Bargagli, R., Smith, R.I.L., Martella, L., Monaci, F., Sanchez-Hernandez, J.C. and Ugolini, F.C. 1999. Solution geochemistry and behaviour of major and trace elements during summer in a moss community at Edmonson Point, Victoria Land, Antarctica. *Antarctic Science* 11(1): 3-12.

Bargagli, R., Wynn-Williams, D., Bersan, F., Cavacini, P., Ertz, S., Freckman, D. Lewis Smith, R., Russell, N. and Smith, A. 1997. Field Report – BIOTEX 1: First BIOTAS Expedition (Edmonson Point – Baia Terra Nova, Dec 10 1995 – Feb 6 1996). *Newsletter of the Italian Biological Research in Antarctica* 1 (Austral summer 1995-96): 42-58.

Baroni, C. and Orombelli, G. 1994. Holocene glacier variations in the Terra Nova Bay area (Victoria Land, Antarctica). *Antarctic Science* 6(4):497-505.

Broady, P.A. 1987. A floristic survey of algae at four locations in northern Victoria Land. *New Zealand Antarctic Record* 7(3): 8-19.

Borchgrevink, C. 1901. *First on the Antarctic Continent: Being an Account of the British Antarctic Expedition 1898-1900.* G. Newnes. Ltd, London.

Cannone, N. and Guglielmin, M. 2003. Vegetation and permafrost: sensitive systems for the development of a monitoring program of climate change along an Antarctic transect. In: Huiskes, A.H.L., Gieskes, W.W.C., Rozema, J., Schorno, R.M.L., Van der Vies, S.M., Wolff, W.J. (Editors) *Antarctic biology in a global context.* Backhuys, Leiden: 31-36

Cannone, N., Guglielmin, M., Ellis Evans J.C., and Strachan R. in prep. Interactions between climate, vegetation and active layer in Maritime Antarctica. (submitted to *Journal of Applied Ecology*)

Cannone, N., Guglielmin, M., Gerdol, R., and Dramis, F. 2001. La vegetazione delle aree con permafrost per il monitoraggio del Global Change nelle regioni polari ed alpine. Abstract and Oral Presentation, 96à Congresso della Societa Botanica Italiana, Varese, 26-28 Settembre 2001.Castello, M. 2004. Lichens of the Terra Nova Bay area, northern Victoria Land (continental Antarctica). *Studia Geobotanica* 22: 3-54.

Cavacini, P. 1997. La microflora algale non marina della northern Victoria Land (Antartide). Ph.D. Thesis. Università "La Sapienza" di Roma. 234 pp.

Cavacini, P. 2001. Soil algae from northern Victoria Land (Antarctica). *Polar Bioscience* 14: 46-61.

CCAMLR. 1999. Report of member's activities in the Convention Area 1998/99: Italy. CCAMLR-XVIII/MA/14.

Clarke, J., Manly, B., Kerry, K., Gardner, H., Franchi, E. and Focardi, S. 1998. Sex differences in Adélie penguin foraging strategies. *Polar Biology* 20: 248-58.

Corsolini, S. and Trémont, R. 1997. Australia-Italy cooperation in Antarctica: Adélie Penguin monitoring program, Edmonson Point, Ross Sea Region. *Newsletter of the Italian Biological Research in Antarctica* 1 (Austral summer 1995-96): 59-64.

Corsolini, S., Ademollo, N., Romeo, T., Olmastroni, S. and Focardi, S. 2003. Persistent organic pollutants in some species of a Ross Sea pelagic trophic web. *Antarctic Science* 15(1): 95-104.

Corsolini, S., Kannan, K., Imagawa, T., Focardi, S. and Giesy J.P. 2002. Polychloronaphthalenes and other dioxin-like compounds in Arctic and Antarctic marine food webs. *Environmental Science and Technolology* **36**: 3490-96.

Corsolini, S., Olmastroni, S., Ademollo, N. and Focardi, S. 1999. Concentration and toxic evaluation of polychlorobiphenyls (PCBs) in Adélie Penguin (*Pygoscelis adeliae*) from Edmonson Point (Ross Sea, Antarctica). Tokyo 2-3 December 1999.

Emison, W. B. 1968. Feeding preferences of the Adélie penguin at Cape Crozier, Ross Island. Antarctic Research Series 12: 191-212.

Ertz, S. 1996. BIOTEX field report: December 1995 – February 1996. Strategies of Antarctic terrestrial organisms to protect against ultra-violet radiation. Unpublished field report in BAS Archives AD6/2/1995/NT3.

Fenice M., Selbmann L., Zucconi L. and Onofri S. 1997. Production of extracellular enzymes by Antarctic fungal strains. *Polar Biology* 17:275-280.

Franchi, E., Corsolini, S., Clarke, J.C., Lawless R. and Tremont, R. 1996. The three dimensional foraging patterns of Adélie penguins at Edmonson Point, Antarctica. Third International Penguin Conference, Cape Town, South Africa, 2-6 September 1996.

Franchi, E., Corsolini, S., Focardi, S., Clarke, J.C., Trémont, R. and Kerry, K.K. 1997. Biological research on Adélie penguin (*Pygoscelis adeliae*) associated with the CCAMLR Ecosystem Monitoring Program (CEMP). In di Prisco, G., Focardi, S. and Luporini, P. (eds) *Proceed. Third Meet. Antarctic Biology,* Santa Margherita Ligure, 13-15 December 1996. Camerino University Press: 209-19.

Frati, F. 1997. Collembola of the north Victoria Land: distribution, population structure and preliminary data for the reconstruction of a molecular phylogeny of Antarctic collembola. *Newsletter of the Italian Biological Research in Antarctica* 1 (Austral summer 1995-96): 30-38.

Frati F. 1999. Distribution and ecophysiology of terrestrial microarthropods in the Victoria Land. *Newsletter of the Italian Biological Research in Antarctica* 3: 13-19.

Frati F., Fanciulli P.P., Carapelli A. and Dallai R. 1997. The Collembola of northern Victoria Land (Antarctica): distribution and ecological remarks. *Pedobiologia* 41: 50-55.

Frati F., Fanciulli P.P., Carapelli A., De Carlo L. and Dallai R. 1996. Collembola of northern Victoria Land: distribution, population structure and preliminary molecular data to study origin and evolution of Antarctic Collembola. Proceedings of the 3rd Meeting on Antarctic Biology, G. di Prisco, S. Focardi and P. Luporini eds., Camerino Univ. Press: 321-330.

Fumanti, B., Alfinito, S. and Cavacini, P. 1993. Freshwater algae of Northern Victoria Land (Antarctica). *Giorn. Bot. Ital.,* **127** (3): 497.

Fumanti, B., Alfinito, S. and Cavacini, P. 1994a. Freshwater diatoms of Northern Victoria Land (Antarctica). 13th International Diatom Symposium, 1-7 September 1994, Acquafredda di Maratea (PZ), Italy, Abstract book: 226.

Fumanti, B., Alfinito, S. and Cavacini, P. 1994b. Floristic survey of the freshwater algae of Northern Victoria Land (Antarctica). Proceedings of the 2nd meeting on Antarctic Biology, Padova, 26-28 Feb. 1992. Edizioni Universitarie Patavine: 47-53.

Guilizzoni P., Libera V., Tartagli G., Mosello R., Ruggiu D., Manca M., Nocentini A, Contesini M., Panzani P., Beltrami M. 1991. Indagine per una caratterizzazione limnologica di ambienti lacustri antartici. Atti del 1° Convegno di Biologia Antartica. Roma CNR, 22-23 giu. 1989. Ed. Univ. Patavine: 377-408.Given, D.R. 1985. Fieldwork in Antarctica, November – December 1984. Report 511b. Botany Division, DSIR, New Zealand.

Given, D.R. 1989. A proposal for SSSI status for Edmonson Point, north Victoria Land. Unpublished paper held in PNRA Archives.

Greenfield, L.G., Broady, P.A., Given, D.R., Codley, E.G. and Thompson, K. 1985. Immediate science report of NZARP Expedition K053 to RDRC. Botanical and biological studies in Victoria Land and Ross Island, during 1984–85.

Harris, C.M. and Grant, S.M. 2003. Science and management at Edmonson Point, Wood Bay, Victoria Land, Ross Sea: Report of the Workshop held in Siena, 8 June 2003. Includes Science Reviews by R. Bargagli, N. Cannone & M. Guglielmin, and S. Focardi. Cambridge, *Environmental Research and Assessment.*

Keys, J.R., Dingwall, P.R. and Freegard, J. (eds) 1988. *Improving the Protected Area system in the Ross Sea region, Antarctica*: Central Office Technical Report Series No. 2. Wellington, NZ Department of Conservation.

Kyle, P.R. 1990. A.II. Melbourne Volcanic Province. In LeMasurier, W.E. and Thomson, J.W. (eds) Volcanoes of the Antarctic Plate and Southern Oceans. *Antarctic Research Series* 48: 48-52.

La Rocca N., Moro I. and Andreoli, C. 1996. Survey on a microalga collected from an Edmonson Point pond (Victoria Land, Antarctica). *Giornale Botanico Italiano*, 130:960-962.

Lewis Smith, R.I. 1996. BIOTEX 1 field report: December 1995 – January 1996: plant ecology, colonisation and diversity at Edmonson Point and in the surrounding region of Victoria Land, Antarctica. Unpublished field report in BAS Archives AD6/2/1995/NT1.

Lewis Smith, R.I. 1999. Biological and environmental characteristics of three cosmopolitan mosses dominant in continental Antarctica. *Journal of Vegetation Science* 10: 231-242.

Melick D.R. and Seppelt R.D. 1997. Vegetation patterns in relation to climatic and endogenous changes in Wilkes Land, continetal Antarctica. *Journal of Ecology* **85**: 43-56.

Meurk, C.D., Given, D.R. and Foggo, M. N. 1989. Botanical investigations at Terra Nova Bay and Wood Bay, north Victoria Land. 1988–89 NZARP Event K271 science report.

Olmastroni S, Pezzo F, Bisogno I., Focardi S, 2004b. Interannual variation in the summer diet of Adélie penguin *Pygoscelis adeliae* at Edmonson Point . WG-EMM04/ 38.

Olmastroni S, Pezzo F, Volpi V, Corsolini S, Focardi S, Kerry K. 2001b. Foraging ecology of chick rearing of Adélie penguins in two colonies of the Ross Sea; 27/8-1/9 2001; Amsterdam, The Netherlands. SCAR.

Olmastroni, S. 2002. Factors affecting the foraging strategies of Adélie penguin (*Pygoscelis adeliae*) at Edmonson Point, Ross Sea, Antarctica. PhD Thesis, Università di Siena.

Olmastroni, S., Corsolini, S., Franchi, E., Focardi, S., Clarke, J., Kerry, K., Lawless, R. and Tremont, R. 1998. Adélie penguin colony at Edmonson Point (Ross Sea, Antarctica): a long term monitoring study. 31 August-September 1998; Christchurch, New Zealand. SCAR. p 143.

Olmastroni, S., Corsolini, S., Pezzo, F., Focardi, S. and Kerry, K. 2000. The first five years of the Italian-Australian Joint Programme on the Adélie Penguin: an overview. *Italian Journal of Zoology Supplement* **1**: 141-45.

Onofri, S. and Tofi, S. 1992. *Arthrobotrys ferox* sp. nov., a springtail-capturing hyphomycete from continental Antarctica. *Mycotaxon* 44(2):445-451.Orombelli, G. 1988. Le spiagge emerse oloceniche di Baia Terra Nova (Terra Vittoria, Antartide). Rend. Acc. Naz. Lincei.

Pezzo, F., Olmastroni, S., Corsolini, S., and Focardi, S. 2001. Factors affecting the breeding success of the south polar skua *Catharacta maccormicki* at Edmonson Point, Victoria Land, Antarctica. *Polar Biology* **24**:389-93.

Pilastro, A., Pezzo, F., Olmastroni, S., Callegarin, C., Corsolini, S. and Focardi, S. 2001. Extrapair paternity in the Adélie penguin *Pygoscelis adeliae*. *Ibis* **143**: 681-84.

Ricelli A., Fabbri A.A., Fumanti B., Cavacini P., Fanelli C. 1997. Analyses of effects of ultraviolet radiation on fatty acids and α-tocopherol composition of some microalgae isolated from Antarctica. In di Prisco, G., Focardi, S., and Luporini P. (eds.), Proceedings of the 3rd meeting on "Antarctic Biology", S. Margherita Ligure, December 13-15, 1996. Camerino University Press: 239-247.

Simeoni, U., Baroni, C., Meccheri, M., Taviani, M. and Zanon, G. 1989. Coastal studies in northern Victoria Land (Antarctica): Holocene beaches of Inexpressible Island, Tethys Bay and Edmonson Point. *Bollettino di Oceanologia Teorica ed Applicata* 7(1-2): 5-17.

Taylor, R.H., Wilson, P.R. and Thomas, B.W. 1990. Status and trends of Adélie Penguin populations in the Ross Sea region. *Polar Record* 26:293-304.

Woehler, E.J. (ed) 1993. *The distribution and abundance of Antarctic and sub-Antarctic penguins.* SCAR, Cambridge.

Wörner, G. and Viereck, L. 1990.   A.I0. Mount Melbourne. In Le Masurier, W.E. and Thomson, J.W. (eds) Volcanoes of the Antarctic Plate and Southern Oceans. *Antarctic Research Series* 48: 72-78.

Wynn-Williams, D.D. 1996. BIOTEX 1, first BIOTAS expedition: field report: Taylor Valley LTER Dec 1995, Terra Nova Bay Dec 1995 – Jan 1996: microbial colonisation, propagule banks and survival processes. Unpublished field report in BAS Archives AD6/2/1995/NT2.

Zucconi L., Pagano S., Fenice M., Selbmann L., Tosi S., and Onofri S. 1996. Growth temperature preference of fungal strains from Victoria Land. *Polar Biology* **16**: 53-61.

Appendix 1

New bibliography and other publications of interest for the research activity at Edmonson Point (Ross Sea)

D. Ainley, V. Toniolo, G. Ballard, K. Barton, J. Eastman, B. Karl, S. Focardi, G. Kooyman, P. Lyver, S. Olmastroni, B.S. Stewart, J. W. Testa, P. Wilson, 2006. Managing ecosystem uncertainty: critical habitat and dietary overlap of top-predators in the Ross Sea. WG-EMM 06/29

Tosca Ballerini, Giacomo Tavecchia, Silvia Olmastroni, Francesco Pezzo, Silvano Focardi 2009. Nonlinear effects of winter sea ice on the survival probabilities of Adélie penguins. *Oecologia* 161:253–265.

Ballerini T, Tavecchia G, Pezzo F, Jenouvrier S and Olmastroni S 2015. Predicting responses of the Adélie penguin population of Edmonson Point to future sea ice changes in the Ross Sea. Front.Ecol.Evol. 3:8. doi:10.3389/fevo.2015.00008

F. Borghini, A. Colacevich, S. Olmastroni 2010. Studi di ecologia e paleolimnologia nell'area protetta di Edmonson Point (Terra Vittoria, Antartide). *Etruria Natura* Anno VII: 77-86.

Cincinelli A., Martellini T. and Corsolini S., 2011. Hexachlorocyclohexanes in Arctic and Antarctic Marine Ecosystems, Pesticides - Formulations, Effects, Fate, Edited by: Margarita Stoytcheva, ISBN: 978-953-307-532-7, Publisher: InTech, Publishing, Janeza Trdine 9, 51000 Rijeka, Croatia, January 2011,453-476, available at http://www.intechopen.com/articles/show/title/hexachlorocyclohexanes-in-arctic-and-antarctic-marine-ecosystems.

Corsolini S., 2011. Contamination Profile and Temporal Trend of POPs in Antarctic Biota. In Global contamination trends of persistent organic chemicals. Ed. B. Loganathan, P.K.S. Lam, Taylor & Francis, Boca Raton, FL, USA, in press.

Corsolini S., 2011. Antarctic: Persistent Organic Pollutants and Environmental Health in the Region. In: Nriagu JO (ed.) *Encyclopedia of Environmental Health*, volume 1, pp. 83–96 Burlington: Elsevier, NVRN/978-0-444-52273-3.

Corsolini S., Ademollo N., Mariottini M., Focardi S., 2004. Poly-brominated diphenyl-ethers (PBDEs) and other Persistent Organic Pollutants in blood of penguins from the Ross Sea (Antarctica). *Organohalogen Compd.*, 66: 1695-1701.

Corsolini S, Covaci A, Ademollo N, Focardi S, Schepens P., 2005. Occurrence of organochlorine pesticides (OCPs) and their enantiomeric signatures, and concentrations of polybrominated diphenyl ethers (PBDEs) in the Adelie penguin food web, Antarctica. *Environ Pollut.*, 140(2): 371-382.

Corsolini S., Olmastroni S., Ademollo N., Minucci G., Focardi S., 2003. Persistent organic pollutants in stomach contents of Adélie penguins from Edmonson Point (Victoria Land, Antarctica). In: Antarctic Biology in a global context, Ed. A.H.L. Huiskes, W.W.C. Gieskes, J. Rozema, R.M.L. Schorno, S.M. van der Vies, W.J. Wolff. Backhuys Publishers, Leiden, The Netherlands. pp. 296-300

Fuoco, R.; Bengtson Nash, S. M.; Corsolini, S.; Gambaro, A.; Cincinelli, A. *POPs in Antarctica; A Report to the Antarctic Treaty in Kiev 2-13 June, 2008*; Environmental Contamination in Antarctica (ECA) Pisa, 2008.

Lorenzini. S., Olmastroni S., Pezzo. F., Salvatore M.C., Baroni C. 2009. Holocene Adélie penguin diet in Victoria Land, Antarctica. *Polar Biology* 32:1077–1086.

Irene Nesti, Yan Ropert-Coudert, Akiko Kato, Michael Beaulieu, Silvano Focardi, Silvia Olmastroni 2010. Diving behaviour of chick-rearing Adélie Penguins at Edmonson Point, Ross Sea. *Polar Biology* 33:969–978.

S. Olmastroni, F. Pezzo, V. Volpi, S. Focardi 2004a. Effects of weather and sea ice on Adélie penguin reproductive performance. *CCAMLR Science* 11:99-109

F. Pezzo, **S.** Olmastroni, V. Volpi, S. Focardi 2007. Annual variation in reproductive parameters of Adélie penguins at Edmonson Point, Victoria Land, Antarctica. *Polar Biology* **31**:39-45.

Bibliography after 2011

Cannone N., Wagner D., Hubberten H. W., Guglielmin M. (2008). Biotic and abiotic factors influencing soil properties across a latitudinal gradient in Victoria Land, Antarctica. *Geoderma*, 144: 50-65

Cannone N., Seppelt R. (2009). A preliminary floristic classification of Northern and Southern Victoria Land vegetation (Continental Antarctica). ANTARCTIC SCIENCE, vol. 20, p. 553-62

Cannone N., Guglielmin M. (2009). Influence of vegetation on the ground thermal regime in continental Antarctica. GEODERMA, vol. 151, p. 215-223

Guglielmin M., Cannone N. 2012. A permafrost warming in a cooling Antarctica? Climatic Change, Climatic Change, 111 p. 177-195

Guglielmin M., Dalle Fratte M., Cannone N. (2014). Permafrost warming and vegetation changes in continental Antarctica. Environ. Res. Lett. 9: 045001

Singh S.M., Olech M., Cannone N., Convey P. (2015). Contrasting patterns in lichen diversity in the continental and maritime Antarctic. Polar Science, 9(3): 311 – 318

Appendix 2   Permits issued

During 2006-2011 Italian Antarctic Campaign have been issued the permits for the Interference or sampling of following living organisms into the Edmonson Point ASPA N° 165:

2006/2007 campaign

Organism denomination	Amount N° or Kg	Sampling System
Pygoscelis adeliae	2000	visual census
" " "	10	tagging
" " "	10	feathers sampling
Stercorarius maccormicki	200	visual census

Have been carried out water sampling from lakes. Permit for entry in ASPA 165 have been performed for 40 days in the field camp.

2007/2008 campaign

Organism denomination	Amount N° or Kg	Sampling System

Have been issued permits for entry in ASPA 165 only for meteo station control for 2 times, 3hours each time

2008/2009 campaign

Organism denomination	Amount N° or Kg	Sampling System

No activity has been performed at Edmonson Point ASPA 165 during 2007/2008 campaign

2009/2010 campaign

Organism denomination	Amount N° or Kg	Sampling System
Pygoscelis adeliae	2000	visual census
" " "	18	feathers and blood sampling
Stercorarius maccormicki	120	visual census
" " "	10	feathers and blood sampling
Mosses	200 g	manual sampling
Algae	200 g	manual sampling

Have been carried out water sampling, mosses and algae from lakes. Permit for entry in ASPA 165 have been performed during 31 days in the field camp and for 3 hours for other sampling.

2010/2011 campaign

Organism denomination	Amount N° or Kg	Sampling System
Mosses	600 g	manual sampling
Algae	400 g	manual sampling
Lichens on rocks and soils	600 g	manual sampling
Colonized rocks and soils by microorganisms and lichens	2 Kg	manual sampling

Sampling and studies activities into the ASPA area have been carried out in 12 different times for a total of 28 hours of work.

Appendix 3   Permits issued

During 2011-2016 Italian Antarctic Campaign have been issued the permits for the interference or sampling of following living organisms into the Edmonson Point ASPA N° 165:

2011/2012 campaign

Organism denomination	Amount N° or Kg	Sampling System
Moses	0.005 kg	manual system
Lichens	0.002 kg	manual system

Permit for entry in ASPA 165 have been performed in the field camp for 4 times, 3 h each time and 3 times for meteo activities 1h heach time. 15 hours in total

2012/2013 campaign

Organism denomination	Amount N° or Kg	Sampling System
Moses	0.08 kg	manual system
Lichens	0.05 kg	manual system

Have been issued permits for entry in ASPA 165 for research activities and meteo station control . The total time inside the ASPA during the 2012-13 campaing has been about 27 h

2013/2014 campaign

Organism denomination	Amount N° or Kg	Sampling System
Lacustrine algae	1 kg	manual system

Moses	1.2 kg	manual system
Lichene	0.1 kg	manual system
Faeces and guano	how need	manual system
Bivalve fossil	3 species for stratigraphic layer	manual system

Have been issued permits for entry in ASPA 165 only for meteo station control for 2 times, 3hours each time . The total time inside the ASPA during the 2013-14 campaing has been about 25 h

2014/2015 campaign

Organism denomination	Amount N° or Kg	Sampling System
Project on Conservation of a polar mesopredator species susceptible to ecosystem change	3000 Pygoscelis adeliae	visual Census
	N° 20 feathers and blood sampling	manual system
	Stercorarius maccormicki 120	visual census
	n°10 feathers and blood sampling	manual system

He was made a field at the ASPA n° 165 (Edmonson Point) for a period of about 60 days. Have been issued permits for entry in ASPA also for meteo station control for 2 times, 3hours each time . The total time inside the ASPA during the 2014-15 campaing has been about 6 h and 60 days

2015/2016 campaign

Organism denomination	Amount N° or Kg	Sampling System
surface with biological crust	1.5 kg	Using sterile spade

Have been issued permits for entry in ASPA also for meteo station control for 5 times, 3hours each time. The total time inside the ASPA during the 2015-16 campaing has been about 21 h .

2016/2017 campaign

Organism denomination	Amount N° or Kg	Sampling System
Collection of tephra No living organism will be		samples by spatula
Algae; Planktonic invertebrates; Fish	5 for species	plankton net, fish line

Have been issued permits for entry in ASPA also for meteo station control for 5 times, 3hours each time. The total time inside the ASPA during the 2016-17 campaing has been about 43 h .

Edmonson Point ASPA 165 Maps

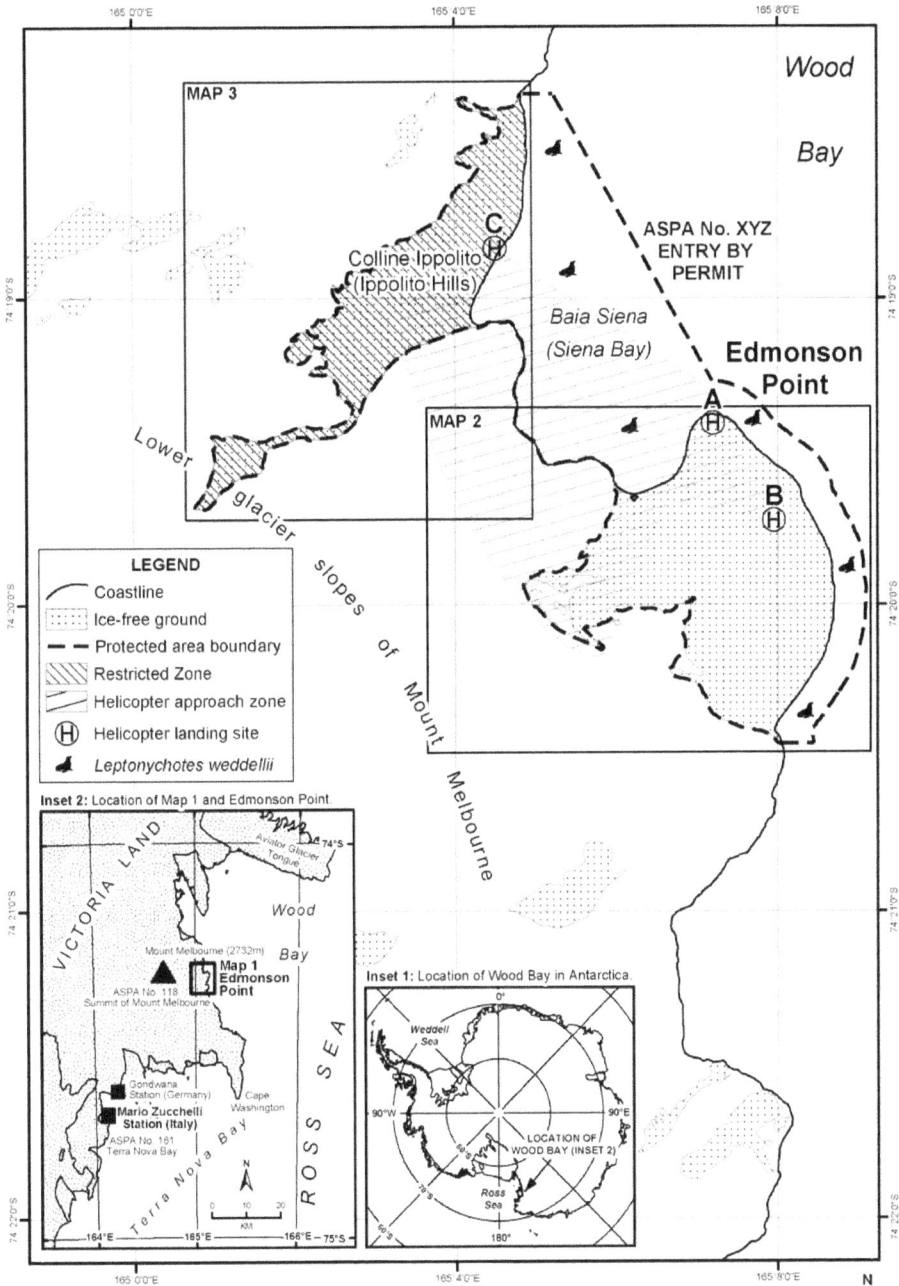

Map 1: Edmonson Point, ASPA No. 165
Wood Bay, Victoria Land, Ross Sea

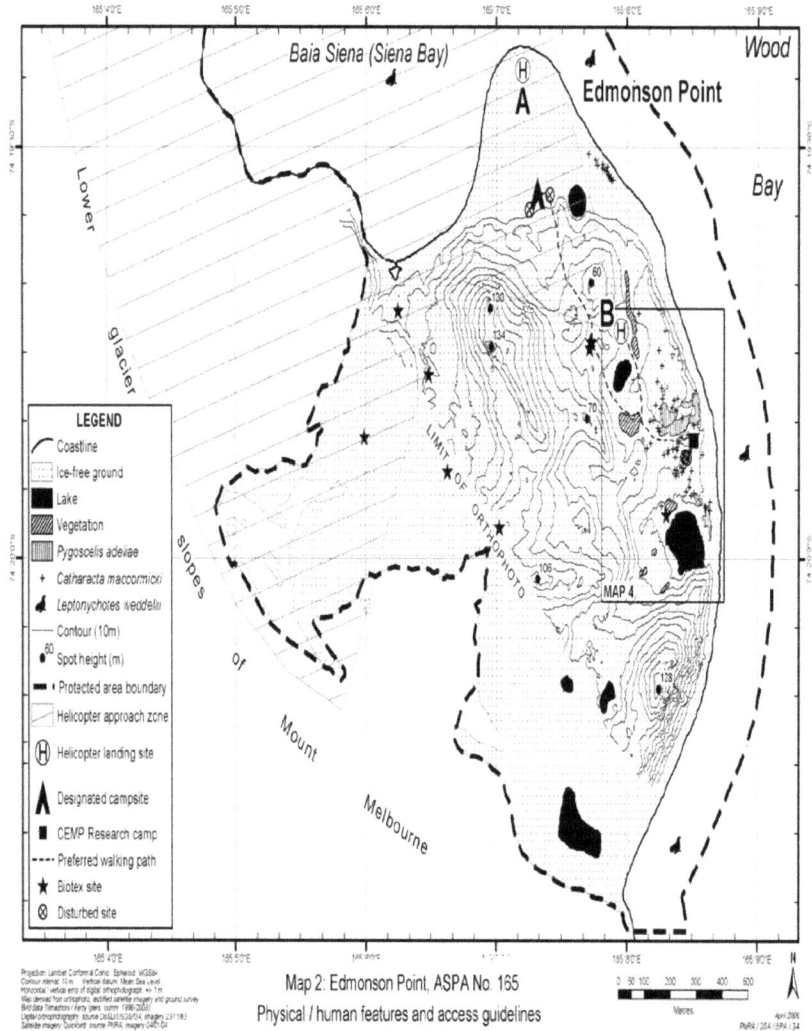

Map 2: Edmonson Point, ASPA No. 165
Physical / human features and access guidelines

LEGEND

- Coastline
- Ice-free ground
- Lake
- Vegetation
- *Pygoscelis adeliae*
- + *Catharacta maccormicki*
- *Leptonychotes weddellii*
- Contour (10m)
- Spot height (m)
- Protected area boundary
- Helicopter approach zone
- (H) Helicopter landing site
- Designated campsite
- CEMP Research camp
- Preferred walking path
- Biotex site
- Disturbed site

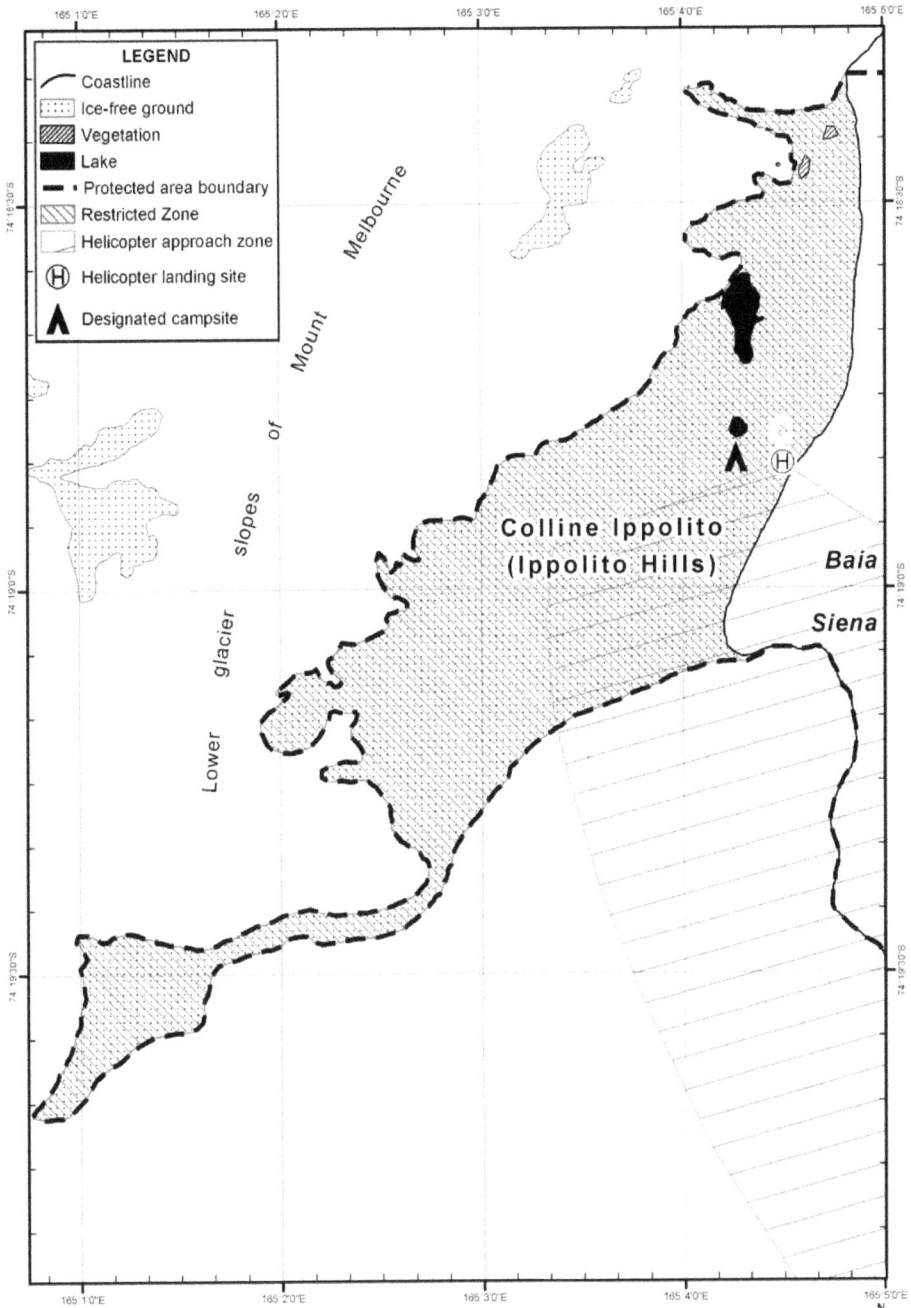

LEGEND

- Coastline
- Ice-free ground
- Vegetation
- Lake
- Protected area boundary
- Restricted Zone
- Helicopter approach zone
- (H) Helicopter landing site
- Designated campsite

Mount Melbourne

Lower glacier slopes of

Colline Ippolito
(Ippolito Hills)

Baia

Siena

Projection: Lambert Conformal Conic Spheroid: WGS84
Map derived from rectified satellite imagery
Source: Quickbird PNRA imagery acquired 04/01/04
Horizontal error of satellite image +/- 10 m
Elevation information unavailable

Map 3: Restricted Zone, Colline Ippolito
ASPA No. 165 Edmonson Point

0 50 100   200   300   400   500
Metres

N

April 2006
PNRA / DSA / ERA

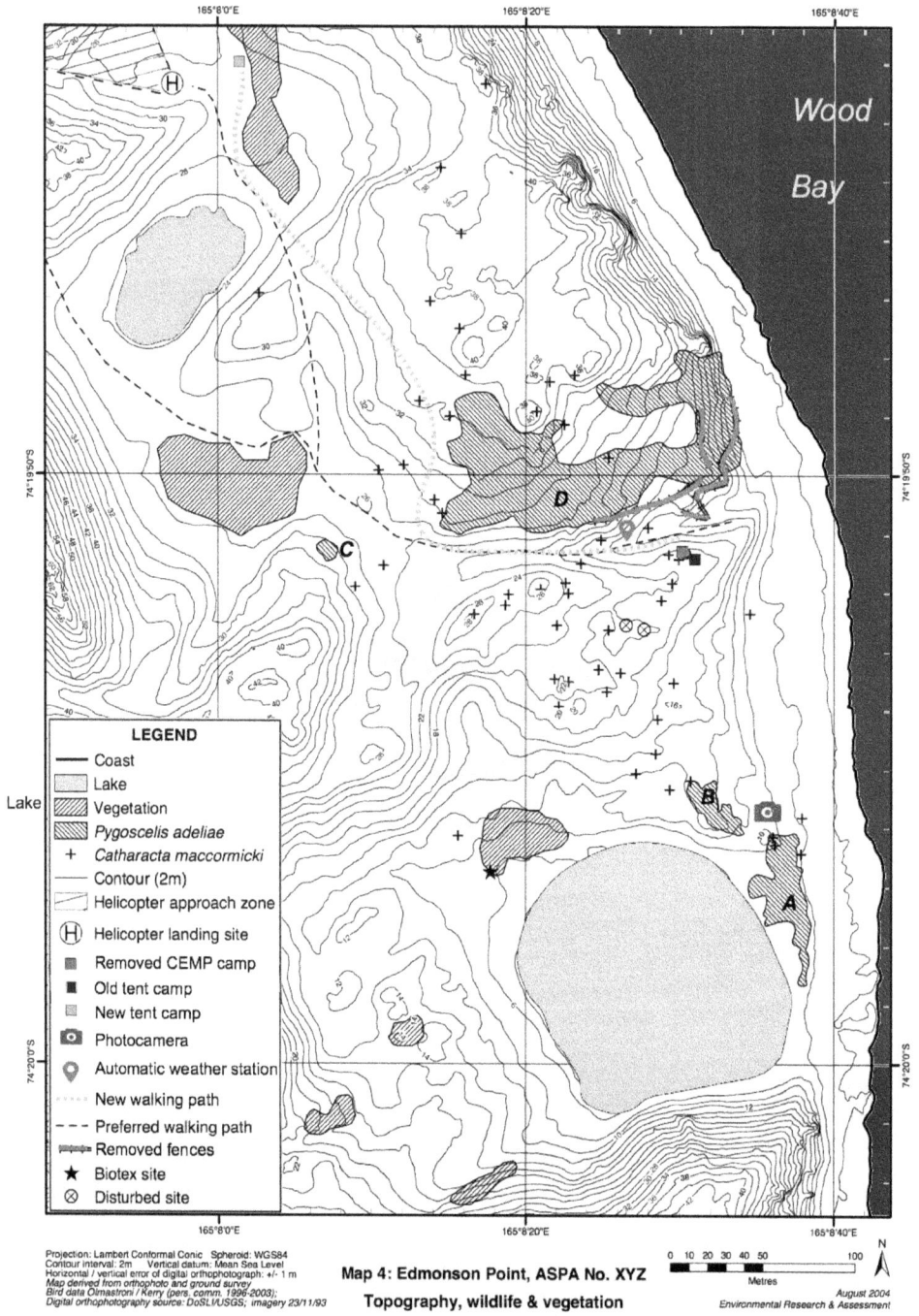

LEGEND

— Coast
▒ Lake
▨ Vegetation
▧ *Pygoscelis adeliae*
+ *Catharacta maccormicki*
— Contour (2m)
▨ Helicopter approach zone
Ⓗ Helicopter landing site
▪ Removed CEMP camp
■ Old tent camp
▫ New tent camp
🄾 Photocamera
📍 Automatic weather station
··· New walking path
--- Preferred walking path
━ Removed fences
★ Biotex site
⊗ Disturbed site

Projection: Lambert Conformal Conic Spheroid: WGS84
Contour interval: 2m   Vertical datum: Mean Sea Level
Horizontal / vertical error of digital orthophotograph: +/- 1 m
Map derived from orthophoto and ground survey
Bird data Olmastroni / Kerry (pers. comm. 1996-2003);
Digital orthophotography source: DoSLI/USGS; imagery 23/11/93

Map 4: Edmonson Point, ASPA No. XYZ

Topography, wildlife & vegetation

0 10 20 30 40 50   100
Metres

August 2004
Environmental Research & Assessment

Management Plan for Antarctic Specially Managed Area No.5 AMUNDSEN-SCOTT SOUTH POLE STATION, SOUTH POLE

Introduction

The Amundsen-Scott South Pole Station (hereafter referred to as South Pole Station), operated by the United States, is located on the polar plateau at an elevation of 2835 m near the geographic South Pole at 90°S. An area of ~26,344 km² around the South Pole Station is designated as an Antarctic Specially Managed Area (hereafter referred to as 'the Area'). The Area has been designated in order to maximize the valuable scientific opportunities at the Pole, protect the near-pristine environment and ensure that all activities, including those to experience the extraordinary qualities of the South Pole, can be conducted safely, environmentally responsibly and without disruption to scientific programs. In order to help achieve the objectives of the Management Plan, the Area has been divided into Scientific, Operations, and Restricted zones. The Scientific Zone is further divided into four sectors: Clean Air, Quiet, Downwind and Dark. The management measures agreed for those areas help coordinate activities and protect the important values of the South Pole.

The Area was originally designated following a proposal by the United States of America and adopted through Measure 2 (2007). The current Management Plan has been comprehensively revised and updated as part of the review process required by the Protocol on Environmental Protection to the Antarctic Treaty (hereafter the Protocol).

The Area is situated within 'Environment Q – East Antarctic high interior ice sheet', as defined in the Environmental Domains Analysis for Antarctica (Resolution 3 (2008)). The Area is not classified under the Antarctic Conservation Biogeographic Regions classification (Resolution 6 (2012)).

Contents

1.   Values to be protected and activities to be managed

Environmental and scientific values

The Area is located in a region of high scientific value and Amundsen-Scott South Pole Station facilitates exceptional scientific research with extensive international collaboration. The unique environmental conditions at the South Pole, including the extremely cold and dry climate, its isolated location high on an ice sheet and being the southern axis point of the Earth, provide ideal conditions to conduct a wide range of scientific observations:

*   Astrophysics, atmospheric and geospace sciences – including near-Earth solar wind, magnetosphere, ionosphere, and astronomy and astrophysical studies including cosmic ray and solar physics. The South Pole's position on the Earth's axis, the Area's climatic conditions and remoteness from light pollution facilitate extended astronomical and astrophysical observations of specific stellar objects. Also, the Area's isolation from sound, vibration, and electromagnetic interference (EMI) is important for astrophysical research. The location is ideal for high-energy particle astrophysics experiments and detection of extreme energy events using instrument arrays installed into the ice sheet. The geophysically stable location of the Area and the operation of the South Pole Station year-round allow for continuous research of upper atmosphere physics, including solar processes, effects of short term geomagnetic phenomena (auroras, induced electrical currents, and radio wave communications interference), and long term events (relating to the ozone layer, ultraviolet radiation, atmospheric composition, stratospheric winds, weather, and climate). Located far from pollution sources and human influence, the air at the South Pole is considered to be the cleanest on Earth. The Area therefore serves as an important monitoring and research location

for global background levels of natural and anthropogenic atmospheric constituents, and also for research into climate change.

- Glaciology – The thick ice sheet contains a natural record of atmospheric constituents, which is researched to understand past changes in the Earth's atmosphere and climate.

- Seismology – Due to its isolation from sound and vibration, one of Earth's most important seismic stations is situated in the Area.

- Medical research – The unique community of people living at South Pole Station allows for specialized medical research on small, isolated groups.

Historic values

The Area has significant historic value and two Historic Sites and Monuments (HSMs) have been designated at the South Pole:

- HSM No.1 was designated in 1972 at 90°S to recognise a flag mast erected at the South Pole by the First Argentine Overland Polar Expedition in December 1965. The flag mast is believed now to lie irretrievably buried deep beneath ice within ~500 m from the geographic South Pole, although its exact location is unknown.

- HSM No.80 was designated in 2005 in the vicinity of 90°S to recognise Amundsen's Tent, which was erected by the Norwegian expedition led by Roald Amundsen on their arrival at the South Pole on 14 December 1911. The Norwegian expedition was the first to reach the South Pole. The tent is believed now to lie irretrievably buried deep beneath ice within several km of the geographic South Pole, although its exact location is unknown.

The United States has established a 'Ceremonial South Pole' close to South Pole Station to commemorate the 1957/58 International Geophysical Year (IGY) and all expeditions that have achieved the South Pole.

Aesthetic and wilderness values

As unique points on the rotational axis of the Earth, the Poles have long captured the imagination of geographers, explorers and the general public. The South Pole has attracted exceptional interest because of its unique and challenging qualities, such as the ice-dominated landscape combined with remoteness, high altitude and extreme cold. The South Pole is one of the most challenging environments on Earth for human survival. Many continue to seek out that challenge for diverse reasons, including for adventure, excitement and for personal discovery and achievement. For many, whether making the journey overland or by air, attaining the Pole represents an extraordinary and highly rewarding experience.

In addition, unusual phenomena such as parhelion or sun dogs, sun pillars and mirages may occur with beautiful effects in polar clouds or in suspended ice crystals in the dry, clear atmosphere. The Aurora Australis may illuminate the sky with dramatic arcs and waves of multicolored light at times of darkness, making a most impressive display.

The extreme environmental conditions, the vast ice-bound landscape, the unusual and beautiful atmospheric phenomena, the deep sense of history of human endurance and perseverance, combined with intangible qualities in people's personal experience and relationship with the South Pole, characterize the site as one of exceptionally high aesthetic and wilderness value.

2.   Aims and objectives

The aim of this Management Plan is to conserve and protect the environment surrounding the South Pole by managing and coordinating human activities in the Area such that the values of the South Pole are protected and sustained in the long term, especially the unique and outstanding scientific values.

The specific objectives of management in the Area are to:

- Facilitate scientific research while maintaining stewardship of the environment;

- Promote and assist with the planning and coordination of human activities at South Pole to manage actual or potential conflicts among different values (including those of different scientific disciplines), activities and operators;

- Ensure the long-term protection of scientific, historic, aesthetic, wilderness and other values of the Area by minimizing disturbance to or degradation of these values, including disturbance to natural features, and by minimizing the cumulative environmental impacts of human activities;

- Minimize the footprint of all facilities and scientific experiments established in the Area, while allowing for necessary modifications and improvements to these in a manner consistent with the other objectives of the Management Plan;

- Minimize any physical disturbance, release of pollutants, contamination and wastes produced within the Area, and take all practical steps to contain, treat, remove or remediate these whether produced in the course of normal activities or by accident;

- Promote use of energy systems and modes of transport within the Area that have the least environmental impact, and minimize as far as practicable the use of fossil fuels for the conduct of activities within the Area;

- Improve the understanding of natural processes and human impacts both locally within the Area and globally, including through the conduct of monitoring programs; and

- Encourage communication and co-operation between users of the Area, in particular through dissemination of information on the Area and the provisions that apply.

- Prevent the unintended introduction of species not native to the Area, and minimize as far as practicable the unintended transfer of native species within the Area;

3.   Management activities

To achieve the aims and objectives of this Management Plan, the following management activities shall be undertaken:

- Parties with an active interest in the Area should convene as required, and preferably annually, a South Pole Management Group (hereafter the Management Group) to oversee coordination of activities in the Area, including to:
    - facilitate and ensure effective communication among those working in or visiting the Area;
    - provide a forum to anticipate, identify and resolve any actual or potential conflicts in use;
    - help minimize duplication of activities;
    - maintain a record of activities and, where practical, impacts in the Area;
    - develop strategies to detect and address cumulative impacts;
    - disseminate information on the Area, in particular on the activities occurring and the management measures that apply within the Area, including through maintaining this information electronically at http://www.southpole.aq/;
    - review past, existing, and future activities and evaluate the effectiveness of management measures; and
    - make recommendations on the implementation of this Management Plan.

- National Programs operating within the Area shall maintain copies of the current version of the management plan and supporting documentation in appropriate station and research facilities and make these available to all persons in the Area, as well as electronically at http://www.southpole.aq/;

- National Programs operating within the Area and tour operators visiting should ensure that their personnel (including staff, crew, passengers, scientists and any other visitors) are briefed on, and are aware of, the requirements of this Management Plan, and in particular the General Environmental Guidelines (Appendix A), the Guidelines for the Scientific Zone (Appendix B) and Restricted Zones (Appendix C), and the Guidelines for Non-Governmental Visitors (Appendices D and E) that apply within the Area;

- National Programs operating within the Area and tour operators visiting should ensure that their personnel are briefed on, and are aware of, the risks and requirements for safety in the extreme environment at the South Pole, including in aircraft operations and in medical emergencies;

- Tour operators and any other group or person responsible for planning and / or conducting non-governmental activities within the Area should coordinate their activities with National Programs operating in the Area in advance to ensure they do not pose risks to the values of the Area and that they comply with the requirements of the Management Plan. In particular, advance coordination should be undertaken with the United States Antarctic Program as operator of Amundsen-Scott South Pole Station;

- National Programs operating within the Area should seek to develop best practices with a view to achieving the objectives of the Management Plan, and to exchange freely such knowledge and information;

- Signs and / or markers should be erected where necessary and appropriate to show the location or boundaries of zones, research sites, landing sites or campsites within the Area. Signs and markers shall be secured and maintained in good condition, and removed when no longer necessary;

- Visits shall be made as necessary (no less than once every five years) to evaluate whether the Management Plan is effective and to ensure management measures are adequate. The Management Plan, Code of Conduct and Guidelines shall be revised and updated as necessary; and

- National Programs operating within the Area shall take such steps as are necessary and practical to ensure the requirements of the Management Plan are observed.

4.   Period of designation

Designated for an indefinite period.

5.   Maps and Photographs

Map 1 – ASMA No.5 South Pole: Location, topography, ASMA boundary, Scientific Zone and Clean Air Sector.

Map 2 – ASMA No.5 South Pole: Management Zones and Sectors.

Map 3 – ASMA No.5 Amundsen-Scott South Pole Station: Operations Zone.

Map 4 – ASMA No.5 Amundsen-Scott South Pole Station.

Map 5 – South Pole Non-Governmental Visitor approach guidelines overview.

Map 6 – South Pole Non-Governmental Visitor approach guidelines detail.

Important notes on South Pole maps

The ice sheet and facilities at the South Pole move at a rate of ~10 m per year. As a result, the true positions of features shown on maps and their GPS coordinates change over time. Therefore a Local Grid is used to define all ASMA, Zone and Sector boundaries, which all move with the Local Grid. Local Grid bearings thus remain consistent relative to permanently installed facilities, which move with the ice. Facility positions remain consistent relative to each other and to the ASMA boundaries, although their true positions shift relative to the geographic South Pole. Local Grid north aligns with the Greenwich Meridian (0 Degrees Longitude). ASMA maps are updated on a regular basis and the most current maps are made available at http://www.southpole.aq/.

6. Description of the Area

6(i) Geographical coordinates, boundary markers and natural features

General description

The landscape at the South Pole comprises an extensive, gently sloping and featureless ice sheet rising to ~2835 m in elevation. The bedrock of the underlying continental landmass has an elevation of ~135 m above sea level, making the ice sheet at this location approximately 2700 m in thickness. The ice sheet over the Pole extending out to 89°S slopes in a Grid NW direction towards the Weddell Sea, ranging from ~3000 m to ~2650 m. The surface near the pole generally comprises windblown snow or sastrugi, and is otherwise featureless and not crevassed.

Boundaries and coordinates

The boundary of the Area is defined as two semi-circles extending with a radius of 20 km and 150 km respectively around the South Pole Station (Map 1). The larger semi-circle extends 150 km from a point of origin defined as the Grid SW corner of the Atmospheric Research Observatory (ARO) building (~365 m from the geographic South Pole (2017)) and is bounded by the Grid 110° and 340° lines from the ARO building. This large semi-circle comprises the Clean Air Sector (CAS) of the Scientific Zone, which shares the outer boundary of the ASMA.

The smaller semi-circle extends 20 km from a point of origin defined as the center of the circular aluminum tower staircase on the main elevated building of South Pole Station (hereafter the elevated station). The center of this staircase is the common origin of three other management sectors (Quiet, Downwind and Dark) which, together with the CAS, comprise the Scientific Zone within the ASMA. The circular aluminum tower staircase is a readily recognizable feature on the maps and on the ground, and the elevated station is expected to be present in the Area longer than any other structure or landmark.

The boundary of the Area comprises all structures and areas of current and planned research at South Pole Station and an area of sufficient size to meet the objectives of the Scientific Zone. The geographic location of the ASMA shifts by ~10 m per year along with all of the facilities as the ice sheet moves.

Climate

The climate at the South Pole Station is extremely cold, windy and arid. The average annual temperature at the South Pole is -49.4°C (-56°F). The highest temperature recorded at South Pole Station is -12.3°C (9.9°F) (on 25 Dec 2011), and the lowest is −82.8°C (−117.0°F) (June 1982).

The sun reaches a maximum elevation of 23.5° above the horizon at midsummer. Snow reflects much of the sunlight reaching the surface of the Polar Plateau.

Air humidity at the South Pole is close to zero, making the environment an extreme polar desert. Snowfall at the South Pole is minimal, with average annual precipitation being only 86 mm liquid equivalent. Winds are persistent and average between 5-15 knots, mainly originating from a Grid northeast / east direction. Wind-blown snow tends to accumulate around structures, causing deep drifts and burying structures even though actual snowfall is low.

An analysis of surface climatology by Lazzara *et al.* (2012) found no statistically significant change in temperature or pressure at the South Pole over the period 1957–2010, although a significant downward trend was observed for wind speeds, decreasing by 0.28 m / s per decade, as well as for average snow accumulation (1983-2010), decreasing by -2.9 mm / year.

Atmospheric sciences

Pollutants from aircraft and other sources in polar regions can travel hundreds of kilometers, affecting measurements of boundary layer air, measurements of gasses and aerosols in the air column, and measurements of contaminants in the snow, thus requiring an extensive area be kept vacant to maintain a site for research on clean air. The Atmospheric Research Observatory (ARO) is situated upwind ~450 m Grid NE of the elevated station, and lies at the Grid SW corner of the Clean Air Sector (CAS). The CAS extends in a semi-circle from ARO 150 km to the outer boundary of the Scientific Zone and the ASMA, which provides the necessary buffer for ensuring accurate measurements. Most of the atmospheric research is conducted within the CAS, which is situated upwind from the station to help to ensure that the air remains as pristine as possible. The research at ARO is carried out by the United States National Oceanic and Atmospheric Administration's Global Monitoring Division (NOAA/ESRL). Measurements are undertaken to determine long-term trends of important trace gases, aerosols, and solar radiation and to investigate the influence of these gases and aerosols on the Earth's climate (Sheridan *et al.* 2016). Stratospheric ozone depletion is also investigated using balloon-borne instrumentation, and both scientific and operational balloon launches are made from the Balloon Inflation Facility located in the Operations Zone.

Astrophysics and Geospace sciences

Most research projects related to astrophysics and geospace sciences are conducted within the Dark Sector, an area which has been set aside with the aim to reduce light and EMI as far as possible within this area.

The Dark Sector Laboratory is home to the South Pole Telescope (SPT). The SPT can detect Cosmic Microwave Background (CMB) Radiation and one of its main aims is to develop understanding of the expansion of the Universe from the time of the 'Big Bang' by identifying galaxy clusters where CMB radiation has been altered by concentrations of dark matter (Carlstrom *et al.* 2011; Reichardt, de Haan & Bleem 2016). The SPT will form part of the Event Horizon Telescope, an array of telescopes distributed worldwide which will synthesise together an earth-sized telescope. The Dark Sector Laboratory also houses the BICEP detectors, which have been operational since 2006. These experiments aim to detect B-mode polarization, with each generation of BICEP increasing the number of detectors and thus the sensitivity to B-mode polarization (Ade *et al.* 2015).

The Martin A. Pomerantz Observatory (MAPO) is also situated inside the Dark Sector. It houses equipment for several research projects, one being the Small Polarimeter Upgrade for DASI (SPUD), which is also designed to measure B-mode polarization.

The IceCube Laboratory, a neutrino detector, is also located in the Dark Sector. IceCube is a form of telescope comprising over 5100 spherical sensors buried in one cubic kilometre of ice. The experiment was built to investigate neutrino properties and the nature of dark matter. Since operation commenced in 2010, IceCube has observed for the first time the astrophysical high-energy neutrino flux, it has measured the cosmic-ray anisotropy for the first time in the southern hemisphere, it has produced the world's best limits on the spin-dependent cross section for weakly interacting dark matter particles, and it has made the most detailed measurements of the properties of light propagation in Antarctic ice (Aartsen *et al.* 2016, 2017).

The Askaryan Radio Array (ARA) is a novel detector under construction in the Dark Sector which aims to discover extreme energy events using sub-surface radio antenna arrays (Allison *et al.* 2015, 2016).

South Pole is part of the Antarctic Gravity Wave Imaging Network (ANGWIN). The aim of ANGWIN is to collect continent-wide gravity wave measurements. At South Pole, measurements are focused on quantifying the temperature signatures of gravity waves deep within the polar vortex (Mehta *et al.* 2017).

A SuperDARN (Dual Auroral Radar Network) array was established at South Pole in the Operations Zone in 2013, and the array helps fill a gap in studies of auroral physics over the Antarctic (Makarevich, Forsythe & Kellerman 2015).

Glaciology

Snow accumulation has been monitored intermittently at the South Pole since the 1957/58 International Geophysical Year (IGY). An extensive network of measurement locations to monitor long-term snow accumulation around the South Pole was established in 1992 (Mosley-Thompson *et al.* 1999). The network of measurement stakes extends out 20 km in all directions from the Pole; it is essential for the research being conducted on snow accumulation that the stakes and the area around the stakes are not disturbed. Data collected between 1958-97 showed net annual accumulation rates increased over this period (Mosley-Thompson *et al.* 1999), which is in contrast to the more recent results reported by Lazzara *et al.* (2012) for the period 1982-2010 showing a decrease.

Ice core drilling is also conducted at South Pole. SPICECORE, which was drilled during the 2014/15 and 2015/16 seasons, will provide records of stable isotopes, aerosols and atmospheric gases dating back ~40,000 years.

Seismology

Seismological data have been collected at the South Pole since the 1957/58 IGY. Conditions at the South Pole are ideal for investigating earthquakes and the structure of the Earth. The energy levels of vibrations from seismic events travelling through the Earth and the polar ice sheet are recorded by seismometers at the South Pole. Because of its position at the Earth's axis of rotation, measurements at the Pole of the energy generated by major earthquakes are not affected by the rotational forces which influence recordings elsewhere on Earth. The South Pole Remote Earth Science and Seismological Observatory (SPRESSO) is situated ~7.5 km from South Pole Station inside the Quiet Sector. The instruments are buried ~300 m deep in the ice recording vibrations of the Earth. Due to the lack of other vibrations in the area which can generate seismic 'noise', the instruments at South Pole can detect vibrations up to four times quieter than other observatories on earth.

Medical research

Due to its isolated environment South Pole Station is ideal for medical research focusing on evaluations of social behaviour and human physiology. Research at the South Pole on sleep patterns has examined the role of total darkness on sleep quality and mood characteristics. Studies have also been undertaken at the South Pole on the effects of isolation and confinement on depression, fatigue, vigor, and anxiety. This research is important for determining the performance capabilities of people working in isolated environments. Research has also been conducted on high altitude illness (Anderson *et al.* 2011).

Historic features

Two Historic Sites and Monuments (HSM) have been formally designated within the Area (HSM No.1 and HSM No.80), and these are described in Section 6(iv).

A marker surrounded by the flags of the original twelve signatory nations of the Antarctic Treaty, known as the Ceremonial South Pole, has been erected by the United States ~150 m grid north of South Pole Station and lies ~200 m from the geographic South Pole. The Ceremonial South Pole commemorates the 1957/58 IGY as well as all expeditions that have reached the South Pole.

Human activities / impacts

Following attainment of the South Pole by the Amundsen and Scott expeditions in 1911/12, no further visits were made to the South Pole until the 1957/58 IGY when a permanent station was established there by the United States. Amundsen-Scott South Pole Station has had several major upgrades, the most recent being the opening of the elevated station in 2008. The main activity at the South Pole is science. The remoteness, scale and types of science being conducted require significant logistical support, including a major ski-way for large transport aircraft, substantial fuel storage and power generation facilities, and accommodation and scientific laboratories. Further information about structures at the South Pole is provided in Section 6(iii).

Non-Governmental Visitors (NGVs) on expeditions or as tourists comprise the other main activity at the South Pole. Over the five-year period between 2006-11 an average of approximately 190 people per season visited the South Pole on private expeditions. The highest number to date was recorded in 2011/12 with 495 visitors, which is almost double the previous high of 266 recorded in 2010/11. This peak was driven by a surge of interest in the South Pole surrounding the centennial years of Amundsen's and Scott's expeditions. Around 230 NGVs were recorded in 2015/16, close to the level seen immediately prior to the centennials.

Approximately 750,000 liters (198,000 gallons) of diesel fuel is stored in tanks at the South Pole, the volume necessary to maintain safe operations at South Pole Station, which is used for power, aircraft, vehicles and heavy machinery. In the winter of 1989 150,000 liters (40,000 gallons) of this fuel leaked into snow at South Pole and was unrecoverable (Wilkniss 1990), which represents the most substantial single contamination event at South Pole to date. Emissions from diesel generators and engines probably account for the majority of contaminants on a continuous basis, although these are dispersed and diluted by persistent winds generally towards the area Grid SW from the station.

6(ii) Restricted and managed zones within the area

This management plan establishes three types of zones within the Area: Operations, Scientific, and Restricted. The management objectives of the different types of zone are set out in Table 1. Maps 1 and 2 show the extent of the Scientific Zone, while Map 3 shows the extent of the Operations Zone and the Restricted Zones.

A new zone or zone type may be considered by the Management Group as the need arises, and those no longer needed may be delisted. Zoning updates should be given particular consideration at the time of Management Plan reviews.

Table 1: Management Zones designated within the Area and their specific objectives.

Management Zones	Specific Zone Objectives	Plan Appendix
Operations Zone	To ensure that science support facilities and related human activities within the Area are contained and managed within a designated area.	-
Scientific Zone	To ensure those planning science or logistics within the Area, and all visitors to the Area, are aware of sites of current or long-term scientific investigation that may be sensitive to disturbance or have sensitive scientific equipment installed, so these may be taken into account during the planning and conduct of activities within the Area. A particular objective of the Scientific Zone is to minimize conflicts between different types of use.	B
Restricted Zone	To restrict access into a particular part of the Area and/or activities within it for a range of reasons, e.g. owing to special scientific values, because of sensitivity, presence of hazards, or to restrict emissions or constructions at a particular site. Access into Restricted Zones should normally be for compelling reasons that cannot be served elsewhere within the Area.	C

The overall policies applying within the zones are outlined in the sections below, while detailed guidelines for the conduct of activities within the Scientific Zone are found in Appendix B and within the Restricted Zones in Appendix C.

Operations Zone

The Operations Zone (Maps 3 and 4) has been established to contain primary human activity in the Area, including science support activities, main station services (e.g. living facilities), ski-way operations, and on-ground support facilities for Non-Governmental Visitors (NGVs).

The boundary of the Operations Zone (Map 3), described clockwise from ARO, extends ~1.85 km Grid SE 110° from ARO, following the southern boundary of the Clean Air Sector. Thence the Operations Zone boundary extends ~3.75 km Grid 243° SW, sharing the boundaries of the Quiet Sector and Downwind Sector. Thence the Operations Zone boundary extends ~1.3 km Grid 202° SSW, following the boundary of the Aircraft Operations Restricted Zone around the Grid southern end of the ski-way. The boundary thence extends ~3.6 km Grid 158° NNE along the Grid western boundary of the Aircraft Operations Restricted Zone, parallel to the ski-way and to its Grid northern end. The Operations Zone boundary continues in the same direction a further ~1.3 km beyond the Grid northern end of the ski-way to the Clear Air Sector boundary. Thence the Operations Zone boundary follows the Clean Air Sector boundary back to ARO ~1.15 km Grid SE (following the Grid 340° line from ARO). The Operations Zone is ~430 ha in area.

The following provisions should be observed within the Operations Zone:

* Waste minimization and management should be considered in the planning, maintenance and decommissioning of facilities within the Operations Zone;

* Alternative energy sources and energy efficiency should be considered in the planning and maintenance of facilities within the Operations Zone;

* Contingency plans for emergencies in the Operations Zone should be developed as appropriate by the National Program(s) operating in the Area;

* The installation of any new structures or modernization of existing structures in the Operations Zone may from time to time be necessary. The National Program(s) operating in the area should review and coordinate any plans for construction or installations to ensure that any impacts on scientific activities and values are minimized. Any change is subject to environmental assessment as required by Article 8 of the Protocol.

* Specific guidelines for Non-Governmental Visitors (NGVs) within the Operations Zone are described in Appendix D of this management plan.

Scientific Zone

The Scientific Zone has been established to avoid mutual interference and / or conflicts between multiple activities, and in particular to protect scientific research from disturbance that could affect results. The Scientific Zone encompasses the majority of the ASMA, with the outer boundary defined by and coincident with the ASMA boundary (Map 1). The inner boundary of the Scientific Zone is defined by, and coincident with, the boundary of the Operations Zone (Maps 2 and 3).

The Scientific Zone is divided into four Sectors – Clean Air, Quiet, Downwind and Dark – to ensure that scientific activities with particular sensitivity are strategically located so the potential for interference is minimized. Of particular concern are interference from sound, light, vibration, contamination from local sources of pollutants, and visual obstruction. Entry to and activities within the Sectors should not interfere with scientific research.

The boundaries of the Sectors and the specific guidelines and operational policies applying within them are defined in Appendix B.

Restricted Zones

Restricted Zones have been designated at sites where access and / or activities need to be restricted to ensure scientific values are maintained, or for reasons of safety. Access to Restricted Zones is prohibited except by authorized personnel for essential scientific, operational or management purposes. There are six Restricted

Zones in the ASMA, all located within or near the Operations Zone (Maps 3 and 4): details of the boundaries and restrictions applying within the Restricted Zones are provided in Appendix C.

The National Program(s) operating in the Area or expedition leaders from other groups should ensure that all visitors to the Area are informed of the boundaries and purposes of the Restricted Zones and the entry restrictions that apply.

6(iii) Structures within and near the Area

The first station at the South Pole was established by the United States in the 1956/57 austral summer for the 1957/58 International Geophysical Year (IGY). A permanent research facility named Amundsen-Scott South Pole Station has been operated at the South Pole continuously by the United States since, although with several major facility replacements and additions. Wind-blown snow accumulation is a perennial problem and without clearance structures can become buried. The first station, now referred to as 'Old Pole', was crushed by the weight of snow and ice and had to be abandoned deep under the surface. More recently, the geodesic dome that replaced 'Old Pole' was removed before it became submerged by ice.

The replacement main building (Map 4), dedicated in 2008, is elevated above ground level in order to minimize snow accumulation, and is referred to as the elevated station. In addition to dining and sleeping accommodation for up to ~150 people, the facilities include a computer laboratory, meeting rooms, lounges, a gym, medical surgery, emergency power plant, and a hydroponic greenhouse. The elevated station has a floor area of ~6000 m² (65,000 ft²). Fuel storage and power generators to support station operations are located in the nearby sub-surface fuel arches.

In the summer South Pole Station accommodates up to a maximum of ~150 scientists and support personnel, while during winter this reduces to ~45 to maintain the station and run experiments. If required, up to ~18 additional personnel can be housed in the nearby 'hypertats' (Map 4). The station is completely isolated between mid-February and late-October, when air and overland support to the Pole are generally not undertaken because conditions are so extreme.

Other structures at the South Pole include the Atmospheric Research Observatory (ARO), located ~450 m Grid NE from the elevated station, air operations facilities and passenger terminal, fuel tanks, antennae, 'Summer camp' buildings, and maintenance offices. Three principal science buildings are located in the Dark Sector, including the IceCube Neutrino Observatory, the Dark Sector Laboratory which houses the South Pole Telescope (SPT), and the Martin A. Pomerantz Observatory (MAPO) where a range of astrophysics and geospace science projects are undertaken.

Two Automatic Weather Stations (AWS) are situated in the Clean Air Sector ~110 km from ARO. AWS 'Henry' is located at Grid north (-89.001° S, -0.391° W) and AWS 'Nico' is located Grid east (-89.0° S, 90.024° E). The AWS were installed in 1993; maintenance access is made by small aircraft, with the most recent in January 2015 when tower heights were increased to account for snow accumulation.

All permanent facilities at the South Pole have been constructed by the United States Antarctic Program. Temporary camp facilities are erected in the summer by Non-Governmental Visitors (NGVs) to the South Pole, and these are located ~1 km Grid north from the elevated station in an area that does not conflict with science or support operations. A second NGV camp typically used by vehicle expeditions is located outside of the Area just over 20 km Grid NW of the South Pole. Each summer, a small temporary building is usually placed by USAP near the aircraft parking area close to the Ceremonial South Pole for use by NGVs as a shelter and for science interpretation.

6(iv) Location of other protected areas within the Area

There are no Antarctic Specially Protected Areas within or near the ASMA.

Two Historic Sites and Monuments have been designated within the Area:

Historic Site and Monument No. 1 (HSM No. 1), located at the South Pole 90°S: Flag mast erected in December 1965 at the South Geographical Pole by the First Argentine Overland Polar Expedition. The precise location or continued existence of the flag mast is not known.

Historic Site and Monument No. 80 (HSM No. 80), located in the vicinity of the South Pole 90°S: Amundsen's tent. The tent was erected at 90°S by the Norwegian group of explorers led by Roald Amundsen on their arrival at the South Pole on 14 December 1911. The tent is assumed to have become buried deep under ice in the vicinity of the South Pole, although the precise location is not known.

7.   General Code of Conduct

7(i) Access to and movement within the Area

Air access to the Area is usually made by ski-equipped fixed-wing aircraft, and visits made by helicopter are rare. Overland access to the Area is made by vehicle, on ski or on foot. For safety reasons, all visitors to the Area should give prior notification of their visit to the National Program(s) operating in the Area. In particular, prior permission is required from the United States Antarctic Program for use of the ski-way. Additional requirements are detailed below for access to the Area by aircraft. Coordination with National Program(s) operating in the Area does not imply any liability of those National Program(s) for any accident or injury incurred at any time during the expedition.

Access to the Area both by air and overland should avoid the Clean Air Sector of the Scientific Zone (Map 1). Access to the Restricted Zones within the Area is generally prohibited except by authorized personnel as detailed below and in Appendix C.

Aircraft access and overflight

The ski-way and associated infrastructure have been established and are maintained by the National Program(s) operating in the Area and are essential to the operations and safety of personnel in the Area. Use of the ski-way and associated infrastructure is therefore restricted to the National Program(s) operating in the Area unless prior permission has been granted by those National Program(s) for aircraft access by other visitors. The entire ski-way and associated aircraft taxi, fuelling and parking areas lie within the Aircraft Operations Restricted Zone (Appendix C), where access is restricted according to the provisions set out below.

Use of wheeled aircraft on the ski-way is prohibited.

All pilots visiting the Area should refer to the latest version of the Antarctic Flight Information Manual (AFIM) for specific details regarding access to the area via aircraft and requirements for prior approval for ski-way use.

Specific restrictions on aircraft access to and overflight within the Clean Air Sector are detailed in the Guidelines for the Scientific Zone (Appendix B).

Aircraft access and overflight by National Programs

- National Program(s) intending to access the Area by aircraft, including for overflight, should coordinate with the National Program(s) operating in the area to ensure there will be no conflicts with ongoing activities.

- Advance planning and communication, consistent with the Antarctic Treaty's Information Exchange requirements, with confirmation at least 24 hours prior to arrival, is necessary to avoid conflicts.

- Pilots approaching the ski-way should notify Amundsen-Scott South Pole Station Communications Center (COMMs) at least 30 minutes prior to landing at the South Pole to allow time to clear the ski-way, and should confirm again their approach 10 minutes before landing.

Aircraft access and overflight by other expeditions

- Approval of ski-way use for an activity not associated with a National Program does not need to include a full safety review of an expedition or its flight plan, and does not imply any liability of those National Program(s) responsible for operating the ski-way for any accident or injury incurred at any time during the expedition.

- Non-Governmental Visitors (NGVs) seeking prior approval to access the Area by aircraft or use the ski-way should refer to the requirements and procedures for approval in the AFIM and contact the appropriate National Authorities.

Ski-way access and crossing

- The ski-way and associated aircraft taxi, refuelling and parking areas are located entirely within the Aircraft Operations Restricted Zone (Appendix C and Map 3) where access is prohibited except by authorized personnel;

- Pilots, logistics personnel, and passengers on aircraft are authorized to move to and from aircraft as necessary and in accordance with operational procedures within the Aircraft Operations Restricted Zone;

- Station personnel and Non-Governmental Visitors are authorized to cross the aircraft taxi area at the Grid northern end of the ski-way at the designated crossing point, located where red beacon lights are installed on the road between the elevated station and Dark Sector science buildings (Map 4);

- Crossing the aircraft taxi area is prohibited when the red beacon lights are flashing, warning that aircraft movements in the vicinity are imminent;

- The ski-way should only be crossed in other areas as absolutely necessary, or as authorized, or in an emergency.

Vehicle access and use

- Vehicles should stay on marked trails to the maximum extent practicable and observe the requirements of the ARO 'No Vehicle' and ARO 'Meteorological Tower' Restricted Zones (Appendix C);

- Vehicles should not be driven within 50 m of the geographic South Pole;

- Vehicles should avoid the Clean Air and Quiet Sectors except as required for essential scientific, operational and management purposes and observe the Guidelines for the Scientific Zone (Appendix B).

Pedestrian access and movement within the Area

- Pedestrians should stay on marked trails to the maximum extent practicable;

- Pedestrians should avoid the Clean Air and Quiet Sectors except as required for essential scientific, operational and management purposes and observe the Guidelines for the Scientific Zone (Appendix B).

Access to buildings and facilities

Access to buildings and facilities in the Area operated by National Program(s) should be made only with permission from the responsible Program. For restrictions on access to specific structures and their surrounding areas, see the Guidelines for the Scientific Zone (Appendix B) and for Restricted Zones (Appendix C).

7(ii) Activities that may be conducted in the Area

All activities in the Area should be conducted in a manner that is in accordance with the requirements of this Management Plan and will preserve the values of the Area to the greatest extent practicable.

Parachute operations from aircraft over or near the ski-way or other infrastructure in the Area should not be conducted unless specific written authorization is provided in advance by the United States Antarctic Program, which operates South Pole Station and the ski-way.

7(iii) Installation, modification, or removal of structures

Care should be exercised when locating and establishing installations to minimize the risk of mutual interference between different scientific activities, or between science and operations activities, and of their impact on the environment. In particular, installation, modification or removal of structures within the Area should be planned taking into account the different objectives of the Scientific Zone Sectors to help ensure that the potential for conflicts is minimized.

Consideration should be given to maximizing the use of existing facilities before new facilities are constructed, and the footprint of all installations should be kept to the minimum practicable. In general, permanent or semi-permanent structures primarily needed for station logistics and operations should be installed within the Operations Zone, unless they are small in size and pose no significant threat to the values of the Area (e.g. an Automatic Weather Station (AWS) or a small radio repeater with minimal associated infrastructure).

All installations should be maintained while operational and removed when no longer necessary. Installations should be identified by the National Program responsible, name of the principal investigator and year of installation. The types of installations and their coordinates should be recorded by the responsible National Program in a facilities database, with this information made available as necessary.

National Programs should exchange information though the Management Group on proposals for new installations in advance of their construction, with the aim of coordinating activities and minimizing the need for new or potentially disruptive or duplicative installations.

7(iv) Field camps

Non-Governmental Visitors (NGVs) to the South Pole should camp at the designated field camp site located within the Operations Zone ~1 km Grid north from the elevated station (Maps 3 and 4).

A small field camp is occasionally established to support NGVs travelling to the South Pole by vehicle, which is located ~300-400 m outside of the boundary of the ASMA, just over 20 km Grid NW from the South Pole.

Field camps shall be maintained while operational and removed when no longer necessary.

7(v) Taking or harmful interference with native flora or fauna

Not applicable.

7(vi) Restrictions on materials and organisms that may be brought into the Area

Long-term research to establish global baselines and trends for atmospheric trace gases and pollutants is being carried out using highly sensitive instruments at ARO. It is important that air sampled remains as pristine as possible. For this reason, those chemicals listed in Table B.1 of the guidelines for the Clean Air Sector (Appendix B), or products and equipment that contain or emit them, are prohibited within the CAS and at ARO. All visitors to the South Pole should, to the maximum extent practicable, seek to avoid bringing those chemicals listed in Table B.1 into the Area.

7(vii) Collection or removal of material found in the Area

Collection and use of snow and ice for water supplies essential to support National Programs or Non-Governmental Visitor (NGV) expeditionary activities is permitted. It is prohibited to damage, remove or destroy any historic artifacts listed as Historic Sites and Monuments under Article 8.4 of Annex V to the Protocol (see Section 6(iv) for a list of designated sites within the Area). All other material found within the Area should only be collected or removed for essential scientific, educational or management purposes and should be limited to the minimum necessary for those needs. Any meteorites taken are to be collected and curated according to accepted scientific standards, and made available for scientific purposes. Material of human origin likely to compromise the values of the Area should be removed unless the impact of removal is likely to be greater than leaving the material in place. If this is the case the appropriate authority should be notified.

7(viii) Waste management

- For the National Program(s) operating in the Area:
    - All waste shall be removed from the Area except human and domestic liquid wastes which may be deposited into deep sewer bulbs beneath the ice surface, or disposed of by other methods in accordance with Annex III of the Protocol;
- For other expeditions to the Area:
    - All wastes, including all human and domestic liquid wastes, shall be removed from the Area.

7(ix) Requirements for reports

Reports of activities in the Area should be maintained by the Management Group to the maximum extent practicable, and made available to all Parties.

In accordance with Article 10 of Annex V to the Protocol, arrangements shall be made for collection and exchange of reports of inspection visits and on any significant changes or damage within the Area.

Tour operators should record their visits to the Area, including the number of visitors, dates, and incidents in the Area, and submit these data in accordance with the procedures for reporting on expeditions adopted by the Antarctic Treaty Parties and the International Association for Antarctica Tour Operators (IAATO).

8. Provisions for the Exchange of Information in Advance of Proposed Activities

In addition to the normal exchange of information by means of the annual national reports to the Parties of the Antarctic Treaty, Scientific Committee on Antarctic Research (SCAR), and Council of Managers of National Antarctic Programs (COMNAP), Parties operating in the Area should exchange information in advance through the Management Group. All National Programs intending to visit or conduct research in the ASMA should contact the National Program(s) operating in the Area sufficiently in advance of the activity to allow for coordination of planned activities with ongoing activities in the Area.

All visitors intending to use the skiway are required to provide advance notification to the United States Antarctic Program, as detailed in Section 7(i) of this Management Plan.

Tour operators and other Non-Governmental Visitors to the Area shall provide advance notification of their visit schedules to National Program(s) operating in the Area.

9. Supporting Documentation

Electronic information

The Management Group has established a website (http://www.southpole.aq) for the purpose of providing additional information and supporting documentation on the environment, science and activities at South Pole, including up-to-date management documents, maps, descriptions and policies.

Because of the steady ice movement at the South Pole there is a need for regular map updates, and the most recent versions are made available at www.southpole.aq/maps.

References

Aartsen, M.G. *et al.* 2016. Search for annihilating dark matter in the Sun with 3 years of IceCube data. *arXiv*: 1612.05949 [astro-ph.HE].

Aartsen, M.G. *et al.* 2017. Neutrinos and Cosmic Rays Observed by IceCube. *arXiv*: 1701.03731 [astro-ph.HE].

Ade, P.A.R. *et al.*2015.BICEP2 / Keck Array V: Measurements of B-mode polarization at degree angular scales and 150GHZ by the Keck Array. *arXiv:*1502.00643v2 [astro-ph.HE].

Allison, P. *et al.* 2015. First Constraints on the Ultra-High Energy Neutrino Flux from a Prototype Station of the Askaryan Radio Array. *arXiv*: 1404.5285v3 [astro-ph.HE].

Allison, P. *et al.* 2016. Performance of two Askaryan Radio Array stations and first results in the search for ultra-high energy neutrinos. *arXiv*: 1507.08991v3 [astro-ph.HE].

Anderson, P.J., Miller, A.D., O'Malley, K.A., Ceridon, M.L., Beck, K.C., Wood, C.M., Wiste, H.J., Mueller, J.J., Johnson, J.B., & Johnson, B.D. 2011. Incidence and Symptoms of High Altitude Illness in South Pole Workers: Antarctic Study of Altitude Physiology (ASAP). *Clinical Medicine Insights: Circulatory, Respiratory and Pulmonary Medicine* **5**: 27–35.

Carlstrom, J.E. *et al.* 2011. The 10 Meter South Pole Telescope. *Publications of the Astronomical Society of the Pacific* **123**: 568-81.

Lazzara, M.A., Keller, L.M., Markle, T. & Gallagher, J. 2012. Fifty-year Amundsen-Scott South Pole station surface climatology. *Atmospheric Research* **118**: 240-59.

Makarevich, R.A., Forsythe, V.V. & Kellerman, A.C. 2015. Electric field control of E region coherent echoes: Evidence from radar observations at the South Pole. *Journal of Geophysical Research: Space Physics* **120**: 2148-65.

Mehta, D., Gerrard, A.J., Ebihara, Y., Weatherwax, A.T. & Lanzerotti, L.J. 2017. Short-period mesospheric gravity waves and their sources at the South Pole. *Atmospheric Chemistry and Physics* **17**: 9141-19.

Mosley-Thompson, E., Paskievitch, J.F., Gow, A.J. & L.G. Thompson. 1990. Late 20th century increase in South Pole snow accumulation. *Journal of Geophysical Research* **104**(D4):3877-86.

Reichardt, C.L., de Haan, T. & Bleem, L.E. 2016. The South Pole Telescope: Unravelling the Mystery of Dark Energy. *International Journal of Modern Physics: Conference Series* **43**: 1-9.

Sheridan, P., Andrews, E., Schmeisser, L., Vasel, B. & Ogren, J. 2016. Aerosol Measurements at South Pole: Climatology and Impact of Local Contamination. *Aerosol and Air Quality Research* **16**: 855-72.

Standing Committee on Antarctic Logistics and Operations (SCALOP) and the Council of Managers of National Antarctic Programs (COMNAP). *Antarctic Flight Information Manual: A Handbook of Antarctic Aeronautical Information*. (See most recent update).

Wilkniss, P. 1990. Fuel spill cleanup in the Antarctic. *Antarctic Journal of the United States* **25**(4): 3-10.

APPENDIX A:

General Environmental Guidelines for the South Pole

The South Pole has unique properties that make it an ideal location for certain types of scientific research. For example, its position remote from human influence makes it ideal for monitoring global background levels of atmospheric constituents. Isolation from light pollution, electromagnetic interference (EMI), sound and vibration, is important for astrophysical research, with the latter two being especially valuable for seismological observations. The thick ice sheet contains a natural record of atmospheric constituents that can be analysed to interpret past climate, and is also an ideal medium for installation of sensitive instruments to detect sub-atomic particles. The position on the Earth's axis of rotation is advantageous for many atmospheric and space science studies. It is important that guidelines are followed so that these qualities may be protected to the fullest extent practicable so that the productivity of the research can be maximized.

Before you travel to the Area:

- Ensure that your planned activities follow the requirements of the Code of Conduct in the Management Plan, the Environmental Guidelines in Appendix A, the specific guidelines that apply within the

Scientific Zone (Appendix B), guidelines for Restricted Zones (Appendix C), and the guidelines for Non-Governmental Visitors in Appendices D and E.

- Plan all activities such as scientific experiments, installation of equipment, travel, camps, fuel handling, and waste management, with the aim of minimizing environmental impacts.
- Ensure that all equipment, supplies and packaging are planned so as to avoid to the maximum extent practicable those compounds listed in Table B.1, Appendix B, as prohibited within the Clean Air Sector (CAS) and at the Atmospheric Research Observatory (ARO).
- Ensure that all equipment, supplies and packaging are planned so as to minimize the amount of waste generated when at South Pole.

Travel and activities within the Area:

- Where practicable, keep to designated or established tracks, and be aware of the site-specific guidelines in Appendices B and C, and in particular avoid the Clean Air and Quiet Sectors and the Restricted Zones, where prior authorization is required for access.
- Vehicles should avoid the ARO 'No Vehicles' and ARO 'Meteorological Tower' Restricted Zones (Appendix C).
- Observe the designated crossing point and beacon warnings on the road between the elevated station and the Dark Sector science buildings.
- Where practicable, vehicles should be parked over a secondary containment unit or a drip tray.
- The ski-way should be marked so it is clearly visible from the air and markers used should be well-secured and durable.

Field camps: location and set up

- Non-Governmental Visitors should use the designated campsite within the Operations Zone when camping within the Area.
- The footprint of the designated campsite should be the minimum size practicable.
- Ensure that equipment and supplies are properly secured at all times to avoid dispersion by wind.

Use of materials and energy:

- Everything taken into the Area should generally be removed to the maximum extent practicable.
- Activities that could result in the dispersal of foreign materials should be avoided (e.g. use of flares) or should be conducted inside a building or tent (e.g. when cutting, sawing or unpacking materials).
- Explosives should not be used within the Area, unless approved by a National Program for use in support of essential scientific or management purposes.
- Where possible, ensure that nothing is left frozen into snow or ice that may ablate out and cause later contamination.
- Use energy systems and modes of travel within the Area that have the least environmental impact as far as practicable, and minimize the use of fossil fuels.

Fuel and chemicals:

- Steps should be taken to prevent the accidental release of fuel or chemicals. For example, regular checks should be made to ensure all fuel valve positions are correctly set, and fuel line couplings are sealed and secure.
- Ensure that spill kits and secondary containment units appropriate to the volume of the substance are available when using chemicals or fuels. Those working with chemicals and fuels should be familiar with their use and with appropriate spill response procedures.
- Chemical and fuel containers should be securely positioned and sealed, particularly when stored outside.
- All fuel drums should be stored with secondary containment.
- Fuel cans with spouts should be used when refuelling generators or vehicles.
- Vehicle oil changes should be carried out with adequate provision for containment and preferably inside.
- Generators and vehicles should be refuelled over drip trays with absorbent spill pads when outside.

Waste and spills:

- Clean up any spills and / or releases to the maximum extent possible and report the location(s) including coordinates, to the appropriate National Program.

APPENDIX B

Guidelines for the Scientific Zone

The Scientific Zone encompasses the majority of the ASMA and is divided into four Sectors – Clean Air, Quiet, Downwind and Dark (Maps 1-4). The Clean Air Sector (CAS) ensures a near-pristine air- and snow-sampling environment for atmospheric and climate systems research. The Quiet Sector is an area where noise and equipment activities are limited to minimize vibration effects on seismological and other vibration-sensitive research. The Downwind Sector provides an area free from obstructions for balloon launches, aircraft operations, and other 'downwind' activities. The Dark Sector aims to provide an area of reduced light pollution and low electromagnetic noise to help facilitate astronomy and astrophysical research. Following are descriptions of the objectives of and special guidelines for activities in each sector of the Scientific Zone.

CLEAN AIR SECTOR

The Clean Air Sector (CAS) is established to preserve the unique conditions that are required for atmospheric research at the South Pole Station. The Earth's atmosphere near the South Pole is remote from worldwide human influence, and a predominant northerly (Grid) wind means the Atmospheric Research Observatory (ARO) is situated upwind of all other facilities more than 90% of the time. These natural conditions allow for nearly continuous measurement of important trace constituents of the atmosphere in a location remote from anthropogenic inputs. The air sampled at the South Pole is representative of the background atmosphere of the planet and may be characterized as the 'cleanest air on Earth'.

Geographic boundaries of the Clean Air Sector

The Clean Air Sector is a wedge-shaped area extending 150 km upwind (grid northeast) of the Atmospheric Research Observatory (ARO) at South Pole Station and the ski-way (Maps 1 to 4). Overland and air access to the CAS are restricted to maintain the scientific value of the Sector. The Clean Air Sector is defined by the following boundaries:

- A line extending 150 km (81 nautical miles) Grid 340° from the SW corner of the ARO building.
- A line extending 150 km (81 nautical miles) Grid 110° from the SW corner of ARO building.
- A semi-circular arc connecting the above two lines, extending ~340 km and maintaining a constant distance of 150 km (81 nautical miles) from the SW corner of the ARO building.

The United States National Oceanic and Atmospheric Administration (NOAA) has conducted many hours of aircraft air pollutant measurements and data show that plumes can be traced for hundreds of miles in stable air. To protect measurements at the ARO and in the snow within the Clean Air Sector it was recommended that aircraft fly above 2000 m (6000 ft) to remain above the boundary layer air and to limit deposition of particles and gas at the snow surface. The 150 km radius was selected as a reasonable buffer distance, although Arctic studies suggest that twice that distance is justifiable.

Aircraft overflight and landing restrictions in the Clean Air Sector

- Aircraft overflight below 2000 m (~6000 ft) and landings within the Clean Air Sector are prohibited except for essential scientific, operational or management purposes (e.g. aviation authority checks (e.g. United States Federal Aviation Authority), scientific missions, aerial photography, emergency flight paths etc.), which must be approved in advance in consultation with the National Program(s) operating within the Area.
- Pilots of any aircraft entering the Clean Air Sector are requested to fly in such a manner that will help to minimize potential contamination (e.g. avoid steep ascents, avoid repeat circling, take the most direct practicable route etc.).

Overland access restrictions to and within the Clean Air Sector

- Activities, structures, and instrumentation located within the Clean Air Sector should not interfere with projects already established, except as specifically authorized by the appropriate National Authority.
- Personnel accessing ARO should follow the marked trail from South Pole Station and observe the requirements of the ARO 'No Vehicle' and ARO 'Meteorological Tower' Restricted Zones (see Appendix C).
- Access to CAS is allowed for scientific purposes such as snow / air sampling. Access may be allowed for occasional or periodic measurement of properties such as snow depth and accumulation, provided this is coordinated in advance to avoid potential conflicts and will not compromise research being carried out within the Sector requiring clean conditions.
- Access to CAS is allowed for snow / trail maintenance, such as occasional excavation of the Met Tower and ARO.
- Access to CAS is allowed for occasional cleaning and maintenance of ski-way visibility markers located along 353° east of grid north (Table D.1).
- All overland access within the CAS should undertake travel and operate in such a manner that will help to minimize potential contamination (e.g. avoid leaving vehicles or machinery running when not necessary, take the most direct practicable route, refuel vehicles outside of the CAS etc.).
- The National Program(s) operating in the Area should document all pedestrian / surface vehicle excursions into the Clean Air Sector.

Additional guidelines for the Clean Air Sector and within ARO

- Access to the roof of the ARO building is restricted. Please contact the United States Antarctic Program (USAP) if access is required for your project. Users of the roof area must note all roof excursions in the Clean Air Sector Log. Structures, objects, etc. are not allowed on the roof of the ARO building in a location that would interfere with air sampling intakes or at a height exceeding 1.3 m (4 ft) above the roof surface, due to interference with the current solar and terrestrial radiation instruments. Do not obstruct the roof hatches with equipment or materials.
- Access to the orange and white meteorological tower and to the snow surface near the tower is restricted. Objects and activity on the tower and on the snow surface in its vicinity (particularly within a distance of approximately three times the tower's height) can interfere with measurements conducted from the tower. Please contact the USAP if access is required.
- Structures should not be placed in a manner that they could cause drifting upwind of, under, or near the ARO building.
- All instrumentation within ARO and the Clean Air Sector must meet the criteria set for current instrumentation as determined by the appropriate National Authority.
- Due to the electromagnetic (EM) sensitivity of solar and thermal atmospheric radiation measurements being conducted at and nearby ARO, the use of EM transmitters near ARO is prohibited except for infrequent but necessary use of handheld radios.
- Any individual or organization wishing to establish an experiment within ARO and/or the Clean Air Sector must coordinate with the National Program(s) operating in the area.

Restricted Chemicals

The use of chemicals listed in Table B.1, or of products and equipment that contain or emit them, is prohibited at ARO and in the CAS (this includes the area beneath the building, the roof of the building, and near the orange and white NOAA meteorological tower, which lies within a Restricted Zone (see Appendix C)). Please contact the National Program(s) operating in the area for help in finding alternatives to their use.

Table B.1 is a partial list of specific chemical substances being monitored at the ARO Clean Air facilities, and may vary over time. The atmospheric concentrations of most are being measured to a precision of parts per trillion, and the measurements are particularly susceptible to contamination from local sources.

Table B.1: Prohibited chemicals at ARO and in the CAS.

Class	Formula	Description	Name	Use
Chlorofluorocarbons (CFCs)	CCl_3F	trichlorofluoromethane	CFC-11	Refrigerants, solvents, foam blowing agents, aerosol propellants, and heat exchange medium (no longer manufactured in the U.S.)
	CCl_2F_2	dichlorodifluoromethane	CFC-12	
	CCl_2FCClF_2	trichlorotrifluoroethane	CFC-113	
Hydrochlorofluorocarbons (HCFCs)	$CHCl_2F$	dichlorofluoromethane	HCFC-21	Refrigerants, solvents, foam blowing agents, aerosol propellants, and heat exchange medium (HCFCs are found in the "blueboard" at South Pole)
	$CHClF_2$	chlorodifluoromethane	HCFC-22	
	CF_3CHClF	chlorotetrafluoroethane	HCFC-124	
	CCl_2FCH_3	dichlorofluoroethane	HCFC-141b	
	$CClF_2CH_3$	chlorodifluoroethane	HCFC-142b	
Hydrofluorocarbons (HFCs)	CF_3CH_2F	tetrafluoroethane	HFC-134a	Refrigerants, foam blowing agents, and aerosol propellants
	CH_3CHF_2	difluoroethane	HFC-152a	
Halons	$CBrClF_2$	bromochlorodifluoromethane	halon-1211	Fire suppression and extinguishing systems (no longer manufactured in the U.S.)
	$CBrF_3$	bromotrifluoromethane	halon-1301	
Chlorocarbons	CH_3Cl	chloromethane	methyl chloride	Solvents, cleaning agents, degreasing agents, and in other less common applications
	CH_2Cl_2	dichloromethane	methylene chloride	
	$CHCl_3$	trichloromethane	chloroform	
	CCl_4	tetrachloromethane	carbon tetrachloride	
	CH_3CCl_3	trichloroethane	methyl chloroform	
	C_2Cl_4	tetrachloroethene	perchloroethene	
Bromocarbons	CH_3Br	bromomethane	methyl bromide	
	CH_2Br_2	dibromomethane	methylene bromide	
	$CHBr_3$	tribromomethane	bromoform	
Idocarbons	CH_3I	iodomethane	methyl iodide	
Others	N_2O	nitrous oxide		Oxidizer
	SF_6	sulfur hexafluoride		Electric transformers

QUIET SECTOR

Sound noise and mechanical equipment activities are limited within the Quiet Sector to minimize vibration effects on seismological and other vibration-sensitive research. The South Pole Remote Earth Science and Seismological Observatory (SPRESSO) was established by the USAP ~7.5 km Grid SE of South Pole Station to provide a remote laboratory for experiments that require a vibration-quiet environment. Seismographic facilities have operated continuously at the South Pole since the 1957/58 International Geophysical Year (IGY).

Geographic Boundaries of the Quiet Sector

The outer boundary of the Quiet Sector is defined by and coincident with the Scientific Zone and ASMA boundary, 20 km from the elevated station (Map 2). The inner boundaries of the Quiet Sector are defined by the Grid 110° line from ARO (shared by the Clean Air Sector) and by the Grid 185° line from the Quiet Sector origin (shared by the Downwind Sector), and by the boundary of the Operations Zone.

Guidelines for the Quiet Sector

- The Quiet Sector is reserved for scientific experiments that require quiet conditions or can operate under stringent quiet conditions. The Quiet Sector has the lowest measured values of seismic noise anywhere on the Earth at periods less than 1 sec. Guidelines for installations and operations within the Quiet Sector are as follows: Activities, structures, and instrumentation located within the Quiet Sector should not produce seismic vibrations at levels greater than the United States Geological Survey (USGS) low noise model (LNM) at periods greater than 1 sec. At periods less than 1 second, levels should not be greater than 12 dB below the LNM (Figure B.1);

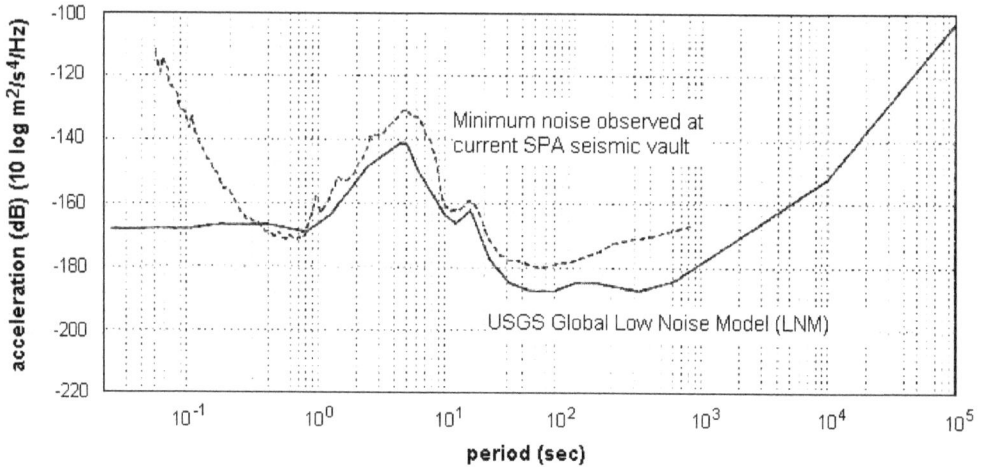

Figure B.1. Noise thresholds for the Quiet Sector. The lowest noise levels achievable at the SPA seismic vault (in 2000) and the USGS LNM based upon quietest noise conditions globally. The seismic band of interest is from 80 Hz to tidal frequencies (<0.001 MHz).

- Structures that potentially may be buffeted by wind, producing extraneous detectable vibrations, should be located below the snow surface;
- All instrumentation located in SPRESSO shall meet the quiet criterion for seismological instrumentation established by National Program(s) operating in the Area;
- All instrumentation located in SPRESSO shall be remotely operable from South Pole Station, particularly during the austral winter;
- Individuals or organizations wishing to establish an experiment within the Quiet Sector shall coordinate in advance with the National Program(s) operating in the Area;
- Transit of motorized vehicles within or across the Quiet Sector for purposes other than support of science or management related to SPRESSO or in the event of an emergency is prohibited except as follows:
  - Access to the Quiet Sector is allowed for trail maintenance, such as when a hard-packed route to SPRESSO is required. This typically requires several passes using heavy equipment to knock down drifts caused by windstorms;
  - Access to the Quiet Sector may be allowed for occasional or periodic measurement of properties such as snow depth and accumulation, provided this is coordinated in advance to avoid potential conflicts and will not compromise seismological and other vibration-sensitive research being carried out within the Sector;
  - Access to the Quiet Sector is allowed for occasional cleaning and maintenance of ski-way visibility markers located along 113° east of grid north (Table D.1).
  - All overland access within the Quiet Sector should undertake travel and operate in such a manner that will help to minimize potential noise and vibration (e.g. avoid leaving vehicles or machinery running when not necessary, take the most direct practicable route, use the lightest

vehicle practicable to meet objectives etc.), and vehicles should avoid operating within 100 m of the SPRESSO facility to the maximum extent practicable.

- National Program(s) operating in the Area may enter the Quiet Sector to remove scientific equipment that is no longer in use, if it will not interfere with other scientific research.

- The National Program(s) operating in the area shall document all travel into the Quiet Sector.

DOWNWIND SECTOR

The Downwind Sector was established to provide an area free from obstructions for balloon launches, aircraft operations, and other activities. Both scientific and operations activities are allowed in the Downwind Sector.

Geographic Boundaries of the Downwind Sector

The outer boundary of the Downwind Sector is defined by and coincident with the Scientific Zone and ASMA boundary, 20 km from the elevated station (Map 2). The inner boundaries of the Downwind Sector are defined by the Grid 185° (shared by the Quiet Sector) and Grid 230° (shared by the Dark Sector) lines from the Downwind Sector origin, and by the boundaries of the Operations Zone and Air Operations Restricted Zone associated with the ski-way.

Guidelines for the Downwind Sector

- Activities in the Downwind Sector should not require any maintenance (e.g. snow removal) and should not otherwise obstruct scientific balloon launches or aircraft operations.

DARK SECTOR

The Dark Sector was established to preserve the conditions of low light pollution and low electromagnetic interference (EMI) at South Pole Station that are important to facilitate many types of astrophysical, astronomical, and aeronomical research.

Geographic Boundaries of the Dark Sector

The outer boundary of the Dark Sector is defined by and coincident with the Scientific Zone and ASMA boundary, 20 km from the elevated station (Map 2). The inner boundaries of the Dark Sector are defined by the Grid 230° line from the Dark Sector origin (shared by the Downwind Sector) and by the Grid 340° line from ARO (shared by the Clean Air Sector), and the boundaries of the Operations Zone and Air Operations Restricted Zone associated with the ski-way.

Guidelines for the Dark Sector

- Science activities in the Dark Sector are restricted to experiments that do not emit light or EMI above levels approved by the National Program(s) operating in the Area.

- Telescopes and other scientific instruments that are light- and / or EMI-sensitive should be located in the Dark Sector.

- Activities both within and outside of the Dark Sector that emit EMI or have potential to obstruct the viewing horizon should take into account their potential to affect scientific values in the Dark Sector. In particular, Electromagnetic Compatibility (EMC) assessments should be undertaken as necessary in advance of the activity to minimize conflicts between uses, including between operational sources of EMI and scientific instruments, and to minimize impacts on science within the Dark Sector whilst allowing for essential operational needs. This applies also to scientific or operational projects operating from aircraft or satellite platforms that require active radio frequency (RF) emissions (e.g. imaging radars such as Synthetic Aperture Radar etc.) or light-emitting instruments (e.g. LiDAR).

- To help protect sensitive scientific observations within the Dark Sector from unnecessary EMI, pilots of any aircraft entering the Dark Sector are requested to minimize, to the extent that is safe and practicable, operational radio frequency (RF) emissions (e.g. navigation radars or other active navaids, altimeters, radar sounders, ice radars, radio communications etc.) while flying within the Sector.

APPENDIX C

Guidelines for Restricted Zones

Six sites within the Area are designated Restricted Zones (Maps 3 and 4), which are defined by boundaries and access policies as follows:

1. Aircraft Operations Restricted Zone:

Description:	An area of ~60 ha within the Operations Zone that includes the ski-way, aircraft taxi, refuelling and aircraft parking areas (Maps 3 and 4).
Boundary:	The boundary is defined as the perimeter of the aircraft operational areas as shown on Map 4.
Access requirements:	Access to the zone is prohibited except by authorized personnel, with access policies applying specifically to pilots, logistics personnel and aircraft passengers and more generally to all other personnel at South Pole detailed in Section 7(i) of this Management Plan.

2. Old Pole Station Restricted Zone:

Description:	An area of ~70 ha within the Dark Sector of the Scientific Zone that includes the former 1957 South Pole station site and the immediate surrounding area up to ~300 – 500 m (Maps 3 and 4).
Boundary:	Clockwise from the SE corner of the zone, the boundary extends Grid NW 1.2 km into the Dark Sector from the Operations Zone, extending past and immediately Grid NE of the Dark Sector Laboratory. Thence the boundary proceeds 1 m Grid NE to a point 200 m from the Clean Air Sector, thence extends for 750 m parallel to and 200 m from the Clean Air Sector to the Operations Zone. The boundary thence shares the Operations Zone boundary for a distance of 440 m Grid SW to the SE corner of the zone.
Access requirements:	Access to the Old Pole Station Restricted Zone is prohibited except by authorized personnel for essential scientific, operational or management purposes. While remediation work has been undertaken at the site, there remain possible subsurface hazards such as voids or structures that should be avoided.

3. ARO 'No Vehicle' Restricted Zone

Description:	A semi-circular area of 0.5 ha within the Operations Zone extending 50 m (150 ft) downwind (Grid SW) of the SW corner of the ARO building (Map 4).
Boundary:	Defined as the perimeter of the semi-circle described above. Part of the southeastern boundary is shared by the Antenna Field Restricted Zone.
Access requirements:	Vehicle access is prohibited without prior authorization by NOAA and the United States Antarctic Program. All vehicles approaching ARO should use the marked trail and park at the 'turnaround' at the edge of the Restricted Zone where a sign states "No Vehicles Beyond This Point". The purpose of the Restricted Zone is to avoid vehicle emissions close to the ARO facility where sensitive atmospheric monitoring instruments are installed.

4. ARO 'Meteorological Tower' Restricted Zone

Description:	A circular area of 0.13 ha within the Operations Zone surrounding the ARO Meteorological Tower extending 20 m (~66 ft) from the center of the facility (Map 4).
Boundary:	Defined as the perimeter of a 20 m circle surrounding the ARO Meteorological Tower.
Access requirements:	Vehicle and pedestrian access is prohibited without prior authorization by NOAA and the United States Antarctic Program. Vehicles and pedestrians should avoid the Grid NW half of the Restricted Zone to prevent disturbance to the snow surface in this area, where albedo is being monitored.

5. Antenna Field Restricted Zone:

Description:	An area within the Operations Zone of ~25 ha located Grid SE of the road to ARO (Map 4).
Boundary:	Clockwise from ARO, the northeastern boundary shares the Grid 110° boundary of the CAS for ~550 m from ARO, thence extends 300 m Grid due south, thence 550 m Grid due west, thence 440 m Grid NW towards but 20 m short of the ARO road, and thence 200 m eastward to the ARO 'No Vehicle' Restricted Zone, and shares this boundary a further ~50 m to the CAS.
Access requirements:	Access to the zone is prohibited except by personnel authorized by the National Program(s) operating in the Area. Personnel operating within the zone should avoid disturbing the area where stakes are installed to measure snow accumulation (Map 4), and should be aware of other sensitive scientific or antenna infrastructure.

6. Communications Restricted Zone:

Description:	An area within the Operations Zone of ~9.5 ha, the center of which is located ~1 km Grid SW of the elevated station (Map 4).
Boundary:	Defined as a rectangle of width ~185 m and of length 510 m.
Access requirements:	Access to the zone is prohibited except by personnel authorized by the National Program(s) operating in the Area.

APPENDIX D

General Guidelines for Non-Governmental Visitors to the South Pole

The South Pole receives a number of visitors associated with Non-Governmental expeditions each austral summer, most of whom are supported by private companies that provide transportation, guides and other logistics. Guidelines have been established to improve coordination between the National Program(s) operating in the Area and Non-Governmental Visitors (NGVs) to the South Pole. The purpose of this Appendix is to inform NGVs about on-site resources, expectations, and hazards at the South Pole, while Appendix E provides specific guidance on overland approach routes.

All visitors to the South Pole shall comply with the Protocol on Environmental Protection to the Antarctic Treaty and with their respective national policies governing activities in Antarctica.

- For the purpose of this management plan, 'Non-Governmental Visitors' includes all individuals or organizations that are not sponsored by a National Antarctic Program.

- Amundsen-Scott South Pole Station is operated by the United States Antarctic Program (USAP), which is not authorized to provide support for NGVs except in an emergency.

- NGVs approaching overland should be aware of ski-way visibility markers located at various distances from the geographic South Pole in four directions around the station (Table D.1). All markers are four feet high by eight feet wide, except the 1 mile markers which are eight feet by eight feet, and mounted four feet off the snow surface.

Table D.1 Visibility markers located around South Pole Station.

Direction	Marker 1		Marker 2		Marker 3		Marker 4		Marker 5		Marker 6	
(° E of grid N)	miles	km	miles	km	miles	km	miles	km	miles	km	miles	km
113	0.5	0.8	1	1.6	1.5	2.6	2	3.2	-		-	
204	0.5	0.8	1	1.6	1.5	2.6	2	3.2	3	4.8	4	6.4
270	0.75	1.2	1	1.6	2	3.2	3	4.8	-		-	
353	0.5	0.8	1	1.6	1.5	2.6	2	3.2	-		-	

- NGVs that intend to fly aircraft into the Area or land on the ski-way shall obtain prior approval to do so from the National Program(s) that operates the ski-way and associated air traffic control. If prior approval is granted, NGV pilots should refer to and follow guidance in the Antarctic Flight Information Manual (AFIM) and information provided by the National Program(s) operating in the Area.

- NGVs shall not conduct a parachute operation from an aircraft and no pilot in command of an NGV aircraft may allow a parachute operation to be conducted from that aircraft over or near the ski-way or other infrastructure in the Area, unless specific written authorization is provided in advance by the National Program(s) that operates the ski-way and associated air traffic control.

- No access to email, telephones, or radios will be provided except as authorized by the appropriate National Program.

- The ideal timeframe for visits to the South Pole Station is on Sunday from 13:00 to 17:00 South Pole Station Time [00:00 to 04:00 GMT/UTC]. This time period is recommended to minimize disruption to station science and operations. Services and access to the station at other times are highly unlikely.

- NGVs are required to be self-sufficient in their provision of transport, camping, food, communications and any other support required by their expedition.

- Within the Operations Zone, NGVs should keep within the designated NGV camping and parking areas (Map 4), or the area immediately surrounding the Ceremonial South Pole and geographic South Pole markers and to move between these sites by a direct line or by following the designated vehicle route, unless otherwise authorized by the National Program(s) operating in the area. The reason for this provision is to ensure hazardous sites such as the Old Pole Station and Aircraft Operations Restricted Zones and areas of scientific research with highly sensitive instrumentation are avoided, as well as to ensure safety in other areas where heavy vehicles or machinery may be operating, often in conditions of poor visibility.

- The designated NGV camping area within the Operations Zone has been selected for the following reasons: it is located near the NGV aircraft parking areas, it is close to medical or other emergency services (if needed), it does not usually interfere with vehicle traffic or USAP aircraft operations, and it is away from most hazardous areas, communications facilities and sensitive scientific instrumentation.

- To avoid disruption of official USAP activities, all South Pole Station buildings and operation and science areas are off limits to NGV personnel except when guided by an individual designated by the USAP or when within the aforementioned areas.

- In the event of an aircraft or medical emergency in the Area, NGVs shall notify Amundsen-Scott South Pole Station Communications Center (COMMS) immediately. Station staff shall notify the on-site U.S. National Science Foundation (NSF) Representative and other personnel as necessary.

- Amundsen-Scott South Pole Station staff shall record NGV arrivals and departures, and make this information available to Antarctic Treaty Party members upon request.

APPENDIX E

Guidelines for Non-Governmental Visitor Overland Approach to the South Pole

No approach to the South Pole through the Clean Air Sector

- The Clean Air Sector extends 150 km Grid NE from the South Pole, its point of origin being the Grid SW corner of the Atmospheric Research Observatory (ARO) building at Amundsen-Scott South Pole Station. The Sector lies between a line extending Grid 340° and a line extending Grid 110° from ARO, which equates approximately to the area lying between W020° and E110° (clockwise).
- Do not approach the South Pole through the Clean Air Sector (see maps).

Approach from Grid northwest – west (Ronne Ice Shelf / Hercules Inlet etc.)

- The Grid northwest and west approach to South Pole lies between W020° and W110°.
- When approaching from this region, on reaching the ASMA boundary at 20 km from the South Pole, proceed directly to 'West Waypoint' at S89° 59.0' W016° 00.0', where a sign is located. Do not enter the Clean Air Sector (see maps).
- Call Amundsen-Scott South Pole Station at least 24 hours in advance of your anticipated arrival at the South Pole to advise of your position and plans. Be prepared to wait and camp if necessary until advised that it is safe to proceed.
- On reaching 'West Waypoint', proceed on the marked trail (bamboo canes and flags) 0.88 km to the non-governmental visitor campsite and thence 1 km to the South Pole (2016), taking care not to cross into the Clean Air Sector, the boundary of which is marked by flags.

Approach from Grid south – southwest (McMurdo / Ross Ice Shelf)

- The Grid south and southwest approach to South Pole lies between E110° and W110°.
- When approaching from this region, on reaching the ASMA boundary at 20 km from the South Pole, proceed directly to the 'Pole Turn 1 Waypoint' at S89° 55.29' W132° 00.0' where a sign is located, following the South Pole Traverse route on the W132° meridian as far as practicable. Do not enter the Quiet Sector (see maps).
- Call Amundsen-Scott South Pole Station at least 24 hours in advance of your anticipated arrival at the South Pole to advise of your position and plans.
- On reaching 'Pole Turn 1 Waypoint', which is 8.8 km from the South Pole (2016), again Stop & Call Amundsen-Scott South Pole Station before proceeding further. Be prepared to camp at 'Pole Turn 1 Waypoint' until advised by Amundsen-Scott South Pole Station it is safe to proceed. This is to ensure safety because the approach route lies close to the skiway.
- From 'Pole Turn 1 Waypoint' proceed 5.2 km on the South Pole Traverse route to the skiway threshold where a sign is located at the Grid south end of the skiway.
- From the skiway threshold, proceed parallel to and along the **Grid west** side of the skiway (i.e. the left side on approach towards the Pole) for 4 km, maintaining a distance of at least 30 m from the line of flags marking the edge of the skiway. Proceed to the road between the elevated station and Dark Sector science buildings, where a red beacon light is installed at the designated crossing point of the aircraft taxi area at the Grid north end of the skiway (see Map 6).
- Do not enter onto the skiway other than at the designated crossing point or in an emergency.
- Do not cross the aircraft taxi area at the end of the skiway if the red beacon light is flashing.
- When safe to do so, cross the aircraft taxi area at the designated crossing point and proceed towards the South Pole markers and onward to the non-governmental visitor campsite.

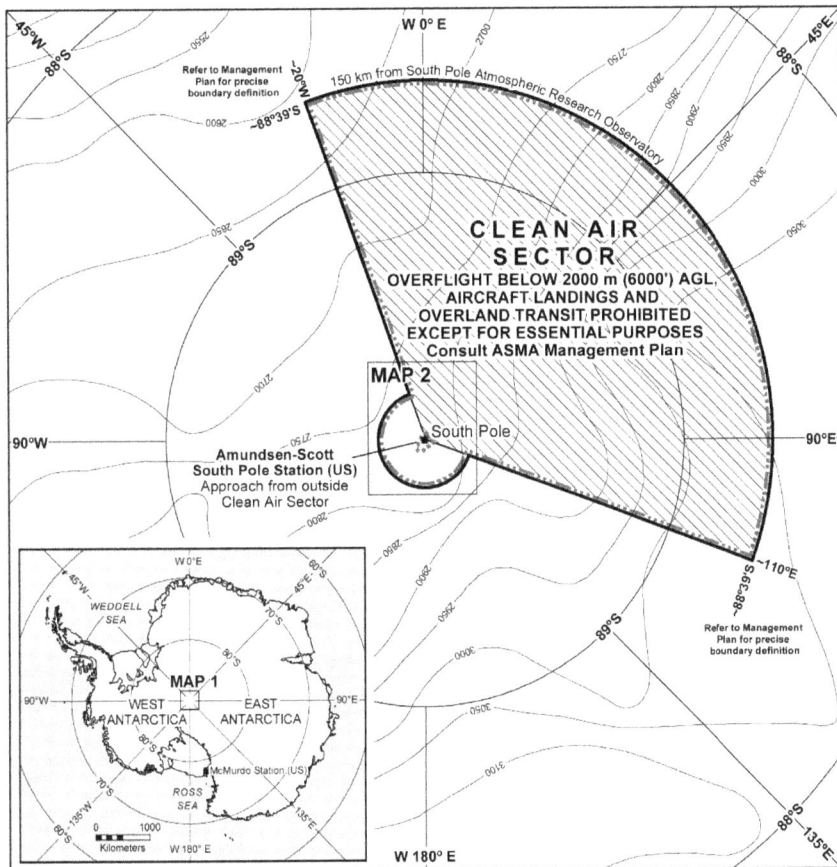

Map 1: ASMA No. 5 - South Pole - Location and topography

23 Mar 2017 (Map ID 10069.010.07)
United States Antarctic Program
Environmental Research & Assessment

Contour (50 m)   ASMA Boundary   Clean Air Sector
Permanent ice   Scientific Zone   Station building

Projection: Polar Stereographic;
Spheroid and horizontal datum: WGS84;
Data source: Coast & topography SCAR ADD (v.6 - 2012);
ASMA boundary, Zones & Sectors: ERA (Feb 2017)

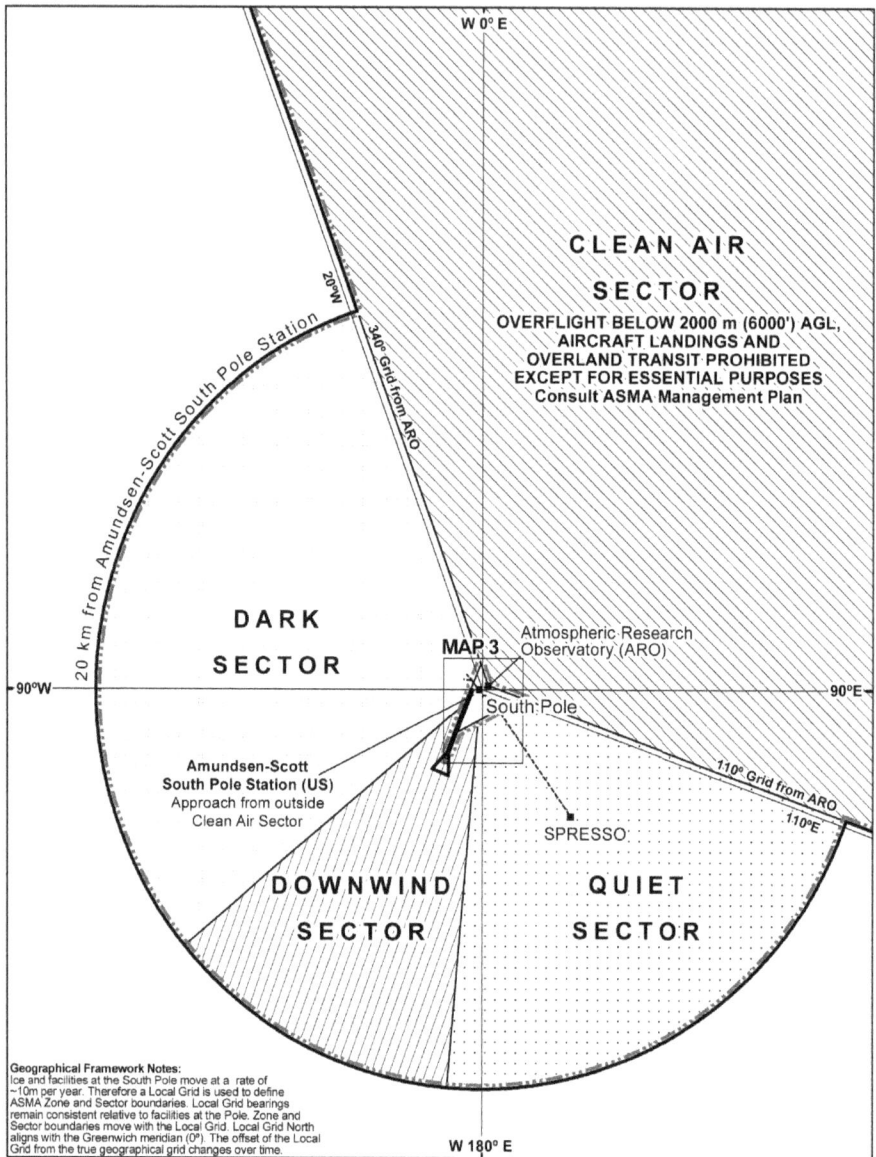

Map 2: ASMA No. 5 - South Pole - Management Zones and Sectors

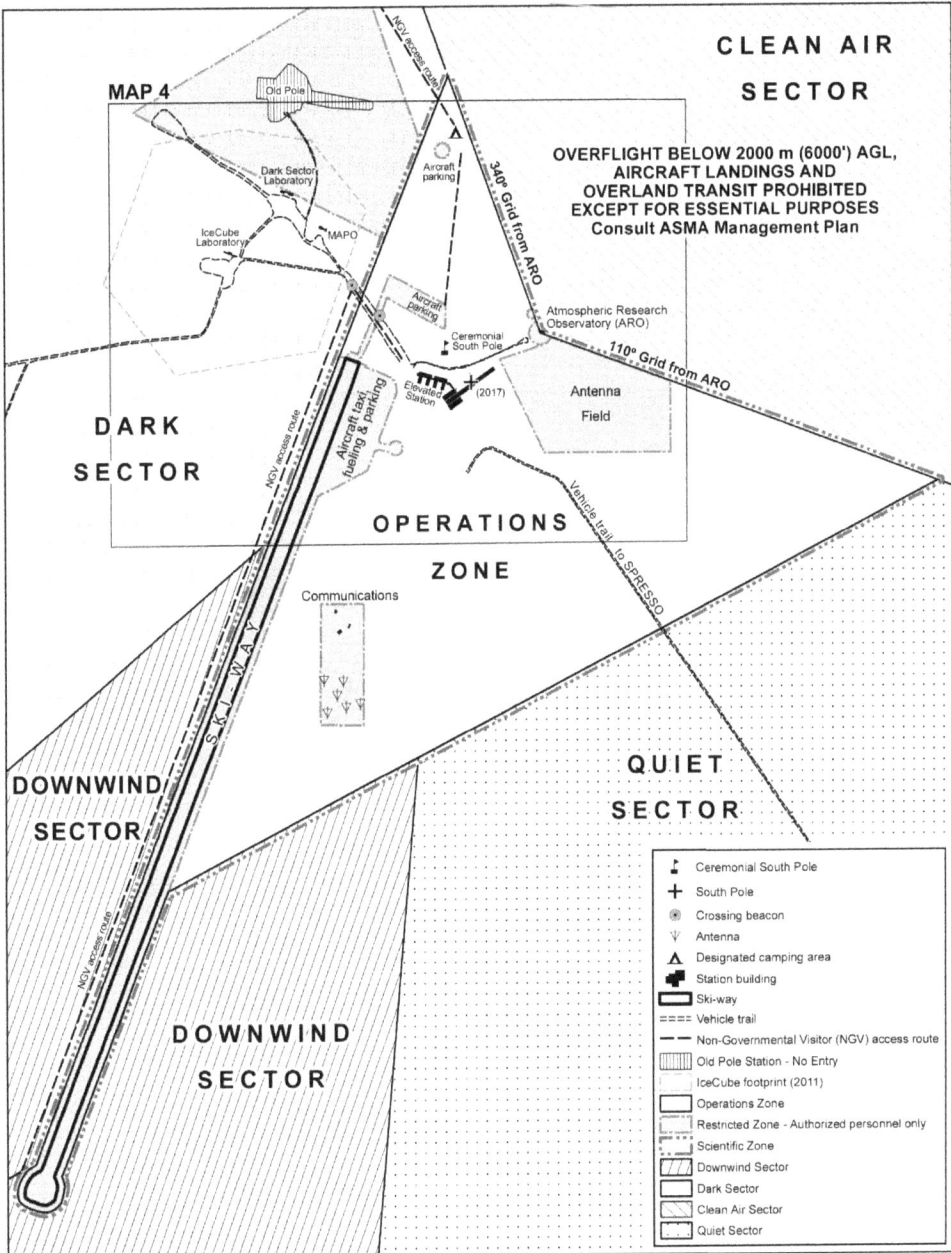

CLEAN AIR SECTOR

OVERFLIGHT BELOW 2000 m (6000') AGL,
AIRCRAFT LANDINGS AND
OVERLAND TRANSIT PROHIBITED
EXCEPT FOR ESSENTIAL PURPOSES
Consult ASMA Management Plan

MAP 4

DARK SECTOR

OPERATIONS ZONE

Communications

DOWNWIND SECTOR

QUIET SECTOR

DOWNWIND SECTOR

Legend:

- ♪ Ceremonial South Pole
- + South Pole
- ⊛ Crossing beacon
- Ѱ Antenna
- △ Designated camping area
- ▟ Station building
- ▭ Ski-way
- ==== Vehicle trail
- – – – Non-Governmental Visitor (NGV) access route
- Old Pole Station - No Entry
- IceCube footprint (2011)
- Operations Zone
- Restricted Zone - Authorized personnel only
- Scientific Zone
- Downwind Sector
- Dark Sector
- Clean Air Sector
- Quiet Sector

Map 3: ASMA No. 5 - Amundsen-Scott South Pole Station - Operations Zone

03 Apr 2017 (Map ID. 10069.013.12)
United States Antarctic Program
Environmental Research & Assessment

0   500   1000
Meters

GRID

Projection: Polar Stereographic.
Spheroid and horizontal datum: WGS84.
Data source: Infrastructure: ASC CAD Survey (2016/17),
Zones & Sectors: ERA (Feb 2017).

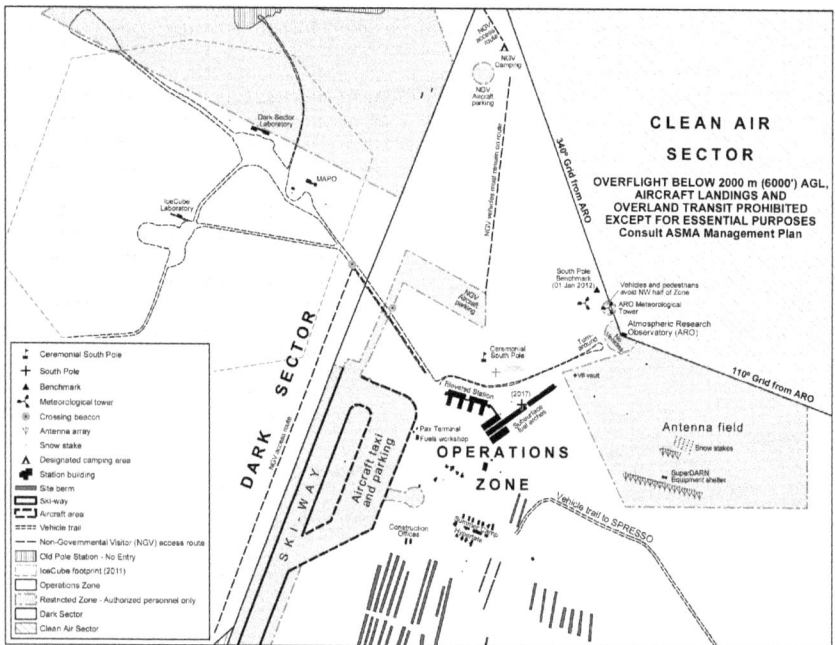

Map 4: ASMA No. 5 - Amundsen-Scott South Pole Station

170

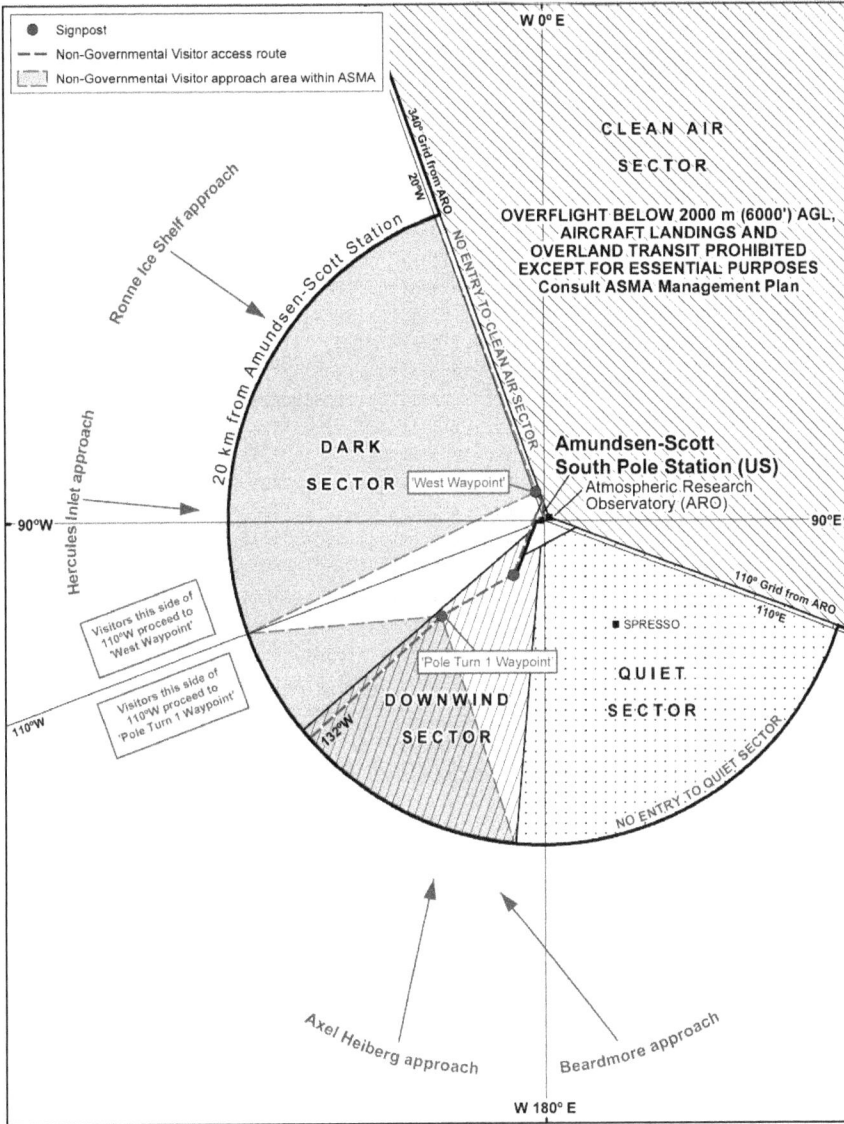

Map 5: South Pole Non-Governmental Visitor approach routes & guidelines overview

Legend:
- Signpost
- Non-Governmental Visitor access route
- Non-Governmental Visitor approach area within ASMA

CLEAN AIR SECTOR

OVERFLIGHT BELOW 2000 m (6000') AGL, AIRCRAFT LANDINGS AND OVERLAND TRANSIT PROHIBITED EXCEPT FOR ESSENTIAL PURPOSES Consult ASMA Management Plan

Ronne Ice Shelf approach

20 km from Amundsen-Scott Station

Hercules Inlet approach

DARK SECTOR

'West Waypoint'

Amundsen-Scott South Pole Station (US)
Atmospheric Research Observatory (ARO)

Visitors this side of 110°W proceed to 'West Waypoint'

Visitors this side of 110°W proceed to 'Pole Turn 1 Waypoint'

'Pole Turn 1 Waypoint'

DOWNWIND SECTOR

QUIET SECTOR

SPRESSO

NO ENTRY TO QUIET SECTOR

Axel Heiberg approach

Beardmore approach

W 180° E

23 May 2017 (Map ID: 10069.006.10)
United States Antarctic Program
Environmental Research & Assessment

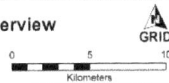

- ASMA Boundary
- Operations Zone
- Downwind Sector
- Dark Sector
- Clean Air Sector
- Quiet Sector
- Station building
- Ski-way

GRID

Kilometers
0   5   10

Projection: Polar Stereographic;
Spheroid and horizontal datum: WGS84;
Data source: Infrastructure: ASC CAD Survey (2016/17);
ASMA boundary, Zones & Sectors, NGV access guidance: ERA (Feb 2017)

171

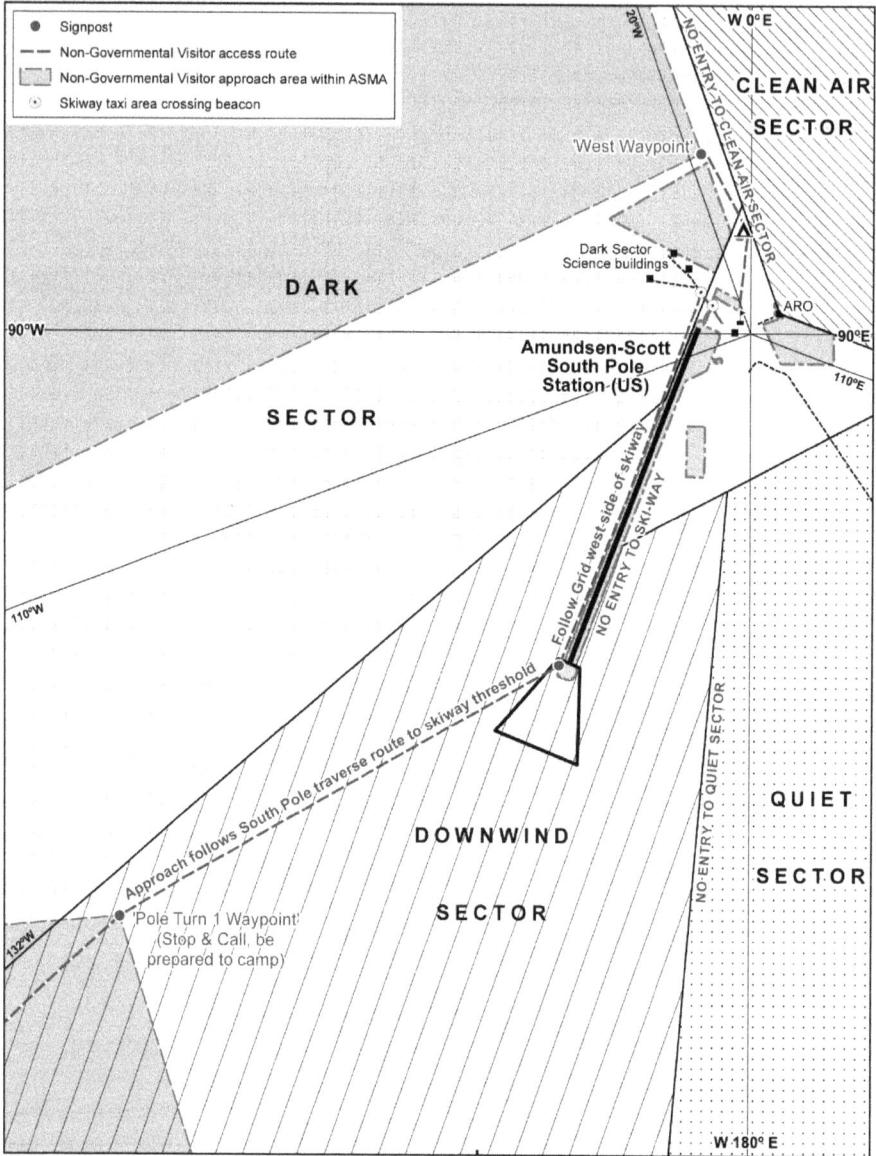

Map 6: ASMA No. 5 - South Pole Non-Governmental Visitor approach guidelines

03 Apr 2017 (Map ID: 10069.007.11)
United States Antarctic Program
Environmental Research & Assessment

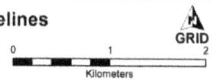

PART III

Opening and Closing Addresses and Reports

1. Opening and Closing Addresses

Remarks by H.E. Zhang Gaoli
Vice Premier of the State Council of the People's Republic of China
At the Opening Session of the 40th Antarctic Treaty Consultative Meeting

Beijing, 23 May 2017

Uphold the Principles of the Antarctic Treaty
And Seek Sustainable Development of Mankind

Chair,

Delegates,

Ladies and Gentlemen,

Friends,

Good morning. May is a time of vigor and vitality in Beijing. Several days ago, we held a successful Belt and Road Forum for International Cooperation. Now we are here for the 40th Antarctic Treaty Consultative Meeting and the 20th Meeting of the Antarctic Committee for Environmental Protection. China attaches great importance to the governance and development of Antarctica. President Xi Jinping noted that Antarctic scientific expedition, a lofty cause that advances human well-being, is of great significance. China stands ready to work with the international community for better knowledge, protection and use of Antarctica. Premier Li Keqiang emphasized that expeditions in polar areas should go deeper, wider and progress at higher levels. This is the first time for China to host the consultative meeting since it acceded to the *Antarctic Treaty* in 1983 and became a Consultative Party in 1985. On behalf of the Chinese government, I would like to offer warm congratulations on the opening of the meeting and extend a sincere welcome to all the distinguished guests present here.

Given its unique geographical location and ecological environment, Antarctica has high importance for global climate change and human survival and development. The *Antarctic Treaty* signed in 1959 established a legal framework for Antarctic governance and opened a new chapter of cooperation in this area. The Antarctic Treaty Consultative Meetings then formulated the *Protocol on Environmental Protection to the Antarctic Treaty* and other conventions and protocols, and adopted relevant decisions and measures. In the past 58 years, the legal system concerning Antarctic governance has been continuously improved. A better governance mechanism has provided a solid legal basis for human knowledge, protection and use of Antarctica. Under the regulation and guidance of the Antarctic Treaty System and following the basic principles, namely Antarctica for peaceful purposes only, freedom of scientific investigation and international cooperation, countries have worked together and produced fruitful results on scientific investigation, environmental protection, logistical support and Antarctic inspections.

The Antarctic Treaty Consultative Meeting is a major platform for discussion and decision-making on Antarctic affairs and the most important multilateral mechanism for Antarctic governance. We should continue to make good use of it, carry forward the spirit of the *Antarctic Treaty* and make unremitting efforts to create a better future for the development of Antarctica and the world at large.

Ladies and Gentlemen,

Friends,

As a Consultative Party to the *Antarctic Treaty*, China has been committed to the purposes and principles of the Treaty and the overall interest of the international community, actively fulfilling its rights and obligations under the Treaty, steadily promoting the cause of Antarctica and contributing wisdom and strength to the human knowledge, protection and use of Antarctica.

China is an important participant in Antarctic governance. Following its accession to the Treaty in 1983, China has taken an active part in Antarctic affairs and contributed to the building of a peaceful, stable and green Antarctic order. China has acceded to almost all important international conventions and instruments in this area. Having joined major international mechanisms on Antarctica, including the Antarctic Treaty Consultative Meeting and its Committee for Environmental Protection and the Commission for the Conservation of Antarctic Marine Living Resources, China has participated in projects and cooperation within relevant frameworks. China advocates equal-footed consultation and joint decision-making on the basis of the Antarctic Treaty System and calls for a more inclusive, rational and cooperative Antarctic governance system. China attaches importance to Antarctica inspections. We have carried out inspections on our own and given support to inspections by other countries in an effort to ensure effective implementation of the purposes and objectives of the *Antarctic Treaty*.

China is a strong contributor to exploration of Antarctica. In order to explore the unknown, acquire knowledge and push for peaceful use of Antarctica, China has pursued research on frontier issues of science and environment in Antarctica for its protection and use. Since 1984, China has successfully conducted 33 scientific expeditions, with more than 5,000 entries made to the Antarctic region, further expanding exploration activities. Chinese scientists have carried out systematic geographical, climatic, glaciological, geological, ecological and oceanographic studies and made important findings. China has also made significant headway in scientific expedition, capacity building and scientific research and application, carried out bilateral and multilateral research cooperation and made due contribution to the exploration of Antarctica and the progress of Antarctic sciences.

China is an active force for Antarctic environmental protection. Protection of Antarctica is one of the principles upheld by the Chinese government. Since 1997, as required by the *Protocol on Environmental Protection to the Antarctic Treaty*, China has submitted 69 assessment reports on the environmental impact of activities in Antarctica, which cover multiple areas such as Antarctic field activities, facility construction and scientific studies. China gives great importance to the protection and management of Antarctica and has proposed on its own or with other countries three special protected areas, one special managed area and two historical sites, and taken a constructive part in the discussions on marine protected areas of Antarctica. To further promote environmental protection in Antarctica, China, the United States and Australia, among others, jointly made the "green expedition" initiative to the Committee for Environmental Protection for promoting cleaner and more environment-friendly expeditions in the future.

Ladies and Gentlemen,

Friends,

"All good principles should adapt to changing times." The future of Antarctica bears on the survival and development of mankind. A peaceful, stable, green and sustainable Antarctica is in the interest of everyone on our planet. And it is what we promise our children and grandchildren. In the spirit of peace, cooperation and rule of law enshrined in the *Antarctic Treaty*, we should make concerted efforts to create a bright future in the development of Antarctica and promote world peace and prosperity. To that end, I would like to make a five-point proposal.

First, we should insist on the peaceful use of Antarctica and work to build a community of shared future for mankind in the region. Peace and stability in Antarctica is a fundamental prerequisite for all human activities in the region. We must bear in mind at all times and abide by the principle stipulated in the *Antarctic Treaty* that "Antarctica shall continue forever to be used exclusively for peaceful purposes", and maintain and promote lasting peace, security and stability in the region, which is in the overall interest of all countries and the international community. We need to further enhance political mutual trust and assume a stronger sense of shared responsibility. In the spirit of inclusiveness and mutual learning, we should step up dialogue and consultation and work out joint plans and solutions to tackle the issues and challenges facing the region, and ensure the sound and inclusive development of Antarctica.

Second, we should uphold the Antarctic Treaty System and improve the rules-based mode of governance of Antarctica. Since the current governance mechanism based on the Antarctic Treaty System functions well, we parties should continue to advance governance of Antarctica within the framework of the Antarctic Treaty System. The principle of consensus should be upheld and the Antarctic Treaty Consultative Meetings should fully play its role in decision making and coordination. In view of changing circumstances in Antarctica, improvements are needed in the formulation of international rules in all fields related to the region. Attention should also be directed to the formulation of such rules beyond the Antarctic Treaty System, in order to enhance the coordination and interaction between the Antarctic governance institutions and other relevant international mechanisms.

Third, we should stress equal-footed consultation and mutual benefit and turn Antarctica into a new arena for international cooperation. The Antarctic Treaty was founded upon cooperation and developed through cooperation. In future governance of Antarctica, we should continue to pursue equal-footed consultation and cooperative governance, make use of the existing bilateral and multilateral institutions and platforms, and further expand the area and scope of Antarctic cooperation. We need to promote long-term, steady, and institutionalized international cooperation through concrete cooperation projects. The level of cooperation should be uplifted and cooperation outcomes should be well implemented in order to deliver needed services and support. This is meant to ensure effective governance of Antarctica and to bring benefits of the protection and utilization of Antarctica to all mankind.

Fourth, we should uphold freedom of scientific investigation in Antarctica and further consolidate the scientific foundation for its protection and utilization. Man's knowledge about Antarctica is still very limited. Scientific investigation in Antarctica is an important field in which we can uncover the secrets of nature and search for new space of development. Today's efforts in this field will have a far-reaching impact on the future. We should continue to adhere to the principle of freedom of scientific investigation stipulated in the *Antarctic Treaty*. We need to focus our efforts on making better plans for scientific research and building stronger capacity of investigation and learning. Our priority should be the research on the impact of global climate and environmental change and in the emerging and frontier fields. We need to learn more about the law of change and development in Antarctica, base our decision making on scientific grounds while making right decisions to promote scientific advancement, thus cementing scientific foundation for the protection and utilization of Antarctica.

Fifth, we should protect the natural environment of Antarctica and ensure the ecological balance and sustainable development in the region. With its unique climate and geography, Antarctica has a delicate natural environment and ecological system that is vulnerable to external impacts. While exploring and utilizing Antarctica, we should seek appropriate and coordinated methods to address issues in all areas of Antarctica and pay great attention to the protection of its ecological system. There needs to be a proper balance between the protection and utilization of Antarctica, in order to achieve green and sustainable development of the continent and unleash its potential and value in promoting scientific progress, economic growth and cultural sustainability for mankind.

To conclude, I wish the 40th Antarctic Treaty Consultative Meeting and the 20th Meeting of the Committee for Environmental Protection a full success. I hope all the guests will have a pleasant stay in Beijing.

Thank you.

2. Reports by Depositaries and Observers

Report of the Depositary Government of the Antarctic Treaty and its Protocol in accordance with Recommendation XIII-2

Information Paper submitted by the United States

This report covers events with respect to the Antarctic Treaty and the Protocol on Environmental Protection to the Antarctic Treaty.

In the past year, there have been no accessions to the Treaty. There was one accession to the Protocol in the past year: Malaysia deposited its instrument of accession to the Protocol on August 15, 2016. In addition, Switzerland deposited its instrument of ratification of the Protocol, including Annex V thereto, on May 2, 2017. The Protocol and Annex V enter into force for Switzerland on June 1, 2017. There are fifty-three (53) Parties to the Treaty and thirty-nine (39) Parties to the Protocol.

The following countries have provided notification that they have designated the persons so noted as Arbitrators in accordance with Article 2(1) of the Schedule to the Protocol:

Bulgaria	Mrs. Guenka Beleva	30 July 2004
Chile	Amb. María Teresa Infante	June 2005
	Amb. Jorge Berguño	June 2005
	Dr. Francisco Orrego	June 2005
Finland	Amb. Holger Bertil Rotkirch	14 June 2006
India	Prof. Upendra Baxi	6 October 2004
	Mr. Ajai Saxena	6 October 2004
	Dr. N. Khare	6 October 2004
Japan	Judge Shunji Yanai	18 July 2008
Rep. of Korea	Prof. Park Ki Gab	21 October 2008
United States	Prof. Daniel Bodansky	1 May 2008
	Mr. David Colson	1 May 2008

Lists of Parties to the Treaty, to the Protocol, and of Recommendations/Measures and their approvals are attached.

Date of most recent action: October 13, 2015

The Antarctic Treaty

Done: Washington; December 1, 1959

Entry into force: June 23, 1961

In accordance with Article XIII, the Treaty was subject to ratification by the signatory States and is open for accession by any State which is a Member of the United Nations, or by any other State which may be invited to accede to the Treaty with the consent of all the Contracting Parties whose representatives are entitled to participate in the meetings provided for under Article IX of the Treaty; instruments of ratification and instruments of accession shall be deposited with the Government of the United States of America. Upon the deposit of instruments of ratification by all the signatory States, the Treaty entered into force for those States and for States which had deposited instruments of accession to the Treaty. Thereafter, the Treaty enters into force for any acceding State upon deposit of its instrument of accession.

Legend: (no mark) = ratification; a = accession; d = succession; w = withdrawal or equivalent action

Participant	Signature	Consent to be bound		Other Action	Notes
Argentina	December 1, 1959	June 23, 1961			
Australia	December 1, 1959	June 23, 1961			
Austria		August 25, 1987	a		
Belarus		December 27, 2006	a		
Belgium	December 1, 1959	July 26, 1960			
Brazil		May 16, 1975	a		
Bulgaria		September 11, 1978	a		
Canada		May 4, 1988	a		
Chile	December 1, 1959	June 23, 1961			
China		June 8, 1983	a		
Colombia		January 31, 1989	a		
Cuba		August 16, 1984	a		
Czech Republic		January 1, 1993	d		1
Denmark		May 20, 1965	a		
Ecuador		September 15, 1987	a		
Estonia		May 17, 2001	a		
Finland		May 15, 1984	a		
France	December 1, 1959	September 16, 1960			
Germany		February 5, 1979	a		2
Greece		January 8, 1987	a		
Guatemala		July 31, 1991	a		
Hungary		January 27, 1984	a		
Iceland		October 13, 2015	a		

India		August 19, 1983	a		
Italy		March 18, 1981	a		
Japan	December 1, 1959	August 4, 1960			
Kazakhstan		January 27, 2015	a		
Korea (DPRK)		January 21, 1987	a		
Korea (ROK)		November 28, 1986	a		
Malaysia		October 31, 2011	a		
Monaco		May 31, 2008	a		
Mongolia		March 23, 2015	a		
Netherlands		March 30, 1967	a		3
New Zealand	December 1, 1959	November 1, 1960			
Norway	December 1, 1959	August 24, 1960			
Pakistan		March 1, 2012	a		
Papua New Guinea		March 16, 1981	d		4
Peru		April 10, 1981	a		
Poland		June 8, 1961	a		
Portugal		January 29, 2010	a		
Romania		September 15, 1971	a		5
Russian Federation	December 1, 1959	November 2, 1960			6
Slovak Republic		January 1, 1993	d		7
South Africa	December 1, 1959	June 21, 1960			
Spain		March 31, 1982	a		
Sweden		April 24, 1984	a		
Switzerland		November 15, 1990	a		
Turkey		January 24, 1996	a		
Ukraine		October 28, 1992	a		
United Kingdom	December 1, 1959	May 31, 1960			
United States	December 1, 1959	August 18, 1960			
Uruguay		January 11, 1980	a		8
Venezuela		March 24, 1999	a		

---

[1] Effective date of succession by the Czech Republic. Czechoslovakia deposited an instrument of accession to the Treaty on June 14, 1962. On December 31, 1992, at midnight, Czechoslovakia ceased to exist and was succeeded by two separate and independent states, the Czech Republic and the Slovak Republic.

[2] The Embassy of the Federal Republic of Germany in Washington transmitted to the Department of State a diplomatic note, dated October 2, 1990, which reads as follows:

"The Embassy of the Federal Republic of Germany presents its compliments to the Department of State and has the honor to inform the Government of the United States of America as the depositary Government of the Antarctic Treaty that, t[h]rough the accession of the German Democratic Republic to the Federal Republic of Germany with effect from October 3, 1990, the two German states will unite to form one sovereign state which, as a contracting party to the Antarctic Treaty, will remain bound by the provisions of the Treaty and subject to those recommendations adopted at the 15 consultative meetings which the Federal Republic of Germany has approved. From the date of German unity, the Federal Republic of Germany will act under the designation of "Germany" within the framework of the [A]ntarctic system.

"The Embassy would be grateful if the Government of the United States of America could inform all contracting parties to the Antarctic Treaty of the contents of this note.

"The Embassy of the Federal Republic of Germany avails itself of this opportunity to renew to the Department of State the assurances of its highest consideration."

Prior to unification, on November 19, 1974, the German Democratic Republic deposited an instrument of accession to the Treaty, accompanied by a declaration, a Department of State English translation of which reads as follows:

"The German Democratic Republic takes the view that Article XIII, paragraph 1, of the Treaty is inconsistent with the principle that all States which are guided in their policies by the purposes and principles of the United Nations Charter have the right to become parties to treaties which affect the interest of all States."

Subsequently, on February 5, 1979, the Federal Republic of Germany deposited an instrument of accession to the Treaty accompanied by a statement, an English translation of which, provided by the Embassy of the Federal Republic of Germany, reads as follows:

"My dear Mr. Secretary,

"In connection with the deposit today of the instrument of accession to the Antarctic Treaty signed in Washington December 1, 1959, I have the honor to state on behalf of the Federal Republic of Germany that with effect from the day on which the treaty enters into force for the Federal Republic of Germany it will also apply to Berlin (West) subject to the rights and responsibilities of the French Republic, the United Kingdom of Great Britain and Northern Ireland and the United States of America including those relating to disarmament and demilitarization.

"Accept, Excellency, the expression of my highest consideration."

[3] The instrument of accession to the Treaty by the Netherlands states that the accession is for the Kingdom in Europe, Suriname and the Netherlands Antilles.

Suriname became an independent state on November 25, 1975.

The Royal Netherlands Embassy in Washington transmitted to the Department of State a diplomatic note, dated January 9, 1986, which reads as follows:

"The Royal Netherlands Embassy presents its compliments to the Department of State and has the honor to request the Department's attention for the following with respect to the Department's capacity of depositary of [the Antarctic Treaty].

"Effective January 1, 1986 the island of Aruba – formerly part of the Netherlands Antilles – obtained internal autonomy as a country within the Kingdom of The Netherlands. Consequently the Kingdom of The Netherlands as of January 1, 1986 consists of three countries, to wit: the Netherlands proper, the Netherlands Antilles and Aruba.

"Since the abovementioned event concerns only a change in internal constitutional relations within the Kingdom of The Netherlands, and as the Kingdom as such, under international law, will remain the subject with which treaties are concluded, the aforementioned change will have no consequences in international law with regard to treaties concluded by the Kingdom, the application of which (treaties) were extended to the Netherlands Antilles, including Aruba.

"These treaties, thus, will remain applicable for Aruba in its new status as autonomous country within the Kingdom of The Netherlands effective January 1, 1986.

"Consequently the [Antarctic Treaty] to which the Kingdom of the Netherlands is a Party, and which [has] been extended to the Netherlands Antilles will as of January 1, 1986 apply to all three countries of the Kingdom of The Netherlands.

"The Embassy would appreciate if the other Parties concerned would be notified of the above.

"The Royal Netherlands Embassy avails itself of this opportunity to renew to the Department of State the assurance of its highest consideration."

The Royal Netherlands Embassy in Washington transmitted to the Department of State a diplomatic note, dated October 6, 2010, which reads in pertinent part as follows:

"The Kingdom of the Netherlands currently consists of three parts: the Netherlands, the Netherlands Antilles and Aruba. The Netherlands Antilles consists of the islands of Curaçao, Sint Maarten, Bonaire, Sint Eustatius and Saba.

"With effect from 10 October 2010, the Netherlands Antilles will cease to exist as a part of the Kingdom of the Netherlands. From that date onwards, the Kingdom will consist of four parts: the Netherlands, Aruba, Curaçao and Sint Maarten. Curaçao and Sint Maarten will enjoy internal self-government within the Kingdom, as Aruba and, up to 10 October 2010, the Netherlands Antilles do.

"These changes constitute a modification of the internal constitutional relations within the Kingdom of the Netherlands. The Kingdom of the Netherlands will accordingly remain the subject of international law with which agreements are concluded. The modification of the structure of the Kingdom will therefore not affect the validity of the international agreements ratified by the Kingdom for the Netherlands Antilles; these agreements will continue to apply to Curaçao and Sint Maarten.

"The other islands that have until now formed part of the Netherlands Antilles – Bonaire, Sint Eustatius and Saba – will become part of the Netherlands, thus constituting 'the Caribbean part of the Netherlands'. The agreements that now apply to the Netherlands Antilles will also continue to apply to these islands; however, the Government of the Netherlands will now be responsible for implementing these agreements."

[4] Date of deposit of notification of succession by Papua New Guinea; effective September 16, 1975, the date of its independence.

[5] The instrument of accession to the Treaty by Romania was accompanied by a note of the Ambassador of the Socialist Republic of Romania to the United States of America, dated September 15, 1971, which reads as follows:

"Dear Mr. Secretary:

"Submitting the instrument of adhesion of the Socialist Republic of Romania to the Antarctic Treaty, signed at Washington on December 1, 1959, I have the honor to inform you of the following:

'The Council of State of the Socialist Republic of Romania states that the provisions of the first paragraph of the article XIII of the Antarctic Treaty are not in accordance with the principle according to which the multilateral treaties whose object and purposes are concerning the international community, as a whole, should be opened for universal participation.'

"I am kindly requesting you, Mr. Secretary, to forward to all parties concerned the text of the Romanian instrument of adhesion to the Antarctic Treaty, as well as the text of this letter containing the above mentioned statement of the Romanian Government.

"I avail myself of this opportunity to renew to you, Mr. Secretary, the assurances of my highest consideration."

Copies of the Ambassador's letter and the Romanian instrument of accession to the Treaty were transmitted to the Antarctic Treaty parties by the Secretary of State's circular note dated October 1, 1971.

[6] The Treaty was signed and ratified by the former Union of Soviet Socialist Republics. By a note dated January 13, 1992, the Russian Federation informed the United States Government that it "continues to perform the rights and fulfil the obligations following from the international agreements signed by the Union of Soviet Socialist Republics."

[7] Effective date of succession by the Slovak Republic. Czechoslovakia deposited an instrument of accession to the Treaty on June 14, 1962. On December 31, 1992, at midnight, Czechoslovakia ceased to exist and was succeeded by two separate and independent states, the Czech Republic and the Slovak Republic.

[8] The instrument of accession to the Treaty by Uruguay was accompanied by a declaration, a Department of State English translation of which reads as follows:

"The Government of the Oriental Republic of Uruguay considers that, through its accession to the Antarctic Treaty signed at Washington (United States of America) on December 1, 1959, it helps to affirm the principles of using Antarctica exclusively for peaceful purposes, of prohibiting any nuclear explosion or radioactive waste disposal in this area, of freedom of scientific research in Antarctica in the service of mankind, and of international cooperation to achieve these objectives, which are established in said Treaty. "Within the context of these principles Uruguay proposes, through a procedure based on the principle of legal equality, the establishment of a general and definitive statute on Antarctica in which, respecting the rights of States as recognized in international law, the interests of all States involved and of the international community as a whole would be considered equitably.

"The decision of the Uruguayan Government to accede to the Antarctic Treaty is based not only on the interest which, like all members of the international community, Uruguay has in Antarctica, but also on a special, direct, and substantial interest which arises from its geographic location, from the fact that its Atlantic coastline faces the continent of Antarctica, from the resultant influence upon its climate, ecology, and marine biology, from the historic bonds which date back to the first expeditions which ventured to explore that continent and its waters, and also from the obligations assumed in conformity with the Inter- American Treaty of Reciprocal Assistance which includes a portion of Antarctic territory in the zone described in Article 4, by virtue of which Uruguay shares the responsibility of defending the region.

"In communicating its decision to accede to the Antarctic Treaty, the Government of the Oriental Republic of Uruguay declares that it reserves its rights in Antarctica in accordance with international law."

PROTOCOL ON ENVIRONMENTAL PROTECTION TO THE ANTARCTIC TREATY
Signed at Madrid on October 4, 1991*

State	Date of Signature	Date deposit of Ratification, Acceptance (A) or Approval (AA)	Date deposit of Accession	Date of entry into force	Date Acceptance ANNEX V**	Date of entry into force of Annex V
CONSULTATIVE PARTIES						
Argentina	Oct. 4, 1991	Oct. 28, 1993 [3]		Jan. 14, 1998	Sept. 8, 2000 (A) / Aug. 4, 1995 (B)	May 24, 2002
Australia	Oct. 4, 1991	Apr. 6, 1994		Jan. 14, 1998	Apr. 6, 1994 (A) / June 7, 1995 (B)	May 24, 2002
Belgium	Oct. 4, 1991	Apr. 26, 1996		Jan. 14, 1998	Apr. 26, 1996 (A) / Oct. 23, 2000 (B)	May 24, 2002
Brazil	Oct. 4, 1991	Aug. 15, 1995		Jan. 14, 1998	May 20, 1998 (B)	May 24, 2002
Bulgaria			April 21, 1998	May 21, 1998	May 5, 1999 (AB)	May 24, 2002
Chile	Oct. 4, 1991	Jan. 11, 1995		Jan. 14, 1998	Mar. 25, 1998 (B)	May 24, 2002
China	Oct. 4, 1991	Aug. 2, 1994		Jan. 14, 1998	Jan. 26, 1995 (AB)	May 24, 2002
Czech Rep.[1,2]	Jan. 1, 1993	Aug. 25, 2004 [4]		Sept. 24, 2004	Apr. 23, 2014 (B)	
Ecuador	Oct. 4, 1991	Jan. 4, 1993		Jan. 14, 1998	May 11, 2001 (A) / Nov. 15, 2001 (B)	May 24, 2002
Finland	Oct. 4, 1991	Nov. 1, 1996 (A)		Jan. 14, 1998	Nov. 1, 1996 (A) / Apr. 2, 1997 (B)	May 24, 2002
France	Oct. 4, 1991	Feb. 5, 1993 (AA)		Jan. 14, 1998	Apr. 26, 1995 (B) / Nov. 18, 1998 (A)	May 24, 2002
Germany	Oct. 4, 1991	Nov. 25, 1994		Jan. 14, 1998	Nov. 25, 1994 (A) / Sept. 1, 1998 (B)	May 24, 2002
India	July 2, 1992	Apr. 26, 1996		Jan. 14, 1998	May 24, 2002 (B)	May 24, 2002
Italy	Oct. 4, 1991	Mar. 31, 1995		Jan. 14, 1998	May 31, 1995 (A) / Feb. 11, 1998 (B)	May 24, 2002
Japan	Sept. 29, 1992	Dec. 15, 1997 (A)		Jan. 14, 1998	Dec. 15, 1997 (AB)	May 24, 2002
Korea, Rep. of	July 2, 1992	Jan. 2, 1996		Jan. 14, 1998	June 5, 1996 (B)	May 24, 2002
Netherlands	Oct. 4, 1991	Apr. 14, 1994 (A) [6]		Jan. 14, 1998	Mar. 18, 1998 (B)	May 24, 2002
New Zealand	Oct. 4, 1991	Dec. 22, 1994		Jan. 14, 1998	Oct. 21, 1992 (A)	May 24, 2002
Norway	Oct. 4, 1991	June 16, 1993		Jan. 14, 1998	Oct. 13, 1993 (B)	May 24, 2002
Peru	Oct. 4, 1991	Mar. 8, 1993		Jan. 14, 1998	Mar. 8, 1993 (A) / Mar. 17, 1999 (B)	May 24, 2002
Poland	Oct. 4, 1991	Nov. 1, 1995		Jan. 14, 1998	Sept. 20, 1995 (B)	May 24, 2002
Russian Federation	Oct. 4, 1991	Aug. 6, 1997		Jan. 14, 1998	June 19, 2001 (B)	May 24, 2002
South Africa	Oct. 4, 1991	Aug. 3, 1995		Jan. 14, 1998	June 14, 1995 (B)	May 24, 2002
Spain	Oct. 4, 1991	July 1, 1992		Jan. 14, 1998	Dec. 8, 1993 (A) / Feb. 18, 2000 (B)	May 24, 2002
Sweden	Oct. 4, 1991	Mar. 30, 1994		Jan. 14, 1998	Mar. 30, 1994 (A) / Apr. 7, 1994 (B)	May 24, 2002
Ukraine			May 25, 2001	June 24, 2001	May 25, 2001 (A)	May 24, 2002
United Kingdom	Oct. 4, 1991	Apr. 25, 1995 [5]		Jan. 14, 1998	May 21, 1996 (B)	May 24, 2002

189

United States	Oct. 4, 1991	Apr. 17, 1997	Jan. 14, 1998	Apr. 17, 1997 (A)	May 24, 2002
Uruguay	Oct. 4, 1991	Jan. 11, 1995	Jan. 14, 1998	May 6, 1998 (B) May 15, 1995 (B)	May 24, 2002

** The following denotes date relating either
to acceptance of Annex V or approval of Recommendation XVI-10
(A) Acceptance of Annex V   (B) Approval of Recommendation XVI-10

State	Date of Signature	Ratification Acceptance or Approval	Date deposit of Accession	Date of entry into force	Date Acceptance ANNEX V**	Date of entry into force of Annex V
NON-CONSULTATIVE PARTIES						
Austria	Oct. 4, 1991					
Belarus			July 16, 2008	Aug. 15, 2008		
Canada	Oct. 4, 1991	Nov. 13, 2003		Dec. 13, 2003		
Colombia	Oct. 4, 1991					
Cuba						
Denmark	July 2, 1992					
Estonia						
Greece	Oct. 4, 1991	May 23, 1995		Jan. 14, 1998		
Guatemala						
Hungary	Oct. 4, 1991					
Korea, DPR of	Oct. 4, 1991					
Malaysia			Aug. 15, 2016	Sept. 14, 2016		
Monaco			July 1, 2009	July 31, 2009		
Pakistan			Mar. 1, 2012	Mar. 31, 2012		
Papua New Guinea						
Portugal			Sept. 10, 2014	Oct. 10, 2014		
Romania	Oct. 4, 1991	Feb. 3, 2003		Mar. 5, 2003	Feb. 3, 2003	Mar. 5, 2003
Slovak Rep.[1,2]	Jan. 1, 1993					
Switzerland	Oct. 4, 1991	May 2, 2017 [7]		June 1, 2017	May 2, 2017	June 1, 2017
Turkey						
Venezuela			Aug. 1, 2014	Aug. 31, 2014		

* Signed at Madrid on October 4, 1991; thereafter at Washington until October 3, 1992.
The Protocol will enter into force initially on the thirtieth day following the date of deposit of instruments of ratification, acceptance, approval or accession by all States which were Antarctic Treaty Consultative Parties at the date on which this Protocol was adopted. (Article 23)

**Adopted at Bonn on October 17, 1991 at XVIth Antarctic Consultative Meeting.

1. Signed for Czech & Slovak Federal Republic on Oct. 2, 1992 - Czechoslovakia accepts the jurisdiction of the International Court of Justice and Arbitral Tribunal for the settlement of disputes according to Article 19, paragraph 1. On December 31, 1992, at midnight, Czechoslovakia ceased to exist and was succeeded by two separate and independent states, the Czech Republic and the Slovak Republic.

2. Effective date of succession in respect of signature by Czechoslovakia which is subject to ratification by the Czech Republic and the Slovak Republic.

3. Accompanied by declaration, with informal translation provided by the Embassy of Argentina, which reads as follows: "The Argentine Republic

declares that in as much as the Protocol to the Antarctic Treaty on the Protection of the Environment is a Complementary Agreement of the Antarctic Treaty and that its Article 4 fully respects what has been stated in Article IV, Subsection 1, Paragraph A) of said Treaty, none of its stipulations should be interpreted or be applied as affecting its rights, based on legal titles, acts of possession, contiguity and geological continuity in the region South of parallel 60, in which it has proclaimed and maintained its sovereignty."

4. Accompanied by declaration, with informal translation provided by the Embassy of the Czech Republic, which reads as follows: "The Czech Republic accepts the jurisdiction of the International Court of Justice and of the Arbitral Tribunal under Article 19, paragraph 1, of the Protocol on Environmental Protection to the Antarctic Treaty, done at Madrid on October 4, 1991."

5. Ratification on behalf of the United Kingdom of Great Britain and Northern Ireland, the Bailiwick of Jersey, the Bailiwick of Guernsey, the Isle of Man, Anguilla, Bermuda, the British Antarctic Territory, Cayman Islands, Falkland Islands, Montserrat, St. Helena and Dependencies, South Georgia and the South Sandwich Islands, Turks and Caicos Islands and British Virgin Islands.

6. Acceptance is for the Kingdom in Europe. At the time of its acceptance, the Kingdom of the Netherlands stated that it chooses both means for the settlement of disputes mentioned in Article 19, paragraph 1 of the Protocol, i.e. the International Court of Justice and the Arbitral Tribunal.

On October 27, 2004, the Kingdom of the Netherlands deposited an instrument, dated October 15, 2004, declaring that the Kingdom of the Netherlands accepts the Protocol for the Netherlands Antilles with a statement confirming that it chooses both means for the settlement of disputes mentioned in Article 19, paragraph 1 of the Protocol.

The Royal Netherlands Embassy in Washington transmitted to the Department of State a diplomatic note, dated October 6, 2010, which reads in pertinent part as follows:

"The Kingdom of the Netherlands currently consists of three parts: the Netherlands, the Netherlands Antilles and Aruba. The Netherlands Antilles consists of the islands of Curaçao, Sint Maarten, Bonaire, Sint Eustatius and Saba.
"With effect from 10 October 2010, the Netherlands Antilles will cease to exist as a part of the Kingdom of the Netherlands. From that date onwards, the Kingdom will consist of four parts: the Netherlands, Aruba, Curaçao and Sint Maarten. Curaçao and Sint Maarten will enjoy internal self-government within the Kingdom, as Aruba and, up to 10 October 2010, the Netherlands Antilles do.
"These changes constitute a modification of the internal constitutional relations within the Kingdom of the Netherlands. The Kingdom of the Netherlands will accordingly remain the subject of international law with which agreements are concluded. The modification of the structure of the Kingdom will therefore not affect the validity of the international agreements ratified by the Kingdom for the Netherlands Antilles; these agreements will continue to apply to Curaçao and Sint Maarten.
"The other islands that have until now formed part of the Netherlands Antilles – Bonaire, Sint Eustatius and Saba – will become part of the Netherlands, thus constituting 'the Caribbean part of the Netherlands'. The agreements that now apply to the Netherlands Antilles will also continue to apply to these islands; however, the Government of the Netherlands will now be responsible for implementing these agreements."

On October 16, 2014, the Kingdom of the Netherlands deposited an instrument, dated September 3, 2014, declaring that the Kingdom of the Netherlands approves Annex V to the Protocol for the Caribbean part of the Netherlands (the islands of Bonaire, Sint Eustatius and Saba).

7. Included in the instrument of ratification of the Protocol by Switzerland is a declaration, in accordance with Article 19, paragraph 1 of the Protocol, that Switzerland chooses the International Court of Justice for the settlement of disputes.

Department of State,
Washington, May 2, 2017.

Approval, as notified to the Government of the United States of America, of measures
relating to the furtherance of the principles and objectives of the Antarctic Treaty

	16 Recommendations adopted at First Meeting (Canberra 1961)	10 Recommendations adopted at Second Meeting (Buenos Aires 1962)	11 Recommendations adopted at Third Meeting (Brussels 1964)	28 Recommendations adopted at Fourth Meeting (Santiago 1966)	9 Recommendations adopted at Fifth Meeting (Paris 1968)	15 Recommendations adopted at Sixth Meeting (Tokyo 1970)
	Approved	Approved	Approved	Approved	Approved	Approved
Argentina	ALL	ALL	ALL	ALL	ALL	ALL
Australia	ALL	ALL	ALL	ALL	ALL	ALL
Belgium	ALL	ALL	ALL	ALL	ALL	ALL
Brazil (1983)+	ALL	ALL	ALL	ALL	ALL	ALL except 10
Bulgaria (1998)+						
Chile	ALL	ALL	ALL	ALL	ALL	ALL
China (1985)+	ALL	ALL	ALL	ALL	ALL	ALL except 10
Czech Rep. (2014)+	1-7, 10 & 12-14	1, 4, 6-7 & 9	1-2, 7 & 11	14-15, 18, 21-24 & 27	2-3 & 6-7	1, 3, 5-7 & 10-13
Ecuador (1990)+						
Finland (1989)+						
France	ALL	ALL	ALL	ALL	ALL	ALL
Germany (1981)+	ALL	ALL	ALL except 8	ALL except 16-19	ALL except 6	ALL except 9
India (1983)+	ALL	ALL	ALL except 8***	ALL except 18	ALL	ALL except 9 & 10
Italy (1987)+	ALL	ALL	ALL	ALL	ALL	ALL
Japan	ALL	ALL	ALL	ALL	ALL	ALL
Korea, Rep. (1989)+	ALL	ALL	ALL	ALL	ALL	ALL
Netherlands (1990)+	ALL except 11 & 15	ALL except 3, 5, 8 & 10	ALL except 3, 4, 6 & 9	ALL except 20, 25, 26 & 28	ALL except 1, 8 & 9	ALL except 15
New Zealand	ALL	ALL	ALL	ALL	ALL	ALL
Norway	ALL	ALL	ALL	ALL	ALL	ALL
Peru (1989)+	ALL	ALL	ALL	ALL	ALL	ALL
Poland (1977)+	ALL	ALL	ALL	ALL	ALL	ALL
Russia	ALL	ALL	ALL	ALL	ALL	ALL
South Africa	ALL	ALL	ALL	ALL	ALL	ALL
Spain (1988)+	ALL	ALL	ALL	ALL	ALL	ALL
Sweden (1988)+						
U.K.	ALL	ALL	ALL	ALL	ALL	ALL
Uruguay (1985)+	ALL	ALL	ALL	ALL	ALL	ALL
U.S.A.	ALL	ALL	ALL	ALL	ALL	ALL

* IV-6, IV-10, IV-12, and V-5 terminated by VIII-2
*** Accepted as interim guideline
+ Year attained Consultative Status. Acceptance by that State required to bring into force Recommendations or Measures of meetings from that year forward.

Approval, as notified to the Government of the United States of America, of measures
relating to the furtherance of the principles and objectives of the Antarctic Treaty

	9 Recommendations adopted at Seventh Meeting (Wellington 1972)	14 Recommendations adopted at Eighth Meeting (Oslo 1975)	6 Recommendations adopted at Ninth Meeting (London 1977)	9 Recommendations adopted at Tenth Meeting (Washington 1979)	3 Recommendations adopted at Eleventh Meeting (Buenos Aires 1981)	8 Recommendations adopted at Twelfth Meeting (Canberra 1983)
	Approved	Approved	Approved	Approved	Approved	Approved
Argentina	ALL	ALL	ALL	ALL	ALL	ALL
Australia	ALL	ALL	ALL	ALL	ALL	ALL
Belgium	ALL	ALL	ALL	ALL	ALL	ALL
Brazil (1983)+	ALL except 5	ALL	ALL	ALL	ALL	ALL
Bulgaria (1998)+						
Chile	ALL	ALL	ALL	ALL	ALL	ALL
China (1985)+	ALL except 5	ALL	ALL	ALL	ALL	ALL
Czech Rep. (2014)+	4 & 6-8	1, 4, 6-10, 12 & 14	1 & 2	1-3 & 8	ALL except 2	ALL except 3-5
Ecuador (1990)+						
Finland (1989)+						
France	ALL	ALL	ALL	ALL	ALL	ALL
Germany (1981)+	ALL except 5	ALL except 2 & 5	ALL	ALL	ALL	ALL
India (1983)+	ALL	ALL	ALL	ALL except 1 & 9	ALL	ALL
Italy (1987)+	ALL except 5	ALL	ALL	ALL except 1 & 9		
Japan	ALL	ALL	ALL	ALL	ALL	ALL
Korea, Rep. (1989)+	ALL	ALL	ALL	ALL	ALL	ALL
Netherlands (1990)+	ALL	ALL	ALL except 3	ALL except 9	ALL except 2	ALL
New Zealand	ALL	ALL	ALL	ALL	ALL	ALL
Norway	ALL	ALL	ALL	ALL	ALL	ALL
Peru (1989)+	ALL	ALL	ALL	ALL	ALL	
Poland (1977)+	ALL	ALL	ALL	ALL	ALL	ALL
Russia	ALL	ALL	ALL	ALL	ALL	ALL
South Africa	ALL	ALL	ALL	ALL	ALL	ALL
Spain (1988)+	ALL	ALL	ALL	ALL except 1 & 9	ALL except 1	ALL
Sweden (1988)+						
U.K.	ALL	ALL	ALL	ALL	ALL	ALL
Uruguay (1985)+	ALL	ALL	ALL	ALL	ALL	ALL
U.S.A.	ALL	ALL	ALL	ALL	ALL	ALL

* IV-6, IV-10, IV-12, and V-5 terminated by VIII-2
*** Accepted as interim guideline
+ Year attained Consultative Status. Acceptance by that State required to bring into force Recommendations or Measures of meetings from that year forward.

Approval, as notified to the Government of the United States of America, of measures
relating to the furtherance of the principles and objectives of the Antarctic Treaty

	16 Recommendations adopted at Thirteenth Meeting (Brussels 1985)	10 Recommendations adopted at Fourteenth Meeting (Rio de Janeiro 1987)	22 Recommendations adopted at Fifteenth Meeting (Paris 1989)	13 Recommendations adopted at Sixteenth Meeting (Bonn 1991)	4 Recommendations adopted at Seventeenth Meeting (Venice 1992)	1 Recommendation adopted at Eighteenth Meeting (Kyoto 1994)
	Approved	Approved	Approved	Approved	Approved	Approved
Argentina	ALL	ALL	ALL	ALL	ALL	ALL
Australia	ALL	ALL	ALL	ALL	ALL	ALL
Belgium	ALL	ALL	ALL	ALL	ALL	ALL
Brazil (1983)+	ALL	ALL	ALL	ALL	ALL	ALL
Bulgaria (1998)+				XVI-10		
Chile	ALL	ALL	ALL	ALL	ALL	ALL
China (1985)+	ALL	ALL	ALL	ALL	ALL	ALL
Czech Rep. (2014)+	1-3, 5-6, 8, 11 & 15-16	1, 3, 5, 7-8 & 10	2, 5, 12-19 & 21	1, 2, 5-6 & 10-12	ALL except 2	ALL
Ecuador (1990)+				1, 2, 5, 6, 10 & 12	ALL except 2 & 3	ALL
Finland (1989)+			ALL	ALL	ALL	ALL
France	ALL	ALL	ALL	ALL	ALL	ALL
Germany (1981)+	ALL	ALL	ALL except 3, 8, 10, 11 & 22	ALL	ALL	ALL
India (1983)+	ALL	ALL	ALL	ALL	ALL	ALL
Italy (1987)+		ALL	ALL	ALL	ALL	ALL
Japan	ALL	ALL	ALL	ALL except 1, 3-9, 12 & 13	ALL except 1-2 & 4	ALL
Korea, Rep. (1989)+	ALL	ALL	ALL except 1-11, 16, 18 & 19	ALL except 12	ALL except 1	ALL
Netherlands (1990)+	ALL	ALL except 9	ALL except 22	ALL	ALL	ALL
New Zealand	ALL	ALL	ALL	ALL	ALL	ALL
Norway	ALL	ALL	ALL	ALL	ALL	ALL
Peru (1989)+			ALL except 22	ALL except 13	ALL	ALL
Poland (1977)+	ALL	ALL	ALL	ALL	ALL	ALL
Russia	ALL	ALL	ALL	ALL	ALL	ALL
South Africa	ALL	ALL	ALL	ALL	ALL	ALL
Spain (1988)+	ALL	ALL	ALL	ALL	ALL	ALL
Sweden (1988)+			ALL	ALL	ALL	ALL
U.K.	ALL	ALL except 2	ALL except 3, 4, 8, 10 & 11	ALL except 4, 6, 8 & 9	ALL	ALL
Uruguay (1985)+	ALL	ALL	ALL	ALL	ALL	ALL
U.S.A.	ALL	ALL	ALL except 1-4, 10 & 11	ALL	ALL	ALL

* IV-6, IV-10, IV-12, and V-5 terminated by VIII-2

*** Accepted as interim guideline

+ Year attained Consultative Status. Acceptance by that State required to bring into force Recommendations or Measures of meetings from that year forward.

Approval, as notified to the Government of the United States of America, of measures relating to the furtherance of the principles and objectives of the Antarctic Treaty

	5 Measures adopted at Nineteenth Meeting (Seoul 1995)	2 Measures adopted at Twentieth Meeting (Utrecht 1996)	5 Measures adopted at Twenty-First Meeting (Christchurch 1997)	2 Measures adopted at Twenty-Second Meeting (Tromso 1998)	1 Measure adopted at Twenty-Third Meeting (Lima 1999)
	Approved	Approved	Approved	Approved	Approved
Argentina	ALL	ALL	ALL	ALL	ALL
Australia	ALL	ALL	ALL	ALL	ALL
Belgium	ALL	ALL	ALL	ALL	ALL
Brazil (1983)+	ALL	ALL	ALL	ALL	ALL
Bulgaria (1998)+					
Chile	ALL	ALL	ALL	ALL	ALL
China (1985)+	ALL	ALL	ALL	ALL	ALL
Czech Rep. (2014)+	ALL except 1 & 2	ALL except 1	ALL except 1 & 2	ALL except 1	
Ecuador (1990)+	XIX-3		XXI-3		
Finland (1989)+	ALL	ALL	ALL	ALL	ALL
France	ALL	ALL	ALL	ALL	ALL
Germany (1981)+	ALL	ALL	ALL	ALL	ALL
India (1983)+	ALL	ALL	ALL	ALL	ALL
Italy (1987)+	ALL	ALL			
Japan	ALL (except 2&5)	ALL (except 1)	All (except 1-2 & 5)		
Korea, Rep. (1989)+	ALL	ALL	ALL	ALL	ALL
Netherlands (1990)+	ALL	ALL	ALL	ALL	ALL
New Zealand	ALL	ALL	ALL	ALL	ALL
Norway	ALL	ALL	ALL		
Peru (1989)+	ALL	ALL	ALL	ALL	ALL
Poland (1977)+	ALL	ALL	ALL	ALL	ALL
Russia	ALL	ALL	ALL	ALL	ALL
South Africa	ALL	ALL	ALL	ALL	ALL
Spain (1988)+	ALL	ALL	ALL	ALL	ALL
Sweden (1988)+	ALL	ALL	ALL	ALL	ALL
U.K.	ALL	ALL	ALL	ALL	ALL
Uruguay (1985)+	ALL	ALL	ALL	ALL	ALL
U.S.A.	ALL	ALL	ALL	ALL	ALL

"+Year attained Consultative Status. Acceptance by that state required to bring into force Recommendations or Measures of meetings from that Year forward."

Approval, as notified to the Government of the United States of America, of measures
relating to the furtherance of the principles and objectives of the Antarctic Treaty

	2 Measures adopted at Twelfth Special Meeting (The Hague 2000)	3 Measures adopted at Twenty-Fourth Meeting (St. Petersburg 2001)	1 Measure adopted at Twenty-Fifth Meeting (Warsaw 2002)	3 Measures adopted at Twenty-Sixth Meeting (Madrid 2003)	4 Measures adopted at Twenty-Seventh Meeting (Cape Town 2004)
	Approved	Approved	Approved	Approved	Approved
Argentina			*	XXVI-1, XXVI-2 *, XXVI-3 **	XXVII-1 *, XXVII-2 *, XXVII-3 **, XXVII-4
Australia	ALL	ALL	ALL	XXVI-1, XXVI-2 *, XXVI-3 **	XXVII-1 *, XXVII-2 *, XXVII-3 **, XXVII-4
Belgium	ALL	ALL	ALL		ALL
Brazil (1983)+	ALL	ALL	ALL	ALL	XXVII-1, XXVII-2, XXVII-3
Bulgaria (1998)+			*	XXVI-1, XXVI-2 *, XXVI-3 **	XXVII-1 *, XXVII-2 *, XXVII-3 **
Chile	ALL	ALL	ALL	ALL	ALL
China (1985)+	ALL	ALL	ALL	ALL	XXVII-1 *, XXVII-2 *, XXVII-3 **
Czech Rep. (2014)+	ALL	ALL	ALL	ALL	ALL
Ecuador (1990)+	SATCM XII-1	XXIV-3	*	XXVI-1, XXVI-2 *, XXVI-3 **	XXVII-1 *, XXVII-2 *, XXVII-3 **, XXVII-4
Finland (1989)+	ALL	ALL	*	XXVI-1, XXVI-2 *, XXVI-3 **	XXVII-1 *, XXVII-2 *, XXVII-3, XXVII-4
France	ALL (except SATCM XI-2)	ALL	ALL	XXVI-1, XXVI-2 *, XXVI-3 **	XXVII-1 *, XXVII-2 *, XXVII-3, XXVII-4
Germany (1981)+	ALL	ALL	ALL	ALL	XXVII-1 *, XXVII-2 *, XXVII-3 **
India (1983)+	ALL	ALL	ALL	XXVI-1, XXVI-2 *, XXVI-3 **	XXVII-1 *, XXVII-2 *, XXVII-3 **
Italy (1987)+			*	XXVI-1, XXVI-2 *, XXVI-3 **	XXVII-1 *, XXVII-2 *, XXVII-3 **, XXVII-4
Japan		ALL	*	ALL	XXVII-1 *, XXVII-2 *, XXVII-3 **, XXVII-4
Korea, Rep. (1989)+	ALL	ALL	*	XXVI-1, XXVI-2 *, XXVI-3 **	ALL
Netherlands (1990)+	ALL	ALL	ALL	ALL	XXVII-1 *, XXVII-2 *, XXVII-3 **, XXVII-4
New Zealand	ALL	ALL	ALL		
Norway		ALL	*	XXVI-1, XXVI-2 *, XXVI-3 **	XXVII-1 *, XXVII-2 *, XXVII-3 **, XXVII-4
Peru (1989)+	ALL	ALL	ALL	ALL	XXVII-1 *, XXVII-2 *, XXVII-3 **
Poland (1977)+		ALL	ALL	XXVI-1, XXVI-2, XXVI-3 **	ALL
Russia	ALL	ALL	ALL		ALL
South Africa	ALL	ALL	ALL		
Spain (1988)+			*	XXVI-1, XXVI-2 *, XXVI-3 **	XXVII-1 *, XXVII-2 *, XXVII-3 **
Sweden (1988)+	ALL	ALL	ALL		XXVII-1 *, XXVII-2 *, XXVII-3 **
Ukraine (2004)+					XXVII-1 *, XXVII-2 *, XXVII-3 **
U.K.	ALL (except SATCM XII-2)	ALL (except XXIV-3)	ALL	ALL	XXVII-1 *, XXVII-2 *, XXVII-3 **, XXVII-4
Uruguay (1985)+	ALL	ALL	*	XXVI-1, XXVI-2 *, XXVI-3	XXVII-1 *, XXVII-2 *, XXVII-3 **, XXVII-4
U.S.A.	ALL	ALL	ALL	XXVI-1, XXVI-2 *, XXVI-3 **	XXVII-1 *, XXVII-2 *, XXVII-3 **

"+ Year attained Consultative Status. Acceptance by that state required to bring into force Recommendations or Measures of meetings from that Year forward."

* Management Plans annexed to this Measure were deemed to have been approved in accordance with Article 6(1) of Annex V to the Protocol on Environmental Protection to the Antarctic Treaty and the Measure not specifying a different approval method.

** Revised and updated List of Historic Sites and Monuments annexed to this Measure was deemed to have been approved in accordance with Article 8(2) of Annex V to the Protocol on Environmental Protection to the Antarctic Treaty and the Measure not specifying a different approval method.

Approval, as notified to the Government of the United States of America, of measures
relating to the furtherance of the principles and objectives of the Antarctic Treaty

	5 Measures adopted at Twenty-Eighth Meeting (Stockholm 2005) Approved	4 Measures adopted at Twenty-Ninth Meeting (Edinburgh 2006) Approved	3 Measures adopted at Thirtieth Meeting (New Delhi 2007) Approved	14 Measures adopted at Thirty-first Meeting (Kyiv 2008) Approved
Argentina	XXVIII-2 *, XXVIII-3 *, XXVIII-4 *, XXVIII-5 **	XXX-1 *, XXX-2 *, XXX-3 **, XXX-4 ***	XXX-1 *, XXX-2 *, XXX-3 **	XXX-1 - XXX-14 *
Australia	XXVIII-1, XXVIII-2 *, XXVIII-3 *, XXVIII-4 *, XXVIII-5 **	XXX-1 *, XXX-2 *, XXX-3 **, XXX-4 ***	XXX-1 *, XXX-2 *, XXX-3 **	XXX-1 - XXX-14 *
Belgium (1983)+	ALL except Measure 1	ALL	ALL	XXX-1 - XXX-14 *
Brazil (1983)+	ALL except Measure 1	XXX-1 *, XXX-2 *, XXX-3 **, XXX-4 ***	XXX-1 *, XXX-2 *, XXX-3 **	XXX-1 - XXX-14 *
Bulgaria (1998)+	XXVIII-2 *, XXVIII-3 *, XXVIII-4 *, XXVIII-5 **	XXX-1 *, XXX-2 *, XXX-3 **, XXX-4 ***	XXX-1 *, XXX-2 *, XXX-3 **	XXX-1 - XXX-14 *
Chile	ALL except Measure 1	XXX-1 *, XXX-2 *, XXX-3 **, XXX-4 ***	XXX-1 *, XXX-2 *, XXX-3 **	XXX-1 - XXX-14 *
China (1985)+	XXVIII-2 *, XXVIII-3 *, XXVIII-4 *, XXVIII-5 **	XXX-1 *, XXX-2 *, XXX-3 **, XXX-4 ***	XXX-1 *, XXX-2 *, XXX-3 **	XXX-1 - XXX-14 *
Czech Rep. (2014)+	ALL except Measure 1	ALL	ALL	ALL except Measure 8
Ecuador (1990)+	XXVIII-1, XXVIII-2 *, XXVIII-3 *, XXVIII-4 *, XXVIII-5 **	XXX-1 *, XXX-2 *, XXX-3 **, XXX-4 ***	XXX-1 *, XXX-2 *, XXX-3 **	XXX-1 - XXX-14 *
Finland (1989)+	XXVIII-1, XXVIII-2 *, XXVIII-3 *, XXVIII-4 *, XXVIII-5 **	XXX-1 *, XXX-2 *, XXX-3 **, XXX-4 ***	XXX-1 *, XXX-2 *, XXX-3 **	XXX-1 - XXX-14 *
France	XXVIII-2 *, XXVIII-3 *, XXVIII-4 *, XXVIII-5 **	XXX-1 *, XXX-2 *, XXX-3 **, XXX-4 ***	XXX-1 *, XXX-2 *, XXX-3 **	XXX-1 - XXX-14 *
Germany (1981)+	XXVIII-2 *, XXVIII-3 *, XXVIII-4 *, XXVIII-5 **	XXX-1 *, XXX-2 *, XXX-3 **, XXX-4 ***	XXX-1 *, XXX-2 *, XXX-3 **	XXX-1 - XXX-14 *
India (1983)+	XXVIII-2 *, XXVIII-3 *, XXVIII-4 *, XXVIII-5 **	XXX-1 *, XXX-2 *, XXX-3 **, XXX-4 ***	XXX-1 *, XXX-2 *, XXX-3 **	XXX-1 - XXX-14 *
Italy (1987)+	XXVIII-1, XXVIII-2 *, XXVIII-3 *, XXVIII-4 *, XXVIII-5 **	XXX-1 *, XXX-2 *, XXX-3 **, XXX-4 ***	XXX-1 *, XXX-2 *, XXX-3 **	XXX-1 - XXX-14 *
Japan	XXVIII-2 *, XXVIII-3 *, XXVIII-4 *, XXVIII-5 **	XXX-1 *, XXX-2 *, XXX-3 **, XXX-4 ***	XXX-1 *, XXX-2 *, XXX-3 **	XXX-1 - XXX-14 *
Korea, Rep. (1989)+	XXVIII-2 *, XXVIII-3 *, XXVIII-4 *, XXVIII-5 **	XXX-1 *, XXX-2 *, XXX-3 **, XXX-4 ***	XXX-1 *, XXX-2 *, XXX-3 **	XXX-1 - XXX-14 *
Netherlands (1990)+	ALL	ALL	ALL	ALL
New Zealand	XXVIII-1, XXVIII-2 *, XXVIII-3 *, XXVIII-4 *, XXVIII-5 **	XXX-1 *, XXX-2 *, XXX-3 **, XXX-4 ***	XXX-1 *, XXX-2 *, XXX-3 **	XXX-1 - XXX-14 *
Norway	XXVIII-1, XXVIII-2 *, XXVIII-3 *, XXVIII-4 *, XXVIII-5 **	XXX-1 *, XXX-2 *, XXX-3 **, XXX-4 ***	XXX-1 *, XXX-2 *, XXX-3 **	XXX-1 - XXX-14 *
Peru (1989)+	XXVIII-1, XXVIII-2 *, XXVIII-3 *, XXVIII-4 *, XXVIII-5 **	XXX-1 *, XXX-2 *, XXX-3 **, XXX-4 ***	XXX-1 *, XXX-2 *, XXX-3 **	XXX-1 - XXX-14 *
Poland (1977)+	ALL	ALL	ALL	XXX-1 - XXX-14 *
Russia	XXVIII-1, XXVIII-2 *, XXVIII-3 *, XXVIII-4 *, XXVIII-5 **	XXX-1 *, XXX-2 *, XXX-3 **, XXX-4 ***	XXX-1 *, XXX-2 *, XXX-3 **	XXX-1 - XXX-14 *
South Africa	XXVIII-1, XXVIII-2 *, XXVIII-3 *, XXVIII-4 *, XXVIII-5 **	ALL	XXX-1 *, XXX-2 *, XXX-3 **	XXX-1 - XXX-14 *
Spain (1988)+	XXVIII-1, XXVIII-2 *, XXVIII-3 *, XXVIII-4 *, XXVIII-5 **	XXX-1 *, XXX-2 *, XXX-3 **, XXX-4 ***	XXX-1 *, XXX-2 *, XXX-3 **	XXX-1 - XXX-14 *
Sweden (1988)+	XXVIII-1, XXVIII-2 *, XXVIII-3 *, XXVIII-4 *, XXVIII-5 **	XXX-1 *, XXX-2 *, XXX-3 **, XXX-4 ***	XXX-1 *, XXX-2 *, XXX-3 **	XXX-1 - XXX-14 *
Ukraine (2004)+	XXVIII-2 *, XXVIII-3 *, XXVIII-4 *, XXVIII-5 **	XXX-1 *, XXX-2 *, XXX-3 **, XXX-4 ***	XXX-1 *, XXX-2 *, XXX-3 **	XXX-1 - XXX-14 *
U.K.	XXVIII-1, XXVIII-2 *, XXVIII-3 *, XXVIII-4 *, XXVIII-5 **	XXX-1 *, XXX-2 *, XXX-3 **, XXX-4 ***	XXX-1 *, XXX-2 *, XXX-3 **	XXX-1 - XXX-14 *
Uruguay (1985)+	XXVIII-2 *, XXVIII-3 *, XXVIII-4 *, XXVIII-5 **	XXX-1 *, XXX-2 *, XXX-3 **, XXX-4 ***	XXX-1 *, XXX-2 *, XXX-3 **	XXX-1 - XXX-14 *
U.S.A.	XXVIII-2 *, XXVIII-3 *, XXVIII-4 *, XXVIII-5 **	XXX-1 *, XXX-2 *, XXX-3 **, XXX-4 ***	XXX-1 *, XXX-2 *, XXX-3 **	XXX-1 - XXX-14 *

"+Year attained Consultative Status. Acceptance by that state required to bring into force Recommendations or Measures of meetings from that Year forward."

* Management Plans annexed to this Measure deemed to have been approved in accordance with Article 6(1) of Annex V to the Protocol on Environmental Protection to the Antarctic Treaty and the Measure not specifying a different approval method.

** Revised and updated List of Historic Sites and Monuments annexed to this Measure deemed to have been approved in accordance with Article 8(2) of Annex V to the Protocol on Environmental Protection to the Antarctic Treaty and the Measure not specifying a different approval method.

*** Modification of Appendix A to Annex II to the Protocol on Environmental Protection to the Antarctic Treaty deemed to have been approved in accordance with Article 9(1) of Annex II to the Protocol on Environmental Protection to the Antarctic Treaty and the Measure not specifying a different approval method.

Approval, as notified to the Government of the United States of America, of measures
relating to the furtherance of the principles and objectives of the Antarctic Treaty

	16 Measures adopted at Thirty-second Meeting (Baltimore 2009) Approved	15 Measures adopted at Thirty-third Meeting (Punta del Este 2010) Approved	12 Measures adopted at Thirty-fourth Meeting (Buenos Aires 2011) Approved	11 Measures adopted at Thirty-fifth Meeting (Hobart 2012) Approved	21 Measures adopted at Thirty-sixth Meeting (Brussels 2013) Approved
Argentina	XXXII-1 - XXXII-13* and XXXII-14**	XXXIII-1 - XXXIII-14* and XXXIII-15**	XXXIV-1 - XXXIV-10* and XXXIV-11 - XXXIV-12**	XXXV-1 - XXXV-10* and XXXV-11**	XXXVI-1 - XXXVI-17* and XXXVI-18 - XXXVI-21**
Australia	XXXII-1 - XXXII-13* and XXXII-14**, XXXII-15	XXXIII-1 - XXXIII-14* and XXXIII-15**	XXXIV-1 - XXXIV-10* and XXXIV-11 - XXXIV-12**	XXXV-1 - XXXV-10* and XXXV-11**	XXXVI-1 - XXXVI-17* and XXXVI-18 - XXXVI-21**
Belgium	XXXII-1 - XXXII-13* and XXXII-14**	XXXIII-1 - XXXIII-14* and XXXIII-15**	XXXIV-1 - XXXIV-10* and XXXIV-11 - XXXIV-12**	XXXV-1 - XXXV-10* and XXXV-11**	XXXVI-1 - XXXVI-17* and XXXVI-18 - XXXVI-21**
Brazil (1983)+	XXXII-1 - XXXII-13* and XXXII-14**	XXXIII-1 - XXXIII-14* and XXXIII-15**	XXXIV-1 - XXXIV-10* and XXXIV-11 - XXXIV-12**	XXXV-1 - XXXV-10* and XXXV-11**	XXXVI-1 - XXXVI-17* and XXXVI-18 - XXXVI-21**
Bulgaria (1998)+	XXXII-1 - XXXII-13* and XXXII-14**	XXXIII-1 - XXXIII-14* and XXXIII-15**	XXXIV-1 - XXXIV-10* and XXXIV-11 - XXXIV-12**	XXXV-1 - XXXV-10* and XXXV-11**	XXXVI-1 - XXXVI-17* and XXXVI-18 - XXXVI-21**
Chile (1985)+	XXXII-1 - XXXII-13* and XXXII-14**	XXXIII-1 - XXXIII-14* and XXXIII-15**	XXXIV-1 - XXXIV-10* and XXXIV-11 - XXXIV-12**	XXXV-1 - XXXV-10* and XXXV-11**	XXXVI-1 - XXXVI-17* and XXXVI-18 - XXXVI-21**
Czech Rep. (2014)+	ALL except 2 and 16	ALL	ALL	ALL	ALL
Ecuador (1990)+	XXXII-1 - XXXII-13* and XXXII-14**, XXXII-15	XXXIII-1 - XXXIII-14* and XXXIII-15**	XXXIV-1 - XXXIV-10* and XXXIV-11 - XXXIV-12**	XXXV-1 - XXXV-10* and XXXV-11**	XXXVI-1 - XXXVI-17* and XXXVI-18 - XXXVI-21**
Finland (1989)+	XXXII-1 - XXXII-13* and XXXII-14**, XXXII-16	XXXIII-1 - XXXIII-14* and XXXIII-15**	XXXIV-1 - XXXIV-10* and XXXIV-11 - XXXIV-12**	XXXV-1 - XXXV-10* and XXXV-11**	XXXVI-1 - XXXVI-17* and XXXVI-18 - XXXVI-21**
France	XXXII-1 - XXXII-13* and XXXII-14** XXXII-15	XXXIII-1 - XXXIII-14* and XXXIII-15**	XXXIV-1 - XXXIV-10* and XXXIV-11 - XXXIV-12**	XXXV-1 - XXXV-10* and XXXV-11**	XXXVI-1 - XXXVI-17* and XXXVI-18 - XXXVI-21**
Germany (1981)+	XXXII-1 - XXXII-13* and XXXII-14**	XXXIII-1 - XXXIII-14* and XXXIII-15**	XXXIV-1 - XXXIV-10* and XXXIV-11 - XXXIV-12**	XXXV-1 - XXXV-10* and XXXV-11**	XXXVI-1 - XXXVI-17* and XXXVI-18 - XXXVI-21**
India (1983)+	XXXII-1 - XXXII-13* and XXXII-14**	XXXIII-1 - XXXIII-14* and XXXIII-15**	XXXIV-1 - XXXIV-10* and XXXIV-11 - XXXIV-12**	XXXV-1 - XXXV-10* and XXXV-11**	XXXVI-1 - XXXVI-17* and XXXVI-18 - XXXVI-21**
Italy (1987)+	XXXII-1 - XXXII-13* and XXXII-14**	XXXIII-1 - XXXIII-14* and XXXIII-15**	XXXIV-1 - XXXIV-10* and XXXIV-11 - XXXIV-12**	XXXV-1 - XXXV-10* and XXXV-11**	XXXVI-1 - XXXVI-17* and XXXVI-18 - XXXVI-21**
Japan	XXXII-1 - XXXII-13* and XXXII-14**, XXXII-15	XXXIII-1 - XXXIII-14* and XXXIII-15**	XXXIV-1 - XXXIV-10* and XXXIV-11 - XXXIV-12**	XXXV-1 - XXXV-10* and XXXV-11**	XXXVI-1 - XXXVI-17* and XXXVI-18 - XXXVI-21**
Korea, Rep. (1989)+	XXXII-1 - XXXII-13* and XXXII-14**	XXXIII-1 - XXXIII-14* and XXXIII-15**	XXXIV-1 - XXXIV-10* and XXXIV-11 - XXXIV-12**	XXXV-1 - XXXV-10* and XXXV-11**	XXXVI-1 - XXXVI-17* and XXXVI-18 - XXXVI-21**
Netherlands (1990)+	XXXII-1 - XXXII-13 and XXXII-14, XXXII-15 - XXXII-16	ALL	XXXIV-1 - XXXIV-10* and XXXIV-11 - XXXIV-12**	ALL	XXXVI-1 - XXXVI-17* and XXXVI-18 - XXXVI-21**
New Zealand	XXXII-1 - XXXII-13* and XXXII-14**	XXXIII-1 - XXXIII-14* and XXXIII-15**	XXXIV-1 - XXXIV-10* and XXXIV-11 - XXXIV-12**	XXXV-1 - XXXV-10* and XXXV-11**	XXXVI-1 - XXXVI-17* and XXXVI-18 - XXXVI-21**
Norway	XXXII-1 - XXXII-13* and XXXII-14**	XXXIII-1 - XXXIII-14* and XXXIII-15**	XXXIV-1 - XXXIV-10* and XXXIV-11 - XXXIV-12**	XXXV-1 - XXXV-10* and XXXV-11**	XXXVI-1 - XXXVI-17* and XXXVI-18 - XXXVI-21**
Peru (1989)+	XXXII-1 - XXXII-13* and XXXII-14**	XXXIII-1 - XXXIII-14* and XXXIII-15**	XXXIV-1 - XXXIV-10* and XXXIV-11 - XXXIV-12**	XXXV-1 - XXXV-10* and XXXV-11**	XXXVI-1 - XXXVI-17* and XXXVI-18 - XXXVI-21**
Poland (1977)+	XXXII-1 - XXXII-13* and XXXII-14**	XXXIII-1 - XXXIII-14* and XXXIII-15**	XXXIV-1 - XXXIV-10* and XXXIV-11 - XXXIV-12**	XXXV-1 - XXXV-10* and XXXV-11**	XXXVI-1 - XXXVI-17* and XXXVI-18 - XXXVI-21**
Russia	XXXII-1 - XXXII-13* and XXXII-14**, XXXII-15	XXXIII-1 - XXXIII-14* and XXXIII-15**	XXXIV-1 - XXXIV-10* and XXXIV-11 - XXXIV-12**	XXXV-1 - XXXV-10* and XXXV-11**	XXXVI-1 - XXXVI-17* and XXXVI-18 - XXXVI-21**
South Africa	XXXII-1 - XXXII-13* and XXXII-14**	XXXIII-1 - XXXIII-14* and XXXIII-15**	XXXIV-1 - XXXIV-10* and XXXIV-11 - XXXIV-12**	XXXV-1 - XXXV-10* and XXXV-11**	XXXVI-1 - XXXVI-17* and XXXVI-18 - XXXVI-21**
Spain (1988)+	XXXII-1 - XXXII-13* and XXXII-14**	XXXIII-1 - XXXIII-14* and XXXIII-15**	XXXIV-1 - XXXIV-10* and XXXIV-11 - XXXIV-12**	XXXV-1 - XXXV-10* and XXXV-11**	XXXVI-1 - XXXVI-17* and XXXVI-18 - XXXVI-21**
Sweden (1988)+	XXXII-1 - XXXII-13* and XXXII-14**	XXXIII-1 - XXXIII-14* and XXXIII-15**	XXXIV-1 - XXXIV-10* and XXXIV-11 - XXXIV-12**	XXXV-1 - XXXV-10* and XXXV-11**	XXXVI-1 - XXXVI-17* and XXXVI-18 - XXXVI-21**
Ukraine (2004)+	XXXII-1 - XXXII-13* and XXXII-14**	XXXIII-1 - XXXIII-14* and XXXIII-15**	XXXIV-1 - XXXIV-10* and XXXIV-11 - XXXIV-12**	XXXV-1 - XXXV-10* and XXXV-11**	XXXVI-1 - XXXVI-17* and XXXVI-18 - XXXVI-21**
U.K.	XXXII-1 - XXXII-13* and XXXII-14**, XXXII-15 - XXXII-16	XXXIII-1 - XXXIII-14* and XXXIII-15**	XXXIV-1 - XXXIV-10* and XXXIV-11 - XXXIV-12**	XXXV-1 - XXXV-10* and XXXV-11**	XXXVI-1 - XXXVI-17* and XXXVI-18 - XXXVI-21**
Uruguay (1985)+	XXXII-1 - XXXII-13* and XXXII-14**, XXXII-16	XXXIII-1 - XXXIII-14* and XXXIII-15**	XXXIV-1 - XXXIV-10* and XXXIV-11 - XXXIV-12**	XXXV-1 - XXXV-10* and XXXV-11**	XXXVI-1 - XXXVI-17* and XXXVI-18 - XXXVI-21**
U.S.A.	XXXII-1 - XXXII-13* and XXXII-14**, XXXII-16	XXXIII-1 - XXXIII-14* and XXXIII-15**	XXXIV-1 - XXXIV-10* and XXXIV-11 - XXXIV-12**	XXXV-1 - XXXV-10* and XXXV-11**	XXXVI-1 - XXXVI-17* and XXXVI-18 - XXXVI-21**

"+Year attained Consultative Status Acceptance by that state required to bring into force Recommendations or Measures of meetings from that Year forward."

* Management Plans annexed to these Measures deemed to have been approved in accordance with Article 6(1) of Annex V to the Protocol on Environmental Protection to the Antarctic Treaty and the Measure not specifying a different approval method.

** Modifications and/or additions to List of Historic Sites and Monuments deemed to have been approved in accordance with Article 8(2) of Annex V to the Protocol on Environmental Protection to the Antarctic Treaty and the Measure not specifying a different approval method.

	16 Measures adopted at Thirty-seventh Meeting (Brasilia 2014)	19 Measures adopted at Thirty-eighth Meeting (Sofia 2015)	9 Measures adopted at Thirty-ninth Meeting (Santiago 2016)
	Approved	Approved	Approved
Argentina	XXXVII-1 – XXXVII-16*	XXXVIII-1 – XXXVIII-18* and XXXVIII-19**	XXXIX-1 – XXXIX-8* and XXXIX-9**
Australia	XXXVII-1 – XXXVII-16*	XXXVIII-1 – XXXVIII-18* and XXXVIII-19**	XXXIX-1 – XXXIX-8* and XXXIX-9**
Belgium	XXXVII-1 – XXXVII-16*	XXXVIII-1 – XXXVIII-18* and XXXVIII-19**	XXXIX-1 – XXXIX-8* and XXXIX-9**
Brazil (1983)+	XXXVII-1 – XXXVII-16*	XXXVIII-1 – XXXVIII-18* and XXXVIII-19**	XXXIX-1 – XXXIX-8* and XXXIX-9**
Bulgaria (1998)+	XXXVII-1 – XXXVII-16*	XXXVIII-1 – XXXVIII-18* and XXXVIII-19**	XXXIX-1 – XXXIX-8* and XXXIX-9**
Chile	XXXVII-1 – XXXVII-16*	XXXVIII-1 – XXXVIII-18* and XXXVIII-19**	XXXIX-1 – XXXIX-8* and XXXIX-9**
China (1985)+	XXXVII-1 – XXXVII-16*	XXXVIII-1 – XXXVIII-18* and XXXVIII-19**	XXXIX-1 – XXXIX-8* and XXXIX-9**
Czech Rep. (2014)+	XXXVII-1 – XXXVII-16*	XXXVIII-1 – XXXVIII-18* and XXXVIII-19**	XXXIX-1 – XXXIX-8* and XXXIX-9**
Ecuador (1990)+	XXXVII-1 – XXXVII-16*	XXXVIII-1 – XXXVIII-18* and XXXVIII-19**	XXXIX-1 – XXXIX-8* and XXXIX-9**
Finland (1989)+	XXXVII-1 – XXXVII-16*	XXXVIII-1 – XXXVIII-18* and XXXVIII-19**	XXXIX-1 – XXXIX-8* and XXXIX-9**
France	XXXVII-1 – XXXVII-16*	XXXVIII-1 – XXXVIII-18* and XXXVIII-19**	XXXIX-1 – XXXIX-8* and XXXIX-9**
Germany (1981)+	XXXVII-1 – XXXVII-16*	XXXVIII-1 – XXXVIII-18* and XXXVIII-19**	XXXIX-1 – XXXIX-8* and XXXIX-9**
India (1983)+	XXXVII-1 – XXXVII-16*	XXXVIII-1 – XXXVIII-18* and XXXVIII-19**	XXXIX-1 – XXXIX-8* and XXXIX-9**
Italy (1987)+	XXXVII-1 – XXXVII-16*	XXXVIII-1 – XXXVIII-18* and XXXVIII-19**	XXXIX-1 – XXXIX-8* and XXXIX-9**
Japan	XXXVII-1 – XXXVII-16*	XXXVIII-1 – XXXVIII-18* and XXXVIII-19**	XXXIX-1 – XXXIX-8* and XXXIX-9**
Korea, Rep. (1989)+	XXXVII-1 – XXXVII-16*	XXXVIII-1 – XXXVIII-18* and XXXVIII-19**	XXXIX-1 – XXXIX-8* and XXXIX-9**
Netherlands (1990)+	XXXVII-1 – XXXVII-16*	XXXVIII-1 – XXXVIII-18* and XXXVIII-19**	XXXIX-1 – XXXIX-8* and XXXIX-9**
New Zealand	XXXVII-1 – XXXVII-16*	XXXVIII-1 – XXXVIII-18* and XXXVIII-19**	XXXIX-1 – XXXIX-8* and XXXIX-9**
Norway	XXXVII-1 – XXXVII-16*	XXXVIII-1 – XXXVIII-18* and XXXVIII-19**	XXXIX-1 – XXXIX-8* and XXXIX-9**
Peru (1989)+	XXXVII-1 – XXXVII-16*	XXXVIII-1 – XXXVIII-18* and XXXVIII-19**	XXXIX-1 – XXXIX-8* and XXXIX-9**
Poland (1977)+	XXXVII-1 – XXXVII-16*	XXXVIII-1 – XXXVIII-18* and XXXVIII-19**	XXXIX-1 – XXXIX-8* and XXXIX-9**
Russia	XXXVII-1 – XXXVII-16*	XXXVIII-1 – XXXVIII-18* and XXXVIII-19**	XXXIX-1 – XXXIX-8* and XXXIX-9**
South Africa	XXXVII-1 – XXXVII-16*	XXXVIII-1 – XXXVIII-18* and XXXVIII-19**	XXXIX-1 – XXXIX-8* and XXXIX-9**
Spain (1988)+	XXXVII-1 – XXXVII-16*	XXXVIII-1 – XXXVIII-18* and XXXVIII-19**	XXXIX-1 – XXXIX-8* and XXXIX-9**
Sweden (1988)+	XXXVII-1 – XXXVII-16*	XXXVIII-1 – XXXVIII-18* and XXXVIII-19**	XXXIX-1 – XXXIX-8* and XXXIX-9**
Ukraine (2004)+	XXXVII-1 – XXXVII-16*	XXXVIII-1 – XXXVIII-18* and XXXVIII-19**	XXXIX-1 – XXXIX-8* and XXXIX-9**
U.K.	XXXVII-1 – XXXVII-16*	XXXVIII-1 – XXXVIII-18* and XXXVIII-19**	XXXIX-1 – XXXIX-8* and XXXIX-9**
Uruguay (1985)+	XXXVII-1 – XXXVII-16*	XXXVIII-1 – XXXVIII-18* and XXXVIII-19**	XXXIX-1 – XXXIX-8* and XXXIX-9**
U.S.A.	XXXVII-1 – XXXVII-16*	XXXVIII-1 – XXXVIII-18* and XXXVIII-19**	XXXIX-1 – XXXIX-8* and XXXIX-9**

"+ Year attained Consultative Status. Acceptance by that state required to bring into force Recommendations or Measures of meetings from that Year forward."

* Management Plans annexed to these Measures deemed to have been approved in accordance with Article 6(1) of Annex V to the Protocol on Environmental Protection to the Antarctic Treaty and the Measure not specifying a different approval method.

** Modifications and/or additions to List of Historic Sites and Monuments deemed to have been approved in accordance with Article 8(2) of Annex V to the Protocol on Environmental Protection to the Antarctic Treaty and the Measure not specifying a different approval method.

Office of the Assistant Legal Adviser for Treaty Affairs
Department of State
Washington, April 25, 2017.

Report of the Depositary Government for the Convention on the Conservation of Antarctic Marine Living Resources (CAMLR)

Information paper submitted by Australia

Abstract

A report is provided by Australia as Depositary of the *Convention on the Conservation of Antarctic Marine Living Resources* 1980.

Background

Australia, as Depositary of the *Convention on the Conservation of Antarctic Marine Living Resources* 1980 ('the Convention') is pleased to report to the Fortieth Antarctic Treaty Consultative Meeting (ATCM XL) on the status of the Convention.

Australia advises Antarctic Treaty Parties that, since the Thirty-ninth Antarctic Treaty Consultative Meeting (ATCM XXXIX), there has been no depositary activity.

A copy of the status list for the Convention is available via the internet on the Australian Treaties Database at the following address:

http://www.austlii.edu.au/au/other/dfat/treaty_list/depository/CCAMLR.html

The status list is also available on request to the Treaties Secretariat of the Australian Government Department of Foreign Affairs and Trade. Requests can be conveyed through Australian diplomatic missions.

Report of the Depositary Government for the Agreement on the Conservation of Albatrosses and Petrels (ACAP)

Information paper submitted by Australia

Abstract

A report is provided by Australia as Depositary of the *Agreement on the Conservation of Albatrosses and Petrels* 2001.

Background

Australia, as Depositary of the *Agreement on the Conservation of Albatrosses and Petrels* 2001 ('the Agreement') is pleased to report to the Fortieth Antarctic Treaty Consultative Meeting (ATCM XL) on the status of the Agreement.

Australia advises Antarctic Treaty Parties that, since the Thirty-Ninth Antarctic Treaty Consultative Meeting (ATCM XXXIX), no States have acceded to the Agreement.

A copy of the status list for the Agreement is available, via the internet, on the Australian Treaties Database at the following address:

http://www.austlii.edu.au/au/other/dfat/treaty_list/depository/consalbnpet.html

The status list is also available on request to the Treaties Secretariat of the Australian Government Department of Foreign Affairs and Trade. Requests can be conveyed through Australian diplomatic missions.

Report by the United Kingdom as Depositary Government for the Convention for the Conservation of Antarctic Seals (CCAS) in Accordance with Recommendation XIII-2, Paragraph 2(D)

Parties to the Convention and new accessions

The United Kingdom, as Depositary Government for the Convention for the Conservation of Antarctic Seals (CCAS), has not received any requests to accede to the Convention, or any instruments of accession, since the previous report (ATCM XXXIX/IP2).

The full list of countries which were original signatories to the Convention, and countries which have subsequently acceded is attached to this report (Annex A).

CCAS Annual Return 2015/2016

Annex B lists all capturing and killing of Antarctic seals by Contracting Parties to CCAS for the reporting year 1 March 2015 to 29 February 2016. All reported captures were for scientific research.

Next CCAS Annual Return

The United Kingdom would like to remind Contracting Parties to CCAS that the Exchange of Information, referred to in Paragraph 6(a) in the Annex to the Convention, for the reporting period of 1 March 2016 to 28 February 2017 is due by **30 June 2017.** CCAS Parties should submit their returns, including nil returns, to both the United Kingdom and SCAR. The UK would like to encourage all Contracting Parties to CCAS to submit their returns on time.

The CCAS report for the reporting period 2016/2017 will be submitted to ATCM XLI, once the June 2017 deadline for exchange of information has passed.

Parties to the Convention for the Conservation of Antarctic Seals (CCAS)

London, 1 June-31 December 1972; the Convention entered into force on 11 March 1978.

State	Date of Signature	Date of Deposit (Ratification or Acceptance)
Argentina*	9 June 1972	7 March 1978
Australia	5 October 1972	1 July 1987
Belgium	9 June 1972	9 February 1978
Chile*	28 December 1972	7 February 1980
France**	19 December 1972	19 February 1975
Japan	28 December 1972	28 August 1980
Norway	9 June 1972	10 December 1973
Russia****	9 June 1972	8 February 1978
South Africa	9 June 1972	15 August 1972
United Kingdom**	9 June 1972	10 September 1974***
United States of America	28 June 1972	19 January 1977

Accessions

State	Date of deposit of Instrument of Accession
Brazil	11 February 1991
Canada	4 October 1990
Germany	30 September 1987
Italy	2 April 1992
Poland	15 August 1980
Pakistan	25 March 2013

*   Declaration or Reservation
**   Objection
*** The instrument of ratification included the Channel Islands and the Isle of Man
**** Former USSR

Annual CCAS Report 2015/2016

Synopsis of reporting in accordance with Article 5 and the Annex of the Convention: Capturing and killing of seals during the period 1 March 2015 to 29 February 2016.

Contracting Party	Antarctic Seals Captured	Antarctic Seals Killed
Argentina	151 (a)	0
Australia	4 (b)	0
Belgium	0	0
Brazil	0	0
Canada	No return received	No return received
Chile	58 (c)	0
France	117 (d)	0
Germany	18 (e)	1 (f)
Italy	0	0
Japan	0	0
Norway	0	0
Pakistan	No return received	No return received
Poland	0	0
Russia	0	0
South Africa	0	1 (k)
United Kingdom	38 (g)	2 (h)
United States of America	2716 (i)	27 (j)

All reported capturing was for scientific research.

(a) **Weddell Seals:** 22 adults (sex unknown). **Crabeater Seals:** 10 adults (sex unknown). **Southern Elephant Seals:** 4 adults, 15 juveniles and 100 weaned (sex unknown).
(b) **Elephant Seals**: 4 (sex and age unknown).
(c) **Antarctic Fur Seals:** 29 female adults, 29 pups (sex unknown).
(d) **Weddell Seals:** 4 male adults, 75 female adults, 19 male pups, 19 female pups.
(e) **Weddell Seals:** 8 male adults, 10 female adults.
(f) **Weddell Seal:** 1 female adult died as a consequence of an irreversible apnoea after unsuccessful pharmacological and mechanical intervention.
(g) **Antarctic Fur Seals:** 31 male adults, 3 female adults, 4 pups (sex unknown).
(h) **Antarctic Fur Seals:** 2 male adults died following anaesthesia process, even though correct procedures were followed in administering it.

(i) **Antarctic Fur Seals:** 46 adults/juveniles and 442 pups (sex unknown). **Leopard Seals:** 11 adults/juveniles (sex unknown). **Southern Elephant Seals:** 50 adults/juveniles and 63 pups (sex unknown) and 76 (age and sex unknown). **Weddell Seals:** 16 adult/juveniles and 26 pups (sex unknown), 246 adult females, 3 (age and sex unknown), 35 pups (both sexes), 12 adults (both sexes), 309 male pups, 330 female pups, 97 adult males, 1 female juvenile, 2 male juveniles and 949 for observation only (age and sex unknown). **Crabeater Seals:** 2 for observation only (age and sex unknown).

(j) **Antarctic Fur Seals:** 2 adult females and 4 pups (sex unknown) all found dead on shore, not previously handled. **Weddell Seals:** 2 unintentional deaths (age and sex unknown); 10 adults and 9 pups (sex unknown) all found dead on shore, not previously handled.

(k) One seal died accidentally from stress during scientific handling to obtain biopsy samples. Now a museum specimen.

Report of the Thirty-fifth
Meeting of the Commission
(Hobart, Australia, 17-28 October 2016)

Opening of the meeting

1.   The Thirty-fifth Annual Meeting of CCAMLR, which was held in Hobart, Australia, from 17 to 28 October 2016, was chaired by Mr Vasily Titushkin (Russian Federation).

2.   Twenty-four Members, two Acceding States, one State Observer and eleven Observers from non-government organisations participated.

Organisation of the meeting

Status of the Convention

3.   Australia, as Depository, reported that the status of the Convention had not changed during the last intersessional period.

Implementation and compliance

4.   The Commission approved the CCAMLR Compliance Report for 2016 – the fourth year of implementation of the CCAMLR Compliance Evaluation Procedure.

5.   Other subjects considered by the Standing Committee on Implementation and Compliance (SCIC) included:

-   the review of notifications received for participation in new and exploratory fisheries for the 2016/2017 season
-   implementation of CCAMLR's catch documentation scheme particularly efforts to strengthen the engagement of non-Contracting Parties in the scheme, analysis of global toothfish trade data and progress towards the deployment of a new electronic web-based CDS (e-CDS) in early 2017. Ecuador was accorded the status of an NCP cooperating with CCAMLR by monitoring toothfish trade through limited access to the e-CDS
-   apparent trends in IUU fishing and the value of cooperation with Interpol's Project Scale

Administration and Finance

6.   The Commission endorsed the advice and recommendations of the Standing Committee on Administration and Finance (SCAF), including supporting further work to examine revenue-generating opportunities and further reduce costs to secure sustainable funding.

7.   The Commission approved the budget for 2017 and the forecast budget for 2018.

Report of the Scientific Committee

A more detailed report that focuses on the five issues of common interest to the CEP and SC-CAMLR, as identified in 2009 at the joint CEP–SC-CAMLR Workshop in Baltimore, USA, will be presented to CEP-XX by the CCAMLR Scientific Committee Chair, Dr Mark Belchier (United Kingdom). The CEP will also discuss the on-going consideration of the outcomes of the second CEP-SC-CAMLR Workshop which was convened in Punta Arenas, Chile, on 19 and 20 May 2016. Additional matters on which the Scientific Committee provided advice to the Commission at its last meeting included:

Krill resources

8. In relation to catches in the 2015/16 season, the Commission noted that up to 14 September 2016, 11 vessels fished in Subarea 48; the total catch was 258 365 tonnes of which 154 461 tonnes was taken from Subarea 48.1; Subarea 48.1 was closed on 28 May 2016.

9. Six Members notified for a total of 18 vessels for the 2016/17 season.

10. The Commission considered that, based on the risk assessment framework, the risks of localised effects of fishing for krill were increasing and that the current distribution of the trigger level for krill in Area 48 described in Conservation Measure (CM) 51-07 should continue for a minimum period of three years. The Commission requested that the Scientific Committee develop annual updates to the risk assessment framework, and after three years, in 2019, provide a substantive review to inform the Commission on the progress towards feedback management and the allocation of trigger level in CM 51-07.

Fish resources

11. In 2015/16, 12 Members fished for toothfish (Patagonian toothfish (*Dissostichus eleginoides*) and/or Antarctic toothfish (*D. mawsoni*)). The reported total catch of *Dissostichus* spp. to 16 September 2016 was 12 211 tonnes. In comparison, the total reported catch of toothfish in 2014/15 was 15 891 tonnes. The Commission endorsed the Scientific Committee's advice on catch limits in 2016/17 for the fisheries for *D. eleginoides* and *D. mawsoni*.

12. Two Members, the UK and Australia, fished for mackerel icefish (*Champsocephalus gunnari*) and Chile conducted research fishing for *C. gunnari*.

13. The Commission endorsed the advice from the Scientific Committee in respect of the need for continued monitoring of CCAMLR fisheries for overcapacity and agreed that, although there was no indication of an excess in capacity at the current time, the Secretariat should continue to monitor the number of vessels notifying and then subsequently fishing in a subarea in each year, in order to detect any increasing trend.

Bottom fishing and vulnerable marine ecosystems

14. The Commission noted the Scientific Committee's discussions on bottom fishing and vulnerable marine ecosystems (VME) and that there was one notification of a VME risk area in Subarea 88.1 during 2015/16, which brings the total number of VME risk areas to 76.

Marine protected areas

15. The Commission noted the Scientific Committee's discussions on MPA planning in Domain 1, preliminary results of research voyages to the South Orkney MPA, and the latest information on the development of the Weddell Sea MPA (WSMPA) (Domains 3 and 4). It further noted that the Scientific Committee had agreed that the extensive information presented in respect of the Weddell Sea is the best science currently available and that it provides the necessary foundation for MPA planning in this region. It also noted that further work was required to develop these analyses and to identify how they are used in the development of a WSMPA proposal, and encouraged the continuation of this work.

16.   The Commission adopted a new conservation measure establishing time-limited special areas for scientific study in newly exposed marine areas following ice shelf retreat or collapse.

Capacity building

17.   The Commission congratulated applicants from Argentina and China who were selected to receive a CCAMLR scientific scholarship in 2017 and 2018.

Priorities of the Scientific Committee

18.   The Commission considered outcomes of the CCAMLR Scientific Committee Symposium, held at the CCAMLR Secretariat, Hobart, Australia, on 13 and 14 October 2016 and noted the discussion on priorities for the Scientific Committee.

CCAMLR Scheme of International Scientific Observation

19.   The Commission endorsed a phased increase in observer coverage for the krill fishery to achieve 100% observer coverage by the 2020/21 fishing season.

Impacts of climate change

20.   On behalf of the Delegations of Australia and Norway, Australia provided an initial report from the Intersessional Correspondence Group (ICG) on considering approaches for enhancing consideration of climate change impacts in CCAMLR. The paper summarised the group's initial work in 2016, including discussions on topics of concern and processes for improving consideration of climate change impacts. This included ideas on assessing status and trends and highlighting key recommendations from the second Joint CEP–SC-CAMLR Workshop on Climate Change and Monitoring which was held in Punta Arenas, Chile, on 19 and 20 May 2016. Discussions were supportive of bringing climate change related work into a cohesive and prioritised framework, such as is exemplified by the CEP's Climate Change Response Work Programme. The work of the ICG will not be restricted to scientific questions and priorities, but will also seek to take account of policy and management considerations.

Conservation measures

21.   The Commission's consideration of revised and new conservation measures and resolutions, and related matters, is recorded in the Schedule of Conservation Measures in Force 2016/17 published in late 2016.

22.   Conservation Measures adopted at CCAMLR-XXXV included one establishing a Ross Sea region MPA which was first submitted to the Commission by New Zealand and the USA in 2012 and subsequently revised in 2013, 2014 and 2015. The MPA, to come into effect on 1 December 2017, seeks to conserve marine living resources, maintain ecosystem structure and function, protect vital ecosystem processes and areas of ecological significance, and promote scientific research including through the establishment of reference areas (see Annex).

Implementation of Convention objectives

The objectives of the Convention

23.   Chile reported on the second CCAMLR Symposium held in Santiago from 5 to 8 May 2015 noting that the Symposium outcomes will be particularly useful in supporting the Commission's further consideration of strategic priorities for the next 5–10 years. Reflecting on these outcomes and the outcomes of the CCAMLR Scientific Committee Symposium which was held in advance of SC-CAMLR-XXXV, the Commission agreed to terms of reference and working arrangements for an intersessional e-group on strategic priorities for the Commission until 2027.

Performance review

24.   The Commission agreed to terms of reference and supporting processes for a second performance review (which will present its report to CCAMLR-XXXVI in October). At the Commission's invitation, the Chair of the CEP, Ewan McIvor, has agreed to participate in the Review Panel.

Cooperation with the Antarctic Treaty System and international organisations

25.   The Executive Secretary provided the Commission with a summary of relevant issues arising from the 39th Antarctic Treaty Consultative Meeting (ATCM XXXIX).

26.   The Commission was advised that a report from the SCAR Observer was presented to SC-CAMLR-XXXV providing an update on SCAR's extensive range of activities relevant to the work of the Scientific Committee and Commission, highlighting the effective engagement between SCAR and CCAMLR.

27.   Noting that the Commission has formal arrangements with the Agreement for the Conservation of Albatrosses and Petrels (ACAP), the Commission for the Conservation of Southern Bluefin Tuna (CCSBT) and the Western and Central Pacific Fisheries Commission (WCPFC) the Commission encouraged the Secretariat to establish MoUs with other relevant regional fisheries management organisations.

Next meeting

Election of officers

28.   The Commission elected South Africa to the position of Chair of the Commission for the 2017 and 2018 meetings.

29.   The Commission confirmed the recommendation from SCIC that Ms J. Kim be elected as SCIC Chair.

Date and location of the next meeting

30.   The Thirty-sixth Meeting will be held in Hobart, Australia, from 16 to 27 October 2017. The Thirty-sixth Meeting of the Scientific Committee will be held from 16 to 20 October 2017.

Annex

The CCAMLR Ross Sea region marine protected area, including the boundaries of the General Protection Zone (areas i, ii and iii), the Special Research Zone and the Krill Research Zone (Conservation Measure 91-05).

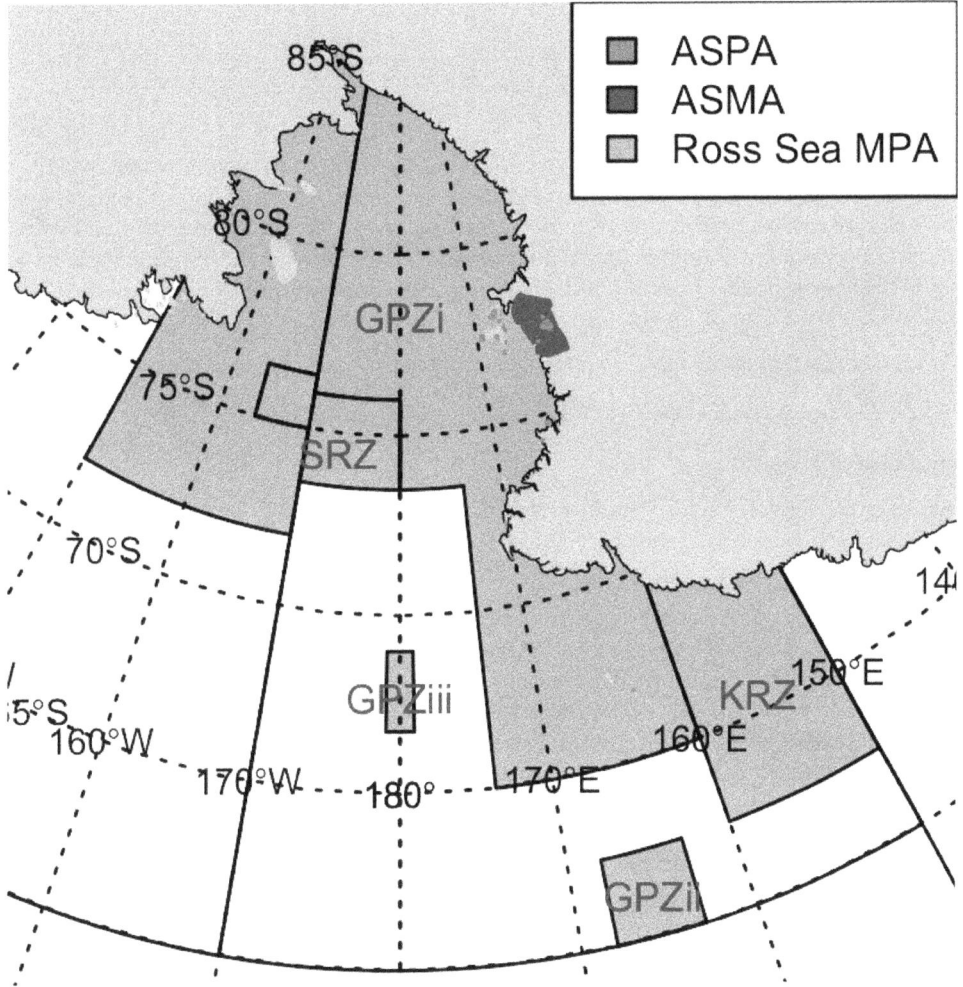

The Scientific Committee on Antarctic Research Annual Report 2016 – 2017 to the XL Antarctic Treaty Consultative Meeting

Information Paper submitted by SCAR

Summary

This paper presents the annual report of The Scientific Committee on Antarctic Research (SCAR) to the Antarctic Treaty Consultative Meeting. For ease of consideration, the main features of the report are presented as an infographic.

Background

The mission of SCAR is to advance Antarctic research, including observations from Antarctica, and to promote scientific knowledge, understanding and education on any aspect of the Antarctic region. To this end, SCAR is charged with the initiation and international coordination of Antarctic and Southern Ocean research beneficial to global society. SCAR provides independent and objective scientific advice and information to the Antarctic Treaty System and other bodies, and acts as the main international exchange of Antarctic information within the scientific community.

Descriptions of SCAR's activities and scientific outputs are available at: *http://www.scar.org/*.

SCAR will celebrate its 60th anniversary in 2018.

Recent Developments

In addition to the synopsis of key outcomes and activities of SCAR presented in Figure 1, SCAR's three science groups, six research programmes, and several specialized subsidiary groups have undertaken a wide variety of activities and produced many outputs, a suite of which are formally presented at this meeting, including in the SCAR Lecture.

At the XXXIV SCAR Meeting and Open Science Conference, held in Kuala Lumpur, Malaysia, a new Executive Committee was elected by the Delegates: Prof Steven L. Chown (President); Prof Dr Karin Lochte (Vice-President), Prof Terry Wilson (Vice-President), Prof Dr Azizan bin Abu Samah (Vice-President), Prof Jefferson Cardia Simões (Vice-President), Prof Jerónimo López-Martínez (Immediate Past President). Dr Jenny Baeseman is SCAR's Executive Director. Dr Aleks Terauds is SCAR's representative to the Committee for Environmental Protection.

Selected Forthcoming Meetings

XII SCAR Biology Symposium. 10-14 July 2017, Brussels, Belgium. http://www.scarbiology2017.org/

Past Antarctic Ice Sheet Dynamics (PAIS) Conference 2017. 10-15 September 2017, Trieste, Italy. http://pais-conference-2017.inogs.it/

IX Congreso Latinoamericano de Ciencia Antártica. 4-6 October 2017, Punta Arenas, Chile. http://www.inach.cl/inach/?p=21366

The XXXV SCAR Meetings and Open Science Conference. 15-27 June 2018, Davos, Switzerland. The Open Science Conference will cover both polar regions, being organized jointly with the International Arctic Science Committee (IASC). *http://www.polar2018.org/*

SCIENTIFIC COMMITTEE ON ANTARCTIC RESEARCH ANNUAL REPORT 2016-2017

XXXIV SCAR MEETINGS AND OPEN SCIENCE CONFERENCE

Participants: 849
Abstracts: 1030
Parallel sessions: 41
Mini-symposiums: 5

AWARDS

Medal for Excellence in Antarctic Research — Dr.Robert Dunbar, USA

Medal for International Scientific Coordination — Dr.Heinrich Miller, Germany

SCAR President's Medal for Outstanding Achievement — Dr.Francisco Herve, Chile

MEMBERSHIP

Full Members
Associate Members
New Associate Members

A YEAR IN NUMBERS

4 Early Career Fellowships

2 Visiting Professor Awards

110 Women in Antarctic Research Wikipedia Bios

1 New Partnership with the Asian Forum for Polar Sciences

1 New Strategic Plan

3 New Research Groups

Graphic: Warren Clark

Find us at: scar.org

213

Annual Report for 2016/17 of the Council of Managers of National Antarctic Programs (COMNAP)

COMNAP is the organisation of National Antarctic Programs which brings together, in particular, the national officials responsible for planning, conducting and managing support to Antarctic science on behalf of their respective governments.

COMNAP is an international association, established in September 1988, whose Members are the 30 National Antarctic Programs from the countries of Argentina, Australia, Belgium, Brazil, Bulgaria, Chile, China, Czech Republic, Ecuador, Finland, France, Germany, India, Italy, Japan, Republic of Belarus, Republic of Korea, Netherlands, New Zealand, Norway, Peru, Poland, Russian Federation, South Africa, Spain, Sweden, Ukraine, United Kingdom, United States and Uruguay. The National Antarctic Programs of Canada (from August 2016), Portugal (from August 2015), and Venezuela (from August 2015) are currently COMNAP Observers organisations.

COMNAP's purpose is to develop and promote best practice in managing the support of scientific research in the Antarctic. As an organisation, COMNAP acts to add value to National Antarctic Program's efforts by serving as a forum to develop practices that improve effectiveness of activities in an environmentally responsible manner, by facilitating and promoting international partnerships, and by providing opportunities and systems for information exchange.

COMNAP strives to provide the Antarctic Treaty System with objective, practical, technical and non-political advice drawn from the National Antarctic Programs' extensive expertise and their first-hand Antarctic knowledge. Since 1988, COMNAP has been an active contributor to ATCM and CEP discussion, with the presentation of 32 Working Papers and 105 Information Papers.

COMNAP continues to have a close working relationship with other Antarctic organisations, in particular with SCAR. A joint COMNAP/SCAR EXCOM Meeting was held in Kuala Lumpur, Malaysia, August 2016. COMNAP was an invited observer to the IAATO Annual Meeting and presented reports to the Forum of Arctic Research Operators (FARO) Annual Meeting, to the Hydrographic Commission on Antarctica (HCA) 14th Conference, and to the 17th International Ice Charting Working Group (IICWG) meetings. A particular highlight for COMNAP in 2016 was the Search and Rescue (SAR) Workshop III convened in co-operation with the Chilean Directorate General of the Maritime Territory and Merchant Marine (DIRECTEMAR) and with Instituto Antártico Chileno (INACH).

The COMNAP Annual General Meeting (AGM) was held in August 2016 in Goa, India, hosted by the National Centre for Antarctic and Oceans Research. Sessions on energy & technology, shipping, and safety were convened. Professor Kazuyuki Shiraishi of Japan's National Institute of Polar Research continues in his three-year term as the COMNAP Chair to AGM 2017 (August). Michelle Rogan-Finnemore continues as Executive Secretary. The University of Canterbury, Christchurch, New Zealand, continues to host the COMNAP Secretariat.

COMNAP Highlights and Achievements for 2016/17

Search and Rescue (SAR) Workshop III - *convened*

In support of safe operations in the Antarctic Treaty region, and as agreed by COMNAP in response to ATCM Resolution 4 (2013), to regularly convene workshops to discuss SAR and emergency response, COMNAP convened the SAR Workshop III on 1–2 June 2016, co-hosted by DIRECTEMAR and INACH. National Antarctic Programs, Rescue Co-ordination Centres (RCCs) IAATO, CCAMLR, and COSPAS–SARSAT delegates participated and a SAR table-top exercise was carried out. The workshop report is submitted as an IP to this ATCM and is also available from
https://www.comnap.aq/Publications/Comnap%20Publications/COMNAP_SAR_WorkshopIII_Final_Report_7July2016.pdf.

COMNAP Symposium 2016 "Winter-Over Challenges" – *convened & Proceedings published*

COMNAP convened its 17th Symposium (August 2016); the theme was "Winter-Over Challenges". The Symposiums are open forums where people involved in managing the support of scientific research in Antarctica can share their experience, expertise and thoughts for the benefit of others. Many National Antarctic Programs are operating wintering/year-round stations and scientific data collected in Antarctica during the winter is critical to inform global studies of the Earth System. The objective of the Symposium recognised that winter-over is challenging and presented solutions to those challenges that are of an operational, technical and personnel nature. There were 112 participants from 30 National Antarctic Programs and others, who contributed to discussions, made presentations or displayed posters. The Symposium Proceedings (published February 2017) can be downloaded from: https://www.comnap.aq/Publications/Comnap%20Publications/Proceedings%20of%20the%20COMNAP%20 Symposium%202016%20Winter-Over%20Challenges.pdf.

Unmanned Aerial Systems Working Group (UAS-WG) – *review of Handbook*

Formed as a sub-group of the COMNAP Air Expert Group, the UAS-WGs purpose is to "…reduce risk to people, infrastructure and environment in the Antarctic Treaty area, while enabling…UAS use in the area for scientific applications and science support purposes." Experts from fourteen COMNAP Member programs are participants. In the intercessional period, post-Antarctic summer science support season, the UAS-WG reviewed the UAS Handbook and carried out an informal survey of COMNAP Members in regards to UAS use in the Antarctic Treaty region (see IP to this ATCM/CEP meeting). Intercessionally, the COMNAP Secretariat remained in close contact with the SCAR SC-ATS in regards to their work on UAS and wildlife.

Station Catalogue – *underway with on-line GIS interface complete*

The COMNAP Station Catalogue, which began as a collaboration with the EU-PolarNet, provides comprehensive information on the National Antarctic Program stations which will be useful to promote future collaboration, exchange of scientists and sharing of infrastructures. The information in the catalogue was provided by National Antarctic Programs and will be updated in the COMNAP database which supports the range of COMNAP products and tools (see additional information on the catalogue and database in an IP to this ATCM). Non-sensitive data are available publicly by way of a GIS interface at: https://www.comnap.aq/Members/SitePages/Home.aspx.

COMNAP Antarctic Research Fellowship – *application round open*

COMNAP established the Antarctic Research Fellowship in 2011 and since that time has awarded eight fellowships, plus four jointly with SCAR. The Fellowship aims to assist early career researchers, technicians and engineers. The 2016 Fellowships were awarded to Ronja Reese (Potsdam Institute for Climate Impact Research, Germany) to undertake research on "Importance of ice buttressing in Antarctica" at the British Antarctic Survey; Blanca Figuerola (University of Barcelona, Spain) to undertake research on "Vulnerability of Antarctic bryozoan communities to environmental change" at the Australian Antarctic Division; and a joint COMNAP/SCAR Fellowship was awarded to Christopher Horvat (Harvard University, USA) to undertake research on " Modelling the Antarctic Sea Ice Floe Size Distribution" at the National Institute of Water and Atmosphere, New Zealand). The 2017 Fellowship round focuses on a list of key projects of value to National Antarctic Programs and closes on 1 July 2017. SCAR and COMNAP are also working with CCAMLR to promote their scholarships. See https://www.comnap.aq/SitePages/fellowships.aspx.

COMNAP Antarctic Roadmap Challenges (ARC) Project – *complete*

The COMNAP ARC project, a follow-on project from the SCAR Antarctic Science Horizon Scan, explored the technology, logistics, operations, funding and international collaboration challenges that will likely be encountered by the National Antarctic Programs in the delivery of Antarctic science in the mid- to long-term. See COMNAP ATCMXXXIX (2016) IP051 for full outcomes of the project. The project was completed in 2016; results are published in *Antarctic Science*, volume 28, issue 6, http://dx.doi.org/10.1017/S0954102016000481.

COMNAP Products and Tools

Search and Rescue (SAR) Webpage   www.comnap.aq/membersonly/SitePages/SAR.aspx

As requested in ATCM Resolution 4 (2013), COMNAP has established a SAR webpage in consultation with RCCs which is regularly updated. SAR contacts have also been publicly listed on the COMNAP website based on SAR Workshop III discussions.

Accident, Incident & Near-Miss Reporting (AINMR) www.comnap.aq/membersonly/AINMR/SitePages/Home.aspx

AINMR was developed to assist in information exchange and is available on the Members-only area of the COMNAP website. The AINMR's primary objective is: to capture information about events that had, or could have had, serious consequences; and/or reveal lessons; and/or for novel or very unusual events. Full reports on accidents can also be posted and shared on the site and can be discussed and reviewed.

Ship Position Reporting System (SPRS) www.comnap.aq/sprs/SitePages/Home.aspx

SPRS is an optional, voluntary system for exchange of information about National Antarctic Program ship operations. Its primary purpose is to facilitate collaboration. It can also make a very useful contribution to safety with all SPRS data made available to the RCCs as an additional source of information complementing all other national and international systems in place. A review of the SPRS led to the testing of a new COMNAP "Asset Tracking System (CATS)" for the 2016/17 summer season. CATS included vessel and some aircraft movements. The results of the CATS test will be discussed at the COMNAP AGM 2017.

Antarctic Flight Information Manual (AFIM) e-AFIM

AFIM is a handbook of aeronautical information published as a tool towards safe air operations in Antarctica as per Resolution 1 (2013). COMNAP no longer publishes the AFIM in loosely-bound paper format, beginning on 1 October 2016, AFIM is published in PDF format and is available to all subscribers by way of a link to the most current version (date-stamped).

Antarctic Telecommunications Operators Manual (ATOM)

ATOM is an evolution of the handbook of telecommunications practices to which ATCM Recommendation X-3 *Improvement of Telecommunications in Antarctica and the Collection and Distribution of Antarctic Meteorological Data* refers. COMNAP Members and SAR authorities have access to the latest version (February 2017) via the COMNAP website. The format of ATOM will be revised to reflect the new format of the COMNAP database.

---

www.comnap.aq

Attachment 1: COMNAP officers, projects, expert groups and meetings

Executive Committee (EXCOM)

The COMNAP Chair and Vice-Chairs are elected officers of COMNAP. The elected officers plus the Executive Secretary, compose the COMNAP Executive Committee as follows:

Position	Officer	Term expires
Chair	Kazuyuki Shiraishi (NIPR) kshiraishi@nipr.ac.jp	AGM 2017
Vice-Chairs	Javed Beg (NCAOR) javed.beg@gmail.com	AGM 2019
	Yves Frenot (IPEV) yves.frenot@ipev.fr	AGM 2017
	John Guldahl (NPI) john.guldahl@npolar.no	AGM 2019
	José Retamales (INACH) jretamales@inach.cl	AGM 2017
	Rob Wooding (AAD) rob.wooding@aad.gov.au	AGM 2017
	[John Hall (BAS) & Hyoung Chul Shin (KOPRI) completed their 3-year Vice-Chair terms in August 2016]	
Executive Secretary	Michelle Rogan-Finnemore michelle.finnemore@comnap.aq	

Table 1 – COMNAP Executive Committee.

Projects

Project	Project Manager	EXCOM officer (oversight)
Antarctic Flight Information Manual (AFIM) – Electronic Format Implementation	Paul Morin & Brian Stone (until May 2016)	John Hall (until August 2016) / Michelle Rogan-Finnemore
Antarctic Roadmap Challenges (ARC) Working Group	Michelle Rogan-Finnemore	Kazuyuki Shiraishi
Test COMNAP Asset Tracking System (CATS)	Robb Clifton	Hyoung Chul Shin (until August 2016) / José Retamales
Facilities Database and Catalogue	Michelle Rogan-Finnemore & Andrea Colombo	Yves Frenot

Table 2 – COMNAP projects currently in progress.

Expert Groups

Expert Group (topic)	Expert Group leader	EXCOM officer (oversight)
Air (includes the UAS-WG)	Paul Sheppard	John Guldahl
Energy & Technology	Felix Bartsch & Pavel Kapler	Rob Wooding
Environment	Anoop Tiwari	Rob Wooding
Medical	Anne Hicks	Javed Beg
Outreach/Education	Dragomir Mateev	Yves Frenot
Safety	Simon Trotter	Kazuyuki Shiraishi
Science (includes the SOOS "Think Tank")	Robb Clifton	José Retamales
Shipping	Miguel Ojeda	José Retamales
Training	Veronica Vlasich	Yves Frenot

Table 3 – COMNAP Expert Groups.

Meetings

Previous 12 months

1–2 June 2016, Search and Rescue (SAR) Workshop III, co-hosted by Instituto Antártico Chileno (INACH) and DIRECTEMAR, Valparaiso, Chile.

16–18 August 2016, COMNAP Annual General Meeting (AGM) XXVIII (2016), hosted by the National Centre for Antarctic and Oceans Research (NCAOR), Goa, India.

19–20 August 2016, COMNAP Symposium 2016 "Wintering-Over Challenges", hosted by the National Centre for Antarctic and Oceans Research (NCAOR), Goa, India.

21 August 2016, Joint SCAR/COMNAP Executive Committee (EXCOM) Meeting, Kuala Lumpur, Malaysia.

21–22 August 2016, Joint Expert Group on Human Biology and Medicine (JEGHBM) Meeting, Kuala Lumpur, Malaysia.

5–6 December 2016, COMNAP Executive Committee (EXCOM) Meeting, hosted by the National Institute of Polar Research (NIPR), Tachikawa, Japan.

Upcoming

31 July–2 August 2017, COMNAP Annual General Meeting (AGM) XXIX (2017), hosted by the Czech Republic National Antarctic Program at Masaryk University, Brno, Czech Republic. Will include the joint COMNAP/SCAR Executive Committee (EXCOM) Meeting 2017 and a workshop session on energy & technology requirements for science support as identified by the ARC project.

3. Reports by Experts

Report by the Secretariat of the International Hydrographic Organization as Chair of the IHO Hydrographic Commission on Antarctica

Introduction

The International Hydrographic Organization (IHO) is an intergovernmental consultative and technical organization. It comprises 87 Member States. Each State is normally represented by its national Hydrographer.

The IHO coordinates on a worldwide basis the setting of standards for hydrographic data and the provision of hydrographic services in support of safety of navigation and the protection and sustainable use of the marine environment. The principal aim of the IHO is to ensure that all the world's seas, oceans and navigable waters are surveyed and charted.

What is Hydrography?

Hydrography deals with the measurement and description of the physical features of oceans, seas, coastal areas, lakes and rivers. Hydrographic surveying identifies the shape and nature of the seafloor and the hazards that lie upon it, together with an understanding of the impact of tides on the depth and on water movement. This knowledge supports all marine activities, including scientific studies, environmental protection and transport.

Importance of Hydrography in Antarctica

Hydrographic information is a fundamental pre-requisite for the development of successful and environmentally sustainable human activities in the seas and oceans. Unfortunately, there is little or no hydrographic information for a number of parts of the world, especially in Antarctica.

In this particular region, where vessels may face the most severe weather conditions, any grounding due to a lack of adequate surveying or nautical charting may have serious consequences. Unfortunately, the grounding of vessels operating outside previously navigated routes in Antarctica is not uncommon.

The Polar Code, adopted by the International Maritime Organization (IMO) in 2014, includes significant cautions concerning hydrography and nautical charting in the polar regions.

As stated, the Polar Code

> ... *"considers hazards which may lead to elevated levels of risk due to increased probability of occurrence, more severe consequences, or both (...)*

and notes in particular:

> *...remoteness and possible lack of accurate and complete **hydrographic data and information**, reduced availability of navigational aids and seamarks with increased potential for groundings compounded by remoteness, limited readily deployable Search and Rescue (SAR) facilities, delays in emergency response and limited communications capability, with the potential to affect incident response ..."*

Most scientific studies and an understanding of the marine environment benefit significantly from a knowledge of the nature and shape of the seafloor and the movement of the water caused by tides. Therefore the lack of such hydrographic knowledge in most Antarctic waters, particularly in the coastal and shallower regions, must compromise many scientific endeavours being undertaken under the auspices of ATCM and individual Member States.

IHO Hydrographic Commission on Antarctica

The HCA comprises 24 IHO Member States (Argentina, Australia, Brazil, Chile, China, Colombia, Ecuador, France, Germany, Greece, India, Italy, Japan, Republic of Korea, New Zealand, Norway, Peru, Russian Federation, South Africa, Spain, United Kingdom, Uruguay, USA, Venezuela), all of which have acceded to the Antarctic Treaty and are therefore also directly represented in the ATCM.

The IHO Hydrographic Commission on Antarctica (HCA) was formed in 1998 aimed at coordinating activities between its Member States to improve the quality, coverage and availability of nautical charting and other marine geospatial and hydrographic information and services covering the region.

Ways and Means to Improve Hydrography and Nautical Charting in Antarctica

The IHO has reported regularly on the unsatisfactory level of hydrographic knowledge in Antarctica since ATCM XXXI (Kiev, 2008) and the inherent risks involved for all seaborne activities taking place around the continent. Barely 5% of the depth in Antarctic waters has been measured. The IHO has consistently indicated the requirement to obtain support at the highest political levels if things are to improve significantly.

It is pleasing that ATCM XXXVII adopted Resolution 5 (2014) on strengthening cooperation in hydrographic surveying and charting of Antarctic waters. However, there has been little noticeable impact or improvement on the previously reported situation.

The IHO HCA attempts to work closely with stakeholder organizations such as COMNAP, IAATO, SCAR, IMO and IOC, However, with the exception of successful work with IAATO, no co-operative programmes or packages using ships of opportunity or other resources have been achieved in order to improve hydrographic data in critical shipping areas.

Depth Measurement to be Included in Environmental Data Observing Programmes

The IHO is committed to the collection and management of reference bathymetric data sets required for modelling the different ocean and coastal mechanisms, in particular through the programme of the General Bathymetric Chart of the Oceans (GEBCO), which is co-governed by the IHO and the IOC, and the IHO Data Centre for Digital Bathymetry (DCDB) that acts as the global data repository for publicly available bathymetry of the world's oceans, seas and coastal waters, including the underpinning data for GEBCO.

The IHO is now encouraging innovative supplementary data gathering and data maximizing initiatives, to increase mankind's knowledge of the bathymetry of the seas, oceans and coastal waters including crowd-sourced bathymetry (volunteered geographic data) including in Antarctica.

The advent of particularly inexpensive data loggers means that it is now possible to use existing equipment in a non-intrusive way for all seafarers to collect and render bathymetric data to the IHO DCDB. Most ships are inherently capable of measuring and digitally recording the depth in coastal waters using existing ship's equipment and an increasing number of vessels are capable of taking measurements in deeper water using existing ship's equipment. This is particularly so for scientific and passenger vessels and supply ships.

The IHO considers that the measurement, recording and rendering of depth data as a routine environmental observing activity should be undertaken at all times when vessels are at sea, and where no restrictions apply.

Proposal for a Seminar on the Importance of Hydrography in the Antarctic Region

At the thirty-ninth Antarctic Treaty Consultative Meeting in Santiago, Chile, the IHO Representative suggested that it would be useful to examine in much more detail the impact of the status of hydrographic surveys and nautical charts covering Antarctic waters. It was proposed that the IHO considers organising a seminar similar to the one offered at ATCM XXXI held in Ukraine in 2008. Chile and Ecuador supported the IHO proposal.

As a result,

... *The Meeting agreed to insert a new priority relating to hydrographic surveying in Antarctica, and agreed to consider the issue in 2018* (see ATCM Final Report paragraph 161).

The IHO proposes that a seminar be arranged during the first days of ATCM XLI in Ecuador in 2018. It would be led by the Secretary General of the IHO, who is also Chair of the IHO Hydrographic Commission on Antarctica (HCA). The seminar would be supported by the national Hydrographers represented in the IHO HCA. Other relevant supporting organizations that operate under the umbrella of the IHO, including the General Bathymetric Chart of the Oceans (GEBCO) project and the International Bathymetric Chart of the Southern Oceans (IBCSO) projects would contribute. Collaborating and supporting Organizations including SCAR, COMNAP, CCAMLR and IAATO will be invited to provide their perspectives as part of the seminar.

In addition to the statement made by Ecuador at ATCM XXXIX in Chile supporting the principle of holding a seminar in Ecuador as part of ATCM XLI in 2018, the IHO Secretariat has received further correspondence[1] from Ecuador as the host country, supporting this position.

The seminar will examine in detail the impact of the currently unacceptable state of hydrographic knowledge, nautical charting and bathymetric mapping covering Antarctic waters, particularly in relation to safety, operations, environmental protection, climate change, oceanographic modeling and research in the region. The seminar will go on to identify several practical, low-cost solutions that States and other Organizations can implement to improve the current situation. The seminar will also draw attention to the existing arrangements in the IHO that enable would-be data providers from the ATCM community to identify specific areas where their own activities can be used to provide much-needed depth data for the common good.

The outcome of the seminar will be a number of recommendations on a coordinated implementation plan for subsequent consideration by the ATCM.

Proposals for Consideration by ATCM

The IHO invites ATCM to include a seminar on the status and the impact of hydrography in the Antarctic to be delivered by the IHO as part of the programme for ATCM XLI in Ecuador in 2018.

The IHO invites ATCM to consider including in its relevant policy/doctrine/regulations covering ship operations (passenger vessels, scientific campaigns, supply activities, etc.), an encouragement that the measurement, recording and rendering of depth data should be undertaken at sea at all times as a routine environmental observing activity unless particular restrictions apply.

---

[1] Letter from Under Secretary of Latin America and the Caribbean, Ministry of External Relations, dated 28 November 2016, to the General Commander of the Navy, Ecuador.

WMO Annual Report 2016-2017

The World Meteorological Organization[2] (WMO) is a specialized agency of the <u>United Nations</u> and includes 191 Member States and Territories. It is the UN system's authoritative voice on the state and behaviour of the Earth's atmosphere, its interaction with the oceans, the climate it produces and the resulting distribution of water resources.

The WMO Polar and High Mountain regions priority activity promotes and coordinates relevant observations, research and services that are carried out in the Antarctic, Arctic and high mountain regions by nations and by groups of nations. It interfaces with all WMO activities (including the World Climate and Word Weather Research Programmes[3]) and other related programmes throughout the world, meeting global needs and requirements for observations, research and services in the polar and high mountain regions.

The Global Cryosphere Watch (GCW) is foundational to WMO's polar initiatives and its observing component is one of the four essential observing systems under the WMO Integrated Global Observing Systems (see IP 113 for further details). Three stations were also added to the Antarctic Observing Network (AntON), which is maintained by WMO and SCAR (see IP 117).

WMO's Polar Space Task Group provides coordination across Space Agencies to facilitate acquisition and distribution of fundamental satellite datasets, and to contribute to or support the development of specific derived products for cryospheric, polar, and high-mountain scientific research and applications. IP 114 gives examples of such products we believe will be of interest to Treaty Parties.

The Year of Polar Prediction (YOPP) is an initiative covering the period 2017 – 2019 centred on 2018, which aims to improve environmental prediction capabilities by coordinating periods of intensive observing, modelling, prediction, verification, and user-engagement and education activities. A special Observing Period is planned in Antarctica from 16 Nov 2018 to 15 Feb 2019 (see associated IP 116).

WMO is planning the development of an Antarctic Polar Regional Climate Centre (PRCC) Network based on the example and lessons learned from the Arctic PRCC Network. We invite Treaty Parties and other interested organisations to engage with the development of an Antarctic PRCC (see associated IP 118).

Through its co-sponsored World Climate Research Programme[2], WMO carries out a number of research activities (often in partnership with SCAR and others) of relevance to Treaty Parties. This year we are submitting two additional papers, on the Polar Climate Predictability Initiative (see IP 115) and on Model Downscaling in the Antarctic (see IP 119).

WMO is committed to a positive, mutually beneficial engagement with Treaty Parties in Antarctic weather and climate observation, services and research.

---

[2] www.wmo.int

[3] The World Climate Research Programme is co-sponsored by WMO, the Intergovernmental Oceanographic Commission (IOC) and the International Council for Science (ICSU). See: <u>www.wcrp-climate.org</u>. The World Weather Research Programme is sponsored by WMO. See www.wmo.int/wwrp

Report of the Antarctic and Southern Ocean Coalition

1.   *Introduction*

ASOC is pleased to be in Beijing for the XL Antarctic Treaty Consultative Meeting. This report briefly describes ASOC's work over the past year, and outlines some key issues for this ATCM.

ASOC's Secretariat is in Washington DC, USA and its website is http://www.asoc.org. ASOC has 24 full member groups in 10 countries and supporting groups in those and several other countries.

2.   *Intersessional activities*

Since XXXIX ATCM ASOC and its member groups' representatives participated actively in intersessional discussions in the ATCM and CEP fora.

ASOC and member group representatives attended a range of meetings relevant to Antarctic environmental protection including the XXXV CCAMLR Meeting, International Maritime Organization meetings relating to the Polar Code, the SCAR Open Science Conference 2016, the IAATO annual meeting, and others. At the 2016 CCAMLR meeting, the Ross Sea Marine Protected Area (RSMPA) was designated, a goal which ASOC has been working towards since 2008. Additionally, from 1st January 2017 the International Code for shipping in polar waters took effect, another goal towards which ASOC has been working since 2008. ASOC has continued to engage with the development of the research and monitoring plan for the MPA, since this is critical to the success of the MPA in accomplishing its objectives.

ASOC member organization WWF released their Tracking Antarctica report at CCAMLR XXXV and has provided information in *Tracking Antarctica: A WWF report on the state of Antarctica and the Southern Ocean* (IP 152). Tracking Antarctica provides a scientific update on the state of Antarctica and the Southern Ocean and highlights recommended solutions. In particular it highlights the need to increase efforts to create a network of MPAs in the Southern Ocean and to develop a more robust response to climate change.

ASOC and WWF are also members of the Antarctic Wildlife Research Fund (AWR), which provided $150,000 to fund three scientific research projects on Antarctic marine ecosystems.

3.   *Priorities for ATCM XL*

ASOC has three major priorities for the ATCM. Below, we detail our recommendations for actions that ATCPs can take at this ATCM under each of those priority areas.

- Expansion of protected areas network

The network of Antarctic Specially Protected Areas (ASPAs) does not fully protect the range of values included in Annex V of the Protocol. In our IP *Considerations for the systematic expansion of the protected areas network* (IP 153), ASOC notes that the adoption of a protected area response that matches current environmental pressures is becoming all the more apparent, and urgent, as human presence in continues to grow across a range of terrestrial, coastal and marine environments; and impacts from climate change increase. ASOC suggests that the ATCM initiates a systematic conservation planning process as soon as possible to expand the network. To assist this process, ASOC has compiled an online database of information relevant to the designation of new areas. We hope the database will be useful to ATCPs and would be happy to receive feedback on how we can improve it.

Furthermore, in *ASOC update on Marine Protected Areas in the Southern Ocean 2016-2017* (IP 149) we provide an update on CCAMLR's work on MPAs, including an MPA discussion at CCAMLR XXXV in 2016, and encourage the ATCM to undertake a process of systematic conservation planning similar to CCAMLR's. This would be important in order to apply the protected area tools of the Environmental Protocol effectively across the Antarctic Treaty area.

- Precautionary management of tourism and other activities

The ATCM has discussed tourism extensively over the past few years, but has made few decisions about how to move forward. To assist the ATCM in taking the next steps on this issue, ASOC has provided *Options for Visitor Management in the Antarctic* (IP 150). This paper discusses some approaches to visitor management in other parts of the world and suggests how the ATCM can apply those approaches to the Antarctic context. Overall, ASOC stresses that it is important for the ATCM to begin a process that will result in consensus decisions about tourism.

Managing non-SOLAS vessels in the Southern Ocean (IP 151) highlights that recent work on the Polar Code at the International Maritime Organization does not cover fishing vessels or private pleasure craft, which represent a significant proportion of the vessels operating in the Southern Ocean. Since many ATCPs have previously noted their concern about the potential risks to human life and the environment from unsafe vessel operations, ASOC recommends that Parties adopt a Decision on the need for concerted action at the IMO to ensure that Phase 2 of work on non-SOLAS vessels at the IMO commences urgently and concludes satisfactorily with no further delay.

- Development of an active ATCM response to Antarctic climate change

ASOC believes that the Antarctic Treaty System, including the ATCM, must take urgent action to address the impact of climate change on the Antarctic environment. In *Antarctic Climate Change Report Card* (IP 147), ASOC summarizes and highlights recent scientific findings on climate change that demonstrate the seriousness of the changes underway in the Antarctic. There are a number of management actions that the ATCM could take, including the designation of protected areas that can serve as climate reference zones, that could increase ecosystem resilience and the ability of scientists to monitor and understand these changes.

Overall, ASOC encourages the ATCM to be proactive on issues that influence significant Antarctic values, and move from discussion to decision.

4.   *Concluding Remarks*

Over the past year, ASOC has engaged with many and varied partners, including IAATO, SCAR, CCAMLR, the Coalition of Legal Toothfish Operators (COLTO), and the Antarctic Wildlife Research Fund (AWR), to work broadly towards identifying strengths and weaknesses existing in the Antarctic Treaty System procedures and practices, while suggesting solutions to these gaps. We value our engagement with these groups, as well as with Antarctic Treaty Parties.

In particular, ASOC would like to highlight our paper with IAATO, *Collaborating on Antarctic Education and Outreach* (IP 148), which describes some successful joint work our organizations have done over the past year. We plan to continue these efforts and thereby expand the knowledge of the public about Antarctica. We welcome further collaborations with other Parties, Observers and Experts.

Report of the International Association of Antarctica Tour Operators 2016-17

Under Article III (2) of the Antarctic Treaty

Introduction

The International Association of Antarctica Tour Operators (IAATO) is pleased to report its activities to ATCM XL, under Article III (2) of the Antarctic Treaty.

IAATO continues to focus activities in support of its mission statement to advocate and promote the practice of safe and environmentally responsible private sector travel to Antarctica by ensuring:

- Effective day-to-day management of member activities in Antarctica;
- Educational outreach, including scientific collaboration; and
- Development and promotion of Antarctic tourism best practices.

A detailed description of IAATO, its mission statement, primary activities and recent developments can be found in the *2017-18 Fact Sheet*, and on the IAATO website: www.iaato.org.

IAATO Membership and Visitor Levels during 2016-17

IAATO comprises 115 Operators and Associates, representing businesses from 66% of the Antarctic Treaty Consultative Party countries. IAATO Operators carry nationals from nearly all Treaty Parties annually to Antarctica, and nationals from a further 50 non-Treaty Party countries. Since 2010, IAATO has represented all passenger vessels operating in Antarctic waters under the International Convention for the Safety of Life at Sea (SOLAS), with two exceptions; Japanese operated cruise-only vessel ASUKA II during the 2015-16 season and Japanese operated cruise-only vessel OCEAN DREAM in 2016-17.

During the 2016-17 Antarctic tourism season the total number of visitors travelling with IAATO Operators was 44,367, representing an increase of 15% compared to the previous season. IAATO numbers have not reached the peak of the 2007–8 season (46,265), however preliminary estimates for the 2017-18 season indicate that IAATO numbers will be close to the peak level of visitation.

Details on tourism statistics including activities and nationalities can be found in ATCM XL / IP163 rev. 1 *IAATO Overview of Antarctic Tourism: 2016-17 Season and Preliminary Estimates for 2017-18*. The Membership Directory and additional statistics on IAATO member activities can be found at www.iaato.org.

Recent Work and Activities

A number of initiatives were undertaken during the year, many of which are focusing on strengthening systems in support of managing activities for expected growth:

- In September 2016, the IAATO Tourism Growth Working Group and the IAATO Executive Committee met in Noto, Sicily for a three-day workshop to develop a proposed strategic approach and priorities for actions for IAATO in order to manage for the anticipated growth in tourism activities. The outcomes of this workshop will be discussed at IAATO's 2017 Annual Meeting.

- IAATO continues to invest in the strengthening and training of field staff, recognising the importance of their role in enforcing Treaty agreements and IAATO standards and guidelines. Specifically:
  - 880 field staff passed the IAATO online Field Staff Assessment and Certification Programme for the 2016-17 season. This represents a 30% increase on last year's participation. Certification is mandatory for many IAATO Operators and 1145 field staff have passed since 2012–13. The Assessment continually evolves, testing staff's knowledge of IAATO's Field Operations Manual which is updated annually and incorporates relevant updates from ATCM and CEP agreements.
  - In September 2017, IAATO, in conjunction with its sister organization in the Arctic, the Association of Arctic Expedition Cruise Operators (AECO), will hold the second combined Field Staff Conference in Iceland. The participation of Treaty Party representatives at the conference is welcomed.

- Educating members, their field staff and clients about Antarctic science and conservation issues is an important component of IAATO's work. During the 2016/17 season IAATO has:
  - Increased frequency in issues of Field Staff Newsletters, designed to disseminate latest information and build community spirit.
  - Instigated and expanded the IAATO Antarctic Ambassador Scheme on various platforms, including social media.
  - Increased participation in citizen science projects, including collaboration with a number of research groups and National Antarctic Programs (NAP).
  - Increased the number of key documents and guidelines translated into different languages and improved the translations used in IAATO's animated films.

- IAATO receives many enquiries on an annual basis from individuals, yachts and private groups who are at various stages of planning expeditions to Antarctica. IAATO explains the Antarctic Treaty System and permitting/authorization process to all of these and passes information to a relevant Competent Authority.

- Efforts to strengthen shipping safety in the region remain a priority within the organization. For example:
  - Crowd sourcing for hydrographic data continues to grow and the data remains available to Hydrographic Offices and research groups as requested.
  - The entry into force of the IMO's Code for ships operating in Polar Waters on 1st of January 2017 has seen the advent of work being completed to support the intent behind these regulations. Working with POLARVIEW and the International Association of Classification Societies (IACS) IAATO is contributing to, and supporting the development of, tools required to implement the Code's requirements, such as a database of ice and temperature information to support operator's risk assessments and Risk Index Systems.
  - In addition to taking part in COMNAP's Search and Rescue Workshop immediately following ATCM XXXIX, IAATO undertook a Search and Rescue Exercise with MRCC Chile in February, 2017 and attended the annual Arctic Search and Rescue Workshop and table top exercise in Iceland in April 2017. All of these initiatives are important in building relationships, trust and understanding as well, of course, as providing critical training opportunities.

IAATO Meeting and Participation at Other Meetings during 2016-17

IAATO's 2017 Annual Meeting will take place May 2-4, 2017 in Edinburgh, UK. This report was written in advance of that meeting. In addition to the above mentioned initiatives, the meeting will include:

- Introduction of IAATO's next Executive Director, Dr Damon Stanwell-Smith;
- Discussions on how to improve and expand the IAATO Yacht Outreach Campaign that is aimed at commercial and private non-IAATO Yacht Operators intending to visit Antarctica. Details of the current campaign can be found at www.iaato.org/yachts;
- Focused discussions on Managing for Growth initiatives in support of the Association's mission statement;
- Additional initiatives to strengthen field staff skills and qualifications framework and training;

- A review of IAATO's draft Unmanned Aerial Vehicle (UAV) policies following feedback from previous seasons and SCAR advice; and
- Proposed new guidelines and updates to existing guidelines such as crevasse awareness and specific advice on understanding fur seal behaviour.

Treaty Party representatives are invited to join any of the open sessions during IAATO's Annual Meeting and subsequent workshops.

IAATO Secretariat staff and Operator representatives participated in internal and external meetings, liaising with National Antarctic Programs, governmental, scientific, environmental and industry organisations. In addition to individual government meetings, IAATO took part in:

- **Council of Managers of National Antarctic Programs (COMNAP) 27ᵗʰ Annual Meeting**, Goa, India, August 2016. IAATO places great merit in good cooperation and collaboration between its Membership and National Antarctic Programs.
- **Association of Arctic Expedition Cruise Operators Conference & Annual Meeting**, , Oslo, Norway, October 2016.
- **Hydrographic Commission for Antarctica**, IHO, Tromsø, Norway June 2016.
- **International Ice Chart Working Group** – Ottawa, Canada, October 2016.
- IAATO continues to be active in the development of the **International Maritime Organisation**'s (IMO) mandatory Polar Code as an advisor to Cruise Lines International Association (CLIA), participating in various IMO meetings.

Environmental Monitoring

IAATO continues to provide ATCM and CEP with detailed information on Operators' activities in Antarctica and works collaboratively with scientific institutions particularly on long term environmental monitoring and educational outreach. This includes the Antarctic Site Inventory, the Lynch Lab at Stony Brook University and the Zoological Society of London/Oxford University. Additionally, IAATO Operators note sightings of fishing vessels for subsequent reporting to CCAMLR in support of the work against IUU fishing.

IAATO welcomes opportunities for collaboration with other organisations.

Tourism Incidents 2016-17

IAATO continues to follow a policy of disclosing incidents to ensure risks are understood and appropriate lessons are learned for all Antarctic operators. The 2016-17 season saw no major incidents involving IAATO Operators.

In all, a total of eight medical evacuations have been reported by IAATO Operators, three via McMurdo Base. In all instances both IAATO and the Operators involved are grateful assistance given.

Scientific and Conservation Support

During the 2016-17 season, IAATO Operators cost-effectively or freely transported over 279 scientific, support and conservation staff, and their equipment and supplies between stations, field sites and gateway ports. This included:

- Transfers of scientists between stations;
- Non-urgent medical evacuations;
- Field support of research projects;
- Collection of scientific samples and other data collection for research programs (all permitted);
- Transport of scientific equipment to/from stations;
- Various citizen science projects including data collection for projects such as HappyWhale.com.

Initial reports indicate that IAATO Operators and their passengers also contributed more than US$830,000 to scientific and conservation organisations active in Antarctica and the sub-Antarctic during 2016-17 season.

Over the past decade, these donations have totalled well over US$5 million.

With Thanks

IAATO appreciates the opportunity to work cooperatively with Antarctic Treaty Parties, COMNAP, SCAR, CCAMLR, IHO/HCA, ASOC and others toward the long-term protection of Antarctica.

PART IV

Additional Documents from ATCM XL

1. Additional Documents

Abstract of SCAR Lecture

What does the United Nations Paris Climate Agreement mean for Antarctica?

Abstract of SCAR lecture

Summary

The SCAR Science presentation to XL ATCM will outline the implications of the 2015 Paris Climate Agreement[1] for Antarctica. Key issues addressed are:

- The relationship between the ATS, its agreements and SCAR and the United Nations Framework Convention on Climate Change (UNFCCC).

- The consequences for Antarctica and the Southern Ocean of 1.5°C, 2°C, and more than 2°C of global warming are presented based on the latest international science, much of which has been conducted under the auspices of SCAR's strategic research programmes[2].

- The poorly understood, and potentially underestimated, contribution of Antarctic ice loss to future global sea-level rise (SLR) is a major uncertainty in policy-relevant climate science. This was highlighted in the Intergovernmental Panel on Climate Change's (IPCC) 5th Assessment Report in 2013[3]. Advances in understanding since 2013 will be presented in the context of future climate pathways where 2°C of global warming is achieved, or alternatively, not achieved.

- Understanding the impacts and avoided impacts of achieving the goal of the Paris Climate Agreement, for ATS members, their activities, and implications for the rest of the world is a key *Future Science Challenge* identified by SCAR[4,5] and the Council of Managers of National Antarctic Programmes (COMNAP)[6] addressed in ACTM XL Working Group 2 agenda item 15a (see Background Paper 20).

The Paris Climate Agreement

- The Paris climate Agreement was signed by 196 member nations of the UNFCCC at the 21st meeting of the Conference of Parties (COP 21) in December 2015.

- The UNFCCC is an international environmental treaty negotiated at the Earth Summit in Rio de Janeiro in 1992, with the objective to "stabilize greenhouse gas concentrations in the atmosphere at a level that would prevent dangerous anthropogenic interference with the climate system".

- The Paris Agreement aims to keep global warming below 2°C - "the safe guardrail for dangerous climate change" identified by the IPCC, and introduced by the UNFCCC at Copenhagen in 2009.

- This will be achieved through nationally determined commitments (NDCs) aimed to reduce all anthropogenic greenhouse gas emissions to zero before the end of this century.

- Following pressure from vulnerable African and low-lying coastal nations, the parties further agreed to "pursue efforts to" limit temperature increase to 1.5°C.

- The Paris Climate Agreement was subsequently signed by 194 countries in New York on Earth Day, 22nd April 2016, and the Agreement went into force on 7th November 2016.

- The Paris Agreement is challenging, especially given, that at the current rate of global emissions ~40Gt per year, Earth's surface temperature could reach an increase of 2°C in the next 15 years.

- The NDCs tabled in Paris, if implemented, will restrict global warming to ~2.7°C. This is still above the UNFCCC safe guardrail and well-above the more ambitious goal of 1.5°C. Moreover, an assessment of current policy settings sees global temperatures stabilizing closer to 3.5°C.

- To be on track to meet the Paris target, all parties need to commit to 40% reduction in global GHG emissions with respect to 1990 levels, by 2030. This is the EU commitment, but many nations NDCs fall well short of this. The Agreement requires parties to increase their commitments during 5-yearly global stock takes, to achieve the target.

The relevance of the UNFCCC and IPCC to the ATS.

- The ATS, charged with the governance of the world's 5th largest continent, has no status within the UNFCCC.

- Less than one third of the 194 member states of the UNFCCC belong to ATS and have direct access to Antarctica for research, yet the UNFCCC, through the IPCC process, requires that scientific knowledge.

- SCAR has observer status within the IPCC, via its membership of the International Council of Scientific Unions (ICSU).

- SCAR/ICSU nominates participants to attend IPCC meetings, as well as candidates to be considered for authorship of special reports and assessment reports.

- More importantly SCAR helps mobilise the international science community to address the impact of climate change on Antarctica, and the role Antarctica plays in the global climate system.

- Two of SCAR's strategic research programmes, *Past Antarctic Ice Sheet Dynamics* (PAIS) and *Antarctic Climate in the 21st Century* (AntClim21) made significant contributions to the IPCC's 5th Assessment Report from the legacy of several large International Polar Year research initiatives, and are positioning themselves to make even more significant contributions to 6th Assessment Report.

- Critical knowledge gaps and research priorities have been identified through strategic assessments carried out by national Antarctic programs and funding agencies[eg. 7] and by the SCAR Horizon Scan process held in New Zealand in 2014[4,5]. These are of direct relevance and interest to the IPCC as it prepares for its 6th integrated assessment report and two newly commissioned Special Reports - "Global Warming at 1.5°C" and "Climate change and the oceans and the cryosphere".

- The ATS and its agreements (e.g. the Protocol on Environmental Protection and the Convention on the Conservation of Antarctic Marine Living Resources) also require evidence-based policy and decision-making, that includes knowledge of the impacts of climate change.

- To meet these challenges the Council of Managers of National Antarctic Programmes (COMNAP) has undertaken the Antarctic Road Map Challenge (ARC), which identifies the resources, infrastructure, logistics and supporting technologies needed to enable priority science objectives to be achieved over the coming decades[6].

References and sources of information

1. http://unfccc.int/paris_agreement/items/9485.php
2. http://www.scar.org/science
3. https://www.ipcc.ch/report/ar5/wg1/
4. Kennicutt, C., Chown, S., 2014. Comment: Six priorities for Antarctic Science. *Nature*, 512, 23-25.
5. Kennicutt, C and 69 others, 2014. A roadmap for Antarctic and Southern Ocean science for the next two decades and beyond. *Antarctic Science*, 27-1, 3-18.
6. https://www.comnap.aq/Projects/SitePages/ARC.aspx
7. http://dels.nas.edu/Report/Strategic-Vision-Investments/21741?bname=prb

2. List of Documents

2. List of Documents

Working Papers								
Number	**Ag. Items**	**Title**	**Submitted By**	**E**	**F**	**R**	**S**	**Attachments**
WP001	ATCM 15a	Future Antarctic Science Challenges – A UK Perspective	United Kingdom					
WP002	CEP 7b	Informal Intersessional Discussion: Implementation of the Climate Change Response Work Programme	New Zealand					
WP003	ATCM 6	Report of the Intersessional Contact Group (ICG) on Criteria for Consultative Status	Chile New Zealand Uruguay					
WP004	ATCM 15a	Future Antarctic Science Challenges	SCAR					
WP005	CEP 10a	Non-native Species Response Protocol	United Kingdom Spain					Figura 1 NNS Response Protocol
WP006	ATCM 6	Approval of Observers to the CEP	United States					
WP007 rev.1	CEP 9a	Revision of the Management Plan for Antarctic Specially Protected Area (ASPA) No. 111 Southern Powell Island and adjacent islands, South Orkney Islands	United Kingdom					ASPA No. 111 Revised Management Plan
WP008	CEP 9a	Revision of the Management Plan for Antarctic Specially Protected Area (ASPA) No. 140 Parts of Deception Island, South Shetland Islands	United Kingdom					ASPA No. 140 Revised Management Plan
WP009 rev.1	CEP 9a	Revision of the Management Plan for Antarctic Specially Protected Area (ASPA) No. 129 Rothera Point, Adelaide Island	United Kingdom					ASPA No. 129 Revised Management Plan
WP010 rev.1	CEP 9a	Revision of the Management Plan for Antarctic Specially Protected Area (ASPA) No. 110 Lynch Island, South Orkney Islands	United Kingdom					ASPA No. 110 Revised Management Plan
WP011 rev.1	CEP 9a	Revision of the Management Plan for Antarctic Specially Protected Area (ASPA) No. 115 Lagotellerie Island,	United Kingdom					ASPA No. 115 Revised Management Plan

Working Papers								
Number	Ag. Items	Title	Submitted By	E	F	R	S	Attachments
		Marguerite Bay, Graham Land						
WP012 rev.1	CEP 9a	Revision of the Management Plan for Antarctic Specially Protected Area (ASPA) No. 109 Moe Island, South Orkney Islands	United Kingdom					ASPA No. 109 Revised Management Plan
WP013	CEP 10c CEP 7a CEP 9a	Antarctica and the Strategic Plan for Biodiversity 2011-2020	SCAR Belgium Monaco					Antarctica and the Strategic Plan for Biodiversity
WP014 rev.1	CEP 9a	Updated Management Plan and maps for Antarctic Specially Managed Area No. 5 Amundsen-Scott South Pole Station, South Pole	United States Norway					ASMA No. 5 Map 1 ASMA No. 5 Map 2 ASMA No. 5 Map 3 ASMA No. 5 Map 4 ASMA No. 5 Map 5 ASMA No. 5 Map 6 ASMA No. 5 Revised Management Plan
WP015	ATCM 15a	The SCAR Antarctic Science Horizon Scan & the COMNAP Antarctic Roadmap Challenges projects	COMNAP SCAR					
WP016	CEP 9e	Guidance Material for Antarctic Specially Managed Area (ASMA) designations	Norway United States					Annex A. Guidance for assessing an area for a potential ASMA designation Annex B. Guidelines for the preparation of ASMA Management Plans
WP017	CEP 9e	SCAR's Code of Conduct for the Exploration and Research of Subglacial Aquatic Environments	SCAR					SCAR's Code of Conduct for the Exploration and Research of Subglacial

Working Papers								
Number	Ag. Items	Title	Submitted By	E	F	R	S	Attachments
								Aquatic Environments
WP018	CEP 9e	SCAR's Environmental Code of Conduct for Terrestrial Scientific Field Research in Antarctica	SCAR	⬇	⬇	⬇	⬇	SCAR's Environmental Code of Conduct for Terrestrial Scientific Field Research in Antarctica
WP019	ATCM 17	Data Collection and Reporting on Yachting Activity in Antarctica in 2016-17	United Kingdom Argentina Chile IAATO	⬇	⬇	⬇	⬇	
WP020	ATCM 13 CEP 10c	State of Knowledge of Wildlife Responses to Remotely Piloted Aircraft Systems (RPAS)	SCAR	⬇	⬇	⬇	⬇	
WP021	CEP 9e	ASPA/ASMA prior assessment process	United Kingdom Norway	⬇	⬇	⬇	⬇	Guidelines: A prior assessment process for the designation of ASPA and ASMAs
WP022	ATCM 17	Non-governmental activity in the Antarctic – current reality, requiring legal regulation	Russian Federation	⬇	⬇	⬇	⬇	
WP023	ATCM 17	New challenges of Antarctic yachting to the Antarctic Treaty System	Russian Federation	⬇	⬇	⬇	⬇	
WP024	ATCM 11	Second report of the Intersessional Contact Group on Education and Outreach	Bulgaria Belgium Brazil Chile Portugal Spain United Kingdom	⬇	⬇	⬇	⬇	
WP025	CEP 4	Antarctic Environments Portal	Australia Japan New Zealand Norway SCAR United States	⬇	⬇	⬇	⬇	
WP026	CEP 10a	Inter-Parties' Action Plan to Manage the Non-Native Flies in King George Island,	Korea (ROK) Chile United	⬇	⬇	⬇	⬇	A Short Questionnaire On Non-

Number	Ag. Items	Title	Submitted By	E	F	R	S	Attachments
Working Papers								
		South Shetland Islands	Kingdom Uruguay					Native Flies at Antarctic Stations
WP027	ATCM 6	Appointment of ATCM Working Group Chairs	Australia Argentina Norway United Kingdom					
WP028	CEP 6	Review of the Antarctic Clean-Up Manual	Australia United Kingdom					
WP029	CEP 9e	Proposed update to the Antarctic Conservation Biogeographic Regions	Australia New Zealand SCAR					
WP030	ATCM 15a	International cooperation to advance shared Antarctic science objectives	Australia					
WP031	ATCM 17	A Strategic Approach to Environmentally Managed Tourism	New Zealand					
WP032	ATCM 6	Establishment of the CCAMLR Ross Sea Region Marine Protected Area	New Zealand United States Argentina Chile France					
WP033	ATCM 17	Updating Resolution 4 (2004) on contingency planning, insurance and other matters for tourist and other non-governmental activities, to reflect the IMO Polar Code	France New Zealand Norway					
WP034	CEP 4	Supporting the work of the Committee for Environmental Protection (CEP): A paper by the CEP Chair	Australia					
WP035	CEP 9a	Report of the Informal Discussion for the intersessional period of 2016/17 on the Proposal for a new Antarctic Specially Managed Area at Chinese Antarctic Kunlun Station, Dome A	China					
WP036	CEP 13	Green Expedition in the Antarctic	Australia Chile China France					Attachment A: some examples of technological

Working Papers

Number	Ag. Items	Title	Submitted By	E	F	R	S	Attachments
			Germany India Korea (ROK) New Zealand Norway United Kingdom United States					innovation
WP037	CEP 9e	Antarctic Specially Protected Areas and Important Bird Areas	United Kingdom Australia New Zealand Norway Spain	▦	▦	▦	▦	
WP038	CEP 9a	Revision of the Management Plan for Antarctic Specially Protected Area (ASPA) No. 165 Edmonson Point, Wood Bay, Ross Sea	Italy	▦	▦	▦	▦	ASPA No. 165 Revised Management Plan
WP039	ATCM 15	Filchner Ice Shelf Project: Scientific and logistic cooperation between the Federal Republic of Germany and the United Kingdom	Germany United Kingdom	▦	▦	▦	▦	
WP040	ATCM 14	Report of the Intersessional Contact Group on Inspections in Antarctica under Article VII of the Antarctic Treaty and Article 14 of the Environmental Protocol	Netherlands Korea (ROK) United States	▦	▦	▦	▦	
WP041	CEP 8b	Environmental Impact Assessments – Update on broader policy discussions	United Kingdom Australia Belgium New Zealand Norway	▦	▦	▦	▦	
WP042	CEP 9e	Prior assessment of a proposed Antarctic Specially Protected Area (ASPA) in the Sør Rondane Mountains	Belgium	▦	▦	▦	▦	
WP043	ATCM 14 CEP 12	General Recommendations from the Joint Inspections Undertaken by Argentina and Chile under Article VII	Argentina Chile	▦	▦	▦	▦	

Working Papers								
Number	Ag. Items	Title	Submitted By	E	F	R	S	Attachments
		of the Antarctic Treaty and Article 14 of the Environmental Protocol						
WP044	CEP 10c	Protection Mechanisms for the Snow Hill Island Emperor Penguin Colony, North East of the Antarctic Peninsula	Argentina	📄	📄	📄	📄	
WP045	CEP 9a CEP 9e	Subsidiary Group on Management Plans Report of activities during the intersessional period 2016-2017	Argentina	📄	📄	📄	📄	
WP046	ATCM 13	Non-governmental operators Infrastructure & Operations related to Air operations – Possible impact on National programs in Antarctica	Norway Australia United Kingdom	📄	📄	📄	📄	
WP047	CEP 9b	Report of the intersessional contact group established to develop guidance material for conservation approaches for the management of Antarctic heritage objects	Norway United Kingdom	📄	📄	📄	📄	

Information Papers								
Number	Ag. Items	Title	Submitted By	E	F	R	S	Attachments
IP001 rev.1	ATCM 4	Report by the Depositary Government for the Convention for the Conservation of Antarctic Seals (CCAS) in Accordance with Recommendation XIII-2, Paragraph 2(D)	United Kingdom	🗋	🗋	🗋	🗋	
IP002	ATCM 13	Belarusian Antarctic Research Station - the current stage of the creation and development perspectives	Belarus	🗋	🗋	🗋	🗋	
IP003	CEP 6	The experience in the reduction of the sources of waste generation in the Belarusian Antarctic Expedition	Belarus	🗋	🗋	🗋	🗋	
IP004	ATCM 13 ATCM 4	Report by the International Hydrographic Organization (IHO) and a Proposal for a Seminar on the Importance of Hydrography in the Antarctic Region	IHO	🗋	🗋	🗋	🗋	
IP005	CEP 8b	Towards establishing of values of critical loads and thresholds for the Antarctic environment	Belarus	🗋		🗋		
IP006	ATCM 15	Antarctic cooperation between Romania and Korea 2015-2017	Romania	🗋				
IP007	ATCM 13	Austral Mid-Winter Medical Evacuation from Amundsen-Scott South Pole Station, Antarctica	United States	🗋				
IP008	CEP 11	Field Project Reviews: Fulfilling Environmental Impact Assessment (EIA) Monitoring Obligations	United States	🗋				
IP009	ATCM 4	Annual Report for 2016/17 of the	COMNAP	🗋	🗋	🗋	🗋	

Information Papers								
Number	Ag. Items	Title	Submitted By	E	F	R	S	Attachments
	CEP 5	Council of Managers of National Antarctic Programs (COMNAP)						
IP010	ATCM 13	Search and Rescue Coordination and Response in the Antarctic: Report from the COMNAP Antarctic SAR Workshop III	COMNAP	🗎				COMNAP SAR Workshop III Final Report
IP011	ATCM 4	Report by the CCAMLR Observer to the Fortieth Antarctic Treaty Consultative Meeting	CCAMLR	🗎	🗎	🗎	🗎	
IP012	ATCM 10	Operational information – national expeditions: Facilities & SAR categories	COMNAP	🗎				
IP013	ATCM 15 CEP 7a	U.K./U.S. Research Initiative on Thwaites: The Future of Thwaites Glacier and its Contribution to Sea-level Rise	United States United Kingdom	🗎				
IP014	CEP 4	Antarctic Environments Portal: Content Management Plan	Australia Japan New Zealand Norway SCAR United States	🗎				
IP015	CEP 9e	Antarctic biogeography revisited: updating the Antarctic Conservation Biogeographic Regions	Australia New Zealand SCAR	🗎				Terauds, A. & Lee, J.R. (2016) Antarctic biogeography revisited: updating the Antarctic Conservation Biogeographic Regions, Diversity and Distributions, 1–5.
IP016	CEP 9e	Representation of Important Bird Areas in the network series of Antarctic Specially Protected Areas	New Zealand Norway United Kingdom	🗎				Attachment A: supporting paper
IP017	CEP 9e	High resolution mapping of human footprint across Antarctica and its implications for the strategic conservation	Spain United Kingdom	🗎				supporting paper

Information Papers								
Number	Ag. Items	Title	Submitted By	E	F	R	S	Attachments
		of bird life						
IP018	ATCM 15	Participación Venezolana en la Antártida 2017	Venezuela				📄	
IP019	ATCM 11	Material divulgativo/educativo: Juega y aprende con el Tratado Antártico	Venezuela				📄	
IP020	CEP 10c	The role of monitoring, education and EIA in the prevention of vegetation trampling within ASPA No. 140, Site C: Caliente Hill	Spain United Kingdom	📄				
IP021	ATCM 15	Absorbing Aerosols Monitoring Over Remote Regions	Spain	📄				
IP022	CEP 11	Trace element contamination and availability within the Antarctic Treaty Area	Portugal Chile Germany Russian Federation United Kingdom	📄				
IP023	CEP 9e	Historical and geo-ecological values of Elephant Point, Livingston Island, South Shetland Islands	Portugal Brazil Spain United Kingdom	📄				
IP024	ATCM 15 CEP 13	Future Challenges in Southern Ocean Ecology Research: another outcome of the 1st SCAR Horizon Scan	Portugal Belgium Brazil France Germany Netherlands SCAR United Kingdom United States	📄				
IP025	CEP 9e	Report of the Antarctic Specially Managed Area No. 6 Larsemann Hills Management Group	Australia China India Russian Federation	📄				
IP026	ATCM 15	Australian Antarctic Science Program: highlights of the 2016/17 season	Australia	📄				
IP027	ATCM	Procedures for Safe	New	📄				New Zealand UAS manual

Information Papers								
Number	**Ag. Items**	**Title**	**Submitted By**	**E**	**F**	**R**	**S**	**Attachments**
	13	use of Unmanned Aerial Systems in Antarctica	Zealand					(Summary version)
IP028	ATCM 11	Enlace web de divulgación y educación: Antártida en la escuela	Venezuela				⬇	
IP029	ATCM 15	Preliminary overview of Canadian Antarctic research contributions (1997 – 2016)	Canada	⬇				
IP030	ATCM 14 CEP 12	Australian Antarctic Treaty and Environmental Protocol inspections: December 2016	Australia	⬇				Australian Antarctic Treaty Inspections December 2016
IP031	ATCM 4	Report of the Depositary Government for the Agreement on the Conservation of Albatrosses and Petrels (ACAP)	Australia	⬇	⬇	⬇	⬇	
IP032	ATCM 4	Report of the Depositary Government for the Convention on the Conservation of Antarctic Marine Living Resources (CAMLR)	Australia	⬇	⬇	⬇	⬇	
IP033	ATCM 6	Gateway Access: Transit Visa Developments in South Africa	South Africa	⬇				
IP034	CEP 11 CEP 9e	Workshop on Environmental Assessment of the McMurdo Dry Valleys: Witness to the Past and Guide to the Future	United States	⬇				
IP035	ATCM 4 CEP 5	The Scientific Committee on Antarctic Research Annual Report 2016 – 2017 to Antarctic Treaty Consultative Meeting XL	SCAR	⬇	⬇	⬇	⬇	
IP036	ATCM 15	The U.S. Antarctic Program Antarctic	United States	⬇				

Information Papers

Number	Ag. Items	Title	Submitted By	E	F	R	S	Attachments
		Infrastructure Modernization for Science Project						
IP037	CEP 10c	Bird Monitoring in the Fildes Region	Germany	🗎				
IP038	CEP 10c	Use of UAVs in Antarctica. A competent authority's perspective and lessons learned	Germany	🗎				
IP039	CEP 10c	Study on monitoring penguin colonies in the Antarctic using remote sensing data	Germany	🗎				
IP040	ATCM 13	Refurbishment and Modernization of the German Antarctic Receiving Station GARS O'Higgins	Germany	🗎				
IP041	ATCM 13 CEP 8b	Final Modernization of GONDWANA Station, Terra Nova Bay, northern Victoria Land	Germany	🗎				
IP042	ATCM 13	DROMLAND - Dronning Maud Land Air Network	Germany	🗎				
IP043	ATCM 13	EDEN ISS: A facility to provide Neumayer Station III overwinterers with fresh food while advancing space technology	Germany	🗎				
IP044	CEP 9e	Significant change to ASPA No 151 Lions Rump, King George Island (Isla 25 de Mayo), South Shetland Islands	Poland	🗎				
IP045	CEP 10c	UAV remote sensing of environmental changes on King George Island (South Shetland Islands): update on the results of the third field season 2016/2017	Poland	🗎				Annex 1. Supporting figures
IP046	CEP 10c	UAV impact – problem of a safe distance from wildlife concentrations	Poland	🗎				Preliminary study on nesting Adélie penguins disturbance by unmanned aerial vehicles. Korczak-Abshire et al 2016

Information Papers								
Number	Ag. Items	Title	Submitted By	E	F	R	S	Attachments
IP047	CEP 10a	Eradication of a non-native grass Poa annua L. from ASPA No 128 Western Shore of Admiralty Bay, King George Island, South Shetland Islands	Poland	☑				First step to eradication of Poa annua L. from Point Thomas Oasis (King George Island, South Shetlands, Antarctica). Galera et al. 2017
IP048	CEP 6	Clean-up of Scientific Equipment and Infrastructure from Mt. Erebus, Ross Island, Antarctica	United States	☑				
IP049	CEP 6	Report on Clean-up at Metchnikoff Point, Brabant Island	United Kingdom	☑				
IP050	CEP 5	Report by the CEP Observer to the XXXIV SCAR Delegates' Meeting	United Kingdom	☑				
IP051	ATCM 11	Creating Awareness: the Role of the Antarctic Legacy of South Africa (ALSA)	South Africa	☑				
IP052	CEP 7a	Integrating Climate and Ecosystem Dynamics in the Southern Ocean (ICED) programme	United Kingdom	☑				
IP053	CEP 5	Report by the SC-CAMLR Observer to the twentieth meeting of the Committee for Environmental Protection	CCAMLR	☑				
IP054	CEP 10a	Detection and eradication of a non-native Collembola incursion in a hydroponics facility in East Antarctica	Australia	☑				
IP055	ATCM 13	Actividades y Desarrollo del Programa Antártico Colombiano - PAC	Colombia				☑	
IP056	ATCM 13	Contribución de Colombia a la Seguridad Marítima en la Antártida	Colombia				☑	
IP057	ATCM 15	Actividades Verano Austral 2016 – 2017,	Colombia				☑	

Information Papers								
Number	Ag. Items	Title	Submitted By	E	F	R	S	Attachments
		Programa de Investigación en Mamíferos Marinos Antárticos: Con especial atención hacia Cetáceos Migratorios a aguas colombianas y Pinnípedos Antárticos						
IP058	ATCM 15	Expediciones Científicas de Colombia a la Antártida	Colombia				🗎	
IP059	ATCM 15	Contribución de Colombia al conocimiento de la biodiversidad y los ecosistemas en algunas áreas de la Península Antártica y de la Tierra Reina Maud, Antártica	Colombia				🗎	
IP060	ATCM 11	Campaña de Educación "Todos Somos Antártica" Actividades 2016 - 2017	Colombia				🗎	
IP061	ATCM 11	Aportes de Colombia al Conocimiento de la Cultura y Adaptación Antárticas	Colombia				🗎	
IP062	ATCM 15	IV Expedición Científica de Colombia a la Antártica Verano Austral 2017-2018 "Almirante Tono"	Colombia				🗎	
IP063	ATCM 13	Benefits of Logistic collaboration in Antarctica in support of Antarctic Science programmes: Australia's experience in 2016-17	Australia	🗎				
IP064	ATCM 10 ATCM 13	Advances to the COMNAP database	COMNAP	🗎				
IP065	ATCM 15	Malaysia's Activities and Achievements in Antarctic Research and Diplomacy	Malaysia	🗎				

Information Papers								
Number	Ag. Items	Title	Submitted By	E	F	R	S	Attachments
IP066	ATCM 17	Blue Ice Runway by Romnæsfjellet	Norway Belgium					
IP067	ATCM 15 ATCM 17	Japan's Antarctic Outreach Activities	Japan					
IP068	ATCM 15 CEP 11	Update on activities of the Southern Ocean Observing System (SOOS)	SCAR					
IP069	CEP 7b	Mapping SCAR affiliated research to the CEP's Climate Change Response Work Programme (CCRWP)	SCAR					Attachment A - Mapping SCAR research to the CEPs Climate Change Response Work Programme.
IP070	CEP 8b	Final Comprehensive Environmental Evaluation for the construction and operation of a gravel runway in the area of Mario Zucchelli Station, Terra Nova Bay, Victoria Land, Antarctica	Italy					
IP071	ATCM 16 CEP 7b	Agreement by CCAMLR to establish time-limited Special Areas for Scientific Study in newly exposed marine areas following ice shelf retreat or collapse in the Antarctic Peninsula region	United Kingdom Belgium Finland France Germany Italy Netherlands Poland Spain Sweden					
IP072	ATCM 13	Antarctic Mass Rescue Operations Response and Preparedness Challenges	United States					
IP073	CEP 9e	Deception Island Antarctic Specially Managed Area (ASMA No. 4) - 2017 Management report	United States Argentina Chile Norway Spain United Kingdom					
IP074	CEP 6	Clean-up and removal of Italy installations at	Italy					

Information Papers								
Number	Ag. Items	Title	Submitted By	E	F	R	S	Attachments
		Sitry airfield camp along the avio-route MZS-DDU, Antarctica						
IP075	CEP 10c	A Report on the Development and Use of UAS by the U.S. National Marine Fisheries Service for Surveying Marine Mammals	United States	🔒				Marine Mammal Commission. 2016. Development and Use of UASs by the National Marine Fisheries Service for Surveying Marine Mammals. Marine Mammal Commission, Bethesda, MD, USA.
IP076	CEP 11	Supporting the analysis of environments and impacts: A tool to enable broader-scale environmental management	New Zealand	🔒				
IP077	ATCM 13 CEP 10c	Update from the COMNAP Unmanned Aerial Systems Working Group (UAS-WG)	COMNAP	🔒				
IP078	ATCM 13	Reconstruction of the Brazilian Station in Antarctica	Brazil	🔒				
IP079	CEP 11	Environmental monitoring of the reconstruction work of the Brazilian Antarctic Station (2015/16 and 2016/17)	Brazil	🔒				
IP080 rev.1	ATCM 16 CEP 7a	Antarctic Climate Change and the Environment – 2017 Update	SCAR	🔒				
IP081	CEP 11	Report of Oceanites, Inc.	SCAR	🔒				
IP082	ATCM 15	Summary of the major research achievements of Chinese Arctic and Antarctic Environment Comprehensive Investigation & Assessment Program for the past five years since its implementation	China	🔒				

Information Papers								
Number	Ag. Items	Title	Submitted By	E	F	R	S	Attachments
IP083 rev.1	CEP 11	Update on work to develop a methodology to assess the sensitivity of sites used by visitors	Australia IAATO New Zealand Norway United Kingdom United States	🗄				
IP084	CEP 7a	Climate change impacts on Antarctic ice-free areas	Australia	🗄				
IP085	ATCM 15	Japan's Antarctic Research Highlights 2016–17	Japan	🗄				
IP086	CEP 9e	Use of UAS for Improved Monitoring and Survey of Antarctic Specially Protected Areas	New Zealand	🗄				
IP087	ATCM 4 ATCM 8	Liability Annex: Financial Security	IGP&I Clubs	🗄				
IP088	ATCM 4 ATCM 8	The International Oil Pollution Compensation Funds	IOPC Funds	🗄				
IP089	ATCM 7	Antarctic Treaty Secretariat Internship Grant for Republic of Turkey	Turkey	🗄				
IP090	ATCM 15	The experience of having SCAR photo exhibition in Turkey as of a new SCAR member	Turkey	🗄				
IP091	ATCM 15	Turkish Antarctic Expedition 2016 - 2017 (TAE - I) Experiences	Turkey	🗄				
IP092	ATCM 15	Turkey-Chile Scientific Collaboration in Antarctica	Turkey Chile	🗄				
IP093	ATCM 15	Turkey - Czech Republic Scientific Collaboration in Antarctica	Turkey Czech Republic	🗄				
IP094	ATCM 6 CEP 4	Ratification of Protocol on Environmental Protection to the	Turkey	🗄				

Information Papers

Number	Ag. Items	Title	Submitted By	E	F	R	S	Attachments
		Antarctic Treaty by Turkey						
IP095	ATCM 15	Opening of Chile-Korea Antarctic Cooperation Center	Chile Korea (ROK)	☑				
IP096	ATCM 11	Programa de Educación Antártica	Chile				☑	
IP097	ATCM 15	Programa de Publicaciones Antárticas del INACH	Chile				☑	
IP098	ATCM 15	The experience in using a remote unmanned underwater vehicle in the Belarusian Antarctic Expedition in 2016-2017	Belarus	☑	☑	☑	☑	
IP099	ATCM 11	Commemoration of the 25th Anniversary of the Protocol on Environmental Protection to the Antarctic Treaty – Presentation of Postage Stamps	Argentina	☑			☑	
IP100	ATCM 13	Fildes Bay Environmental Monitoring Coastal Environmental Observation Program (P.O.A.L.) 2017	Chile	☑			☑	
IP101	ATCM 13	Support to Antarctic Campaigns Meteorological Service of the Navy	Chile	☑			☑	
IP102	ATCM 13	Maintenance of Aids to Navigation in Antarctica, Summer Season 2016 - 2017	Chile	☑			☑	
IP103	ATCM 13	Search and Rescue Cases in the area of the Antarctic Peninsula Period 2016 / 2017 MRCC Chile	Chile	☑			☑	
IP104	ATCM 13	Production of an Antarctic Nautical Chart by the Hydrographic and Oceanographic Service of the Chilean Navy: Nautical Chart 15350 (INT 9104)	Chile	☑			☑	

Information Papers								
Number	Ag. Items	Title	Submitted By	E	F	R	S	Attachments
		"Estrecho de Gerlache - Islote Useful a Isla Wednesday"						
IP105	ATCM 13	Chile in the Southern Antarctica Joint Scientific Polar Station "Union Glacier"	Chile	📄			📄	
IP106	CEP 8b	Auditoría Ambiental de Cumplimiento de la XX Campaña Antártica Ecuatoriana (2015-2016)	Ecuador				📄	
IP107	ATCM 13	Capacidad logística de la Estación Científica Ecuatoriana "Pedro Vicente Maldonado"- Año 2017	Ecuador				📄	
IP108	CEP 6	Gestión de los desechos sólidos generados en la Estación Maldonado - XXI Campaña Antártica (2016-2017)	Ecuador				📄	
IP109	ATCM 13	Aplicación de la Norma de Operación en la XXI Campaña Antártica Ecuatoriana (2016-2017)	Ecuador				📄	
IP110	ATCM 13 CEP 13	Plan de contingencias y riesgos durante la XXI Campaña Antártica Ecuatoriana (2016-2017)	Ecuador				📄	
IP111	ATCM 15	XXI Expedición Científica Ecuatoriana a la Antártida (2016-2017)	Ecuador				📄	
IP112	ATCM 4 CEP 5	WMO Annual Report 2016-2017	WMO	📄	📄	📄	📄	
IP113	ATCM 15 CEP 11	The Global Cryosphere Watch and CroNet	WMO	📄				
IP114	ATCM 15 CEP 11	The Polar Space Task Group: Coordinating Space Data in the Antarctic Region	WMO	📄				
IP115	CEP 7a	The Polar Climate Predictability Initiative of the World Climate Research	WMO	📄				

Information Papers								
Number	Ag. Items	Title	Submitted By	E	F	R	S	Attachments
		Programme						
IP116	ATCM 15 CEP 5	Southern Hemisphere Key Activities and Special Observing Periods during the Year of Polar Prediction	WMO	🗋				
IP117	ATCM 15	The Antarctic Observing Network (AntON) to facilitate weather and climate information: an update	WMO SCAR	🗋				
IP118	ATCM 16 CEP 7a	Progress Update on WMO Polar Regional Climate Centres	WMO	🗋				
IP119	CEP 7a	Regional climate downscaling through the Antarctic-CORDEX project	WMO	🗋				
IP120	ATCM 15	Finland´s international collaboration in the Antarctic field work with different stations and other actors	Finland	🗋				
IP121	ATCM 15	Status Report 2017: Ongoing and Recently Ended Antarctic Research Funded by the Academy of Finland	Finland	🗋				
IP122	ATCM 15a	The Future Challenges of Antarctic Research – The Finnish Perspective	Finland	🗋				
IP123	ATCM 13	The Polar Code – Finnish Views	Finland	🗋				
IP124 rev.1	ATCM 17	Action taken following unauthorized presence of a French yacht in the Treaty Area during the 2015/2016 season	France	🗋				
IP125	ATCM 13	Report on the 19th edition of the Joint Antarctic Naval Patrol between Argentina and Chile	Argentina Chile	🗋			🗋	
IP126	ATCM	Report of the Joint	Argentina	🗋			🗋	Inspection Report

Information Papers								
Number	Ag. Items	Title	Submitted By	E	F	R	S	Attachments
	14 CEP 12	Inspections' Program undertaken by Argentina and Chile under Article VII of the Antarctic Treaty and Article 14 of the Environmental Protocol	Chile					
IP127	CEP 9d	Update on the process of designation of a Marine Protected Area (MPA) in the West Antarctic Peninsula and South of the Arc of Scotia (Domain 1)	Argentina Chile	◩			◩	
IP128 rev.1	CEP 10a	Prevention of the Introduction of Non-native Species to the Antarctic Continent. Argentine Antarctic Program Operations Manual	Argentina	◩			◩	Manual para las operaciones del Programa Antártico Argentino
IP129	ATCM 11	Primeras Jornadas Antárticas, 2016	Ecuador				◩	
IP130	ATCM 13	XXVII Reunión de Administradores de Programas Antárticos Latinoamericanos, 2016	Ecuador				◩	
IP131	ATCM 17	Areas of tourist interest in the Antarctic Peninsula and South Orkney Islands region. 2016/2017 austral summer season	Argentina	◩			◩	
IP132	ATCM 13	Aids to navigation, beaconing and Antarctic cartography - (2016-2017)	Argentina	◩			◩	
IP133	ATCM 13	Report on the installation of Aids to Navigation on the Antarctic Continent	Argentina	◩			◩	
IP134	ATCM 11 ATCM 15	Actividades del Programa Nacional Antártico de Perú Período 2016 – 2017	Peru				◩	
IP135	ATCM 13	Campaña Antártica ANTAR XXIV Verano	Peru				◩	

Information Papers								
Number	Ag. Items	Title	Submitted By	E	F	R	S	Attachments
		austral 2016 - 2017						
IP136	ATCM 15	COMNAP Antarctic Station Catalogue Project	COMNAP	☑				COMNAP Station Catalogue examples
IP137	ATCM 17	Report on Antarctic tourist flows and cruise ships operating in Ushuaia during the 2016/2017 Austral summer season	Argentina	☑			☑	
IP138	ATCM 11 ATCM 15	Polar Scientific and Outreach Cooperation Between Bulgaria and Turkey	Bulgaria Turkey	☑				
IP139 rev.1	ATCM 13	An overview of the International Code for Ships Operating in Polar Waters	IMO	☑				
IP140	ATCM 13	Brazilian XXXV Antarctic Operation	Brazil	☑				
IP141	ATCM 15	Russian-Swiss Antarctic Circumnavigation Expedition 2016–2017	Russian Federation	☑		☑		
IP142	ATCM 15	To question on the project of the international scientific drifting station "Weddell-2"	Russian Federation	☑		☑		
IP143	ATCM 13	On use of the blue ice area in the vicinity of Romnaes Mount as a reserve airstrip	Russian Federation	☑		☑		
IP144	ATCM 8	Russian legislation on regulation of activities in the Antarctic	Russian Federation	☑				Russian Federal Law
IP145	ATCM 8	Approximate list, scope and character of response actions	Russian Federation	☑				
IP146	ATCM 4	Report of the Antarctic and Southern Ocean Coalition	ASOC	☑	☑	☑	☑	
IP147	ATCM 16 CEP 7a	Climate Change Report Card	ASOC	☑				
IP148	ATCM 11	Collaborating on Antarctic Education and Outreach	ASOC IAATO	☑				Pdf version of the IUCN poster produced by IAATO, ASOC and WWF
IP149	CEP 9e	ASOC update on Marine Protected	ASOC	☑				

Information Papers								
Number	Ag. Items	Title	Submitted By	E	F	R	S	Attachments
		Areas in the Southern Ocean 2016-2017						
IP150	ATCM 17	Options for Visitor Management in the Antarctic	ASOC	🔲				
IP151	ATCM 13	Managing non-SOLAS vessels in the Southern Ocean	ASOC	🔲				Legal memo on the potential application of the Polar Code to fishing vessels and yachts
IP152 rev.1	ATCM 16 CEP 7a	Tracking Antarctica - A WWF report on the state of Antarctica and the Southern Ocean	ASOC	🔲				
IP153	CEP 9e	Considerations for the systematic expansion of the protected areas network	ASOC	🔲				
IP154	ATCM 15	MADICE –Joint Initiative of Scientific Programme at CDML by India and Norway	India Norway	🔲				
IP155	ATCM 15	Creating spaces of collaboration: Meeting of Administrators of Latin American Antarctic Programs	Peru Argentina Brazil Chile Ecuador Uruguay	🔲			🔲	
IP156	ATCM 13	Greening of established infrastructure and logistics in Antarctica	Norway	🔲				
IP157	CEP 4	Committee for Environmental Protection (CEP): summary of activities during the 2016/17 intersessional period	Australia	🔲				
IP158 rev.2	ATCM 4	Report of the Depositary Government of the Antarctic Treaty and its Protocol in accordance with Recommendation XIII-2	United States	🔲	🔲	🔲	🔲	Antarctic Treaty Status Table List of Recommendations/Measures and their approvals Protocol Status Table
IP159	ATCM 13	Decarbonizing Antarctic Operations	ASOC	🔲				
IP160	ATCM 17	Maritime Antarctic tourism through Ushuaia: from the beginning of the activity to present	Argentina	🔲			🔲	

Information Papers								
Number	Ag. Items	Title	Submitted By	E	F	R	S	Attachments
		times						
IP161	ATCM 15a	What does the United Nations Paris Climate Agreement mean for Antarctica?	SCAR	🗎	🗎	🗎	🗎	
IP162	ATCM 4	Report of the International Association of Antarctica Tour Operators 2016-17	IAATO	🗎	🗎	🗎	🗎	
IP163 rev.1	ATCM 17	IAATO Overview of Antarctic Tourism: 2016-17 Season and Preliminary Estimates for 2017-18	IAATO	🗎				
IP164	ATCM 17 CEP 9c	Report on IAATO Operator Use of Antarctic Peninsula Landing Sites and ATCM Visitor Site Guidelines, 2016-17 Season	IAATO	🗎				
IP165	ATCM 17	Document Withdrawn	South Africa	🗎				
IP166	ATCM 17 CEP 9e	Systematic Conservation Plan for the Antarctic Peninsula	SCAR IAATO	🗎				
IP167	ATCM 13 ATCM 17	New IAATO Guidelines for Submersibles and Remote Operated Vehicle activities	IAATO	🗎				
IP168	ATCM 9	An Update on Status and Trends Biological Prospecting in Antarctica and Recent Policy Developments at the International Level	Netherlands	🗎				
IP169	ATCM 6	Statement by Iceland	Iceland	🗎				
IP170	ATCM 15	The Kazakh Geographical Society	Kazakhstan	🗎				
IP171	ATCM 11	Romanian Antarctic Education and Outreach Activities during 2015-2017	Romania	🗎				
IP172	ATCM 15	Cooperation of Romania with Australia, China, India	Romania	🗎				

Information Papers								
Number	Ag. Items	Title	Submitted By	E	F	R	S	Attachments
		and Russian Federation within ASMA No. 6 Larsemann Hills, East Antarctica						
IP173	ATCM 15	Cooperation of Romania with Argentina in Antarctica – Romanian RONARE 2017 Expedition in cooperation with Argentina	Romania	🔏				
IP174	ATCM 15	Report from Asian Forum for Polar Sciences to the ATCM XL	China	🔏				
IP175 rev.2	ATCM 6	Chair's Summary of the Special Meeting "Our Antarctica: Protection and Utilisation"	China	🔏				

Background Papers									
Number	Ag. Items	Title	Submitted By	E	F	R	S	Attachments
BP001	ATCM 13 CEP 10c	Best Practice for Minimising Remotely Piloted Aircraft System Disturbance to Wildlife in Biological Field Research	SCAR	🖹				Hodgson and Koh article
BP002	ATCM 15	Scientific and Science-related Cooperation with the Consultative Parties and the Wider Antarctic Community	Korea (ROK)	🖹				
BP003	CEP 8b	Information on the Progress of the Renovation of the King Sejong Korean Antarctic Station on King George Island, South Shetland Islands	Korea (ROK)	🖹				
BP004	CEP 9b	Antarctic Historic Resources: Ross Sea Heritage Restoration Project. Conservation of Hillary's Hut, Scott Base, Antarctic HSM 75	New Zealand	🖹				
BP005	ATCM 13	Plans for the revitalization of the Dobrowolski Station	Poland	🖹				
BP006	ATCM 15	South African National Antarctic Program (SANAP): Science Highlights 2016/7	South Africa	🖹				
BP007	ATCM 14 CEP 12	Measures taken on the recommendations by Inspection team at Arctowski Polish Antarctic Station in 2016/2017	Poland	🖹				
BP008	CEP 11	Using virtual reality technology for low-impact monitoring and communication of protected and historic sites in Antarctica	New Zealand	🖹				
BP009	ATCM 11	Piloto Luis Pardo Villalón: Rescatando del olvido a un héroe chileno	Chile				🖹	
BP010	ATCM 11	Celebración de la Semana Antártica en Punta Arenas	Chile				🖹	
BP011	ATCM 15	Monitoring of Antarctic flora – new Ukrainian-Turkish cooperation, a key for understanding biodiversity in the Argentine Islands, West Antarctica	Ukraine Turkey	🖹				
BP012	ATCM 15	Sightings of cetaceans during the First Joint Ukrainian-Turkish Antarctic Scientific Expedition 2016	Ukraine Turkey	🖹				
BP013	ATCM 11	The Practice of Holding International Scientific and Practical Conferences on the	Belarus	🖹	🖹	🖹	🖹	

Background Papers									
Number	Ag. Items	Title	Submitted By	E	F	R	S	Attachments	
		Problems of Antarctic in the Republic of Belarus							
BP014	ATCM 14 CEP 12	Follow-up to the Recommendations of the Inspection Teams at the Eco-Nelson Facility	Czech Republic	📄					
BP015	ATCM 15	Incidencia de factores bióticos y abióticos en la composición y abundancia de la comunidad fito planctónica y las migraciones zoo planctónicas en la Antártida, las islas Galápagos y el Ecuador continental	Ecuador				📄		
BP016	ATCM 15	Estudio de la dinámica poblacional y adaptación al cambio climático de microorganismos acuáticos de los cuerpos de agua dulce en la Isla Dee, Islas Shetland del Sur	Ecuador				📄		
BP017	ATCM 15	Estudio comparativo de la diversidad liquénica antártica versus andina con fines de bioprospección y biomonitoreo	Ecuador				📄		
BP018	ATCM 15	Inventario y caracterización preliminar de la biodiversidad de moluscos marinos en transeptos litorales de la estación antártica ecuatoriana Pedro Vicente Maldonado	Ecuador				📄		
BP019	ATCM 15	Tratamiento de lodos de la planta de aguas residuales de la Estación Científica Pedro Vicente Maldonado (2016-2017)	Ecuador				📄		
BP020	ATCM 15a	The SCAR Lecture: What does the United Nations Paris Climate Agreement mean for Antarctica?	SCAR	📄				Figures referenced in the document	
BP021	ATCM 15	The Polish Programme on Polar Research and Strategy of Polish Polar Research – concept for years 2017-2027	Poland	📄					
BP022	ATCM 13	Capacidades y limitaciones de la Base Antártica "Pdte. Eduardo Frei M." en apoyo a los Programas Antárticos Nacionales y Extranjeros	Chile				📄		
BP023	ATCM 6	Ingreso no Autorizado a la Estación Machu Picchu	Peru				📄		

Background Papers								
Number	Ag. Items	Title	Submitted By	E	F	R	S	Attachments
		Período 2016 – 2017						

Secretariat Papers								
Number	**Ag. Items**	**Title**	**Submitted By**	**E**	**F**	**R**	**S**	**Attachments**
SP001 rev.1	ATCM 3	ATCM XL - CEP XX Agenda and Schedule	ATS					Multi-year Strategic Work Plan 2016 (MYSWP)
SP002	CEP 2 CEP 3 CEP 7b	CEP XX Preliminary Agenda, Five-Year Work Plan (5YWP) and Climate Change Response Work Program (CCRWP)	ATS					
SP003	ATCM 6	List of measures with status "not yet effective"	ATS					Status report
SP004 rev.3	ATCM 7	Secretariat Report 2016/17	ATS					Appendix 1: Audited Financial Report 2015/16 Appendix 2: Provisional Financial Report 2016/17 Appendix 3: Contributions Received by the Antarctic Secretariat 2016/17
SP004 rev.4	ATCM 7	Secretariat Report 2016/17	ATS					Appendix 1: Audited Financial Report 2015/16 Appendix 2: Provisional Financial Report 2016/17 Appendix 3: Contributions Received by the Antarctic Secretariat 2016/17
SP005 rev.1	ATCM 7	Secretariat Programme 2017/18	ATS					Contribution scale 2018/19 Provisional Report for the Financial Year 2016/17,

Secretariat Papers								
Number	Ag. Items	Title	Submitted By	E	F	R	S	Attachments
								Budget for the Financial Year 2017/18, Forecast Budget for the Financial Year 2018/19 Provisional Report for the Financial Year 2016/17, Budget for the Financial Year 2017/18, Forecast Budget for the Financial Year 2018/19 Salary Scale 2017/18
SP005 rev.2	ATCM 7	Secretariat Programme 2017/18	ATS	🔖				Contribution scale 2018/19 Provisional Report for the Financial Year 2016/17, Budget for the Financial Year 2017/18, Forecast Budget for the Financial Year 2018/19 Provisional Report for the Financial Year 2016/17, Budget for the Financial Year 2017/18, Forecast Budget for the Financial Year 2018/19 Salary Scale 2017/18

Secretariat Papers								
Number	Ag. Items	Title	Submitted By	E	F	R	S	Attachments
SP006	ATCM 7	Draft Five-Year Forward Budget Profile 2017-2022	ATS	⬇	⬇	⬇	⬇	Five-Year Forward Budget Profile 2017/18-2021/22
SP006 rev.1	ATCM 7	Draft Five-Year Forward Budget Profile 2017/18-2021/22	ATS	⬇				Five-Year Forward Budget Profile 2017/18-2021/22
SP007 rev.2	CEP 8b	Annual list of Initial Environmental Evaluations (IEE) and Comprehensive Environmental Evaluations (CEE) prepared between April 1st 2016 and March 31st 2017	ATS	⬇	⬇	⬇	⬇	
SP008	ATCM 16 CEP 7a	Actions taken by the CEP and the ATCM on the ATME recommendations on climate change	ATS	⬇	⬇	⬇	⬇	
SP009	ATCM 17 CEP 11	Update on the current state of recommendations of the 2012 CEP Tourism Study	ATS	⬇	⬇	⬇	⬇	
SP010	ATCM 10	Report for the review of the functioning of the EIES	ATS	⬇	⬇	⬇	⬇	
SP011	ATCM 1 ATCM 18 ATCM 19 ATCM 2 ATCM 20 ATCM 21 ATCM 3 ATCM 4 ATCM 5	ATCM Plenary Schedule, Annotated Agenda and Summary of Papers	ATS	⬇				
SP012	CEP 2	CEP XX Schedule, Annotated Agenda and Summary of Papers	ATS	⬇				
SP013	ATCM 10 ATCM 11 ATCM 12 ATCM 6 ATCM 7 ATCM 8 ATCM 9	ATCM Working Group 1 Schedule, Annotated Agenda and Summary of Papers	ATS	⬇				
SP014 rev.2	ATCM 13 ATCM 14 ATCM 15 ATCM 15a	ATCM Working Group 2 Schedule, Annotated Agenda and Summary of Papers	ATS	⬇				

Secretariat Papers								
Number	Ag. Items	Title	Submitted By	E	F	R	S	Attachments
	ATCM 16 ATCM 17							

3. List of Participants

3. List of Participants

Consultative Parties			
Party	**Title**	**Name**	**Position**
Argentina	Sec	Barreto, Juan	Delegate
Argentina	Ms	Capurro, Andrea	Delegate
Argentina	Sec	Cortelletti, Juan Manuel	Delegate
Argentina	Sec	D'onofrio, María Guillermina	Delegate
Argentina	Min	Gowland, Máximo	Head of Delegation
Argentina	Amb	Guelar, Diego Ramiro	Delegate
Argentina	Mr	Humarán, Adolfo Ernesto	Advisor
Argentina	Amb	Kralikas, María Teresa	Head of Delegation
Argentina	Min	Millicay, Fernanda	Alternate
Argentina	Mr	Musso Soler, Carlos Claudio	Advisor
Argentina	Lic	Ortúzar, Patricia	CEP Representative
Argentina	Mr	Sánchez, Rodolfo	Delegate
Argentina	Sec	Sartor, Jorge	Delegate
Argentina	Lic	Vereda, Marisol	Advisor
Argentina	Mr	Videla, Enrique	Advisor
Australia	Ms	Buttermore, Erin	Delegate
Australia	Mr	Clark, Charlton	Alternate
Australia	Ms	Cooper, Katrina	Head of Delegation
Australia	Ms	Crosbie, Sophie	Delegate
Australia	Dr	Fenton, Gwen	Delegate
Australia	Mr	Gales, Nicholas	Advisor
Australia	Mr	Googan, Michael	Delegate
Australia	Dr	Kiessling, Ilse	Delegate
Australia	Ms	Kingston, Melissa	Delegate
Australia	Ms	Lewis, Alicia	Delegate
Australia	Ms	Mason, Jennifer	Delegate
Australia	Mr	McIvor, Ewan	Delegate
Australia	Prof	Rayfuse, Rosemary	Advisor
Australia	Prof	Stephens, Timothy	Advisor
Australia	Dr	Tracey, Phillip	CEP Representative
Australia	Mr	Westcombe, Alexander	Delegate
Belgium	Mr	André, François	CEP Representative
Belgium	Dir	Touzani, Rachid	Delegate
Belgium	Ms	Vancauwenberghe, Maaike	Delegate
Belgium	Dir	Vanden Bilcke, Christian	Head of Delegation
Belgium	Ms	Wilmotte, Annick	Advisor
Brazil	Mr	Batista De Melo, Renato	Alternate
Brazil	Couns	Chiarelli V. de Azevedo, Paulo José	Head of Delegation
Brazil	Mr	Da Costa Pereira Junior, Eduardo	Advisor
Brazil	Mr	Gaspar Fernandes, Ronald Alexandre	Advisor
Brazil	Mr	Leite, Marcio Renato	Advisor
Brazil	Mr	Pazeto, Flavio	Advisor
Bulgaria	Mr	Chakarov, Danail	Head of Delegation
Bulgaria	Prof	Kuchev, Yuriy	Advisor
Bulgaria	Mr.	Mateev, Dragomir	CEP Representative
Bulgaria	Mrs	Petrova, Elena	Advisor
Bulgaria	Prof	Pimpirev, Christo	Alternate
Bulgaria	Amb	Porozhanov, Grigor	Alternate

Consultative Parties			
Party	**Title**	**Name**	**Position**
Bulgaria	Ms.	Raycheva, Sasha	Delegate
Chile	Amb	Berguño, Francisco	Head of Delegation
Chile	Mr	Figueroa, Miguel	Advisor
Chile	Mr	Gamboa, César	Advisor
Chile	Mr	Gonzalez, Gustavo	Delegate
Chile	Mr	Heine, Jorge	Delegate
Chile	Mr	Leppe, Marcelo	Advisor
Chile	Coronel	Marchessi Acuña, Rodrigo	Advisor
Chile	Sr	Mendez Olave, Julio	Alternate
Chile	Dr	Retamales, José	Alternate
Chile	Mr	Sepulveda, Victor	Advisor
Chile	Mr	Silva, Manuel	Advisor
Chile	Mr	Vega, Edgardo	Advisor
Chile	Mr	Velásquez, Ricardo	Delegate
China	Mr	Ao, Shan	Delegate
China	Ms	Bai, Jiayu	Advisor
China	Ms	Chen, Danhong	Delegate
China	Mr	Chen, Jianzhong	Delegate
China	Ms	Chen, Yue	Delegate
China	Mr	Ding, Huang	Advisor
China	Mr	Dong, Yue	Advisor
China	Mrs	Fang, Lijun	Delegate
China	Ms	Fu, Sha	Delegate
China	Mr	Gao, Zhiguo	Advisor
China	Mr	Gou, Haibo	Delegate
China	Ms	Lan, Hua	Advisor
China	Mr	Li, Hanyu	Delegate
China	Ms	Lin, Dan	Delegate
China	Mr	Lin, Shanqing	Alternate
China	Mr	Liu, Yang	Delegate
China	Mr	Liu, Zhenmin	ATCM Chairman
China	Ms	Liu, Ying	Delegate
China	Mr	Long, Wei	Delegate
China	Prof	Lu, Zhibo	Advisor
China	Mr	Ma, Xinmin	Delegate
China	Mr	Mu, Zhilin	Delegate
China	Mr	Qin, Weijia	CEP Representative
China	Mr	Shao, Yong	Delegate
China	Mr	Sun, Shengzhi	Delegate
China	Mr	Xia, Liping	Advisor
China	Mr	Xu, Hong	Alternate
China	Mr	Yang, Jian	Advisor
China	Ms	Yang, Fan	Delegate
China	Mr	Zhai, Yong	Delegate
China	Ms	Zheng, Yingqin	Advisor
Czech Republic	Ms	Filippiova, Martina	Alternate
Czech Republic	Dr	Nyvlt, Daniel	Advisor
Czech Republic	Dr	Smolek, Martin	Head of Delegation
Czech Republic	Dr	Štěpánek, Přemysl	CEP Representative
Czech Republic	Dr	Válek, Petr	Alternate
Czech Republic	Mr	Venera, Zdenek	CEP Representative
Ecuador	Amb	Baus Palacios, Mauricio Efrain	Head of Delegation

		Consultative Parties	
Party	**Title**	**Name**	**Position**
Ecuador	Capt	Proaño, Juan	Advisor
Ecuador	Ms	Rochina, Marcia	Delegate
Finland	Ms	Lahti, Johanna	Delegate
Finland	Ms	Mähönen, Outi	CEP Representative
Finland	Ms	Valjento, Liisa	Head of Delegation
Finland	Mr	Valtonen, Veli Pekka	Advisor
France	Mrs	Bellemere, Olivia	Alternate
France	Dr	Frenot, Yves	CEP Representative
France	Ms	Guillemain, Anne	Delegate
France	Mr	Lebouvier, Marc	CEP Representative
France	M	Olivier, Guyonvarch	Advisor
France	Mr	Ortolland, Didier	Head of Delegation
Germany	Mr	Duebner, Walter	Delegate
Germany	Prof Dr	Gaedicke, Christoph	Delegate
Germany	Dr	Hain, Stefan	Delegate
Germany	Dr	Herata, Heike	CEP Representative
Germany	Ms	Heyn, Andrea	Delegate
Germany	Dr	Lassig, Rainer	Head of Delegation
Germany	Dr	Läufer, Andreas	Delegate
Germany	Mr	Liebschner, Alexander	Delegate
Germany	Dr	Nixdorf, Uwe	Delegate
Germany	Ms	Reppe, Silvia	Delegate
India	Ms	Jayakumar, Rocheus S.	Delegate
India	Ms	John, David Thelma	Head of Delegation
India	Dr	Ravichandran, Muthalagu	Head of Delegation
Italy	Dr	Fioretti, Anna	Delegate
Italy	Ing	Mecozzi, Roberta	Delegate
Italy	Counselor	Sgrò, Eugenio	Head of Delegation
Italy	Dr	Torcini, Sandro	CEP Representative
Japan	Mr	Hokari, Toshiyuki	Alternate
Japan	Ms	Nakano, Akiko	CEP Representative
Japan	Prof	Shiraishi, Kazuyuki	Delegate
Japan	Officer	Takehara, Mari	Alternate
Japan	Senior Dep	Tanaka, Kenichiro	Head of Delegation
Japan	Prof	Watanabe, Kentaro	Delegate
Kazakhstan	Mr	Daulet, Sharipov	Delegate
Kazakhstan	Mr	Mukushev, Murat	Head of Delegation
Korea (DPRK)	Mr	Ri, Chol Ho	Head of Delegation
Korea (DPRK)	Mr	Ri, Kum Song	Delegate
Korea (ROK)	Mr	Cho, Minjun	Delegate
Korea (ROK)	Mr	Cho, Namdeuk	Delegate
Korea (ROK)	Ms	Choi, Song A	Delegate
Korea (ROK)	Dr	Kim, Ji Hee	CEP Representative
Korea (ROK)	Ms	Kim, Min-Sun	Delegate
Korea (ROK)	Dr	Kim, Jeong Hoon	Delegate
Korea (ROK)	Dr	Seo, Wonsang	Delegate
Korea (ROK)	Dr	Shin, Hyoung Chul	Delegate
Korea (ROK)	Mr	Song, Kwan-Sung	Delegate
Korea (ROK)	Mr	Yoon, Ho Il	Delegate
Korea (ROK)	Mr	Yun, Sang Hun	Delegate
Netherlands	Dr	Badhe, Renuka	Advisor
Netherlands	Prof dr	Bastmeijer, Kees	Advisor

Consultative Parties			
Party	Title	Name	Position
Netherlands	Mr	Breukel, Sebastiaan	Advisor
Netherlands	Drs	Eijs, Arthur	CEP Representative
Netherlands	Mrs	Elstgeest, Marlynda	Advisor
Netherlands	Drs	Kroef, van der, Dick A.	Advisor
Netherlands	Prof dr	Lefeber, René J.M.	Head of Delegation
Netherlands	Mr	Peijs, Martijn	Advisor
Netherlands	Mr	Splinter, Jorden	Advisor
Netherlands	Mr	Van Bracht, Gerard	Advisor
New Zealand	Mr	Beggs, Peter	Advisor
New Zealand	Dr	Gilbert, Neil	Advisor
New Zealand	Ms	Laurenson, Amy	Head of Delegation
New Zealand	Dr	Morgan, Fraser	Advisor
New Zealand	Ms	Newman, Jana	CEP Representative
New Zealand	Ms	Stent, Danica	Advisor
New Zealand	Mr	Townend, Andrew	Advisor
New Zealand	Mr	Trotter, Simon	Advisor
New Zealand	Ms	Wilkinson, Kelsie	Advisor
New Zealand	Mr	Wilson, Gary	Advisor
Norway	Ms	Abrahamsen, Sunniva Helen	Advisor
Norway	Mr	Breidal, Ola	Advisor
Norway	Mr	Fliflet, Jon Gudbrand	Delegate
Norway	Mr	Gabrielsen, Trond	Delegate
Norway	Mr	Guldahl, John Erik	Advisor
Norway	Mr	Halvorsen, Svein Tore	Delegate
Norway	Ms	Heggelund, Kristin	Delegate
Norway	Ms	Høgestøl, Astrid Charlotte	Delegate
Norway	Ms	Johansen, Therese	Delegate
Norway	Ms	Krutnes, Anniken Ramberg	Head of Delegation
Norway	Ms	Njaastad, Birgit	CEP Representative
Norway	Ms	Strengehagen, Mette	Alternate
Norway	Dr	Winther, Jan-Gunnar	Delegate
Peru	Ms	Bello Chirinos, Cinthya	Delegate
Peru	Mr	Capunay, Juan Carlos	Head of Delegation
Peru	Mr	Casafranca, Jaime	Delegate
Peru	Mr	Celis, David	Delegate
Peru	Mr	Vargas Murillo, Ignacio Alejandro	Delegate
Poland	Dr	Bialik, Robert	Alternate
Poland	Mr	Dajda, Aleksander	Delegate
Poland	Mr	Jakukowicz, Tomasz	Delegate
Poland	Dr	Kidawa, Anna	Delegate
Poland	Ms	Krawczyk-Grzesiowska, Joanna	Delegate
Poland	Prof	Lewandowski, Marek	Delegate
Poland	Dr	Marciniak, Konrad	Head of Delegation
Poland	Prof	Szumowski, Lukasz	Delegate
Russian Federation	Ms	Chernysheva, Larisa	Delegate
Russian Federation	Mr	Lukin, Valerii	CEP Representative
Russian Federation	Mr	Pomelov, Victor	Delegate
Russian Federation	Mr	Tarasenko, Sergey	Delegate
Russian Federation	Mr	Timokhin, Konstantin	Delegate
Russian Federation	Mr	Titushkin, Vasily	Head of Delegation
Russian Federation	Mr	Tsaturov, Iury	Delegate
South Africa	Mr	Abader, Moegamat Ishaam	CEP Representative

		Consultative Parties	
Party	**Title**	**Name**	**Position**
South Africa	Mr	Bapela, Sonnyboy	CEP Representative
South Africa	Ms	Brammer, Romi	Advisor
South Africa	Mr	Dopolo, Mbulelo	CEP Representative
South Africa	Dr	Mphepya, Jonas	Head of Delegation
South Africa	Ms	Pretorius, Hester	Delegate
South Africa	Dr	Siko, Gilbert	Advisor
South Africa	Mr	Skinner, Richard	Advisor
Spain	Mr	Aguilera, Francisco	Alternate
Spain	Mr	Catalan, Manuel	Alternate
Spain	Mr	López, Jerónimo	Advisor
Spain	Mr	Muñoz De Laborde Bardin, Juan Luis	Head of Delegation
Spain	Mr	Ojeda, Miguel Angel	Advisor
Spain	Dr	Quesada, Antonio	Delegate
Spain	Mrs	Ramos, Sonia	Delegate
Sweden	Dr	Carman, Rolf	Head of Delegation
Sweden	Dr	Johnsson, Mats	Advisor
Sweden	Dr	Maud, Bergkvist	Advisor
Sweden	Dr	Selberg, Pia Cecilia	Advisor
Ukraine	Mr	Cheberkus, Dmytro	Head of Delegation
Ukraine	Mr	Fedchuk, Andrii	Delegate
Ukraine	Mrs	Mykhalchenkova, Olena	Delegate
Ukraine	Mr	Rozhdestvenskyi, Artem	Delegate
Ukraine	Mrs	Savchenko, Valeriia	Delegate
United Kingdom	Ms	Clarke, Rachel	Delegate
United Kingdom	Mr	Doubleday, Stuart	CEP Representative
United Kingdom	Mr	Downie, Rod	Delegate
United Kingdom	Prof Dame	Francis, Jane	Delegate
United Kingdom	Mr	Garrod, Simon	Delegate
United Kingdom	Ms	Griffiths, Lowri	Delegate
United Kingdom	Mr	Howes, James (Jamie)	Delegate
United Kingdom	Dr	Hughes, Kevin	Delegate
United Kingdom	Ms	Rumble, Jane	Head of Delegation
United Kingdom	Capt	Stockings, Tim	Delegate
United States	Dr.	Bergmann, Trisha	Delegate
United States	Mr	Bloom, Evan T.	Head of Delegation
United States	Mr	Edwards, David	Delegate
United States	Dr	Falkner, Kelly	Delegate
United States	Mr	Ganser, Peter	Alternate
United States	Mr	Kill, Theodore P.	Delegate
United States	Ms	Knuth, Margaret	Delegate
United States	Dr	McGinn, Nature	Delegate
United States	Dr	Penhale, Polly A.	CEP Representative
United States	Mr	Rudolph, Lawrence	Delegate
United States	Mr	Titmus, Andrew	Delegate
Uruguay	RA	Nuñez, Daniel	Alternate
Uruguay	Mrs	Casavalle Bonilla, Agustina	Delegate
Uruguay	Mrs	Caula, Nicole	CEP Representative
Uruguay	Mr	Lluberas, Albert	Delegate
Uruguay	Amb	Lugris , Fernando	Head of Delegation
Uruguay	Mrs	Silva Garcia, Laura Elena	Delegate
Uruguay	Mr	Torres Gutierrez, Miguel Angel	Delegate

		Non Consultative Parties	
Party	Title	Name	Position
Belarus	Dr	Gaidashov, Aleksei	Head of Delegation
Belarus	Dr	Kakareka, Sergey	Delegate
Belarus	Mr	Pilshchikov, Igor	Delegate
Belarus	Mr	Vergeichik, Sergei	Delegate
Canada	Ms	File, Susan	Advisor
Canada	Mr	Scott, David	Alternate
Canada	Mr	Taillefer, David	Head of Delegation
Canada	Ms	Wark, Jutta	Advisor
Colombia	Mr	Diaz Sanchez, Christian Michael	Advisor
Colombia	Mr	Mesa Salazar, Daniel	Advisor
Colombia	Mr	Molano, Mauricio	Advisor
Colombia	Mr	Montenegro Coral, Ricardo	Head of Delegation
Colombia	Mr	Rueda García, Oscar Orlando	Delegate
Colombia	Mr	Torres Parra, Rafael Ricardo	Advisor
Denmark	Ms	Steenberg, Eva	Head of Delegation
Iceland	Mr	Ragnarsson, Tómas Orri	Head of Delegation
Malaysia	Mr	Abd Rahman, Mohd Nasaruddin	Delegate
Malaysia	Mr	Adinan, Norazizi	Delegate
Malaysia	Ms	Kassim, Syarina	Delegate
Malaysia	Mr	Kua, Abun	Head of Delegation
Malaysia	Dr	Mohd Nor, Salleh	Delegate
Malaysia	Prof	Mohd Shah, Rohani	Advisor
Malaysia	Ms	Shuib, Nor Azimah	Delegate
Monaco	Dr	Le Bohec, Céline	Head of Delegation
Pakistan	Mr	Abbas, Shozab	Advisor
Portugal	Dr	Baptista, Alexandra	Delegate
Portugal	Dr	Espada, Maria De Jesus	Delegate
Portugal	Amb	Pereira, Jorge Torres	Delegate
Portugal	Dr	Xavier, José Carlos Caetano	Head of Delegation
Romania	Mr	Lupeanu, Adrian-Daniel	Alternate
Romania	Ms	Sascau, Giorgiana	Delegate
Romania	Dr	Sidoroff, Manuela Elisabeta	Head of Delegation
Romania	Dr	Toparceanu, Florica	Delegate
Romania	Ms	Tusa, Iris Maria	Delegate
Slovak Republic	HE Mr	Bella, Dušan	CEP Representative
Slovak Republic	Mr	Gajdoš, Lukáš	Alternate
Switzerland	Mr	Krebs, Martin	Delegate
Turkey	Ms	Bayar, Eda	Advisor
Turkey	Mr	Durak, Onur Sabri	Advisor
Turkey	Mr	Oktar, Ozgun	Advisor
Turkey	Mr	Önder, Ali Murat	Advisor
Turkey	Dr	Ozalp, Egemen	Delegate
Turkey	Mr	Ozdem, Mustafa Ilker	Delegate
Turkey	Ass Prof	Özsoy Çiçek, Burcu	Advisor
Turkey	Mr	Şahinkaya, Ibrahim Cem	Advisor
Turkey	Ms	Unal, Eda	Advisor
Turkey	Ms	Unal, Elife	Head of Delegation
Turkey	Mr	Uykur, Teoman	Advisor
Venezuela	Mr	Bardinet, Mauricio	Advisor
Venezuela	Capt	Carlos , Castellanos	Delegate
Venezuela	Lic	Quintero, Juan Pablo	Delegate

Non Consultative Parties			
Party	**Title**	**Name**	**Position**
Venezuela	Dr	Sira, Eloy	Head of Delegation
Venezuela	Ms	Yao, Tongyu	Staff
Belarus	Dr	Gaidashov, Aleksei	Head of Delegation
Belarus	Dr	Kakareka, Sergey	Delegate
Belarus	Mr	Pilshchikov, Igor	Delegate
Belarus	Mr	Vergeichik, Sergei	Delegate

Observers, Experts and Guests			
Party	**Title**	**Name**	**Position**
CCAMLR	Dr	Belchier, Mark	CEP Representative
CCAMLR	Mr	Wright, Andrew	Head of Delegation
COMNAP	Ms	Colombo, Andrea	Delegate
COMNAP	Ms	Rogan-Finnemore, Michelle	Head of Delegation
IAATO	Dr	Crosbie, Kim	Head of Delegation
IAATO	Ms	Hohn-Bowen, Ute	Advisor
IAATO	Ms	Kelley, Lisa	Alternate
IAATO	Mr	Li, Zhenyu	Advisor
IAATO	Mr	Liu, Fubin	Advisor
IAATO	Mrs	Lynnes, Amanda	CEP Representative
IAATO	Mr	Rootes, David	Advisor
IAATO	Ms	Schillat, Monika	Advisor
IAATO	Dr	Stanwell-Smith, Damon	Advisor
IAATO	Ms	Yuan, Ru	Advisor
ICAO	Mr	Ha, Huho	Delegate
IGP&I Clubs	Dr	Wu, Chao	Head of Delegation
IHO	Mr	Ward, Robert	Head of Delegation
IMO	Mr	De Boer, Jan Engel	Head of Delegation
IOPC Funds	Mr	Liebert, Thomas Alain	Alternate
IOPC Funds	Mr	Maura, José	Head of Delegation
SCAR	Dr	Baeseman, Jenny	Head of Delegation
SCAR	Prof	Chown, Steven L.	Head of Delegation
SCAR	Prof	Karentz, Deneb	Delegate
SCAR	Prof	Naish, Timothy	Delegate
SCAR	Dr	Terauds, Aleksandrs	CEP Representative
WMO	Mr	Charpentier, Etienne	Delegate
WMO	Dr.	Sparrow, Mike	Head of Delegation
ASOC	Ms	Arthur, Lindsay	Advisor
ASOC	Ms	Bai, Yunwen	Advisor
ASOC	Dr.	Brooks, Cassandra	Advisor
ASOC	Mr	Chen, Jiliang	Advisor
ASOC	Ms	Christian, Claire	Head of Delegation
ASOC	Mr	Dolan, Ryan	Advisor
ASOC ·	Ms	He, Liu	Advisor
ASOC	Ms	Kavanagh, Andrea	Advisor
ASOC	Ms	Lau, Winnie	Advisor
ASOC	Mr	Li, Shuo	Advisor
ASOC	Mr	Liu, Nengye	Advisor
ASOC	Dr	O'reilly, Jessica	Advisor
ASOC	Dr	Roura, Ricardo	Advisor

Observers, Experts and Guests			
Party	Title	Name	Position
ASOC	Mr	Tamm-Buckle, Sune	Advisor
ASOC	Mr	Walker, Mike	Advisor
ASOC	Mr	Werner Kinkelin, Rodolfo	Advisor
ASOC	Ms	Xue, Guifang	Advisor
ASOC	Ms	Xue, Yi	Advisor
ASOC	Ms	Yao, Songqiao	Advisor

Host Country Secretariat			
Party	Title	Name	Position
Host Country Secretariat	Mrs	Guo, Xiaomei	HC Executive Secretary
Host Country Secretariat	Mr	Hai, Qian	Staff
Host Country Secretariat	Mr	Jing, Li	Staff
Host Country Secretariat	Ms	Qiaoping, Lyu	Staff
Host Country Secretariat	Ms	Xiaofei, Sun	Staff
Host Country Secretariat	Ms	Yang, Xiaoning	Staff
Host Country Secretariat	Mr	Yeqing, Zou	Staff

Antarctic Treaty Secretariat			
Party	Title	Name	Position
ATS	Mr	Acero, José Maria	Alternate
ATS	Mr	Agraz, José Luis	Staff
ATS	Ms	Balok, Anna	Staff
ATS	Ms	Dahl, Justiina Miina Ilona	Staff
ATS	Mrs	Dahood-Fritz, Adrian	Staff
ATS	Mr	Davies, Paul Ronald	Staff
ATS	Ms	Erceg, Diane	Staff
ATS	Mr	González Vaillant, Joaquín	Staff
ATS	Mrs	Hodgson-Johnston, Indiah	Staff
ATS	Mr	Hokkanen, Eero Juhani	Staff
ATS	Mr	Joblin, Scott Grant	Staff
ATS	Ms	Nielsen, Hanne Elliot Fonss	Staff
ATS	Mr	Phillips, Andrew	Staff
ATS	Ms	Portella Sampaio, Daniela	Staff
ATS	Dr	Reinke, Manfred	Head of Delegation
ATS	Mr	Wainschenker, Pablo	Staff
ATS	Prof	Walton, David Winston Harris	Staff
ATS	Mr	Wydler, Diego	Staff
Translation & Interpretation	Ms	Alal, Cecilia Viviana	Head of Delegation
Translation & Interpretation	Ms	Ávila, Patricia Evelin	Staff
Translation & Interpretation	Mrs	Bachelier, Karine Lydie Alice	Staff
Translation & Interpretation	Ms	Bouladon, Sabine	Staff
Translation & Interpretation	Mrs	Christopher, Vera	Staff
Translation & Interpretation	Ms	Cook, Elena	Staff
Translation & Interpretation	Ms	Coussaert, Joelle Rose	Staff
Translation & Interpretation	Mr	Falaleyev, Andrei Gerkurievich	Staff
Translation & Interpretation	Ms	Garteiser, Claire	Staff
Translation & Interpretation	Ms	González García, Erika	Staff

Antarctic Treaty Secretariat			
Party	**Title**	**Name**	**Position**
Translation & Interpretation	Ms	Hale, Sandra Beatriz	Staff
Translation & Interpretation	Ms	Kasimova, Zouchra Aikaterini	Staff
Translation & Interpretation	Ms	Malofeeva, Elena	Staff
Translation & Interpretation	Mrs	Martínez, Silvia Renee	Staff
Translation & Interpretation	Ms	Mullova, Ludmila Dietrich	Staff
Translation & Interpretation	Mr	Orlando, Marc	Staff
Translation & Interpretation	Mr	Salvadori, Claudio Ezequiel	Staff
Translation & Interpretation	Ms	Speziali, Maria Laura	Staff
Translation & Interpretation	Mr	Tanguy, Philippe Josue Samuel	Staff
Translation & Interpretation	Ms	Vignal, Edith	Staff

www.ingramcontent.com/pod-product-compliance
Lightning Source LLC
Chambersburg PA
CBHW061616210326
41520CB00041B/7472